BASIL BUNTING

MAN AND POET

THE MAN AND POET SERIES

Louis Zukofsky: Man and Poet, 1979
Basil Bunting: Man and Poet, 1981

In Process

George Oppen: Man and Poet, editor, Burton Hatlen
May Sarton: Woman and Poet, editor, Constance Hunting
H.D.: Woman and Poet, editor, Burton Hatlen

FOR BASIL BUNTING

BASIL BUNTING

NATIONAL
POETRY
FOUNDATION, INC.

Man and Poet

Edited
with an introduction by
Carroll F. Terrell

1980

Published by

The National Poetry Foundation
University of Maine at Orono
Orono, Maine 04469

Printed by

The University of Maine at Orono
Printing Office

Library of Congress No. 80-84942
ISBN 0-915032-51-1

PREFACE

In all the arts, time is required to discriminate among those of the first order who are truly great. With a longer perspective, time present can clarify the work of time past and with more careful focus present more accurate records for time future. So it was with the work of Louis Zukofsky, the subject of the first of this series, so it is with Basil Bunting, the oldest of the still living poets who followed in the Pound tradition; and so it is with George Oppen the third of the series now in process.

The success of the book, *Louis Zukofsky: Man and Poet*, published in 1979 by the National Poetry Foundation, indicated that it filled a need which was not otherwise being met. We were, therefore, prompted to establish a series to fill similar needs as they exist with respect to other poets whose work, although considered by other poets and the most perceptive critics to be truly great, has been until recently unavailable and whose names, therefore, have been little known to academia and the general public. Of course, the names of Louis Zukofsky and Basil Bunting have long been familiar to students of Pound, Eliot, and Yeats because Pound dedicated his *Guide to Kulchur* to them in 1937. But to most readers they were names only because their work was always out-of-print and pointedly neglected by most critics. Most critics have been concerned with the latest fads practiced by one brief generation after the other, generations which since WW II may be labeled as Stunned, Beat, Stoned, Flowered, Zenned, Revolutionized, until coming full circle we have the Stunned again.

Happily, the situation is now improved. Happily, Guy Davenport's estimate of the publishing industry, that it should be indicted "on charges of critical dullness, terminal stupidity, and general mopery," does not apply to all publishers. Norton for years kept the shorter poems of Zukofsky available, and the University of California Press under the perceptive direction of August Frugé brought out his complete *"A"* in 1978. Similarly, the Oxford University Press picked up from a minor publisher *The Collected Poems* of Basil Bunting in 1978 and made his remarkable work, including *Briggflatts*, available to a growing and dedicated audience.

As with the Zukofsky book, to produce this one from the initial decision to do it, through the search for funding, to actual publication within a year was no easy task. This book too needed the help of many people. First I must acknowledge the subsidy given by the Faculty Research Funds Committee of the University of Maine at Orono. Without the financial assistance they provided, the book could not have been done at all, let alone so quickly. But I am even more indebted to many others: Basil Bunting himself, who tolerated my assaults upon his privacy with patience and resignation; who accepted me as a guest filled with trepidation in the wilds of northern England; who traveled to this country to serve for a week on the faculty of The Great Living Poets Institute here at Orono during the summer of 1980; who read *Briggflatts* under the glare of television cameras, helped through the confusion only by a modicum of wine; and who continued to provide information about his life and work with amiable good humor. Hugh Kenner's advice and encouragement given to both Bunting and to me has been invaluable. As with the Zuk book, the work of the writers here speaks for itself, but does not show the deadlines many of them met which cannot be described as indulgent. Again, it was the urgent need perceived by all that acted as a most powerful stimulant to speedy production of this book.

To several of my colleagues in the English Department here, especially Burton Hatlen, Robert Hunting, and Cathleen Bauschatz, I owe thanks for help in the chores of indexing, and proofreading. I am absolutely beholden to a most helpful library staff: James MacCampbell, Director, and Frances Hartgen, problem-solver; Lorraine LeBlanc, Purchasing; Margaret Menchen, Interlibrary Loans; Charlotte Huntley, Reference Department, all have helped quickly when called upon. My immediate staff must be praised for doing this job in addition to their regular duties: Sharon Stover, IBM Selectric Composer; Nancy Nolde, Research Assistant; Marilyn Emerick, Executive Secretary; JoAnn DeGrasse, Office Manager; and Roland Nord and Dana Wilde, graduate students in English, who were patient workers for many months.

Several pieces in the book appeared elsewhere in substantially their present forms. The first half of "The Sound of Sense" by Hugh Kenner appeared in an issue of *Paideuma* (Vol. 9, No. 1) dedicated to Basil Bunting's 80th birthday. "An Acknowledged Land," here revised, corrected, and up-dated appeared first in

Poetry Information (No. 19, Autumn, 1978) as did "Basil Bunting's Persian Overdrafts: A Commentary" by Parvin Loloi and Glyn Pursglove. The two pieces by Sister Victoria Marie Forde, S.C., "The Odes" and "The Translations and Adaptations of Basil Bunting" were taken with a few changes from her doctoral dissertation *Music and Meaning in The Poetry of Basil Bunting*, Notre Dame, Indiana, 1973. The dissertation is scheduled for publication in England by Colin Simms of the Genera Press some time in the near future.

Special acknowledgement is due to Basil Bunting and the Oxford University Press for permission to quote from the works of Basil Bunting; to New Directions Publishing Corporation to quote from the works of Ezra Pound; and to the University of California Press for permission to quote from the works of Louis Zukofsky.

C.F.T.
Orono, Maine
November, 1980

TABLE OF CONTENTS

CARROLL F. TERRELL

INTRODUCTION

Kenneth Cox, an astute critic in both mind and ear, said, "Bunting was at twenty-five among the most accomplished poets of his time" for in that year he wrote "Villon." Cox was measuring Bunting's work against new work of that time: *"Hugh Selwyn Mauberley* and *The Waste Land* had been published only a few years before. "Villon" is a masterpiece not in the conventional but in the original sense of the word: work done by an apprentice to demonstrate his mastery of the craft, though a man as yet un-formed" [*Agenda*, 36]. Cox's opinion is now shared by a growing number of critics and professors. But in the twenties and thirties, it could be found only among practicing poets: Pound, Zukofsky, and with some reservations, T.S. Eliot. Thus, until recently Bunting has been seldom read and studied intensively except by other poets earnest to learn all the tricks of their trade. Thus, as were Pound and Zukofsky, Bunting has been a poet's poet. And as with the work of Zukofsky, Bunting's work has been until recently almost totally unavailable. In the last fifty years, many a poetic fad has been clamored in magazines and the press and passed into the early obscurity it deserved. But Bunting's work had to be kept alive through small presses like Fulcrum, who did *Briggflatts* as a separate book in 1966. This remarkable work produced an im-mediate impact. It created the interest of a small but new audience in Bunting's work and led Fulcrum Press to issue the first *Collected Poems* in 1968. Wider critical acclaim over the next decade resulted in Oxford University Press re-issuing *The Collected Poems* in 1978. Since 1966, nearly 10,000 copies of Bunting's work have been sold. New editions are presently in the offing.

To many an astute critic, Bunting is now considered to be England's greatest living poet. To all critics of any consequence, he is *one* of the greatest of the Twentieth Century. Thus, the time may have come when his life and work may be of some interest even to a few astute English professors. English professors, by and large, are shall we say peons, followers, or hangers-on of the literary establishment, distinguished more for endurance than intelligence. Although they may have little creative ability, almost no imagination, and not a jot or tittle of poetic taste, they compensate for these lacks by a highly developed sense of duty and a great sense of justice. If they have the texts and the tools available, they will in time see to it that those who are truly great will receive appropriate attention. The intent of this book is to provide a basic tool for this now rapidly growing audience for Bunting's work.

The division of the book into sections is only a contrivance because neither a poet nor his work can be divided into parts labeled The Man, The Poet, The Thinker, and so forth. "The Poet" cannot avoid being also the man. But such an organizational device is likely better than none or better than resorting to the alphabet of author or title. The first piece, "Basil Bunting An Eccentric Profile," and the final piece, "A Bibliography of Works about Basil Bunting with Extended Commentary," were written last and after editorial work on all the rest of the book was done. The first piece is called "Eccentric" because it was not written to be read alone: it was deliberately written to emphasize materials not found elsewhere in the book and to leave out materials which are. In a word, it is supplementary. The same thing is true of the "Annotated Checklist" at the end of the book. Its subtitle, "Occasional Extended Commentary," indicates that articles containing valuable information and stimulating opinions not found elsewhere in the book are summarized at greater length than are some others.

Hugh Kenner's piece might well be sub-titled "Basil Bunting in Action." Kenner's own keen ear and eye pounce on the relevant details in both sights and sounds and move us closer to Basil's ideas about music and meaning. When it dawns on us that "the sound of sense" is by no means the same as "the sense of sound," we have one minor but helpful insight into Basil's ideas of the music of poetry. Similar feelings and reactions are to be found in Ted Enslin's piece. Here we have a practicing poet reflecting on the significance of Bunting's theories of prosody and remembering the man talking and reading and reacting to questions in interviews. Bunting the man is Bunting the poet. Here is the unity of vision and action.

In the first piece of "The Poet" section, Eric Mottram shows how long and thoughtfully he has considered the Bunting corpus. With the nicest and easiest of art, he steps back, looks at the whole, and then considers in order the various parts as they appeared, ending with a number of telling observations on *Briggflatts*, seeing the end of this work implied in the beginning not only of the single work but of Bunting's life work. The Alma Venus of the early Lucretius lines is present at the conclusion of *Briggflatts* bringing this generative poem into light. Neither Mottram nor Bunting rushes into conclusions. It takes time, as does a fine wine, for the poet's acknowledged land to be developed in crisp and unblurred lines. And by the way, Mottram sketches in the names of poets and their works which have been most vital in the development of Bunting's eclectic but "highly personal" poetic. Thus, Mottram's overview makes a fine lead-in to the more specialized studies which follow.

Since the twenties, Bunting has made much of the musical structure of his poetry as well as the musical cadence of the lines as sounds traced in the air. When he encountered Eliot's "Preludes" in 1919, he was much taken with the idea as he had for some years been thinking along similar lines. It's become a critical commonplace that Bunting's sonatas, early and late, are structured on Scarlatti sonatas. But this concept of relating one art form so closely to another is difficult to spell out. In "The Structure of Bunting's Sonatas," David Gordon faces the difficulty squarely and spells it all out. Mr. Gordon is perhaps the best equipped person in this generation to do that. He has been familiar with Bunting's work and theories since the early fifties and had years of exposure to Pound's talk about the subject as well. With his astute presentation, the ideas of fugue, *fugato*, and sonata all began to gel. Without wasting words he strikes into the solar plexus of the matter with the early work and follows through to the heart and spirit of the matter as it works out and culminates in *Briggflatts*.

Sister Forde probes Bunting's theories of sound and rhythm and illustrates by examples drawn from the First and Second Book of Odes. Quite remarkably, his performance in the earliest odes done in the twenties and the final ones done in the sixties is technically and in sound and shape quite similar: differences are to be found in new subtleties of tone, timbre, coloration, and perhaps distance. But the same master-ear is at work, early and late.

Peter Quartermain, a student and devotee of Bunting's work for some fifteen years, has had the advantage few others have had of hearing Bunting talk about his craft and sullen art for over a year while Bunting was in residence at the University of British Columbia in 1966. Thus, he was able to soak up slowly and brood about intensely a wide variety of the poet's oral commentary about his own work and the work of others he liked or disliked. In his piece, "To Make Glad the Heart of Man," he steps back from the Bunting canon and looks at it in the larger context of its roots in early English masters such as Wyatt and Spenser, 19th century masters such as Wordsworth, Swinburne and Whitman, as well as in the more immediate context of the early 20th century.

These several articles on Bunting's poetics lead neatly into a *Briggflatts* Symposium where we find three commentaries by other major poets followed by two articles by distinguished critics. Donald Davie with characteristic patience and wit opens the dialog by setting the critical record straight. The several "howlers" committed by the unfortunate commentator he cites might have been charitably passed over in silence, except for the fact that his article on *Briggflatts* had such wide distribution. Innocent students cannot be allowed to go on thinking that "Rawthey" is the name of the sweet tenor bull. The Rawthey is a river which flows past the Quaker meeting house at Briggflatts. If the bull dancing and singing on the river's bank had a name, it is not recorded in the poem. Davie does great service also by bringing the critical tradition back to its appropriate Bunting place: a massive phalanx of particulars. Philosophers take note—or even better, warning!

After Davie, we are prepared for the more detailed examination of each of the five sections of *Briggflatts*, seriatim, given us by John Peck whose blunt thesis is that the poem "must be defended against claustration within discussions of music and tone, so that its edge can be felt." His commentary casts strong light on dozens of edges in the poem, edges that cut sharp. Peck also discriminates moods and tones Bunting has in common with other poets of Orkney and the dales, such as Sorley Maclean and George Mackay Brown.

M.L. Rosenthal then gives us an evaluative criticism in the traditional mode, but it is the kind of technical look that only a master craftsman in the art can give to the work of another master. He finds problems but concludes, "Bunting's real reputation will surely hang on *Briggflatts*. It is his one masterpiece of affective balancing, despite the problems I have suggested."

L.S. Dembo, for many years now the distinguished editor of *Contemporary Literature*, and one of the few academic critics who could write appreciatively of both Zukofsky and Bunting when most others had not even heard of them, gives us also an interpretation and an evaluation in the traditional mode. As a point of departure he takes on the querulous statements of Peter Dale, who castigates Bunting for being a writer of "the quonk

and groggle school of poetry." Dembo finds Dale's examination to
be what he accuses Bunting's poetry to be: both primitive and simplistic. Rather than the "syntactical boredom" Dale finds in *Briggflatts*, Dembo finds a display of "linguistic virtuosity," and "a
strong song" that tows us, even though like many other modern
quest poems it "tows us to nowhere."

Anthony Suter adopted Bunting as his main research interest
over a dozen years ago and has written and published more about
him than have any other dozen critics together, not only in
England and America but also in France. As do most other students of Bunting's work, he finds *Briggflatts* to be the *summa* of
the whole canon. He finds the poem to be "a presentation of a
protagonist's journey through the wilderness of life, just as St.
John Perse's *Anabase* describes a spiritual 'journey into the interior.'" Suter's examination of the five parts of the poem casts
provocative light upon the whole: we are stimulated to react and
sometimes come to different conclusions from his own, but in the
process we have been led closer to the poem. But ambiguity is
one of the dimensions of the work. Where did we or the work
come from? Who knows? "Who . . . guesses where we go?" Perhaps Suter is right: "Nothing is certain in life, except the work
of art."

Taken together the five writers of the Symposium (one from
England, one from Canada, two from the United States, and one
from France) give us both a panoramic view of the work and an
accumulative glance at its details. I am reminded of one of Henry
James's prefaces, I think to *The Awkward Age*, where he sees the
matter of his novel to be like a statue in a dark garden. As novelist, his business is to bring to the garden many lighted candles and
so place them that in the end the statue is fully illuminated. So
with these five writers. They have each brought a light and placed
it at a different angle in relation to the work and have thereby
brought the reader, according to his own lights, a great way out
of the darkness of ambiguity so that he can see, understand, and
judge for himself.

A feeling of reluctance and a spirit of temerity informed the
decision to continue the format of the series by calling the next
section "The Thinker." The reader must be warned that "thinker"
here does not imply "philosopher." We will not get from Bunting
any generalizations of a philosophical or religious kind, except
statements denigrating the value of such generalizations on the
part of philosophers who can't say anything unless it has become
so over-simplified as to be necessarily false. Thus did Bunting ap-

preciate the early Wittgenstein, who ironically thought and wrote himself out of business in the *Tractatus*, and the later Zukofsky, who wrote *Bottom: on Shakespeare* to put an end to philosophy.

By "thinker" here we limit the word to concern thoughts about poets, poetry, critics and criticism, and Bunting's thoughts and evaluations about them. Dale Reagan has collected over the years a massive file of Bunting's pronouncements on these subjects taken from unpublished letters, interviews, classroom notes, as well as published sources. He has done the literary world a great service by selecting from this mass of statements, made over a fifty- year period, the most pithy and characteristic ones and organizing them into coherent patterns. His "Basil Bunting: obiter dicta" is a singularly effective overview of the poet in mental action. His piece is followed by a selection similar in form done by William S. Milne. The two pieces together suggest a remarkable consistency in Bunting's precepts which he formed early and still holds to late. Here, consistency is neither foolish nor a hobgoblin of any kind.

From the no-ideas-but-in-things dicta of the thinker, we turn to questions of the poet as translator. Since Pound listed translation as one of the legitimate kinds of criticism and set the pace by renditions "after the manner of" Oriental poets or as "homage" in the *Propertius*, other poets have followed suit and have been followed in turn by the hoots of dismay of pedants who are concerned mainly with literal meaning or questions of grammar and/ or philology. Poetry as an art is not one of their concerns. The patterns of praise by some and villification by others which attended upon Pound's work were repeated with the work based on other languages done by Bunting. Together, Cid Corman and Sister Forde give an overview of Bunting's intentions within the history of the controversy. Their work is followed by a close examination of his "Persian Overdrafts" done by two Persian students, Parvin Loloi and Glyn Pursglove. The reader is thus effectively informed about the problems and issues and introduced to this part of the Bunting canon.

"The Testament" gives us two valuable working tools: a year by year bibliography of all of Bunting's published work from the first in 1924 to the most recent in 1978; and "A Bibliography of Works about Basil Bunting with Extended Criticism." The first done by Dana Wilde is based upon the official bibliography of Roger Guedella. It gives us a quick look at the whole prose-poetry canon. The second done by Roland Nord, a graduate student in English at Orono, first involved months of meticulous work of the listing, locating, obtaining, Xeroxing, and organizing kind. That had to be followed by intensive study of Bunting in order to be able to write knowledgeable annotations. After his work was done, I read through all the articles and his annotations. Only a few required alterations of any kind. Several required much more extended treatments. Items which received such additions are indicated by initials at the end. The 85 items are indexed first, alphabetically, but they are numbered and considered in the order and time they appeared. With this organization, the flow of thought and change of attitude about Bunting and thus a fuller realization of his significance may be evoked in the reader's mind. For "nothing matters but the quality of affection, dove sta memora, that carves its trace in the mind."

THE MAN

CARROLL F. TERRELL

BASIL BUNTING: AN ECCENTRIC BIOGRAPHY

I

Some poets object to any writer who wants to probe into their private lives. It makes little difference whether the prober is a critic, thesis writer, biographer, or scandalmonger. Dislike of misplaced emphasis rather than fear of exposure usually motivates their objections. A poet is a poet is a poet. Or he is not. If he is, then the music of the poetry carving its trace in the air is the only reasonable subject of inquiry. Palaver about the poet's life, relatives, idiosyncracies, sexual indiscretions, or whatever, falls wide of the point: it leads the reader away from what should be his major concern without arriving anywhere else.

Other poets are quite the opposite. They gladly encourage the scholar and biographer. They make efforts to preserve their letters and papers for posterity and leave their libraries to libraries. Pound may be included in this latter category. He seemed to believe that he was singled out for a high destiny and that the gift, granted to him by the gods, should be held in sacred trust. Because of this sense of high mission, he was glad to encourage the scholar and biographer and quite willing to be publicized if the process would result in celebrating the art of poetry, the visibility of the many other writers he wanted to promote, or the propagation of ideas he wanted to spread.

But most of Pound's friends and followers, such as Eliot, Zukofsky, and Bunting, were of the opposite persuasion. To Zukofsky concern with his private life was an annoyance, to Eliot it was an impertinence, but to Bunting—that other struggler in the desert—it was and is anathema—or, more precisely, "bloody" anathema. And still is. For over a half-century, he has destroyed personal letters from other people, and has tried to persuade his friends to destroy any letters he has written to them. Unhappily, most have obliged. Therefore, because of his feelings, I undertake

to write about his personal life with mixed feelings: a conviction
that a great poet is in part a possession of the public and the process of introducing his work to a wider and growing audience entails
a legitimate interest in the life of the poet; but also a regret that
such work must be done in defiance of the poet's preferences.*

II

So that: we'll begin at the beginning! Basil Bunting was born
March 1, 1900 at Scotswood, a village on the southern fringe of
Newcastle-on-Tyne: born, as he told Jonathan Williams, "amid
rejoicings for the relief of Ladysmith during the Boer War." His
father was a medical doctor who received his degree from Edinburgh University. Although he had a local practice, he spent much
of his time as a research scientist doing primary work on the histology of mammalian lymphatic glands. Thus, he not only haunted
pet shops and zoos to remove the glands of animals who had died,
but he also harbored animals at home. Basil grew up in a house
sometimes overrun by lizards that had escaped from boxes in the
cellar. But finding it impossible to earn a living doing histology,
Dr. Bunting took up radiography only to find there, too, that he
was ahead of his time. Besides that, the doctor was not a very
good bill collector. Said BB: "I think he spent more on machines
than he ever got back from practice." But he stayed in general
practice and worked hard at it until he died of a coronary in
1925 [JW, 9].

Basil's mother was the daughter of a local mining engineer
and was brought up in a genteel tradition. His aunt was a pianist,
his uncle a Quaker, and his father a poetry reader so that Basil was
brought up in an atmosphere of music, poetry, and Quakerism. His
earliest memories involve hearing his father read poetry. The
sounds and rhythms so affected him that by the time he was six
he had resolved to be a poet himself. He also heard good music
continually from the cradle on and as he told JW: "I was brought
up entirely in a Quaker atmosphere." Most of the schools he

---

*The factual materials of this account were compiled from several sources: the taped
interviews with Jonathan Williams entitled *Descant on Rawthey's Madrigal*, Gnomon
Press, 1968 [identified in the text as JW plus page]; *Madeira and Toasts for Basil Bunting's 75th Birthday*, Jargon Society, 1977 [*MT* plus page]; interviews published in the
Memorial edition of *Agenda*, Vol. 16, No. 1, Spring, 1978 [*Agenda* plus page]; the
Bunting issue of *Poetry Information*, No. 16, 1977 [*PI* plus page]; the university micro-
film of the Ph.D. thesis of Sister Victoria Marie Forde, *Music and Meaning in the Poetry
of Basil Bunting*, Notre Dame, 1973 [*VF* plus page]; and interviews I've had with Mr.
Bunting in Northumberland and Cumbria in the fall of 1979 and in Orono during the last
week of August, 1980.

attended were run by Quakers, except for the first one. That was a kind of kindergarten which a housemaid started taking him to when he was six:

> It was a long walk, about a mile and a half to the tram terminus, and then a considerable ride in the tram, and away up the hill to a part of Newcastle that is now all slums, which was then slightly shabby middle-class. There was an old lady who kept a school, a very old-fashioned kind. You learned your ABC and got thoroughly rapped on the knuckles if you made mistakes. You learned by copying pot hooks into exercise books. You were supposed to learn good manners by eating up everything that was put in front of you, but I couldn't do that because she included a great deal of tapioca pudding in her menu—and tapioca is something I could never endure. I spent an awful lot of time sitting and look-ing at platefuls of tapioca. It would be there in front of me from the beginning of dinner time until the middle of the afternoon. If I hadn't eaten it by then I got spanked [JW, 7-8].

The old lady had an assistant, a young girl "with long black ring-lets," called Miss Winny. She helped with coats and shoes when the students were going home. And then there was another little girl, a quite special one:

> She was a couple of years older than me and took me under her protection. We sat around the table and read in turn verses from the Bible. It was very hard on the youngest, who had just got as far as deciphering c-a-t, *cat*, and she would sit there with her arm around me and when my turn came she would whisper in my ear what the verse was! I would get it right—to the great astonish-ment of Miss Bell, the school mistress.

At home, Basil and his sister were trained by a governess named Miss Wraith. In the spirit of the times, she was considered a nice woman, but she used the cane "fairly frequently" not wanting to spoil the child.

After the private school, he spent about a year and a half at Newcastle Royal Grammar School and then, according to custom, was sent away from home to be educated. But, not according to custom, Basil was sent to a Quaker boarding school at Ackworth in the West Riding of Yorkshire. It was an old fashioned place even in pre-WW I days. But its emphasis on the Bible, with all its sonorous and redolent language, had an effect on Bunting. Basil said of it:

> It had changed scarcely any rules since its foundation in the early part of the 18th century. It had finally introduced holidays. Twenty years or so before I went there, you didn't get home on holidays at all. You went to school at the age of twelve and came home permanently at the age of sixteen—meanwhile, you never saw home . . . And the other main change was that they had

unfortunately stopped issuing two pints of beer per day per boy.
They did, about up to 1880. . . . I suppose that the chief permanent influence of Ackworth, besides instilling the general
Quaker attitude, was the enormous amount of Bible that had to
be read. Every morning you had to get a large lump of the Bible
by heart before breakfast. At breakfast the Bible was read to you.
At dinner the Bible was read to you. At tea time, after tea, the
Bible was read to you again. And on Sunday there were *very* large
lumps of the Bible, besides Scripture lessons in between. And
with that, and some other accidents, I came to be far better acquainted with the Bible than any of my juniors that I have come
across. Although, there were other people mostly in Noncon-
formist schools of one sort or another of my own age who at-
tained much the same grounding in the Holy Scriptures; the
rhythms of the translation in the authorized version of Job, of
the Song of Songs, some of the Prophets, all the extraordinary
narrative skill of some chapters of the Book of Kings. I remember
the early chapters of the Second Book of Kings in particular—
things you won't get better anywhere else, and which I feel
people of this generation lack [JW, 9-10].

From Ackworth, Bunting went to another Quaker school
which was located at Leighton Park in Berkshire: "one of the
expensive public schools for the rich." He stayed at Leighton Park
until he was about seventeen and a half years old. WWI was soon
to be over, but Basil returned home to Newcastle and waited for
the police to arrest him because he had decided on principle to
refuse military service. The police obliged soon after he became
18. His family didn't support his position and neither did anyone
else except for one old Quaker woman:

So far as I can remember only one person approved of me at that
time. She was an oldish lady. She was long past the proper re-
tiring age of mistress on the staff of the girls school at Ackworth.
A Miss Fry. Her sister was a very famous member of the Society
of Friends, in charge of most of their relief work. But she herself
found more interest in plain education. She was a very pene-
trating woman with children. She found out a great deal more
about me in the course of a very few conversations than I think
anybody else has done in the whole of my life. And she certainly
encouraged me to take Quaker doctrine seriously [JW, 10].

Bunting was arrested in Newcastle shortly after he became
18, probably, therefore, by April of 1918. He spent what he later
referred to as "a long spell in jail," adding, "which I don't want to
talk about." He still doesn't. Perhaps it was half a year. At least,
Pound mentions it years later in a letter: "I think Bunting is about
the only man who did six months in jail as a conscientious objector
during the armistice, i.e., after the war was over, on principle that
if there was a war he wouldn't go..." [VF, p. 2; cited from Stock,

The Life of Ezra Pound, 1970, p. 283]. Bunting's testimony about his prison experience had positive result. He later wrote footnotes for a Graham Wallas book on prisons "which was the main evidence before the Royal Commission that reformed the prisons." But as a prisoner he was uncompromising and didn't get out until he went on a hunger strike. After he hadn't eaten anything for eleven days, the prison officials let him go, but not before pulling a rather dirty trick. To break his will, they put a hot, roasted chicken in his cell everyday. Basil looked upon the chicken with contempt and anger and never ate. In the British penal system of the time, the warden was left with the alternative of force-feeding or letting him go. Perhaps it was with a note of admiration for so strong a will in one so young that they took the easy way out and turned him loose.

The prison experience did not change the essential man. Rather it intensified the qualities of conviction there from the beginning: outrage at injustice; a sense of the cruelty of not the individual man but institutional man; an awareness of the power, beauty, and sanctity of the earth and all creatures in it.

III

Bunting's experience during his childhood and youth was both the same as that of other boys and different. Bad vision denied him the ability to indulge in sports which required good eyes. But with glasses, he observed the processes of all nature around him very closely, from the smallest to the largest. His sense of sound, cadence, and rhythm was always highly developed. Different from many of his peers, he listened hungrily to all the good music available from his earliest years: his aunt's piano playing; the Newcastle Bach choir conducted by Dr. Whittaker, from whom he learned a lot not only about music but art in general; Dr. Fellows, who had just discovered at Durham Cathedral the Manuscript of Byrd's Great Service, lost for over 300 years. As a young boy, he heard the Great Service often as he sat in on many of the rehearsals at Durham Cathedral while Whittaker trained his Bach choir in the newly-discovered work. Basil said later, "I was able to see more than I dare say most hearers did of the extreme complexity of that work." These experiences provided him with a technical understanding which paved the way for his later enthusiasm for Scarlatti, Corelli, and Schoenberg.

Bunting insists that all anyone needs to know about him may be found in *Briggflatts*. He says the poem is autobiographical, but

it is not historically biographical: that is, it does not deal in facts
so much as the emotional and intellectual qualities of his life. Thus,
we may deduce from the poem much about the emotional and
scenic experiences of his childhood. The qualities of the various
landscapes near the Tyne Valley, the Midlands, the Yorkshire
Riding, and Cumbria are dramatic: the moors, fells, fogs, great
dells, barren hills, and vast distances leave one feeling open, exposed, unprotected. Most of the people made a living on the land.
Farming and animal husbandry at the turn of the century required
most farm people to live close to a continuous process of life,
death, and sexuality. All living things seemed bound to the cycle
of "birth, and copulation and death." But different from Eliot's
Sweeney that was not all. Hidden behind the visible processes
there exists for some a divine and mysterious force which shapes
the ends of all. Bunting early in youth became convinced that all
living creatures are beautiful if looked at steadily and seen whole.
All seem to move in a rhythm of their own and celebrate the
creation in a dance of life and a dance, perhaps, even of death.

The concepts here are distinctly Whitmanesque. Whether
Bunting formed them before he became a student of Whitman or
afterwards would be hard to say. At the age of 15, he received
a "more or less national prize" for an essay on Walt Whitman.
Before that he came across an early (around 1870) edition of
Leaves of Grass which had been pushed behind other books in
the school library. Said Basil, "Whitman was in very poor repute
everywhere. English people were scarcely aware of his existence,
and Americans would dismiss him as a useless sort of fellow"
[*PI*, 6]. But the book was a revelation to the young poet. He saw
in Whitman's lines *cadences* which were "in a way parallel to what
was being done by his contemporaries in music, particularly Liszt."
Bunting's prize brought him "the great annoyance" of his teachers,
but also brought him a visitor, "an old gentleman living in Shef-
field who got on his pushbike and rode thirty or forty miles in
order to call on the fifteen year old critic of Whitman. That was
no less a person than Edward Carpenter, who'd been one of
Whitman's close friends" [*PI*, 6].

Whitman celebrated all living things as instinct with a healing
power which turns the corruption of death into new health and
life. In "This Compost" Whitman says, "Now I am terrified at
the Earth, it is that calm and patient,/It grows such sweet things
out of such corruptions,/ . . . It gives such divine materials to men,
and accepts such leavings from them at last." Perhaps such lines
as "The resurrection of the wheat appears with pale visage out of

its graves" and "probably every spear of grass rises out of what
was once a catching disease" are behind a similar sentiment in
Briggflatts:

> Decay thrusts the blade,
> wheat stands in excrement
> trembling.

And maybe such lines from *Leaves of Grass* as

> And the cow crunching with depress'd head surpasses any statue,
> And a mouse is miracle enough to stagger sextillions of infidels.

are antecendent to the dozens of living creatures celebrated in
Briggflatts. With such inhabitants of the poem as vultures, snakes,
crabs, and maggots, we must be alert not to read a personal "anti"
emotion into the text. To some people the obscene looking buzzards and vultures of French Guiana have little to commend them
even though they are the main instrument of sewage disposal for
the city. But to Basil they are creatures of great beauty as well as
utility. I questioned him quite closely about both buzzards and
maggots. He told me about the beautiful heads, colors, wings,
and eyes of buzzards and how graceful they are in flight. Maggots are even more beautiful and remarkable: if watched closely
they may be seen doing a sort of rhythmic ballet dance while they
work. The idea that beauty is in the eye of the beholder is most
unlikely to receive a better illustration. These lines,

> Ax rusts. Spine
> picked bare by ravens, agile
> maggots devour the slack side
> and inert brain, never wise.

should be read with no negative connotation. In a clear Whitmanesque manner the raven and maggots are there working in a natural
dance of life to restore the earth to health. Whitman wrote:

> Behold this compost! behold it well!
> Perhaps every mite has once form'd part of a sick person—yet behold!
> The grass of spring covers the prairies,
> The bean bursts noiseless through the mold in the garden . . .
> What chemistry!

In his impressionable youth Bunting encountered Whitman
and came away from the encounter a different person. It seems to
have been as dramatic a change as that which transformed Whitman on the beach at Paumanok from Walter Whitman Esquire
into Walt Whitman, celebrator of nature. Both Whitman's music
and ideas can be found worked into the texture of Bunting's
poetry, early and late. Sadness at the death which must come to

all living things is balanced by rejoicing that death does not win
over life: resurrection comes with returning spring and makes all
deathless. We have the theme in Bunting's first ode from 1924:

> Weeping oaks grieve, chestnuts raise
> mournful candles. Sad is spring
> to perpetuate, sad to trace
> immortalities never changing.
>
> Weary on the sea
> for sight of land
> gazing past the coming wave we
> see the same wave;
>
> drift on merciless reiteration of years;
> descry no death; but spring
> is everlasting
> resurrection.

The last ode in the *Collected Poems* restates the theme:

> Boasts time mocks cumber Rome. Wren
> set up his own monument.
> Others watch fells dwindle, think
> the sun's fires sink.
>
> Stones indeed sift to sand, oak
> blends with saints' bones.
> Yet for a little longer here
> stone and oak shelter
>
> silence while we ask nothing
> but silence. Look how clouds dance
> under the wind's wing, and leaves
> delight in transience.

But we must be alert not to go to far. When Bunting encountered Whitman, he was equipped by experience not to discover
but to recognize what he'd encountered before in such diverse
writers as Lucretius and Wordsworth. Bunting read Lucretius
"quite early" and had "high respect for him, both as a thinker
and a poet." What he found there also was the idea of love as the
propulsive power in "control of landscape and its creatures" [*PI*,
9]. He distilled complex ideas and emotional reactions about life
into his 1927 "overdraft" from Lucretius, in whom he recognized
a kindred spirit. What the Latin poet called Alma Venus, Bunting
saw as the powerful sexual drive all nature is instinct with:

> In the first days of spring
> when the untrammelled allrenewing southwind blows
> the birds exult in you and herald your coming.

> Then the shy cattle leap and swim the brooks for love.
> Everywhere, through all seas mountains and waterfalls,
> love caresses all hearts and kindles all creatures
> to overmastering lust and ordained renewals.

But the young poet already had similar ideas from observing nature itself. Although *Briggflatts* contains many recollections from his childhood there, Bunting saw the particular bull on a farm near Throckley where he was living then. In a later interview he said about the scene:

> it struck me, at once, nobody had noticed the bull has a *tenor* voice. You hear of the bull bellowing. . . . But in fact he bellows in the most melodious tenor, a beautiful tenor voice. In spring, the bull does in fact, if he's with the cows, dance, on the tip of his toes, part of the business of showing off, showing that he is protecting them. . . . He's not really doing anything, but he sees somebody walking by the hedge and he begins to dance at once, just to demonstrate to the cows what an indispensable creature he is. It is delightful, and it bears such a strong resemblance to the behavior of young men in general and . . . well all creatures.

These observations went into Bunting's notebooks not to be used until 50 years later. Thus did the dancing bull come to be part of the ceremonial landscape of *Briggflatts*. But first either Lucretius prepared the young poet to observe the bull or the bull prepared the poet to understand Lucretius.

The idea of dance here is fundamental to what became cadence and rhythm in modern poetry generally. The ballet dance done by maggots is repeated in the mating dance of male birds as well as bulls in spring. As Bunting has often said, the impulse to dance even before puberty is seen in children: if left alone they don't walk, they skip and dance to school expressing some sense of individual rhythm. The idea of a personal rhythm, Pound came to call great bass: each person's rhythm is different from the rhythm of all others. A poet's business is to find his own rhythm and then find means to express that rhythm or dance: by this means he expresses himself, a self that is intimately tied up with his total being—a concept Pound found in Cavalcanti's *Virtu*.

We find it in Yeats. Ones labor in life is to find his own dance. If he expresses it fully, the dancer cannot be distinguished from the dance:

> Labor is blossoming or dancing where
> The body is not bruised to pleasure soul,
> Nor beauty born out of its own despair,
> Nor blear-eyed wisdom out of midnight oil.
>
> O chestnut tree, greet rooted blossomer,

> Are you the leaf, the blossom or the bole?
> O body swayed to music, O brightening glance,
> How can we know the dancer from the dance?

Not long after Bunting wrote the Lucretius, we find Yeats feeling the same overpowering sexuality which he calls sensual music:

> The salmon-falls, the mackerel-crowded seas,
> Fish, flesh, or fowl, commend all summer long
> Whatever is begotten, born, and dies.
> Caught in that sensual music all neglect
> Monuments of unaging intellect.

And not long after that we find it even in Eliot who sees "the dance along the artery" to be equivalent to sap in trees and boarhounds chasing boars. But Eliot makes mystic connections and with Dante finds these patterns "reconciled among the stars":

> The dance along the artery
> The circulation of the lymph
> Are figured in the drift of stars
> Ascend to summer in the tree
> We move above the moving tree
> In light upon the figured leaf
> And hear upon the sodden floor
> Below, the boarhound and the boar
> Pursue their pattern as before
> But reconciled among the stars.

These patterns of experience, reading, and perception out of Bunting's adolescence and teens formed convictions which remained with him the rest of his life. Also they prepared affinities he and Pound could recognize in each other, not only in their poetry but also in their religious intuitions. Pound's strong and permanent reactions against dogma find a counterpoint in Bunting's attitude to his Quaker experience:

> fortunately it is a religion with no dogma at all—and consequently there's very little you can quarrel with, and I don't have to believe this or that or the other. . . . The real essence of the Quaker business is exactly as it was at the beginning: if you sit in silence, if you empty your head of all the things you usually waste your brain thinking about, there is some faint hope that something, no doubt out of the unconscious or where you will, will appear—just as George Fox would have called it, the voice of God, and that will bring you, if not nearer God, at any rate nearer your own built-in certainties [*PI*, 9].

Bunting's belief has much in common with that of Pound. Pound believed that no statement in words, either few or millions, could come close to expressing the immensity of the divine presence acting in the world. Or put another way, neither the universe nor God can be caught in a net of words. Since Pound also believed that one of the many ways that divinity acts in man is via his aesthetic sense [Tὸ καλόν], he would respond to questions about what he believed by saying such things as "if I had the material means, I would restore the goddess to her pedestal at Terracina": the presence of a beautiful statue might evoke feelings which derive from one's deepest religious nature—perhaps, tap a still, inner voice. But dogma, under the guise of logic or otherwise, leads to the hunt for heretics, the odor of burned flesh in the marketplace, and periodically war sanctioned by one dogma-ridden god or another.

As did Pound, Bunting in his youth freed himself of destructive orthodoxies. The point is vital. Most writers are "unenterprising," according to Bunting, because they are brought up "in schools, or parts of schools, or traditions of schools." Take a bright person and train him thoroughly in any orthodoxy, whether it be religion, economics, money and banking, music, painting or poetry, and if he is really intelligent he will soon not be able to see or hear anything around him.

Thomas Wentworth Higginson was a giant on the 19th century American literary scene. It wasn't because he didn't know any better; it was because he knew very well indeed the current orthodoxy about how poetry had to be written that he felt free to rewrite Emily Dickinson. Looking at her lines, "But I know what the heather's like/And what a billow be," he could only throw up his hands, say "It cannot go in so," and change it to "And what a wave must be." Or "Not all the Frankfort berries/ Yield such an alcohol" had to be changed to the heavy-footed iambic "Not all the vats upon the Rhine." Even worse, orthodoxy about exact rhymes required him to change the marvellous music and cadence of

> To see the little tippler
> From Manzanilla come

to

> To see the little tippler
> Leaning against the sun.

The drunkenness of Emily's butterfly is conveyed by the Cuban port, whence Boston imported most of its rum. But worse than that, butterflies do not lean against the sun. Emily, a true poet, one who could look and see, could not have written such a line.

Similarly, Barrett Wendall, the great Harvard anthologist, was no fool. Orthodoxies he'd spent his life acquiring allowed him no

margin to treat Whitman's verse as anything but unformed, undis-
ciplined rantings. In his *Literary History of America*, Wendall
spoke of Whitman's "eccentric insolence of phrase and temper"
and said he was "In temperament and style . . . an exotic member
of that sterile brotherhood which eagerly greeted him abroad."*
But younger men, not conditioned by old orthodoxies, could hear
something new and began to speak of it in musical terms as did
Louis Untermeyer, who became the major anthologist after
Wendall. Said Untermeyer: "None can deny the music in this
poetry which is capable of the widest orchestral effects. It is a
music accomplished in a dozen ways—by the Hebraic 'balance'
brought to perfection in Job and the Psalms, by the long and
extraordinarily flexible line suddenly whipped taut . . . by following his recitatives with a soaring aria. . . . 'No counting of syllables,' wrote Anne Gilchrist, 'will reveal the mechanism of this music.' But the music is there, now rising in gathering choirs of
brasses, now falling to the rumor of a flute" [*Ibid.*, 38].

New poets such as Bunting who were concerned with technique and craft hailed Whitman as a creator of new forms. Untermeyer summarized: "they placed their emphasis on his flexible
sonority, his orchestral *timbre*, his tidal rhythms, his piling up of
details into a symphonic structure" [*Ibid.*, 6]. Bunting read poets
such as Whitman on his own, but he also read a lot of others required by the traditional curriculum. In all, his eyes and ears saw
and heard much the ordinary student was impervious to and in
time came to distinguish a few in the English tradition who invented new forms or brought old forms close to new perfections.

First comes Spenser who, according to Bunting, provided
Sidney and Shakespeare as well as all their followers with a whole
bag of new poetry-making "tricks," or tools. He said "Sidney's
slightly older contemporary, Spenser, invented a new thing which
has given a complexion to English verse ever since. . . . Spenser
made the words produce their own music, instead of depending
on the musician to do it." Spenser's inventions transformed the
art and amazed the very faculties of his audience's eyes and ears:

> It was utterly astonishing to his contemporaries. There's an ac-
> count in one of Ludowick Briskett's letters of a poetry reading at
> some village outside Dublin where Spenser read some bits from
> *The Faerie Queene*. They were extremely astonished and worried
> and called on Spenser to justify doing this sort of thing. Spenser
> began, just as Ezra Pound began, by trying every possible mode
> that was known to poetry, seeing what could be done in it. In

*Reported by L. Untermeyer in the *Preface to Modern American Poetry*, 1950, p. 5.

The Shepheardes Calendar you have a wonderful collection of possibilities which served English poets for nearly 300 years after Spenser wrote it [*PI*, 41].

After Spenser, high on Bunting's list of inventor-masters come Wyatt, Campion, Wordsworth and Swinburne. While still a small boy, he came to feel a special kinship with the last two who came from his own north country and spoke in broad accents which paralleled his own. One of the regrets of his life is that even though as a child he walked where Swinburne often walked, he never encountered him:

> My father used to take me up to Capheaton sometimes and he knew some of the Swinburnes. We walked about the park and looked at the lake and so forth and it's just chance that when I was a small boy Swinburne never had met me. He'd do what he would always have done, what he did to all the children on Putney Heath: he'd pat me on the head and present me with half a crown. And that would have been very interesting to me because when *he* was a little boy of eight or nine, as I, he was taken to Grasmere where he met an old gentleman who patted him on the head, but did not offer him half a crown—he was too frugal— and that was William Wordsworth! And I thought that a splendid thing!

In talking about what poets Bunting would include in an anthology of his own, Jonathan Williams asked him, "Where do you pick up after Wordsworth?" and he replied:

> I think Swinburne is the next. Ezra knew about Swinburne all right. He says . . . that Swinburne is the only 19th century poet who showed any interest in rhythm, and it is true that Swinburne has been misread steadily ever since he wrote, and his peculiar qualities, before he became sodden with drink, have also been missed. He was a weaver of patterns, of very abstract patterns, without caring if you ever got what was behind the patterns or not. He certainly never underlines it, but he has a greater rhythmic variety than I think has ever been suspected by the people who write books about him—astonishing variety, if you will only take the pains to read him slowly and according to syntax, instead of according to some idea of metrics derived from George Saintsbury or somebody like that.

As for Wordsworth himself, what can be said? Wordsworth was the greatest poet of them all for Bunting, who knew in the ways others could not what Wordsworth meant when he wrote of the landscape Bunting also inhabited. In his "boyish days," he too had experienced "aching joys" and "dizzy raptures" in the presence of "the sounding cataract." In him, too, "the tall rock,/the mountain, and the deep and gloomy wood" created "a feeling and a love." Bunting, too, learned to look on nature and feel a presence and a joy and

> a sense sublime
> Of something far more deeply interfused,
> Whose dwelling is the light of setting suns

and to hear, indeed, "the still sad music of humanity."

In summary, Bunting's experiences when young, in both life and letters, cannot be found in quite the same way in any other poet. If we believe that poets are 90% born and not made, we must be impressed by the extraordinary and very special kind of experiences he had as a school boy: the sound of poetry and the sound of music; Quakerism, Whitman, and Lucretius; life close to the soil with real fire, wild water, and a whole spectrum of animal life on a dramatic landscape; Wyatt, Spenser, Campion, Swinburne and above all Wordsworth. When he was free to seek his fortune in London and the literary world at large, he was prepared to become the poet he was born to be.

IV

Not long after he got out of prison, Bunting seems to have faced the facts of life and decided that since poets can't make a living writing poetry he would have to get money to live on some other way. So in 1919, he went to London to see if he could cage a job, but instead he spent most of his time on the fringes of the literary world. In that year, he read his first Pound and Eliot. The musical idea expressed by Eliot in his title "Preludes" struck a bell because, as he put it later, he "had been thinking along similar lines." And it was his alertness to musical analogies that made him one of the earliest readers to see the extraordinary, complex music and rhythm in Pound's *Homage to Propertius*. He continued to write poetry himself as he had for nearly ten years, but it was all practice and he threw everything away. Pound had done the same: he had written a large but unknown number of sonnets and discarded them as practice exercises. When he was 17 and still at Ackworth, Bunting did send one poem to a London editor. Years later he recalled the results in these words:

> . . . the editor, a kind-hearted fellow though an extremely bad poet himself, sent for me and said, well, we can't print this, it's not good enough. But it's getting on for it, you know. You must just try a little harder and you'll have it. . . . So that was encouraging. But mostly I had the sense to destroy them before I got to showing them to anybody. And I think the earliest poem that I preserved is only a fragment of one that I wrote in 1923.

Perhaps it was this encouragement that prompted him to try to make it in London. After he arrived he spent most of his time in the Bloomsbury and Soho areas: Russell Square, the British Museum, cafes near the Tottenham Court Road, Charlotte Street, and the University of London. Whatever odd jobs he had, he decided they were not enough to provide for a worryless future. So, in the fall of 1920, he matriculated at the London School of Economics. He kept his nose on this uncongenial grindstone for three terms and then gave up. Why? Said Basil, thinking back on those years: "I was too bored with economics—I got enough of all that to last me a lifetime in a year and a half. Ultimately, I cleared off to France with no money at all. I landed in Paris and, well, had the usual sort of adventures that young men have until Pound got me a job as one of Ford's young men for the time being" [JW, 13]. The chronology becomes imprecise here. He probably left the London School by the middle of 1922. But he probably didn't "clear off" for Paris until the summer of 1923. Sometime during that summer he became an acquaintance of Pound, who took enough interest in his ideas to recommend him to Ford. In a letter to a friend written in 1932, Bunting said he first met Pound "playing a swashbuckling kind of chess" and added:

> I believed then, as now, that his "Propertius" was the finest of modern poems. Indeed, it was the one that gave me the notion that poetry wasn't altogether impossible in the XX century. So I made friends. I was digging roads outside of Paris for a living. I got locked up for a colossal drunk. It was Ezra who discovered me . . . and perjured himself in the courts to try to get me off. When I came out of quod, and was working at the Jockey, he introduced me to Ford Madox Ford and I became sub. ed. and sec. to the *Transatlantic Review* [VF, 3].

More about the colossal drunk—quod—and perjury events later.

Since the *Transatlantic Review* didn't really get underway or have office space until September of that year, we can conclude that Bunting took up his duties sometime in October. To Jonathan Williams' question, "What was this job with Ford Madox Ford—secretarial work?" Bunting said:

> No, not a bit. It was the strangest type of set-up you can imagine. One young man after another performed the same functions, oh, for many years. I think I lasted rather less time than any of the others. My successor was Ernest Hemingway, and I forgot who went immediately before me. The one who is supposed to have lasted longest is Douglas Goldring. He was several years Ford's young man. You did all sorts of things. I acted as assistant-editor, and sub-editor, and various other things for the *Transatlantic Review*, which he was starting. I also bathed the

baby, and answered the telephone. I corrected the proofs and
made various alterations of my own—some of them with and
some of them without his knowledge. I changed a few words in
a Ford-Conrad novel which I was reading the proofs of at that
time too. Nobody troubled. . . . What else did I do? Chiefly I kept
him company. He liked eating and drinking expensively and well
and he wanted somebody to talk to meanwhile. Now Ford may
have been the biggest liar you like. No doubt he was quite a considerable one, but he was always exceedingly entertaining and the
untruths were there not for the sake of untruth but for the sake
of turning a mediocre story into a very good one. To feed in his
company while he talked was always a pleasure. I'd say he was a
kind-hearted man, and I'm fairly sure that the root reason behind
a large party he gave that year was not so much that he was anxious to entertain his literary friends as that he thought it a good
opportunity for me to dance with the daughter of one of his
American colleagues whom I suddenly had a fancy for. Unfortunately, he didn't ask me before hand whether I could dance!
It was rather a failure.

Stella Bowen's recollections of Bunting and Ford in her
memoir, *Drawn From Life*, are similar:

> The early days of the *Transatlantic Review*, before it became ap-
> parent that by no conceivable chance could it be made to pay,
> were great fun. The whole thing was run in conditions of the ut-
> most confusion. Everything that could possibly go wrong with
> regard to the printing, paper, packing, forwarding and distribu-
> tion did go wrong. An elegant White Russian colonel offered his
> services for a pittance, and was sent to make all sorts of arrange-
> ments with printers, bookshops and forwarding agents. All his
> arrangements fell through. A nice young man called Basil Bunting
> also offered his services—in exchange for his keep. He slept in a
> damp little store-room beyond our kitchen and was kept on the
> run by Ford for eighteen hours a day. He endured much in the
> cause of literature, and indeed everybody seemed to be over-
> worked and underpaid in the good cause.*

Ford himself wrote to prospective visitors in this vein:

> If you let us know the route you are coming by and the time of
> the train we will either meet you or have you met by Bunting—a
> dark youth with round spectacles, in a large Trilby hat and a blue
> trench coat with belt who shall hold up a copy of the *Transatlan-
> tic Review* towards passengers arriving at the barrier and smile
> [*Ibid.*, 28] .

Bunting's most careful estimate of Ford is given in a letter he
wrote to Bernard Poli:

> All Ford's biographers miss the point: what's it matter if he told

---

*Cited in *Ford Madox Ford and the Transatlantic Review* by Bernard J. Poli, Syracuse
Univ. Press, 1967, p. 27.

lies? He was a writer of fiction. What does matter is his kindness
to young men and men in distress, his readiness to talk to them at
length, without being patronising or pedantic, his willingness to
consider everything, the tolerance in his frivolity, the care for
living English, the generosity, the fun. Ford did a great deal of
good one way and another, and has never been given full credit
for it. He was a good poet and a good novelist too. To dwell on
what was comical or exasperating in him is to mislead a generation that cannot meet him [*Ibid.*, 144].

But through no fault of his own, Mr. Poli makes some errors about
Bunting's Paris experience:

Basil Bunting was the young English poet and conscientious objector designated by Pound to become a member of the staff; he
spent the first ten shillings Ford gave him as an advance on his
meager salary to celebrate his new appointment and ended up at
the "Santé" prison, actually very close to Ford's house. Perhaps
on account of this recent achievement, he was promoted to the
post of subeditor when the White Russian disappeared with the
manuscript of Ford's first editorial. As Ford's secretary, Basil
Bunting wrote letters for him, but he also had to keep the accounts of the company and run all kinds of errands, including
meeting honored guests at the railroad station [*Ibid.*, 27].

This account is reasonably accurate except for details about
the "Santé" prison experience. This escapade might well be included under the rubric of not the "usual" but the "unusual sort
of adventures that young men have" in Paris. Basil finally told the
whole story which goes something like this.*

A friend of mine had received a hundred pounds which in
those days was quite a lot of money so he invited me along with
another friend on a party to celebrate. We went out on the town.
Around midnight the other friend gave up and left, but we kept
on drinking and celebrating until quite late in the morning until
he gave up. After that, I had nothing to do but go home. The
Paris streets laid out in the time of the Empire often had four corners which looked exactly alike, so that my hotel on one corner
looked like the one on the next corner. My taxi driver drove up
in front of one which I took to be mine. I got in and found my
room but the damn key wouldn't work! That got me quite frus-
trated and furious. Finally, I had to relieve myself on the wall of
the stairs, but I went back and tried to knock the door down.
Eventually the noise aroused the concierge whose husband appeared. He'd never seen me before so concluded I was a burgler

---

*At Orono in 1980, Bunting complained about the inaccuracy of the account I'd given
in the journal in which I confused an evening which he spent drinking with Brancusi with
the events leading to his landing in jail. They were two separate events. So, in answer to
my question, "What did happen? Tell me the whole story," he gave this account. But the
reader should be warned. I have no skills in shorthand and could not write down his
story until some hours after he told it. Thus, it is at best, impressionistic: accurate in the
facts given, but not a word-by-word transcription.

who had broken in. I'd never seen him before, and couldn't imagine what he was protesting about or why he should be trying to kick me out of my own hotel. Finally, he threatened to call the cops if I wouldn't leave quietly. I invited him to do so and while he was gone jumped into bed with his wife. She was fairly old but made up for a lack of youth by a whole lot of enthusiasm. Imagine my chagrin and surprise, right at the height of my own enthusiasm, to be dragged out of bed by the police, who for some mysterious reason wanted to take me to jail. Well, now, as an innocent man, it was my duty to refuse to go. I was outnumbered, but while they were trying to restrain me, I managed to give one of them a good swift kick in the pants. In the end, they overpowered me. By this time I could be charged with a number of crimes: minor ones such as disturbing the peace, but also serious ones such as resisting arrest and what the French call "rebellion."

The next day I was herded into the *grande salle* along with a flock of petty thieves, pickpockets, prostitutes, pimps, and other assorted characters. I happened to have a copy of Villon in my pocket, so while waiting my turn, I sat on a bench reading him, quite aware of the ironies. For Villon himself, centuries before, had sat in this same salon and waited his turn before the magistrate. Here it was that Ezra found me. He was always interested in helping young writers in trouble; but I think it was seeing me reading Villon that really got him. After he heard my story, he rushed away to get lawyers and money or whatever to get me off and see justice done.

The case came to trial. But since a key witness in the prosecution's case was the wife of the hotel keeper, I was saved. She refused to say anything against me or support any of the story the police were telling. She told them that I was a very nice, polite, young man and she hadn't seen me do any horrible things they were accusing me of. Thus, I was only sentenced to two weeks in jail. But it was probably lucky things happened the way they did. If the hotel keeper hadn't come and got me away from the door I was hell-bent to break down, I'd have doubtless been killed. I found out afterwards that sitting in the middle of the room facing the door was an old man with a loaded pistol. If I had come through it, he had every intention of shooting to kill.

Some discrepancies in detail litter the record about Bunting's first months in Paris. From his own memories, we can now deduce what happened. He first had manual labor jobs constructing roads outside the town. He inhabited the cafes where literary figures of the lost generation gathered. He met Pound casually somewhere there during the summer of 1923. During this time he also met Brancusi and ate oysters and drank white wine with him all of one night [*Paideuma*, 9-1, p. 65]. He ended up in "quod" and impressed Pound mightily when he found him reading Villon in the *grande salle* waiting his turn to come before the magistrate. After he got out of prison in late September, Pound got him his job with

Ford. But in January of 1924, he quit and, Pound not being in Paris, took off for Rapallo.

By 1923, Pound had already spent many months in Rapallo and was in the process of becoming a permanent resident so that he was in Paris more as a vistor and to do business than as a permanent resident. In May of 1923, he was consulting with William Bird of the Three Mountains Press, who had agreed to publish the first book of cantos. Since Bird had also given space in a gallery back of his offices to Ford for the *Transatlantic Review*, the Ford-Pound-Bunting connections were in the cards. In the fall and early winter of that year, Pound was much involved in music. He had met George Antheil in June, he finished his opera before that, and he wrote violin music for an Olga Rudge concert in September. But sometime after the January, 1924, issue of the *Transatlantic Review* was out, Pound and Dorothy were back in Italy. His health was not good and he had a troublesome appendix, which he wrote to Yeats about from Assisi on the 8th of May, but by June he was back in Paris again. On July 7th Olga Rudge gave a concert at the Salle Pleyel and did two pieces by Pound. But in October, 1924, Pound took up permanent residence at Rapallo and lived there for the next twenty years.

After the first issue of the *Transatlantic Review* was out in January, Bunting gave up his job as jack-of-all-things to Ford and took off for Italy, probably in February, 1924. He gave Jonathan Williams a brief account of his arrival in Italy:

> When I left there for Italy I called in Rapallo because I had an address for Pound and I thought I would like to say how do to him. But, he'd gone and I didn't expect to see him. I found the place likeable and I stayed on. It was little in those days, not what it is now of course. One day I walked up the mountain. I had to walk in those days, there were no cable railways and no roads. I walked up the mule track and there was a little inn at the top. As I passed the inn somebody rushed out of the doorway and began shouting "Bunting!" "Bunting!" And I looked around and there to my astonishment was Ezra Pound, followed almost immediately by Dorothy, running after me up the mountain. Ezra was very pleasant, and it was from that meeting that I can say that I became one of Pound's friends.

Bunting stayed on for something like a year. During that time he made a living by sailing. He first sailed on sand boats, which brought sand for building purposes along the Tuscany coast, and he learned to handle the big lateen sails they were rigged with. This new skill took him quite a distance because he told Jonathan Williams that he "sailed a fair amount at Amalfi in a little lateen rig." By this time, he had developed a Thoreau-like attitude. If he didn't need much money, he'd not have to spend much time making it. And life on a boat could be very inexpensive:

> Then I bought a boat on the beach near Rapallo—quite a large boat, 26 or 28 feet long I think, undecked, a heavily built fishing boat. Perfectly good once I'd repainted her. She'd looked pretty bad on the beach. I bought her for four pounds and sailed that for some years [JW, 25].

Sailing, working with things, enjoying the striking weather and congenial climate of the Italian Riviera, and talking with Pound and his friends was for Bunting an idyllic life, one that he would not have left willingly without compelling reasons. Such reasons prevailed sometime in 1925. Perhaps it was the death of his father that took him from the land of the sun back to the London of fogs.

V

The year 1925 was a bad one for most people in England because of the nationwide depression caused by the return to the gold standard. But it was lucky for Bunting. He happened to be at Kleinfeldt's public house when he was called to the telephone:

> It was Otto Theiss, the literary editor of the *Outlook*, saying to me, "Bunting, do you know anything about music?" To which I answered, "Not a damn thing!" Theiss then said, "You'd better find out quick, you're our music critic now."

The *Outlook* was an English conservative paper something like *The Nation* in the USA. Or something on the order of *The New Statesman*. Otto Theiss was an American, out to do good in the world, but his interests were broad rather than distinctly political. The job gave Bunting the chance to make an excellent living. He said of the job,

> It was a very good one for a young man of that time of that age. I suppose I made, between what the *Outlook* paid me and what other jobs I was able to get on the strength of that one—writing music for a monthly magazine, an occasional review for the *Musical Times*, sometimes standing in for one of the daily newspaper critics, and so on—I made something like 250 pounds a year. You multiply that by five and you've got the present [1966] equivalent. It's not bad for a youngster of 27 [JW, 15].

At the time, a room in London cost 10.bob [$1.40] a week.

Bunting started with *Outlook* as music critic, but by 1927 he had the title of music editor. His success widened his circle of

acquaintances but he did not know or seek to meet the big ortho-
dox music critics such as Neville Cardus:

> I occasionally met W. J. Turner, who was music critic for *The
> New Statesman*, and, of course, an older man with a musical edu-
> cation such as I hadn't got. Our manner of writing was not dis-
> similar and we were both interested in getting the public to take
> notice of composers despised at that time. The Sunday papers
> in those days were dominated by a whole lot of old academic
> critics who thought in terms of the more abstruse musical and
> technical terms and musical examples on the page, but never
> went beyond the repertory of the Viennese School.

It also gave him the opportunity to learn a lot about music which
in time he was able to read:

> . . . in my early twenties I couldn't really make much of a Bach
> sonata. Before my twenties ended, after I had that spell as music
> critic on the *Outlook* and was able to spend some money on
> scores and to listen with the scores before me, I could for a num-
> ber of years—I've lost the art now—read a score and hear in my
> mind pretty roughly, but accurately enough for my general pur-
> poses, how the thing goes. So I read quite a lot of music of that
> period. Not precisely the same as is now fashionable—Vivaldi was
> not above the horizon at that time.

During 1925, Bunting first met T. S. Eliot. His appointment
was for an interview which Bunting would use in some article he
was writing, but his memory of exactly what the article was about
has become vague. The official reason was in a sense a pretext
anyway. Bunting wanted to see Eliot and Eliot was certain to be
sympathetic to any young poet being encouraged by Pound. In
later days, Bunting remembered most clearly Eliot's tendency to
be oracular and his recommendations about Dante:

> So far as I remember that conversation, he spent a long time
> urging upon me the necessity to read Dante. And being a modest
> young man and not wanting to put him off his stride, I never
> once mentioned that I had already read Dante and knew a good
> deal of the *Inferno* by heart. So that, perhaps, I wasted that first
> interview.

Eliot was a role player. Sitting in the Faber offices as editor of
The Criterion, he played the part with more than a hint of oracular pomposity. But he played other roles. Later this same year,
Bunting saw Eliot at a party wearing an enormous cape lined with
red and eyebrows painted green. He responded to Bunting's expression of amazement with these words: "thought the party needed
hotting up."*

---

*When Basil told me this I could hardly conceal my own amazement. I said, "Basil, you're
kidding, aren't you?" He protested that he wasn't. Then I recalled my own surprise in

The *Outlook* years allowed Bunting some time to write poetry and to experiment with his concepts of musical analogies. He went from Eliot's idea of "Preludes" to his own idea of sonata form in verse, but it took a little time to get the right musical models:

> I had thought all along that the sonata was the more likely one to be of use. But I got off on the wrong foot trying to imitate Beethoven's sonatas, using extremely violent contrasts in tone and speed which don't actually carry well onto the page, and I had to puzzle about that for awhile before I discovered it was better to go back to a simpler way of dealing with the two themes and to take the early or mid-eighteenth-century composers of sonatas— John Christian Bach and Scarlatti—as models to imitate [JW, 14].

During his years with *Outlook*, Bunting's ideas about the music-poetry connection firmed up and became more precise. In 1928, he expressed convictions about the business of the critic which have not changed since. In a piece entitled "Criticism and Music" [*Outlook*, LXI (April 28, 1928), 526-527], he made precise connections between music and poetry:

> No art depends principally or even largely on its appeal to the intellect, and in the Age of Reason itself Pope was preferred to Young for melody, not for sense; Voltaire's style gained for him more admirers than his doctrines, and Chardin was appreciated not for the realism of his rabbits but for the nobility of his rhythm and design. . . .
> . . . it may be due to the deficiency of my intellect that it gets but little more from one art than from another. If music speaks first to the emotions, so, it seems to me, do poetry, sculpture, painting, architecture, even the prose art of fiction, whether in the drama or in the novel. . . . All arts are of a party against the intellect, and if music does outrun the others it is by a very short lead [VF, 13].

But the man who later is going to conclude flatly, "There is no excuse for literary criticism," is already a little uneasy in the role he is playing:

> The principles of criticism must be looked for in a realm that embraces all the arts and where the intellect, however important to the critic as the regulator of his other faculties, plays a limited and subordinate part. This realm is hardly explored at all, and least by the critics who confine their attention to music. It is probable that the principles that may be found in it will be inexpressible in the language of logic. If Beauty and Sublimity escape easy definition how shall their ingredients be tabbed? But until

---

the early 50s while reading a lot of the Eliot correspondence at Harvard. After years of seeing Pound and Yeats referred to as just Pound and Yeats, but seeing Eliot always described as Mr. Eliot, it took time to get used to letters which started "Dear Tom" or "Dear Tommy."

some attempt has been made to describe them criticism must remain more a matter of luck than cunning, of an inborn sympathy
than of acquired technique [*Ibid.*].

One of his steps along the way was to agree with Pound that only
the practitioner of an art can understand the technical problems
it presents:

As you would not seriously consider a man's knowledge of tennis
until either he could make or had made some sort of show in a
tournament, we can assume that until a man can actually control
a given set of procedures there must be many elements in them of
which he has but an imperfect knowledge [VF, 14].

Of all the poetry he wrote during these years, he kept only the
sonata called "Villon" [dated 1925] and a few odes: "To Peggy
Mullett" and "After the Grimaces" [1926], "To Helen Egli" and
"Personal Column" [1927]; and "The Day Being Whitsun"
[1928]. The subject matter of the next ode, also dated 1928, indicates that sometime during that year he left *Outlook* for Simonsides.

An unfortunate event brought about the demise of the magazine. Said Basil: "The *Outlook* died of a libel action that it didn't
want to face and we were out of work. It was very rough going
for awhile" [JW, 17].

Fortunately, through Otto Theiss Bunting had met a quite
remarkable woman who became his patron and subsidized his
freedom to work on several occasions during the next decade.
Margaret de Silver was the widow of an American, one of the
founders of the Civil Liberties Union, who had left her a great deal
of money. Said Basil: "She spent this money in the course of her
lifetime very largely on subsidizing artists, poets, politicians, lawyers, civil liberties, etc. Before she died, I believe she got rid of
practically all of it, just giving it away in this very wonderful and
rather discriminating, generosity" [JW, 18]. After the demise of
Outlook, Otto Theiss told Bunting that she had left him a subsidy
of £200 a year for two years so that he would have a chance to
concentrate on his writing. Typically, he chose to get away from
London and back to the land. When Jonathan Williams asked if
the subsidy kept him in London, he said,

No! With that I said goodbye to London. I was tired of London.
I knew London very well, but I never did like towns, especially
big ones. My first instinct was to get as far away from towns as
possible. I went up to a shepherd's cottage in the hills in central
Northumberland. It was seven miles walk to the cigarette shop
and four miles walk to the pub. It was a very pleasant place up
there. I learned a little about how they train sheep dogs.

The two year grant from Margaret de Silver thus started a new life of freedom. It allowed him to start with a journey to the north followed by travel through Germany and then back to Rapallo, Pound, and the Mediterranean.

VI

Bunting elected to start his new life in isolation at a place in the Simonsides about seven miles south of Rothbury. But practicing his art alone without the stimulation of other poets and artists near was not so successful in reality as it had seemed as an idea. Life at Simonsides was inexpensive and allowed him to husband his resources, but even so he gave up after six months and travelled south. He went first to Germany in 1929, but after a brief stay in Berlin he found he couldn't tolerate the Germans. In a letter to a friend he said: "I tried my own North country for a while, and it wasn't so bad. But I got very little done that I wanted to keep, so I took advice and went to Berlin and it was the worst thing I ever did. In the end to save my sanity I went suddenly to the station and bought a ticket for Italy to look up Pound again" [VF, 5]. But out of the Berlin experience came the sonata entitled "Aus dem zweiten Reich," a sharp condemnation of a sterile, plastic society in the process of being created. *Schrecklich*, the German word used in the poem, is probably stronger than the various English words used to translate it: frightful, dreadful, horrible or hideous.

From his arrival in 1929 to his departure for the Canary Islands at the end of 1933, Rapallo became Bunting's base of operations. But while he still had some of Margaret de Silver's bounty, he was able to seek his fortune in other places. He spent part of 1929 and 1930 in the United States. Louis Zukofsky was in Rapallo when he arrived and he became fond of him both as person and poet. Since Bunting was equipped to write music criticism for anyone who would employ him, Zuk urged him to try his luck in The States. At the crest of the boom decade the idea seemed good, but a month or so after he arrived the October crash of the stock market occurred. By the time he was looking for a job none existed. He placed a few free-lance pieces: "I think I did some for one of the Philadelphia papers. There were some for the *New York Times* and some in *The Nation*, but you didn't get much for them and there weren't many of them in the first place. There certainly was no living in it" [JW, 20].

In early September, Zukofsky had to leave for the University of Wisconsin at Madison where he had a year's appointment in the English Department. Sometime close to the turning of the year Bunting visited Zuk there, an event that changed his life completely: he fell in love and got married. But Margaret de Silver's money was running out so he decided that if he were going to have to live on nothing he'd better return to Italy with his bride: "It was better to go back and see how long we could live on nothing in Italy—rather than the very short time you can live on nothing in the United States" [JW, 20]. Bunting and his new wife settled down in a little place at Rapallo which was "halfway up the mountain." The next two years were one of the happiest interludes in his life. He said of those days:

> I got a good deal of poetry written, I enjoyed conversation, enjoyed sailing my boat, enjoyed the sunshine. And enjoyed having a baby. My first daughter. Pound was there then and various other people. Yeats was there. I saw a good deal of Yeats. But of few others. I don't enjoy literary society or literary conversation [JW, 21].

During these years Bunting, with the help of both Pound and Zukofsky, published quite a lot of poetry. In March, 1930, *Redimiculum Matellarum* came out in Milan. In 1932, an anthology called *Profile*, edited with commentary by Pound, contained parts of "Villon." Also in 1932, *Whips and Scorpions*, a collection by Sherard Vines, and *An "Objectivists" Anthology*, edited by Zukofsky, contained work by Bunting. In 1933, Faber and Faber published *Active Anthology*, edited by Pound, which contained 50 pages of Bunting's poetry.

During these years two other events occurred which had long-range consequences. Bunting's interest in music led him to the discovery of a cache of unpublished Vivaldi manuscripts. Immediately Pound and Olga Rudge took over the project. Basil was also involved in the series of musical events Pound organized for the citizens of Rapallo. Even more consequential was the accidental way he was led to learn Persian. Jonathan Williams asked how it happened. He explained that he had found a little book along the quays in Genoa which was a translation by two Italians of the *Hojoki*. That led him to write "Chomei at Toyama."

> So, when I finished turning that into a poem, I thought, well, I'd go back and have another look at the quays. I found a book—tattered, incomplete—with a newspaper cover on it marked "Oriental Tales." I bought it, in French. It turned out to be part of the early 19th century prose translation of Firdausi, and it was absolutely fascinating. I got into the middle of the story of the education of Zal and the birth of Rustam—and the story came to

> an end! It was quite impossible to leave it there, I was desperate
> to know what happened next. I read it, as far as it went, to Pound
> and Dorothy Pound, and they were in the same condition. We
> were yearning to find out, but we could think of no way. The
> title page was even missing. There seemed nothing to do but learn
> Persian and read Firdausi, so, I undertook that. Pound bought me
> the three volumes of Vullers and somebody, I forget who, bought
> me Steingass's dictionary, and I set to work. It didn't take long.
> It's an easy language if it's only for reading that you want it. It's
> difficult to speak. . . .

When later he did learn to speak modern Persian and hear the
sound of the classics, he found it to be a most musical language.
We may say that the dramatic effect the Chinese written character came to have on Pound's poetic practice is repeated in the
effect Persian poetry had on the poetic practice of Bunting. Even
more than that, his knowledge of Persian changed the whole
course of his life during WW II.

Although he wrote thousands of lines and dozens of separate
poems during these Rapallo years, he kept only "Chomei at
Toyama" and fifteen short odes [9-23]. He believes that on the
average he keeps no more than one line out of any dozen he writes,
a practice which leads him to tell students a poet's most important tool is his wastebasket. So, he wrote, discarded, polished, and
wrote some more. And listened to Pound and Yeats. Although he
didn't like literary talk, he liked listening to them. The whole
dialog with Jonathan Williams on this point is striking:

> W.   What kind of conversation did Yeats like? Did he like to talk
>   poetry?

> B.   Yeats liked gossip. He was ready to talk about anything at
>   anytime. He was always entertaining, often very intelligent
>   on whatever you chose to talk about.

> W.   And Pound?

> B.   Pound was wit and brilliance. He's so rapid it makes him a
>   most excellent conversationalist. All he requires from any-
>   body is a fact or an observation or an argument set in front
>   of him and he'll go off at once and talk magnificently. I
>   believe, nowadays, he's gone quite silent. That is a loss to
>   the world.

> W.   It didn't have to be High Culture?

> B.   Oh, no. Anything would set him going.

> W.   I didn't know that Yeats had spent much time down there.

B. For three years he spent half the year at Rapallo. He had a flat which he let indefinitely. He was still there when I left— that would be the end of 1933. I left Rapallo and went to the Canaries [JW, 21].

Bunting didn't want to leave Rapallo, but poverty forced the move. Prices in Italy were on the increase, but the pay he received for free lance writing was not. He made some money doing manual labor jobs; Margaret de Silver provided some "on various pretexts"; and some money came occasionally from his wife's family. Thus, the pattern Bunting had developed was repeated: if you can't increase your income to cover increased expenses, you must decrease your expenses. At the end of 1933, that could best be done in the Canary Islands.

Bunting and his family stayed in the Canaries for about three years and found the place both good and bad. The tradewind climate is hot and humid, but there is little rain: clouds blown off the sea condense on the mountains and the water trickles into the ground where it has to be mined from galleries. The sky is continually overcast, but enough sunshine comes through to sunburn you faster than the bare sun does on the Mediterranean.

Bunting formed no close friendships there. He played chess sometimes with a man from St. Helena, who was a friend of Francisco Franco. Once he played with Franco, who was then military governor of the Canaries. "Occasionally, there were all three of us at the table with a drink and a chess board" [JW, 22]. But Bunting did not find himself temperamentally sympathetic with the people:

I don't like Spaniards at all as a rule. I like them better than Germans, but they are a cruel people, the Spaniards. One gets tired of their cruelty, one gets tired of the neglect of comfort, of the horrible food the Spaniards find good enough for themselves even when they're rich enough to afford very decent food. But, the climate in the Canaries is delightful. The scenery is very good. The girls are very pretty.

The only work he preserved from his years there is "The Well of Lycopolis," which he wrote because he got very gloomy. He says, "The Well" is "about as gloomy a poem as anyone would want" [*Ibid.*]. But an event which caused joy as well as problems was the birth of a second child. Money was scarce; the international situation was worsening; his wife was getting increasingly uneasy with more responsibilities and more insecurity. She wanted to get the family out of the Canaries and onto a more secure basis. Thus came a dramatic change and upheaval. Thirty years later Bunting could summarize the trauma in offhand terms:

We left there just a day or two before the outbreak of the Spanish

> Civil War, and went back to London, where my wife presently
> quit me and took the children with her and went to America.

After she left, he turned once again to boats and the sea:

> Yes . . . I thought the best way to face up to the difficulty of life
> was to get a little boat and live on that. At least you were away
> from the mass of apes that call themselves mankind. I had a year
> aboard the *Thistle* and enjoyed it very much. One can live awfully
> cheaply that way.

He bought the *Thistle* in Essex and after getting used to the boat
sailed it down the channel on the way to France. But to get the
papers necessary for foreign waters was impossible. A complete
pedigree required knowing all the owners from the time the boat
was built, and he couldn't get the list completed. But the result
was all right: "I got stuck in Devonshire and spent a very pleasant
winter going out with the herring fishermen and helping the seine-
net men on the shore."

The *Thistle* was a six tonner which Bunting could handle
alone. After handling it, he was "able to take on much bigger
boats." He bought it for a hundred pounds and used it for a year.
But then he had to have money so he sold it for two hundred
pounds. He then went back to school at "a very peculiar place
called Nellist Nautical Academy." His account of the place has a
flavor of its own:

> It's in Newcastle, and it's a cramming school for people who want
> certificates to be mates or masters. And it used to turn out nearly
> half of all the Merchant Navy officers in Britain. When I first
> saw it I couldn't believe my eyes. I walked in asking for Mr. Nellist
> and was shown into a room in an old house across which I
> couldn't see because of the thickness of the tobacco smoke—all
> these men smoking pipes. No window was ever opened, the
> smoke just accumulated and got thicker and thicker like London
> fog. . . . You learned the routine things, how to handle the nauti-
> cal tables and the theory of navigation and so forth. I picked and
> chose. Because of my eyes I couldn't hold a certificate, so that
> didn't enter into the matter at all. I just wanted to know enough
> to handle a boat intelligently. They were very pleased, for they
> had not had anybody wanting to read sailing stuff as against
> steamship stuff for a long time. That brought me into classes
> where I would not otherwise have been at all, of course; and into
> one class where I was with a number of shipmasters reading for
> the extra masters certificate. And there old Mr. Nellist explained
> to us the various ways of correcting the error of the sextant.
> There was one way, now outdated, called taking the angle off the
> arc, about which you were required to know something. He ex-
> plained this. He said: "Now, ye dinna need to knaw much aboot
> it, cause its outa date. And if the examiner say to ye, what aboot
> the angle off the arc, ye just say to that Board of Trade Examiner,

bugger the angle off the arc, there's a new method!" I wonder how many of them did that? . . . I remember once when we had a mock examination. The man—a mate reading for master—sitting next to me was given two or three old charts of the Red Sea and the Indian Ocean and told to make a bridge-book for a ship from Suez to Karachi. The obvious thing, of course, was simply to take the ship down the Red Sea, noting the various lights you'd see on the way, any special dangers, and around the bottom of Arabia and up again to Karachi. This man next to me had not had an opportunity yet during the examination of showing off his knowledge of the way to set out a great circle route. So he set to work. He took the latitude and the longitude of both places, applied his mathematics and worked out the great circle route. And it was only when he came at last—towards the end of the time allowed for the question—to transfer it to the chart that he discovered he'd taken his ship across the middle of the Arabian Desert [JW, 23].

After finishing at the Nellist Academy, Bunting returned to the US where he got jobs sailing other men's boats, including "a big schooner," but there were not enough such jobs to keep going. He was in Los Angeles when the Germans went into the Sudeten-land and saw a handwriting on the wall different from that seen by the British government of the time. William Carlos Williams [*Autobiography*, p. 264] wrote:

Bunting had been a conscientious objector in the First World War and they had given him some rough treatment. It is worth noting, however, that for the Second World War he rushed across the United States from California to go to England, as fast as he could, to enlist [VF, 6].

Although he was back in England by May Day of 1939, he couldn't get into any of the services. While waiting, he did "six solid, stolid lectures" on history from Alexander the Great to the Middle Ages for "W.E.A." classes. These were completed by December 1939. In August he complained to Zukofsky: "I am idle; . . . no nearer job, on waiting lists of army (intelligence), air force (balloons), . . . but nothing comes of it" [VF, 7]. Bunting's account of these days as he gave it to Jonathan Williams some 24 years later has his typical sense of irony and verve:

And then the War came. First of all I couldn't get into any of the service units. I finally wangled my way into the Royal Air Force by coming across a doctor on one of the boards who had known my father, was friendly, and allowed me to get the letters on the eye-chart by heart before I had to read them out. And all that would have been dull, for they considered me too old for any-thing except the damned balloons after I had been trained. The squad were all Welshmen and many of them didn't understand English. Amusing blokes. After training I was sent to a balloon

site in Hull—terrible bore. But the very first day I was there a
notice appeared asking for volunteers for what was described as
difficult and dangerous work at sea. And I thought, well, that's
the job for me. And went for it. The people I left behind at Hull
were killed in the great raid on the docks which took place almost
immediately after I left. I found that the "dangerous and difficult work at sea" turned out to be the most comfortable you
could find in the Royal Air Force. We worked on these large
yachts that millionaires had built before the War. The masts had
been taken out of them, of course. They were running on diesel
engines. We lived in berths that had been built for Rothschilds,
and we ate very well. The crews were mixed—partly RAF, partly
Navy, partly civilian fishermen. We got on very well together. On
my boat, the *Golden Hind*, it was extremely difficult to get anybody to take the day off when they had a day in harbor. We had
to make it compulsory to go ashore, otherwise they wouldn't.
Oh yes, I enjoyed that year. That was 1940 and some of 1941....
After that I went to Persia, ultimately. Somebody invented a lot
of little balloons that ships could carry for themselves and our big
balloons weren't needed any more. And I was going to have to
go back to this damned old business of flying balloons ashore. So,
I wrote a letter to the Air Ministry. I told them the only thing
I knew was very old, mediaeval, classical Persian. Curiously, they
were sufficiently impressed by that to send me on to Persia as
interpreter for a squadron [JW, 26].

Bunting had never heard a word of Persian spoken until he
arrived in Persia and was immediately called upon to interpret for
a court martial. He did. But his performance was more inventive
than precise. Afterwards, he could only hope that "they put the
right man in jail" and consoled himself that the case was not one
which required "shooting or hanging." But even with so halting a
start, Basil was very glad to get to Persia. He has always since
called it "one of the most civilized countries in the world" and
"one of the pleasantest to live in." Of Isfahan, he says, it's "the
pleasantest city I've ever been in. . . ." To Jonathan Williams
marveling about such wonders, Bunting had good answers:

W. And you got there on the basis of your classical Persian.
That's great. Was it understandable?

B. Well, it was understandable, but it was queer, no doubt. The
same thing had happened to me much earlier with Italian. I
learned Italian from Dante. And when I went to Italy and
tried to talk to people, obviously, it was as if someone came
along in England speaking a Chaucerian mode. With the wild
men of the Luri tribes and Bakhtiari tribes I got on very
well. Their dialect is very similar to early mediaeval Persian.
With the Teheranis it was much harder.

W. And you were interpreting for the British troops?

B.   Yes. In fact I found myself in charge of a vast number of
     Luri workmen, and that was simple enough. I got on very
     well with them. We wandered about the country a bit, then
     went off in pursuit of the Eighth Army. We had to take in
     some shells, because it had become obvious that the Germans
     were not going to get down through the Caucasus while
     there was Stalingrad on the flank.

W.   How is that?

B.   They were simply unable to capture Stalingrad, so we could
     be spared. There was a hell of a great convoy of lorries full
     of shells waiting for anyone that would take them. Our
     squadron leader, without asking whether anybody could
     drive or not, said oh, we'll take them. Then they found that
     by putting on everybody who had ever taken a milkcart a
     hundred yards down the street and by making all the officers
     drive, we could just manage. We had to take on a few Indian
     drivers as well to cross the desert. We set off and were a
     month getting from Basra to Tripoli. A month of very hard
     fare, yet one of those I've enjoyed most in my life. Seeing
     vast stretches of the desert; and from El Alamein onwards
     there was this vast pile in all directions of abandoned, broken
     arms, broken guns, broken airplanes, broken cars and lorries,
     lying about. One of the two or three most astonishing things
     I've ever seen in my life—I've described it in "The Spoils."
     As I said, we went to Tripoli, and one or two of us went as
     far as Wadi Aqarit, where the fighting was going on at that
     moment. There I was obliged to take a commission, which
     I'd never wanted, and I set off to Cairo.

W.   Let's take a tea break.

B.   Thank God . . . [JW, 27-28].

VII

Bunting's love affair with the Persian people, their land, and
their culture grew with the years. He approved of their easy going
life and values. He liked the way they kept untouched by modern
advertising and the lusts it creates for omnivorous consumption.
They were diametrically opposite to the plastic modern Germany
he couldn't tolerate. The Bakhtiari and Luri workmen of his unit
sensed his feelings and returned them. They could talk to him because their dialect was close to the early medieval Persian of the
Sha Namah. In a letter to Zukofsky [May 9, 1943] he wrote:

> My men became the envy of other units. And out of hours (and
> out of bounds) they entertained me now and then as Bakhtiaris
> should, with pipes and drums, dancers and singers, sweetmeats

and rice and strong drink, and a man to fan me all the evening—
very welcome in the terrific heat of Khuzistan (139° in the shade
—and it had been 145° a little earlier) [VF] .

Later he helped lead a convoy across the Arabian desert to
Tripoli. The commission he never wanted but felt obliged to take
involved espionage. Under some kind of secrecy code he was not
supposed to talk about it then or, as far as he is concerned, now.
But when he was back in Northumberland, he wrote in general
about his former duties in a letter to Zukofsky, dated July 23,
1944:

> I found myself practically in charge of a unit working beyond its
> strength. . . . I've even signed documents as Medical Officer! . . .
> I planned operations, interpreted orders from above, ruled every-
> thing without official authority or backing. I even started and
> regulated a civilian market (not black, but stripy), caught and
> punished thieves, traced a spy, instituted liaison with an Italian
> regiment.

But in an interview at St. Andrews in the USA in 1976,
when he was asked about the treatment of Pound as if he had been
a spy for Mussolini, Bunting told some of his own experiences as
a spy during the war. He led into his remarks by observing "American behavior in that sort of thing shocked English people horribly,"
and then he went on to illustrate:

> During the war I captured, for instance, a very famous Ger-
> man spy and I was asked, what should we do with him? I said
> send him to Australia, he'll make a damn good immigrant, and
> this was accepted by the English government and the Australian
> government. Unfortunately our treaty with the Russians obliged
> us to send him back to Germany. But he escaped—we probably
> arranged for him to escape. That's the way we dealt with spies.
> Of course, when he was captured and being sent for interrogation
> and he asked me what was going to happen to him, I said, "Of
> course we usually hang spies." But nobody ever had the slightest
> intention of doing that sort of thing to him.
>
> But I captured an American girl once. She was a silly bloody
> girl. It's true that she had done extraordinary things, but always
> by the folly of other people, not because of her own cleverness.
> She came from Chicago and imagined that she could be like Mata
> Hari. She went off to Mexico City. She had no papers, so they
> chucked her straight out. She managed to get into Brazil and then
> into Argentina—still with no papers. Then she got to South Africa,
> where she managed to become the mistress of a British official.
> She at last got some information and she sent it to the Japanese
> —it wasn't very much. Then she went, with the help of the British
> official, to India. She couldn't do very much in India, so she ar-
> rived in Persia where she had the brazen cheek to go and make
> herself the mistress of an intelligence officer in the South of

Persia and he sent her up to Teheran finally where she became the mistress of a man in the Embassy. I still hadn't heard of her yet, you see. Then one of my Russian colleagues in Isfahan said: "There's a queer specimen coming down here this weekend. You'd better look into her." I began making enquiries and we had her letters looked at and so on and here she was in constant correspondence with the Japanese to try and do down the United States. I'm sure it was purely a matter of silly girl vanity, you see, nothing more. But I caught her, as she'd obviously got to be stopped, and I sent her back to Teheran. My impression was, since we always treated all these people with extreme gentleness, that nothing much could happen to her. She'd get a spanking and go back to Chicago. But in fact we handed her over to the Americans and I was told that three days afterward they shot her. That's the way they behaved. We were absolutely frightened of them.

In 1945, Bunting was back in Isfahan, this time as Vice-Consul, and he wrote to Zukofsky about his war experiences on April 21:

. . . my taste for variety has certainly been gratified in this war. I have been on almost every British front worth being on except Dunkirk, traveled through every rank from Aircraftsman First Class to Squadron-Leader (equals Major, to forestall your question), seen huge chunks of the world that I wouldn't otherwise have visited, been sailor, balloon-man, drill instructor, interpreter, truck driver in the desert, intelligence officer to a busy fighter squadron, recorder of the doings of nomadic tribes, labour manager, and now consul in a more or less crucial post [VF, 8].

But on June 10, 1946, Bunting was on his way home to England, where he planned to spend some of the money he had saved in the service "to buy a boat and to live again at sea—it's cheap there—and to write." From a transit camp in Cairo, he wrote again to Zukofsky:

So my responsibility for telling our two governments what happens in Western Asia—between the Jordan and the Indian border, between the Hadhramand and the Ukraine—is ended at last. So are the pleasant journeys ended, amongst mountain tribes, long trips on horseback, moufflon hunts, banquets with provincial governors and cocktail parties with diplomats. . . . All the tribesmen ask the same question: "Why are you taking these officers away from us? Who will be left to understand the Kurds and tell the Powers what we need? . . . The Bakhtiari sent a note to the British Government asking for my return to Persia [*Ibid.*].

Maybe it was the note from the Bakhtiari which resulted in the change of plans. He didn't get his boat because the Foreign Office sent him back to Persia, this time to the British Embassy in Teheran. What exactly he did is not known, but he reported to Zuk on

May 5, 1947 that the job required "all the astuteness and tact" he could muster. But by November he had left the Embassy to work as a correspondent for the *London Times*. The change seems to have come about at least partly because of a new love and a new marriage [1948], this time to a beautiful Persian girl named Sima. The evidence suggests that he had found paradise on earth and planned to live there for a long time. Robert Payne, an American visitor, has given us a glimpse of him luxuriating expansively in his Persian garden, as if on a permanent honeymoon in paradise gained:

> I spent the days bathing in this waterfall in the garden of an English poet not far from Shamran, up the sloping road which eventually loses itself in the snows of the Elbruz mountains. It was a small garden, full of dying roses, for summer was coming on. There was a red-tiled swimming-pool, and the poet was credited with possessing the best cook and the best collection of whisky in Teheran. He possessed a passionate love of Persia, translated their poetry superbly, knew many Persian dialects and thought the world and ambition well lost as long as he could remain in his garden, with his exquisitely handsome Armenian wife, his books and his pipes. He had been in the British Secret Service, held—and this was one of the most astonishing things about him—the rank of squadron-leader in the R.A.F. and was known in Teheran for the wisdom of his political judgments. He had known everyone, and was afraid of no one. He looked like an intelligent monkey, and there was something in the quick sharp voice which reminded you of Socrates. He had known Yeats and Pound in their heyday in Paris, starved under Paris bridges, written and rarely published some of the best poetry of our time. He had quelled a German-aided revolt of the Bakhtiari tribesmen almost singlehanded, and to that extent he may have altered the course of the war, for the Germans were within an ace of succeeding in creating a foothold in Persia. I had heard about him in China. Ezra Pound had said once: "If I was a younger man, I would go to Teheran just to see him."
>
> He puffed on his evil-smelling pipe and gazed at the blue water in the pool, where three Armenian girls were splashing one another. Yellow butterflies ran wild over the scented garden, and no sounds came from the street outside. He raised his shaggy eyebrows, and said quickly: "You're quite wrong. You say the best is Persepolis, but it isn't—the best is the people. The people are entrancing. There is nothing in the world like them. I don't know what it is—a strange mixture of licence and dignity. They live their lives without subterfuges: they have all the dignity of the desert Arabs without the Arab hysteria. It is the only place in the world where it is impossible to be bored. Do you remember the inscription on the tomb of Hafiz:
>
>> When thou passest by the head of this tomb, invoke a blessing,
>> For this is a place of pilgrimage for all the libertines of the world.

They are gay and charming and effervescent—much more than the French. They know their own minds. They have decided what is due to God, and what is due to themselves. And they cannot be completely serious: as soon as they make the effort, they realise how ridiculous they are. They give the impression of knowing all the answers, as perhaps the Chinese do, and so they play, even when they are most miserable—" . . .*

But the paradise had to be lost, again because of money problems. In 1950, the cost of living forced him to take his new wife and a new child back to Northumberland.

In a letter to Zuk [Nov. 12, 1950] he said that he had convinced the *London Times* to send him as their first foreign correspondent to Italy but that he had to spend "six dreary weeks" in London "pretending to learn what [he] already knew about newspaper offices" [VF, 9]. The dreariness was ameliorated somewhat by the chance to see old friends such as T. S. Eliot and visit old hangouts and cafes within the neighborhood of the British Museum. But toward the end of 1950, he was on the job in Italy. Although Bunting knew little about it, at this same time Dallas Simpson of Galveston, Texas, at the behest of Pound, was publishing a collection of his poetry. In June of 1951, his job in Italy came to an end and he returned to Northumberland. This time he did buy a boat, but his plans were interrupted by a new job offer from the *Times*: foreign correspondent in Persia. He said to Jonathan Williams: "Yes, I was back in England. I did buy a boat and it was being fitted out for sea when this job was offered me and I had to sell it again" [JW, 29]. Bunting returned to Teheran with Sima and the child. It was toward the end of 1951 that the confrontation between Bunting and Mosaddeq occurred. Jonathan Williams asked: "And Mosaddeq got rid of everyone, of all the foreign journalists?" Bunting's response must be given in full in his own words:

Oh no, the journalists mostly ran away. They were terrified, by mobs and by other threats. I have never seen people like them. Very few of them showed the slightest spunk of any sort. There was just one from the *Daily Express* who was not afraid to go with me into the middle of a big riot. But, after the Greek journalist got hit on the head and was killed during a riot, the rest departed. It was shocking. I think all the cheap English papers and the American papers, without exception, disappeared within the next two or three days. In fact, all these kind of things are much less dangerous than people imagine. You can go about with threats against your life for a long time and nothing happens at all—there's no use taking the slightest notice of them. I've been

---

*Reprinted with the author's permission from *Journey to Persia*, 1951.

shot at once or twice, and often had people looking for me supposed to be going to kill me if they could, but they never got
around to it. If somebody hires a man to kill you, that man
doesn't want to earn the money. He wants to get the money, but
once he kills you he's taking a risk for it and he's not likely to
kill you at all. One time there was a mob. I don't know quite
who had hired them but I've no doubt they were hired all right.
They came around and began shouting outside the door of the
Ritz in Teheran for my life. They *wanted* to kill me. And I sat
in the flat of the Reuter's correspondent and watched for some
time and then said I want to go hear what they're saying. And
Reuter's man was a bit afraid to go out. I said what the hell, no
one knows what I look like or anything. I went out. I walked into
the crowd and stood amongst them and shouted DEATH TO MR.
BUNTING! with the best of them, and nobody took the slightest
notice of me. Another time, two men with pistols arrived at our
door while I was taking an afternoon nap. My wife told them I
wasn't in. That was all; they accepted that and went away again.
There's no great determination on the part of hired assassins
[JW, 29].

Mosaddeq got his way and Bunting was expelled as a suspicious
person. But Bunting believes he was really expelled because he
refused to doctor the news to fit Mosaddeq's theories. The dic-
tator tried to persuade Sima to stay on with her child, but British
authorities were able to clear them and they all returned to
Throckley, Northumberland. Here in 1952, his son Thomas Fara-
marz was born. And here in various places in his northern home
country, Bunting has lived most of the time since. Because he had
no university degrees and because he was muzzled by the official
secrets act from detailing his experiences, he was unable to get
work in which his amazing creative talents could be used. To support wife and family, he was reduced to "proofreading a column
of suburban train times, then seedsmen's catalogs, and finally
electoral lists" [VF, 10]. For years he commuted everyday to
Newcastle to produce the financial page and write copy for the
Evening Chronicle, a job which required living among a bunch
of walking zombies:

Provincial journalists are not capable of any thought of any sort
at all. No doubt he writes what he thinks is expected of him and
his notions are framed on God only knows what. Certainly, *not*
on any experience of life. By now I've had a long life. I've seen
very many odd situations and I have never at any time seen
people so wholly without experience of life as journalists. They
go to newspaper offices from the most ignorant parts of secon-
dary-modern schools. That's where they're recruited. And they
are never outside the newspaper office again for the rest of their
days, except to do a little shorthand writing in the police court

or something like that. They see nothing and their notions of life are probably adopted from out-of-date novels. The stupid things you see in newspapers are going to be there as long as newspapers are run the way they are. Like anything else that lives upon advertising—they'll be run the same way. That is the horror of all these attempts to extend the sphere of advertising to television and so on [JW, 30].

One of the worst consequences of such an enervating existence was that the born poet could no longer find the time and energy to write poetry. He had been able to write very little since the beginning of the war. The *Collected Poems* contain only one brief ode for each of the years 1947, 1948, and 1949, and the five Persian Overdrafts out of the same period. These brief works were followed by a silence which lasted for thirteen years. Then Bunting, the poet, came back to life and work because of a miracle which took place in 1963. In that year, a young poet-to-be named Tom Pickard began writing for help and advice to such poets as Jonathan Williams, Louis Zukofsky, and Robert Duncan. They all told him that since he lived in Newcastle the poet to see was Basil Bunting who lived nearby. So, Tom Pickard arrived: the effect of that meeting and the many that followed was catalytic and charismatic for both the old man and the young one. Bunting was re-born as a poet and went on to write his greatest work, and Tom Pickard got seriously down to business, trying to become one. What happened after, including the belated fame that has come to Bunting, is told elsewhere in this book.

HUGH KENNER

THE SOUND OF SENSE*

The busy reviewer's cliché, "a distinct voice," is like most clichés after all based on *something*. Poets, as we encounter them face to face, sound different from one another, and have learned much of their craft by listening to themselves. Pound's gamin theatrics were supported by a habit of intonation; Williams's phrases ran upscale in headlong short-breathed surprise. And the tune of Basil Bunting's voice is gay in its cherishing of Tyneside phonemes; nowhere in his English tongue are there inconspicuous syllables.

> *Remember, imbeciles and wits . . .*

He takes a minatory pause after "Remember," puts a sinister rising inflection on "and": wits are not to suppose themselves exempted from the whims of Death, that Guignol headmaster. Most readers would slur over the "and."

His are Northern habits of speech, he is quick to specify: as, in his version of English literary history, have been those of poets you'd not think of that way. Swinburne was a northerner. So was Wordsworth, who "composed his poems by shouting them aloud," and shouted deliberate vowels much like Bunting's. There are Wordsworth rhymes only northern intonation will preserve; there's also an hour of Bunting reading Wordsworth preserved in the BBC archives: "The Brothers" and "Michael," taletelling in a voice that comes out of the dark. Even Spenser (Bunting claims) was taught by schoolmasters come south from Durham, and the deliberate tapestry of his stanzas is ablaze with small words rendered richly audible:

> *The dapper ditties, that I wont devise*
> *To feed youth's fancy, and the flocking fry*
> *Delighten much; what I the bett for-thy?*
> *They han the pleasure, I a slender price . . .*

---

*Part of this essay appeared in the issue of *Paideuma*, Vol. 9, No. 1, which celebrated Bunting's 80th birth year.

That *The Shepheardes Calendar* affects north-country dialect is an annotator's commonplace; that Spenser's mouth may have been adept with north-country sounds—cherished in Ireland, where he read aloud stanzas of *The Faerie Queene* in progress—is a possibility likely to enter no one's head but Bunting's, where those sounds are alive to guard little words from slurring.

> *Brag, sweet tenor bull . . .*

In the opening line of *Briggflatts* his reading—preserved on a Stream recording (P 1205)—accords "sweet" as much time as any of the other words. The line is not metrically equivalent to "Bag the tender wool."

The year he taught at Santa Barbara, Basil would turn up from time to time at our dinner-table, to the repeated delight of one of my daughters, who thought that for once a poet looked like a poet. He looked trim and twinkly-eyed, with a white moustache, and I suspect she was projecting on his features the undoubted fact that he *sounded* like a poet.

The poet's voice didn't recite poetry, save a snatch now and then in illustration. It told endless stories: Persian stories, secret service stories. "Wing-Commander Bunting" was one form of address to which he had been entitled, part of his role in Intelligence. There was a vivid hilarious account of a plane bumping down, its fabric blown loose from its struts, crucial parts of its framework held together by the clenched fists of the passengers. There were dog-stories, camel-stories. And there was the story of Fordie and Kipling, whom he alleged to have been in some way related. And Kipling was coaching his younger charge in his Sunday School lesson, and as he spoke of the clouds, the halos and the harps, Ford's face grew longer and longer.

"And that, Fordie," quoth Kipling, "is where you will go if you are good.

"But if you are *bad*—

"You will go to a *much worse place*."

He has a story too—I heard it only years later—about one of his Santa Barbara classes, where he'd gotten them reading Wordsworth's "Idiot Boy" aloud, overcoming their impatience by making them linger. And as first one, then another, took up the reading, they gradually began to find that tall tale—funny. (It has *never* been officially acknowledged that Wordsworth might anywhere be funny.) And the laughter grew contagious, and the roomful of California adolescents were helpless with hysterics, and from the next classroom there came bangs on the wall to get them to shut up.

He told that in a BBC studio in Newcastle, where we were making a tape. The idea was to record about an hour of Basil, out of which could be edited a half-hour NPR program for American audiences. I was not there to "interview"—that had been stipulated in advance. I simply prodded, suggested subjects, handed him passages to read as the whim took me.

Sound and voice of course, and the rooting of poetry in these, were natural topics for an acoustic medium. He talked of the primacy of dance—"Watch your children when they are going to school; they don't walk—they dance!" He had even known, he said, a naturalist who came upon a tribe of gorillas dancing. The dance is in our animal blood, and so is the rhythmic chanting of unintelligible sounds; and the poet is he who can gather up this blood-rite and miraculously contrive that the words shall make gestures of meaning as well.

(I have just this moment come upon Donald Davie's TLS article [23 Nov. '79] on Edward Thomas, where we read of Robert Frost speaking in 1914 "about 'the sound of sense,' " meaning by that what comes over of a conversation that is heard "from behind a door that cuts off the words." And Frost also said, "A sentence is a sound in itself on which other sounds called words may be strung." Those are Bunting's priorities too: the tune, then the words.)

Bunting thought Yeats's "I am of Ireland . . ." had very little meaning but was a fine poem for all that; its show of meaning sufficed.

> 'I am of Ireland
> And the Holy Land of Ireland,
> And time runs on,' cried she.
> 'Come out of charity,
> Come dance with me in Ireland.'

Paraphrase, anyone?

Rhyme, he said, was a binder, a weaver-together; sometimes also a prompter. For he quoted Eliot, a long-ago mentor, who admonished him that young poets especially should cultivate rhyme. "For when you have nothing to say—and when you are very young you *have* nothing to say—rhyme will suggest something." He suspected that the young Eliot had acted on that principle:

> I grow old . . . I grow old . . .
> I shall wear the bottoms of my trousers rolled.

And he was anxious that we include one clarification, which he enunciated carefully. "People sometimes suppose me to be saying that music is the only thing in poetry. Not at all. It is not the only thing. But it is the only *indispensable* thing."

Like everyone who uses the word "music" in statements like that, Basil assumes that we know what it means. Certainly, as a sometime music critic, he knows what he means, and he does not mean mellifluousness. For verse is apt to be judged "musical" when the words in a line sound as much alike as possible—

> *The moan of doves in immemorial elms*

—and it seems not to be reflected that an array of like sounds is not at all what anyone expects of music. You get an array of like-sounding words by paring off the raspy-edged consonants (expunging the sound of "s" in particular was called by Tennyson "kicking the geese out of the boat"), to leave your vowels immersed in a syrup of l's and m's and n's. But the identity of a word is contained in its consonant structure—hence the phone-book abbreviations, plmbr, tchr—and insofar as a poet renders consonants unnoticeable he renders words indistinguishable.

Late 19th-century English verse in particular was apt to be marked by a compulsive fastidiousness over what the phonetician calls junctures: occasions when consonants abut. You can avoid them completely if the successor to any word ending with a consonant is a word commencing with a vowel—

> *In the afternoon we came unto a land*
> *In which it seemed always afternoon.*

"S must not meet s," George Moore recalls Yeats proclaiming at the turn of the century, though by 1938 Yeats was willing to write

> *Swear by what the sages spake.*

Now consonantal junctures so characterize human speech that a boxful of electronic parts can be made to distinguish speech from instrumental music by no other criterion.* It follows that the poetic of mellifluousness pushes poetry far away from natural utterance, so much so that to ears trained on the early Yeats the Pound "Seafarer" actually sounds unnatural:

> *May I for my own self song's truth reckon*

—self#song's#truth! Unspeakably unmusical! And though sensibility may alter terminology lags, and "musical" is not a word people apply unprompted to

> *Brag, sweet tenor bull*

though its five discrete vowels, held apart from one another by

---

*I built one years ago. It silences radio commercials with about 95% sureness.

consonantal junctures, resembles a musical phrase from the keyboard more closely than what usually gets called musicality.

A phrase from the keyboard; one thing by which the poet
can be guided is the quality of specific instruments. When Pound
wrote "libretto" in the margin of a passage in Canto 81, he invited
us to hear in the A-E-I-O of

> *Ere the season died a-cold*

and the I-O-U of

> *I rose through the aureate sky*

a singer running through the scale, the scale of the five vowels,
not the scale of musical notes. And when he came to

> *Has he tempered the viol's wood*
> *To enforce   both the grave   and the acute?*

plucked strings were in his ear, as we can tell by comparing the
consonantal junctures—enforce #both, and #the—with those in
Mauberley's

> *Go, dumb-born book,*

where context tells us to hear the boom of a grand piano. Alter
the line from the Canto by omitting one article—

> *To enforce   both the grave   and acute.*

Its effect collapses.

These are details, but poetry is made of details. They have
this quality in common, that they hover on the borders of onomatopoeia, a bull, a lute, a piano being named in the vicinity to help
us collect our acoustic attention. Bunting has a little tour-de-force
in this genre:

> *A thrush in the syringa sings.*
>
> *'Hunger ruffles my wings, fear,*
> *lust, familiar things.*
>
> *Death thrusts hard. My sons*
> *by hawk's beak, by stones,*
> *trusting weak wings*
> *by cat and weasel, die.*
>
> *Thunder smothers the sky.*
> *From a shaken bush I*
> *list familiar things,*
> *fear, hunger, lust.'*
>
> *O gay thrush!*

That's as densely packed as 50 words can be. "My sons by hawk's beak, by stones, trusting weak wings, by cat and weasel, die"—so runs the fourth sentence word for word in prose, and it makes mannered prose indeed.

But it isn't prose; one thing Bunting means when he calls music "the only indispensable thing" in poetry is that the syntactic structure, though present and formal, is a secondary principle of organization. Be guided by the lineation, and mark the accretion of sounds. "Syringa sings" tells us to listen for "—ing(s)," a sound which duly recurs five times (wi*ngs*, thi*ngs*, trusti*ng*, wi*ngs*, thi*ngs*), with consonances in hu*ng*er and thu*nd*er. Also *thrush* gets echoes in *ruffles*, then again in *thrusts, trusting, bush, list, lust*. Then *beak*, introduced as late as the fifth line, finds its echo in *weak*, is dissociated into *shaken*. . . .

It's an obsessed little tune, in short, that carries the burden of the thrush, and if "O gay thrush" is an irony it is also a dissonance. For there has been no acoustic preparation for "gay," nor for "O." Those three strong terminal monosyllables would seem strayed in from some other poem but for the principle the American poet Ronald Johnson invoked when he quoted Charles Ives to elucidate this very line: "All the wrong notes are right."

That was one of the poems Basil read into the Newcastle microphone. Within a few minutes he had something else to say about music. You obviously cannot imitate the sound of a harpsichord with words. But you can imitate the structure of a harpsichord sonata in the structure of a poem. I wish I'd gotten him to elaborate on this, but he was tiring and the studio clock was running out.

The technician handed me the big tape, which I eventually hand-carried back to Washington, ever watchful of airport metal-detectors. Basil and I dined at an Indian restaurant (his appetite was for the hotter curries), and we parted toward midnight: he for a bus back to his council home, I for the airport hotel which I had some hope of finding from mid-town where we were, but not from his labyrinthine suburb if I were to drive him there first.

That was March, 1979. We were to have met again in June for a drive to Briggflatts, and there was a failure of mails, and a foul-up of telephones, and we could establish no contact. I still have hope of Briggflatts. Meanwhile there's the radio program. Beautifully produced by Bob Montiegel, now of WBGH-Boston, it preserves Basil's best speaking and reading voice. If your local NPR station didn't ghettoize it into some such forlorn time-slot as Saturday at dawn you heard it, I trust, in February 1980, and if you heard it what you have just read is mostly superfluous. The voice of Basil Bunting was not shaped by all those decades of craft to the end that its simulacrum might lie pressed flat on a page.

THEODORE ENSLIN

AS HOMAGE TO BASIL BUNTING:
SOME ARTICLES OF FAITH

Many years ago, Louis Zukofsky suddenly broke off a conversation, and said, "You look like Basil Bunting," and Celia produced a photograph in which there was, undeniably, a resemblance, though perhaps not enough to claim close kinship, more, a certain air—a bearing. Years later, when I finally met Bunting, there was nothing that I could see remaining of that resemblance—to either one of us—only Bunting's eyes were still those of the photograph. I had never forgotten them, quite obviously eyes which examine sharply, whether minutiae close at hand, or the sweep of a far horizon—a sailor's eyes. Always with the dictum, "condensare"—never *more* than is adequate, but supremely adequate in voice and sparing choice. The words and the movement/articulation of those words. Clarity, and insistence upon clarity in every action and reaction. Small wonder that the man protested when Jonathan Williams asked him for autobiographical reminiscences: "Why Jonathan, I'm surprised at you. It's all there in *Briggflatts*."

This dictum—condensare—was almost the only war cry of those who became known as Objectivists, as it had been earlier for Pound, and T.E. Hulme who once said that all a man really had to say could be given in half a page. True, I would quarrel with some of this, and say that one tightens/condenses to the essentials at times through the just opposite—by loosening. It is the process of enantiosis once more—the same thing in essence, and it may account somewhat for my personal devotion to the work of the Objectivists, while in the same breath I could not be accused of brevity in my own procedures. At any rate, Bunting, as the only English representative of that circle of friends is necessarily at a slight remove from them. His flavor is not that of Oppen, nor of Rakosi—not of Zukofsky·or Reznikoff. He is thoroughly grounded in the best of English traditions, and where one at times senses conscious scholarship in Zuk, in Bunting it is the heritage of English schooling—that enviable (to us) tradition which is available to any "educated" Englishman, and was lost long ago in our pathetic attempts to streamline and specialize. Thus a man who has a working acquaintance with Latin and Greek is an uncommon man here in the States, but very ordinary in Great Britain. Not that Bunting is in any way a common man in any context, but that he can move with ease and grace through translations from Horace to classical Persian. Such a man here always runs the risk of being considered a pedant—at least in certain circles—while in England any country vicar or Midland businessman might have such interests without altering a very usual life—or it might be the particular delight of a man who once lived in a houseboat in the English Channel—one, who, according to Zukofsky via Lorine Niedecker, "arrived in New York with yeoman's muscles and a sextant." It is the same man who walked away from a crowd of irate Iranians out to kill him. As he explains it, "No one gets hurt in situations of mob violence except those who are afraid of it." A clear head, and a very practical one—hardly the absent-minded professor or "impractical" artist. The same intelligence, diamond hard, which is brought to bear in the poems.

Beyond these autobiographical facts, more important in the case of a man like Bunting than with many—they do apply to his work, and inform his poetic intelligence. There are three kinds of writers—of artists—that come to mind (not ruling out many others, and shades of others). There are those who are divinely inspired, and erupt in a kind of intoxication which may not be always intelligent, or particularly knowledgeable of the craft itself—largely intuited without being worked through consciously. And at the other end of the scale there are those who produce through sheer will and dogged determination, where every move is calculated. This is not necessarily oppressive, and sometimes rises to a kind of genius, but it must necessarily lack some of the fluidity of the spontaneous outpouring of the first. Then there is the man who has both the gift of the spontaneous, and the intelligence to control it. It would be absurd to attempt to rank any of these, but it is interesting at times to see who belongs where, with no ultimate attempt at categorization.

Certainly Bunting is of this last type. Beethoven was. Melville was the first (but even Hawthorne gave up trying to teach him grammar as unnecessary to what he accomplished superbly without it.) We need them all. In connection with this intelligence, it is possible for Bunting to say, "Emotion first—but only *facts* in the poem." The emotion generated by these facts comes through and informs the poem, *not* psychological or other special pleading. Basil is able to talk about this lucidly—there are many who cannot. But in the end, it is knowledge of *how* the work functions, and any valid example does come through its facts, no matter which type created it. We are all far too familiar with the other method. I am conscious of Bunting using basically the same material again and again in different contexts, and with widely differing intent and result—a tribute to his craftsmanship—the unique poem coming through exactly each time. This is the privilege of mastery. I am less attracted to his stated dislike of "organic form" as a unifying principle, as it has become important to us to think of it these past years (not merely via Olson). It is a valid reaction to reiteration which has become cliché, but I am never satisfied that one can plan formal structure, except in the broadest terms, and pull it off successfully or at least without some loss, unless the material itself has dictated this particular form in advance. This may be a largely unconscious process, as it probably was historically with Haydn's sonata form. He *thought* that way; therefore, such a form was right for the material he used, but it was extremely varied in internal shape as anyone can discover by analyzing his quartets. The arbitrary setting of form in advance had gotten out of hand and increasingly perfunctory—at least in the case of poetry in English a good century and a half ago—which made some sort of reaction inevitable and salutary. Bunting has not needed this cautionary, at least as a signpost—that much is evident in his work, but it is interesting, and at first a bit puzzling, to hear him apparently harking back to a possibility which had become threadbare three or four generations before his own. So I believe it is much more the catch phrase itself, and its implied limits to which he objects, than to what it legitimately means. I seem to remember another statement of Bunting's in an interview which I have mislaid, to the effect that it makes very little difference if the *facts* are falsified facts. They are still the facts. It takes bravery to say that, and I echo my admiration for one who has had the occasion to say it legitimately.

There is, too, the sense of music. It is not crankiness or a parochial sense that prompts Basil to read *Briggflatts* in Northumbrian accent—the music of language so used demands it. As powerful a structure as *Briggflatts* would withstand *any* reading (as one could play Mozart on pennywhistles), but much would be lost. His speculation: That Wordsworth, similarly, would sound best in that accent, or that Keats might in cockney, gives me pause for reflection—he may just be right. Do we hear Bach at optimum —or Bunting's beloved Scarlatti—at *"A"* 440? It was certainly not *their* pitch.

Several years ago, when he gave a reading at Orono, Bunting mentioned at dinner that there was something almost amusing in the American interest in current politics, and had there been no other reason in that meeting, that would have been enough to warm me. In that same mislaid interview he went even further, disclaiming interest of any sort, except the broadest (most humane) in the current world "situation." Despite the fact that this is a distasteful attitude (which I share) to many of our friends, who despair the lack of responsibility in this direction, I must say, once more, "Bravo!", as I did when I first read that interview. We have enough to do, and our concerns as writers are too deep to clutter with the latest jargon. Politics, even the frightening politics of our own time, won't do it. Right living may, and that right living is concerned, ultimately, with the individual, not with statistical reports on the "masses." It is not disdain or hauteur that drives a man to isolation from the various fads and movements, but a far deeper concern for the roots of life. They grow deep, and are not so easily swayed as we pretend to think.

I would not want to say more, specifically, of Basil Bunting's work. It is with me constantly, and for many reasons—the whole way from pleasure to example. I return to it again and again—hardy—ordinary at the right places—and superlative, always, in a just measure.

THE POET

ERIC MOTTRAM

"AN ACKNOWLEDGED LAND":
LOVE AND POETRY IN BUNTING'S SONATAS*

The eighteen lines of Lucretius which Bunting translated in 1927, when he was twenty-seven, articulate hopes that were not to be fulfilled, to judge by the six "sonatas" composed between 1925 and 1965—or rather, fulfilled in *Briggflatts* in ways not entirely predicated in earlier work. His characteristic personal reticence and self-depreciation are not only responding to a sense of unfulfilled technical ambition. Indeed, *Briggflatts*, passages in the sonatas and a number of the shorter poems reach standards of sound and measure unsurpassed in this century, and only equalled in his friends and peers—Williams, Zukofsky, Yeats and Pound. The Lucretius articulates a belief in the possibility of love being with landscape and its creatures a natural order, the generation of a pantheistic, epicurean life and poetry of that life, in which what Wordsworth would consider "eternal forms," together with the tender sensualities of love, would cohere inseparably. Place would be experienced as community and given the form of art. Clear language in clear structures would mobilize uncomplicated mystery, that oneness which Wordsworth and Coleridge believed to be the possible subject for epic. Bunting's father not only read him Wordsworth but Spenser, but Bunting's sensibility is not allegorical and not political in the sense *The Faerie Queene* is, although he, too, is obsessed with "mutabilitie." The Lucretius lines address generative Venus:

> Everywhere, through all seas mountains and waterfalls,
> love caresses all hearts and kindles all creatures
> to overmastering lust and ordained renewals.
> Therefore, since you alone control the sum of things
> and nothing without you comes forth into the light
> and nothing beautiful or glorious can be
> without you, Alma Venus! trim my poetry
> with your grace, and give peace to write and read and think.

*A revised and corrected version of the article which originally appeared in the Basil Bunting issue of *Poetry Information* (No. 19, Autumn 1978).

But by the mid-1930s Bunting's poetry concentrates on threats of impotence, incompetence and war. In 1965 the power of *Brigg-flatts* emanates from its control of self-doubt and castrating forces by music and structure, the plaiting of skills through which a radical mistrust of the muse of Love and Poetry is overcome. Bunting's deflection of interviews away from the connotative meaning is partly an understandable need not to be personally investigated in such areas of experience which he has taken pains to transmute into art, not to have his commitments of the 1930s too closely exposed, especially his themes of poetic and personal failure, the double undermining of love and craft. In the Horace translations of the 1930s he writes scornfully of conventional sportsman manhood, the "tough guy," the "first-class middle-weight pug," especially in their disruption of steady love:

> Only the thrice blest are in love for life,
> we others are divorced at heart
> soon, soon torn apart by wretched bickerings.

Other, later poems ambivalently regret time spent in physical man-hood prowesses, when value really lies in "a tale of mine (that) may remain in the world" (Ferdosi, 1935). In a translation from Rudaki (1948):

> Bright wine and the sight of a gracious face,
> dear it might cost, but always cheap to me.
> My purse was my heart, my heart bursting with words,
> and the title-page of my book was Love and Poetry.
> Happy was I, not understanding grief,
> any more than a meadow.
> Silk-soft has poetry made many a heart
> some before and heavy as an anvil.

From Manuchehri in 1949:

> Happy is he whose she is singlehearted! . . .
>
> If tears rain from my eyes, say: Let them rain!
> Spring rains make fair gardens. And if then
> she has cast me into the shadow of exile, say:
> Those who seek fortune afar find it the first.

In 1933, during the Depression and when fascism became a world force, Bunting composed his poetry in the company of Pound and Zukofsky in Italy, and then in Teneriffe. In October, Pound's *Active Anthology* contained fifty of his poems, including "How Duke Valentine Contrived . . . ," a long virtuosic poem in which sixteenth century politics is given as an example of recur-rent general wasted energy and criminal rascality in rulers. The poem places Machiavelli in the present—for example, the Duke "thought he might stave things off / with a few men and a lot of negotiations / until he could raise a reliable army." The poems in Pound's collection dramatize a constant theme in Bunting: the strong chance that a man's life will be wasted in rulers' stratagems and wars. But this material is fused with themes of lost opportunities in love, with penury and lack of potentially creative circumstances, and the chances of resisting the resultant depletion, avoiding impotence, achieving something through craft with which to challenge erosion. As Bunting's stoic contemporary Hemingway put it in *Death in the Afternoon* (1932):

> . . . to put down what really happened in action; what the actual things were which produced the emotion that you experienced. . . the real thing, the sequence of motion and fact which made the emotion and which would be valid in a year or in ten years or, with luck and if you stated it purely enough, always.

Bunting would agree with the general tenor of Ford Madox Ford, whom he assisted on the *Transatlantic Review* in 1923, writing in *The Critical Attitude* (1911):

> Poetry with the note of greatness would seem to demand a simplicity of outlook upon a life not very complex. The poet is a creature of his emotions, and seldom or never is his intellect very powerful or very steady. For there can be no doubt that the more emotional play there is demanded of a man's brain the less rigidity will it have for the following of logical thought-trains. Thus, the last really great poet working in a very complex age may be said to have been Lucretius. To Dante the digesting of all the knowledge in the world was a comparatively simple matter. And having assimilated it he could write fearlessly, with assurance, and with composure.

To Ford—and Bunting's stated opinions on Lucretius, Dante and other writers come very near to his—Kipling came near greatness by versifying clear emotions in the vernacular and in "the rhythm of popular music." For a poet "who knows too much," there is "no end of generalizations." Bunting would also agree with Ford that "the poets have not the courage to lead their own lives. They seem to shut themselves up in quiet book-cabinets, to read forever, and to gain their ideas of life for ever from some very small, very specialized group of books, or to dream for ever of islands off the west coast of Ireland." Bunting's poetry, on the contrary, has been generated from a life of various employments and led as adventure —hence his admiration for Raleigh and Wyatt, for Renaissance men of varied action, for whom poetry was a man's accomplishment among other accomplishments. This goes for Spenser as well, a poet Bunting takes as the type of the serious poetic inventor

who influences his fellow poets. But such men either had aristo-
cratic incomes, or depended on state jobs or patronage and were
therefore vulnerable to rulers—which is the condition of Machiavelli's world and that of Bunting's "Villon," "Attis," "Chomei at
Toyama," "The Complaint of the Morpethshire Farmer" and "Gin
the Goodwife Stint" (a range, that is, from fifteenth century
France to 1930s Northumbria—all poems in the *Active Anthology*
of 1933). In "They Say Etna" (omitted from the Fulcrum *Collected Poems*) the targets are armaments manufacturers, a slave-
ship skipper, Boris Godunof, Stalin, British landowners, and men
who turn land and air into capital. Miners underground exemplify
expenditure of energy in the gears of capitalism, and the poem
ends with three assertions—"Man is not an end-product, / Maggot
asserts," and

> Waste accumulates at compound interest.
> Man is an end-product affirms
>   Blasphemous Bolshevik.

The six sonatas which open the *Collected Poems* of 1968
date from between 1925 and 1965 and articulate Bunting's
coming to terms with the society of competition, war and waste,
without yielding to it, or plumping for an ideology or indulging
in that sentimental liberal stoicism which governs in the popular
middle-class poets of the 1960s and 70s. That in itself is a considerable poetic achievement, cutting across the grain of a period
addicted to conformity of one kind or another. Breadth of experience is placed in Bunting's poetry at the disposal of skilled
craft, and its dominant urge is to retrieve and create value through
poetry as chiselled as masonry or the mosaics of "Ode 36": "no
cement seen and no gap / between stones." But it is in that ode in
particular that a transcendental factor in his work is given, the
point at which, as in the conclusion of *Briggflatts*, words through
musical form become vehicles for non-verbal vitality, as they do
so profoundly in Dante, and from time to time in Wordsworth,
Bunting's other main guide here. The poem is architectonically
given as a mosaic apse (1948):

> the rays of many glories
> forced to its focus forming
> a glory neither of stone
> nor metal, neither of words
> nor verses, but of the light
> shining upon no substance;
> a glory not made
> for which all else was made.

The only other place where Bunting is that direct rather than directly implicit is in his interview with Paul Johnstone (*Meantime*, no. 1, 1977); here, too, he relates logic to experience and language towards the non-verbal, but the context is his Quakerism:

> Quakerism is a form of mysticism no doubt, in that it doesn't put forward any logical justification whatever, only the justification of experience. It is comparable pretty easily with a pantheistic notion of the universe. . . . What you believe is your own affair so long as you follow out the process of simply waiting quietly and emptying your mind of everything else to hear what they would call in their own language the voice of God in your inside. We don't use that kind of language nowadays, but it is a simpler one than the various psychological phrases which we would use.

In Wordsworth, this sense of the whole speaking in silence is also "the justification of experience." In 1799, the waterfalls and crags of the Simplon pass become "working of one mind, the features / Of the same face, blossoms upon one tree, / Characters of the great Apocalypse, / The types and symbols of Eternity, / Of first, and last, and midst, and without end." But that kind of verse has the tactless abstraction which Bunting, a poet who has learned from Mallarmé and Pound, would reject. But the sense of eternal forms is present in his poetry constantly. Wordsworth's isolated human beings do not necessarily draw nourishment from the non-human landscape, and nor do they in Bunting. The opening of "The Brothers," on the other hand, is probably where to notice a declarative tone which Bunting often uses.

> These tourists, heaven preserve us! need must live
> A profitable life . . .

It is not only Wordsworth's dense, variedly paced and detailed, forwarding movement that Bunting could employ, but certain of Wordsworth's emotions, still active. Ennerdale works for him as West Yorkshire does for Bunting:

> Strange alteration wrought on every side
> Among the woods and fields, and that the rocks,
> And everlasting hills themselves were changed . . .

"The Brothers" concerns waste and nostalgia, major themes in Bunting. The enforced traveller, Leonard Ewbank, returns to and leaves the "native soil" which is his basis, but his life is no longer practically rooted from day to day. That kind of tension plays throughout *Briggflatts*. But Bunting of course knows Wordsworth far beyond one work, and all major poets take up what they need from the poetic inheritance. We only need to know their bearings. It is not a question of "influences" in the common academic usage of the term. Dante, Wyatt and Wordsworth have all dealt with the damaged soul, the crippling waste that hinders achievement, the need for lyrical tenderness as a stay against eroded love. As Bunting says in his preface, the poems were "written here and there now and then over forty years and four continents," and those from whom he acknowledges he "learned the trick of it" are not restricted to a narrow range of English poets. Nothing narrowly national pressed him, nothing in the nature of hunting for a patriotic tradition, such as obsesses British middle-class establishment poetry today.

But "trick" means artifice and stratagem as well as craft, and it also means semblance and deception. Bunting is using the classical sense of art as fiction: a trick is a contrivance, a feat of dexterity, a knack or faculty for action. That is, his poetry lies firmly within the modern poetic tradition from Baudelaire and Mallarmé, the tradition of crafted artifice.

He also speaks of "sleights learned from others and an ear open to melodic analogies," words "pricked" as a score. It is an action remote from Tennyson's Virgilian musical verse, and nearer to Tudor and early seventeenth-century fusions of music and words, when "prick" meant to write down music by pricks or notes. But the term also means to trace on a surface by pricks or dots—that is, notation as design in space, or as Bunting says: "to trace in the air a pattern of sound." Sonata is from *sonare*, to sound: a sound structure pricked for performance.

But the sound is not that of nineteenth-century ebullience. Beethoven's sonatas contained too many dynamic and contrasting changes to be available for poetry, Bunting says in his interview with Dale Reagan (in *Montemora*, no. 3, 1977). "*Briggflatts* was written with certain sonatas of Domenico Scarlatti in mind, and is heard best when those sonatas alternate with the movements of the poem"—so Bunting prefaced his 75th birthday reading at the National Poetry Centre in 1975 (before it became a dull adjunct of the Arts Council). The performance field of the poem comprises the sound of the poet's voice, the sound of a harpsichord, the graph of musical form signified by the printed text. Sonata means sound-form, as the etymology suggests, but, as Wilfred Mellers points out, "it is not so much a form as a principle, an approach to composition. . . . a principle which perpetually renews itself under the pressure of experience." (*The Sonata Principle*, London, 1957, p. 3). In fact Scarlatti evolved a new keyboard style with a wide emotional range and extraordinary technical invention. So that Bunting's choice infers compositional procedure which is far from conventional, although Scarlatti's innovations take place within a relatively simple form, within which, as Bunting observes (Reagan, op. cit.) "an enormous variety of movement, of life" did not interfere with simplicity.

In a similar way, Bunting's poetry develops principles of sound form without dogma. His fairly rare statements on principles confirm his poetic texts, whether the extended forms of the "sonatas" in the *Collected Poems*, or in the small form of his epitaph for Lorine Niedecker (*Epitaphs for Lorine*, ed. Jonathan Williams, 1973):

> To abate what swells
> use ice for scalpel.
> it melts in its wound
> and no one can tell
> what the surgeon used.
> clear lymph, no scar,
> no swathe from a cheek's bloom.

This poem exactly demonstrates both Bunting's admiration for Niedecker—"No one is so subtle with so few words"—and his principles in "A Statement" (Northern Arts Association *Arts Diary*, April/Summer 1966; Jonathan Williams—*Descant on Rawthey's Madrigal: Conversations with Basil Bunting*, 1968); principles which are part of a poetics which he shares with Yeats, Pound and Eliot:

> Poetry, like music, is to be heard. It deals in sound—long sounds and short sounds, heavy beats and light beats, the tone relations of vowels, the relations of consonants to one another which are like instrumental colour in music. Poetry lies dead on the page, until some voice brings it to life, just as music, on the stave, is no more than instructions to the player. . . . Without the sound, the reader looks at the lines as he looks at prose, seeking a meaning. [Poetry's "meaning"] lies in the relation to one another of lines and patterns of sound, perhaps harmonious, perhaps contrasting and clashing, which the hearer feels rather than understands; lines of sound drawn in the air which stir deep emotions which have not even a name in prose.

Those "patterns" Bunting relates to a particular tradition. He began a reading of British poetry in 1977 by saying that "cultures are extraordinarily long-lived; they lie dormant in the soil and come out again in an astonishing way." The Angles amalgamated with the Celts in the North East; the early kings of Northumberland married Celtic women; the resultant Celtic-Teutonic culture was "the most splendid art of the Dark Ages," examplified by the Lindisfarne book. The pattern in the designs of the latter is not immediately obvious, "it only gradually dawns on you," and the local crosses of the northeast have a similar patterning (Bunting was probably remembering, for instance, the cross at Bewcastle). Bunting cited "The Dream of the Rood" (passages of which appeared on the Ruthwell Cross, as W. P. Ker recalls in *The Dark Ages*, 1904, chapter 4). Patterning appears again strongly in the *Gawain* and *Pearl* poems, and much nearer our own time in Swinburne, who considered himself a Northumbrian poet. When Bunting reads Swinburne's "Itylus" at the right pace and with the proper musical stressing of vowel and consonant, the patterning is clear (it is related to what has more recently been called "rime," in the writings of Robert Duncan, to mean the pattern of recurrence and variation in word order, image and cadence). That his own poetry is musically related to Swinburne's can be heard in a number of works, and the subject material of "the birth of Venus" semi-chorus in *Atalanta in Calydon* is closely related to main preoccupations in Bunting's work.

The Niedecker epitaph, in fact, could only be properly analyzed as a chart of sound points with unforced melodic measures: an imperative sentence—a descriptive-analytical sentence—a verbless statement with two negatives—and a rhyme structure which is best described as patterning, producing a music rather than a system. The poem's buoyant confidence rests in such firm architectonics. The bogus good manners of metrical formalists are rejected, along with those practices arising from the belief that poetry decorates prior prose meaning (the current British poetic gold-standard). Being within the main tradition of modern poetry since Mallarmé, the poem does not refer back primly to some preconceived origin, nor does it point to itself except in pleasure of form. It generates an object out of a sound-performance in patterned language. But as Bunting insists about technique, "let it stay invisible. It's the effect on the reader which matters" ("A Man for the Music of Words: Basil Bunting talks to Edward Lucie-Smith," *Sunday Times*, 1965).

Such obviousnesses have to be restated because of the degenerate state of official poetry and poetic theory among the academics and reviewers in this country, who either reject or are ignorant of the main tradition of modern poetry. This dominance refuses the sound-form principles demonstrated by Yeats, Pound, Eliot and Bunting (and Zukofsky and Olson in the United States, and Duncan in the next generation). It also refuses the range of materials and the idea of an extended form to hold them, preferring the ironical, the confessional and the descriptive; in a word, the small scale.

Eliot put the issue bluntly in his 1922 essay, "The Lesson of Baudelaire": "the lack of curiosity in technical matters of the academic poets today (is) only an indication of the lack of curiosity in moral matters." The present dominance in poetry fatally lacks ambition of form and materials. Bunting's sound structures are the projection of a scope it flinches from. As he said ten years ago, after reiterating poetry as "the shape you can make with sound" (Lucie-Smith, op. cit.):

> But you musn't put water with the whisky. You musn't be afraid
> to be prodigal with your material. It's for this reason that my out-
> put is very small. It takes the experience and reading of a number
> of years to provide material for a serious poem.

Bunting indeed writes out of an experience and reading which is today incomparable. The kind of experience can be seen at a glance from the *Chronology* which Garth Clucas provided for the Bunting exhibition organized by Roger Guedalla in March of 1978. His reading has been above all practical. In his conversation, books and poems take their place as events energizing a lifetime, and it is evident in the poems themselves as a scaffolding provided by specific tradition. When Bunting states his belief in the qualities of Malherbe, that opinion is reinforced by recited text. Since he is encumbered neither with political or religious ideology, nor the need to express humanistic faith in "man" in some dream calm future beyond the present anguish, his poetry has not contracted the twentieth century diseases of propaganda and whining irony, the cheap alibis of "committed" or "confessional" verse. It follows that his work has been dismissed by the Movement mob, who do not have to pay attention to poetry, to spend time and energy on it, nor even, when necessary, to go into special training to read it. From the 1920s Bunting's poetry has been compressed rather than discursive. If the sound patterns are clear, the connotative verbal patterning requires more than sensuous reception.

II

The poet against authority is the binding theme of "Villon": the skilled man's exceptional abilities at the mercy of rulers. The iconic vision of kingship, as in an illuminated manuscript or painting, betrays him away from the truth of his sound—"my tongue is a curve in the ear." Sonata counters false vision. Imprisonment is physical, economic and literary: "my sound box" (the body and a gramophone's) "lacks sonority" (the quality of deep and carrying sound). Ironically, his condition is what he wants from poetic truth—"Naked speech! Naked beggar both blind and cold!" The "Emperor with magic in darkness" is the poet's "fetters"; the "eyes lie"; the poet anchors on Averrhoes, analyst, believer in intelligence, in methods of understanding rather than arcane and religious symbols. The Emperor hastens Death, final authority, the final royal hand. Bunting's sense of death is constant from this point in 1925, an inherent sense of the tenuous grip of sensibility and intelligence under pressure from non-human and inhuman forces. Only in art is divine authority truly present, the man-made object, semi-permanent as against the Earth's seasons and man's impermanence.

The poem's account of imprisonment is first hand, but also the enclosure represented by systematic and abstracted knowledge —again, always resisted in Bunting's work: "they have named all the stars . . . run the white moon to a schedule." The parallels with the twentieth century are explicit: interrogations from every kind of authority, and endless measuring that postures as value. But Part Three concludes with experience which will repeatedly recur in Bunting's work: some kind of paradisal glimpsed world— in this instance, Mediterranean—natural and civilized, a kind of order, which is here as threatened as Troy: "because of the beauty of Helen."

The generative interior theme, then, is the nature of enclosures both wasting and productive:

> precession clarifying vagueness;
> boundary to a wilderness
> of detail; chisel voice
> smoothing the flanks of noise . . .

It is a paradigm of Bunting's design right through to the chiselled stones and "unnoted harmonies" of *Briggflatts*. The human body is more trusted in the art of marble than the life of Helen—or of Circe, who appears in Part Two; and nature, in a tradition which extends from Baudelaire, through Mallarmé, into a number of symbolist poetic procedures, and to *Paterson* in the 1940s, is like the sea (and by association like the sea goddesses) a deathly singularity—"no renewal, no forgetting, / no variety of death"—the sterility of a poet as out of season as an untimely salmon: "silent with the silence of a single note."

The "trick" of "Villon" combines the Browning persona, open-measure lines, quatrains, the Villon *ubi sunt?* method, rhymed pairs of lines in a single paragraph, speech rhetoric and design or patterning rhetoric, and divided and undivided lines. The technique therefore is an initial stage in the apparatus which Bunting will develop towards the high skills of *Briggflatts*. But "Villon" also begins to project Bunting's dialectic between nature, including human nature, and art, between death and the semi-permanence of art, the love and lust for women and what lasts from sensuality—materials treated with sardonic humour in "Attis: Or, Something Missing." This poem parodies Lucretius and Cino da Pistoia (a poet Ford cites in *The Critical Attitude*), and Milton's shorter poems; and the title and epigraph refers both to Catullus's "Attis" —"great goddess, goddess Cybele, goddess mistress of Dindyma, from me be all your madness taken; drive others mad, drive others rabid"—and to the Phrygian castrated and bled to death: Cybele was the Phrygian Aphrodite of Mount Ida, whose priests castrated themselves in memory of her lover. (Dindyma is a shrine in Asia Minor.)

By 1931, Bunting's Alma Venus has the attributes and effects of both Helen and Circe in Cybele. In Part Two of "Attis," the struggle against mother goddess and eunuchery is given as decayed vitality, declined love, the onslaught of the goddess on the very men who worship her for fertility, and castration. The two-faced venereal power generates the evils of submissions both erotic and social (political and economic), and encourages a streak of masochistic emasculation, stronger in Part Three where she becomes Medusa, goddess of enclosure, and enforced rigidification which is the opposite of chiselled stone.

The music of the Tyne at Bywell does not exorcize the myth of Orfeo. Perhaps the poem is recalling Monteverdi's version of the myth in which the poet-hero is rescued from both Hell and Eurydice by Apollo. Nor does the river harmony eliminate the two Erinyes, daughters of Mother Earth from the blood of Uranus castrated by Cronos, furies who avenge parricide and perjury. The poem summons Medusa in the voice of Dante (the city of Dis in the *Inferno*), and her "method" is shown at work in corrupt city life (this section might be compared with section six of Ford's "Antwerp"), and on the poet explicitly, through a girl in a pub. In Part Three the castrated, stiffening male—the male reduced to passivity in a "pastorale arioso (falsetto)," gelded by religion and sex—becomes a shade in Hell, like Orpheus a shade among shades. Impotence follows seduction and the abortive loss of virginity: "Attis grieving for his testicles! / Attis stiffening amid the snows. . . ." Through a pun on "rooted" (which Bunting will use again in later work), the goddess is shown taking the poet's phallus; but nothing grows. She ironically rebukes him: pride and rewards "defraud" her. The "allegorical oracle" implies that submissively sensual art and erotic sensuality are alike in leading to non-existence: "Nonnulla deest." Something is missing indeed in this pastoral of reduced vitality. Echoes of "Lycidas" and "Methought I saw my late espoused saint" reinforce the absence of redemption, ideological or otherwise.

But, again, the poem's vitality lies in its exuberant formal controls—a variety of measures for an over-all sardonic scorn for anyone who allows himself to be such a Phrygian, frigid to rigidity, but containing an underlying inevitability, a real chance of nonentity. It is this that gives the poem its main seriousness. The artist has offended the purity of divine art which alone is permitted— hence the parodies of Lucretius and Milton, and Cino da Pistoia's poems of prostration before love. And no paradisal culture is nostalgically resorted to in "Attis," nor in "Aus dem Zweiten Reich," which also dates from 1931, a poem out of the pre-Nazi Berlin world which attracted Christopher Isherwood later.

This is the corrupt city culture of Georg Grosz, "rapid, dogmatic, automatic and efficient," the superficially modern and incipiently aggressive. Pudovkin's *Storm over Asia* is replaced by any relaxing flick distributing teasing sex, mediocre existence and indolence. A Berliner offers to show the poet Old Berlin, but it is defined as "naked cabarets" and a departmental store rivalling Macy's. Literature is reduced to a prolific and preening but famous author. These elements are then moved towards Bunting's characteristic theme: "Stillborn fecundities, / frostbound applause," and a chronic sense of Arnold's castrating fear of "the buried life."

Technically the poem's carefully restricted accuracy of tone articulates the seedy and decayed. Again, it is the sheer articulacy which rescues the speaker from immersion, enclosure and the overwhelming drifts of decadence.

The myth—perhaps the fact— of "The Well of Lycopolis" (1935) is mentioned, as Bunting notes, in one of Gibbon's footnotes: a malign spring in Egypt in the days of the Roman conquest, a draft of which, says the epigraph, teareth away the signs of virginity. The poem exposes the heroics of World War I; the epigraph to Part One is from the opening of Villon's "Lament of the Belle Hëaulmiere"—"It seemed I heard the one they called the Belle Hëaulmiere complain, longing for the days when she was young . . ." (Anthony Bonner's translation). The French woman was rich and kept a young man—now as Alma Venus, in the poem, she looks back to her past from the horror of old age. (Between 1931 and 1935, the Japanese had penetrated the Great Wall and occuped Shanghai; Salazar was elected premier of Portugal; Franco and Stalin signed a non-agression pact; Adolf Hitler was appointed Chancellor of Germany and conferred with Mussolini; and Moseley fascism was rife in Britain). In Part One, the "unlovely labour of love" what is made of love by precautions and socially imposed inhibitions, resulting in puritanical erotic failure. Venus and Polymnia, love and poetry, are aspects of a single goddess, a single energy, the centre of this taunting failure (one focus is a necessarily sharp pun on "tool"). Polymnia demands to know why the poet has introduced Venus into the work—"you who / finger the goods you cannot purchase," "a tool not worth the neglible price," handled by a man of "barren honesty."

Again, it is a poetry of defeated sensuality, of erotic-poetic failure, of art needing to be recognized, whether love is a success or not. The form is a sardonic dialogue on time's decay of human powers—the "mutabilitie" theme. The horror is that Venus herself has grown old, that the goddess ages. Bunting's vision, related to the polluting well, is that the forces of renewal are themselves decayed.

In Part Two, the poet addresses his "devoutly worshipped ladies" of impotence, and asks "am I answerable?"—that is: how far is a man personally responsible for his talent (as in Milton's sonnet on "that one talent which is death to hide"), or, in a sense both puritan and Quaker, how far can he be held accountable? (again as in the Christian parable of the talents). And the question is asked not only with regard to the constancies of mutability but in the context of competitive and warring society. Nostalgia for virgin love in another era of taste, Daphnis and Chloe, "wine without headache," simple songs, a place other than the region between High Holborn and Euston, and sailing "closehauled," "stubborn against the trades," are elements of enclosure and the Medusa-effect. So that "proud, full sail" becomes in Part Three "infamous poetry, abject love," the "cuckolding" of flowering trees in autumn, Sirius as god of the New Year turned into a hellish tank reflection rather than a god above the sea: "I shall never have anything to myself." (Sirius regains his power years later in the conclusion of *Briggflatts*). Song becomes "tweedle" and "twat," bad verse and slanged sex, "squalid acquiescence in the cast-offs of repeated poetry." Bellerophon's Pegasus is now "a livery hack, a gelding."

At thirty-five Bunting's theme is not maturity, health and achievement but "abject poetry, infamous love," "scamped spring, squandered summer," mildewed grain and bad bread, "the

cunnilingual law" which governs tongue in poetry and sex. "Clap
a clout on your jowl for / Jesus sake!" cries the self-punishing
public—"Hack off his pendants!"—and in a brief parody of Eliot:
"Can a moment of madness make up for / an age of consent?"
After involuntary or ecstatic passion, the constraint of impotence
and passivity, disgust at sexual restraints, and men under Circe's
indictment, men possessed by the devils of lust—these themes
move to the containing biblical image: "The Gadarene swihine
have got us in tow."

      But this guilt and abhorrence are part of "the age," as "E.P.
Ode Pour L'Election de son Sepulchre" would term it. In Part
Four, paradise is invoked, but seen from Hell, so that the Dante
epigraph is active in the poem, referring to those who believe that
a breathing people lives under the marsh. In Canto 7 of the *Inferno* Virgil points out to Dante souls stupified by anger—"And you
should understand for sure that sighing under the water are people
who make the surface bubble and churn." This section of Bunting's
poem presents people stuck in the hellish mud of anger and ac-
cidie—a punishment for impotence and idleness, in the poem's
context, as the exhaustion and death of language: "words die in
their throat; / they cannot speak out" (in Dante: "che dir nol
posson con parola integra"). The fertile rivers of Paradise are impossible as an active myth for Bunting at this stage, but the Styx-
Paradise polarity remained central to his poetry. The paradox of
his work is clear in this 1935 work, in fact: "the bright peaks have
faded" and his is to be a poetry of regret and nostalgia, an inter-
war poetry of insecurity whose point of view is that of classicist
perfection, the poets cited in the *Collected Poems* preface. Pollution and impotence must be countered by achieved prosody or not
at all. Villon and Dante are guides to the Inferno of punishment
and a nostalgically based Purgatorio, the fundamental pairing in
his work. But in "The Well of Lycopolis" it is Styx that is "eternal, a dwelling," even if the chances of change are never actually
relinquished: "Who had love for love / whose love was strong or
fastidious?" "The college of Muses reconstructs / in flimsy drizzle
of starlight" only crippled verse, cheaply made for cheap praise.
Masculine poetry under Venus Aphrodite is turned into a manhood determined by the armed services (the services of those
malignant forces in Swinburne's Venus)—"one of the ragtime
army, / involuntary volunteer, / queued up for the pox in Rouen,
What a blighty!" That is, VD gets you sent home from the Front
but as a cure for self-doubt it is a fraud. War is mustard gas, lung
schrapnel, shell shock, self-inflicted wound, tetanus, and Styx is

only too clearly analogued as the needs of the Front in World
War I, which is in turn the condition of futile combat (in 1918
Bunting was imprisoned as a conscientious objector). In literature,
this futility becomes "barren, dependent . . . this page ripped from
Love's ledger and Poetry's."

Once again the religious sense of accountability plagues the
poet. The ironic horror of Styx is that the glittering surface is
caused by the sighs of those boiling eternally beneath. The Well
has become the Styx. A reversal of Dante's indictment could only
occur if the people were aroused. The religious basis of the myth
used here infers inevitability, or even a decree from some external,
eternal force: "the spoils are for God." But that curt enforcement
at the head of "The Spoils" (*Poetry* [Chicago], 1951) is from the
Koran. The poetic energies of "The Well of Lycopolis" are de-
ployed in forms which barely contain their malignant propulsions.
The scornful, angry rhetoric tends to be its own adequate form.
In the opening speech of Asshur in "The Spoils" you can hear
Bunting's new achievement in sound and measure organization,
an ability which he will carry through to the beauties of *Briggflatts*:

> . . . so in his greaves I saw
> in polished bronze
> a man like me reckoning pence,
> never having tasted bread
> where there is ice in his flask,
> storks' stilts cleaving sun-disk,
> sun like driven sand.

"The Spoils" is Bunting's most complex work because it operates
frequently through inferential meanings below the firmly controlled surfaces. After an introduction on Death as the one secure
fact in life, of "little worth" in any case, Part One is shaped as an
exchange between four Semitic or Indo-European figures each
speaking three times in the same order, the four sons of Shem,
chosen in fact at random by Bunting and not deliberately referring to the cities in Abraham's world. They represent aspects
of semitic attitudes and Islamic virtues. Asshur, assessor of the
people's property and money, sees himself reflected in a soldier's
greaves and contrasts his life with military privations: it is a time
of war and lust again—"lean watches, then debauch: / after long
alert, stupidity." Men are debased. Asshur recalls earlier bondage
to Leah and Rachel (twin daughters of Laban who married Isaac's
son Jacob—a history of family bargaining in property, marriage
and sex). Lud (presumably the ancient Luz) speaks of the sullen
Euphrates city—Bagdad now, Ctesiphon then—under a frugal,

accounting God, and Arpachshad of "bought deference," "apt to
no servitude, commerce or special dexterity," "recited the sacred
/ enscrolled poems, beating with a leaping measure / like blood in
a new wound." Fertile poetry is opposed to the "parched Arabian."
From Aram's second short speech onwards the Babylonian exile
is parodied (the Tigris city, Babel); Asshur and Arpachshad are
Mesopotamian towns; Aram is Syrian (Damascus). Farming is
opposed to the sterility of usury, country to city, farmers to
tailors, hairdressers, perfumers and jewellers. The future religious
poet-ruler David is "dancing before the Ark, they toss him pennies"
as if he lived for gain: "they were seeking to hire us to a repugnant trade." All that is left of the flock is the "sterile ram." Soldiers' money for sex in brothel style is "tossed" aside by a woman. Married sex is natural culture, part of an agrarian coherence,
without usury. Breasts are either sterile sexual pleasure or fertile
(there are three usages of this issue). Such are, in brief, the main
elements of this section.

Bunting has here transposed his themes of sterility in cap-
tivity to the area of his Persian experience (he began learning
Persian in 1930 and worked in Persia between 1942 and 1950).
The prosody, however, is that of his later condensed procedures
(the first speech of Arpachshad for example). The Paradise-Medi-
terranean imagery of a desired life becomes, in Part Two of "The
Spoils" the value of a Persian civilization (*paradeisos* is used by
Xenophon for Persian royal parks) whose architecture is the metaphor of the architectonics of both poetry and society: "lines nowhere broken, / for they considered capital / and base irrelevant."
The economic terms are rapidly transposable into architectural
terms, just as passion and poetry are in "Their passion's body was
bricks and its soul algebra. / Poetry / they remembered / too
much, too well." And this last line contains the threat to a dream-
historical world: a degeneration into academicism, faked ability,
repetition and patronage, exactly the condition of official British
poetry and culture from 1900 until the present day. The invading
Seljuks at least built and organized before "withering" out of
"patience and public spirit." This culture was a God-based durability of building and law, "domination and engineers." It did not
last.

Bunting's model here, as always, is a pattern of arts in an
agrarian-based small town society—not the heroic virtues but comfort and ease. It quickly ends with the falcon of absolute invasion
which attacks the harvest—sudden death, but not simply to be
feared—a Sophoclean "were we not better dead," and the

characteristic inter-war and post-war imagery of omnipotent and predatory power. Part Three offers the poet as an agrarian in an ideal pastoral scene: exchanged goods, barter without money. But the plough is soon blunted by tribute and levy, and architecture is a bank. Water is sterilized and taxed, and artists are sterilized by a number of methods. Energy is dispersed and corrupted: "flares on a foundering barque, / stars sputtering still sea under iceblink" ("iceblink" is a luminous appearance on the horizon caused by the reflection of light from ice). So that the poet, planting, pruning and bartering his goods, has to recall the fact that wheat cannot "sprout through a shingle of Lydian pebbles"—which are not only plough-blunting stones but refer to an Asia Minor people and to a mode in ancient Greek music with a soft, so-called feminine character. Lydia was also reputed to have invented coinage, in the poem's context another restraint on creative productivity. The poet also resumes the facts of the Mediterranean turned into a field of war in World War II—"broken booty" on the seashore of Asia Minor and Tripoli under "a cone of tracers," ancient civilizations of Rome and the Eastern Mediterranean peoples again under war: "old in that war after raising many crosses." Noncreative public figures always "lie in wait for blood, / every man with a net," trapping workers and poets alike.

The wartime naval bases of Rosyth and Chesapeake project other uses for the sea than fishing ("the sprool" here is an instrument for single-line fishing with large hooks which foul the fish). The wartime convoy man hears the surf in his memory, an image of release from filthy harbour water—and here the verse has the recurrent music of Bunting's reconciliatory cadences, those lyrical measures of nostalgia for peace which will bring *Briggflatts* to it conclusion:

> In watch below
> meditative heard elsewhere
> surf shout, pound shores seldom silent
> from which heart naked swam
> out to the dear unintelligible ocean.

But his watch is carried out on the north side of the Firth of Forth and his marshalled convoy will move north to the Lofoten Islands, Spitzbergen and the frozen Arctic. The sea cannot remain beneficent for long—at least until certain passages in *Briggflatts*:

> Cold northern clear sea-gardens
> between Lofoten and Spitzbergen,
> as good a grave as any, earth or water.

What else do we live for and take part,
we who would share the spoils ?

Spoils are goods taken from an enemy or a captured city, confiscated goods or property or territory, loot, booty, plunder. The poem dramatizes a fact recurrent in Bunting: there is no guarantee of benefit from combat or anguish, no rule of recompense, no humanistic blessing on suffering. But spoils also means that which is acquired by special endeavour—art, books, treasure—as well as public offices or positions of emolument distributed among the supporters of a party or a power. The poem defines its title therefore: spoliation is always authoritarian; it is God's right not man's supposed right, seizable from God, or taken by permission. It is a catastrophic part of things as they are. The dream of ideal nature and culture is invaded. You may, if you wish, hope or desire to share the spoils with God. The rest is endurance—for poet, service-man, would-be lover, hoping to avoid the humiliating dangers of being hired by some limiting paymaster and the threatening enclosure of impotence. The paradisal gardens of Persia and the South are severely counterpointed by the layered plants and jellyfish in the frozen sea-gardens of the North.

"Chomei at Toyama" (*Poetry* [Chicago], 1933) is not part of Bunting's sonata series but it is worthwhile noting here its articulation of recurrent materials, without reaching into further analysis. The twelfth-century Chinese nobleman retired to Toyama on Mt. Hino and in old age wrote a prose work which Bunting condenses and completes, from an Italian translation, as the poet Chomei apparently wanted to write. The poem opens with a characteristic Bunting image of water: he frequently presents tides, pools, harbours, open sea, whirlpools, waterfalls and streams as instances of clarity and pollution, freedom and stagnation, mobility and clogged fixity, fertility and sterility. They are associated with moon and stars, ships, boats, and with time-flow and timelessness, a navigational sense of life as recurring transience, which the artist necessarily resists if he is to create anything to last. Bunting's opening is an ideogram of mobility, a dialectic between appearance and disappearance, clarity and scum. The focussing irony is that since it recurs, dew outlasts the hibiscus petals. In literature, therefore, recording events provides a sense of process within eternity. The Kyoto fire instances transitory civilization, paralleled by a New York cyclone. Kyoto, the capital, is replaced: "the soil returned to health," the new site resisting recalcitrant nature. The urban and governmental is arbitrary, an imposition of men on nature and men on men. Nature and men are to be stoically endured, a recurrent theme in Bunting and here sealed with an aphorism: "To appreciate present conditions / collate them with those of antiquity."

After disaster a priest marks the dead with an A for Armida, ironically the compassionate Buddha. Natural events, such as "the great earthquake of Genryaku," may cause "a religious revival," but it is soon forgotten. In this "unstable world" apparent help is mere enclosure: "Whoever helps him encloses him / and follows him crying out: Gratitude!" Where may a man settle, choose a "trade," and "the body rest"? Chomei is the figure who at fifty leaves his city—"I perceived there was no time to lose, / left home and conversation"—and at sixty builds his "last home" as "a lodging, not a dwelling, / omitted the usual foundation ceremony." But the simple mountain home does contain "lute and mandolin." Bunting's lifelong search for a tolerable life—a form of the inter-war poets' deep need for stability and an end to conflict—is imaged through Chomei's need for a home, a hearth, in exile: not "a private fortress" but a Quaker simplicity, detached from the urban, from objects, a practical form of stability within transience. Eliot's over-ambitious need for philosophical and religious security is parodied by simplicity: "Between the maple leaf and the cornflower / murmurs the afternoon." Bunting's fondness for epigrammatic forms is played here within the interior monologue of Chomei, and in fact reaches *haiku*-like structures:

> A fine moonlit night,
> I sit at the window with a handful of old verses.

The poet retreats, actively, into memory—his dissociation is not a form of imprisonment:

> Neither closed in one landscape
> nor in one season
> the mind moving in illimitable
> recollection.

This tone of reconciliation with the terms of life prefigures the conclusion of *Briggflatts*:

> A man like me can have neither servants nor friends
> in the present state of society.
> If I do not build for myself
> for whom would I build? . . .

> If you keep straight you will have no friends
> but catgut and blossom in season. . . .

> I do not enjoy being poor,
> I've a passionate nature.

My tongue
clacked a few prayers.

The characteristic Bunting note here is pride in independence, and the trade of poetry as a praxis of reconciliation within that persistence which makes endurance tolerable. Chomei's paradise is convincing for the post-passionate man, even if, unlike the Persian version, it is not social but a form of internal exile.

The flexible measures and patterns of this poem can articulate disaster, the ironies of city life, and the quiet passion of solitude with equal ease. Bunting once said that he thought there was "merit in the shape of the thing, and very little in the line by line run of it." In fact, the poem is a considerable work—in shape, line by line, and in its clarification of lifelong preoccupations, its flexibilities of procedure which prefigure strengths in *Briggflatts*.

III

In retrospect, Bunting's work moves towards the abundance of the 1965 poem in which a lifetime's experience of travel and employment is shaped under the energies of a craft which itself contains not only the practice of four decades but a theoretical consideration of how writing is actually committed. It is not the least moving experience of *Briggflatts* that it also embodies a commitment to the great British tradition of lyrical poetry from Wyatt and Spenser to Swinburne and Yeats, concretely audible in the sound and movement of the work. That is what its subtitles infer: "an autobiography" and, translating a thirteenth-century Portuguese troubadour, "the spuggies are fledged" (But the "Peggy" of the dedication is not the "Peggy Mullett" to whom the 1926 "Ode 3" is dedicated).

Briggflatts is impregnated with the memory of an early love which did not corrupt (opening his 1975 birthday reading, Bunting said: "the poem is an autobiography, but you musn't suppose that it is an historical autobiography"). The paradise of the poem occurs in West Yorkshire—neither the warm South nor the frozen North. In technique, the poem represents, as in a late Titian or Cezanne, an artist whose methods themselves are a major part of the pleasure in his accomplishment. Its abundance is too richly patterned to be opened in the space of a short essay; indeed part of its skill is a clarity which makes too obvious an analysis laughable. But it might be worthwhile placing the work at the head of Bunting's achievement, mainly through a fairly close look at Parts One and Two.

The twelve thirteen-line verses in fairly short measures which make up Part One are a beautifully organized pattern of sounds which is self-produced—that is to say, it does not inherit a formal mold. Two terms used there relate it to Tudor musical forms: to descant is to sing a tune in harmony with a fixed theme—a descant is harmonized imposition; and a madrigal, originally a pastoral song, is both a lyrical love poem and a contrapuntal part-song. (So we could relate this opening passage to Williams' "triple pile," Pound's "pleasure in counterpoint," and Zukofsky's idea of poetic concord as "an integral / Lower limit speech / Upper limit music"). Marlowe wrote of "shallow rivers, to whose falls melodious birds sing madrigals," and Bunting's initial set is a perception of things together in nature—not symbols but things in their relationships, with a wonderful sense of fertile interactive forms, layered as they are, for instance, in David Jones' drawings. "Brag" means not only boast and a form of poker but the bray of a trumpet, and "bull" is not only the animal but something said which the speaker does not see is foolish, and also an edict. "Pebble" will recur later with an explicitly sexual meaning of balls, and the bull will be present in Part Five in Aldebaran, star and bull-god, in the marvellous music of the night fishing which precedes the memory of a fifty-year-old love, celebrated initially in Part One. So the bull's descanting on the Rawthey at Briggflatts village is both "ridiculous and lovely," spring flowers on its black hide as it bellows and dances, preceding the creature at the other end of Bunting's scale, the slowworm.

The coherence and plaiting of sounds and modifications of meaning analogue the coherence of the hamlet: "a mason times his mallet / to a lark's twitter." The name in stone ironically memorializes decay as the pun suggests: "he lies. We rot." Out of decay, the carver's skill and the wheat alike. Speech is inhibited by the very conditions of generation, as love can be hindered. The smooth cold stone and the dead on "a low lorry" (a local word for cart) are in apposition to two children in love. The scene of death is the scene of love as the lorry journeys eastwards, reaching Garsdale at dawn, then Hawes. But it is also the scene in which history, inhabitants and landscape are in harmony— stones, birds, becks, Baltic speech sounds and the Danish Northumbrian king who was killed at Stainmore (according to some chronicles). The sound of becks, "felloe" (part of the wheel rim) and other parts of the cart, human song, sheep and peewit harmonize, and likewise the simple food and the children indoors finally, drying off, making love: "shining slowworm part of the marvel."

Each object is in its place, juxtaposed, held in the lyrical flow and in what Williams defined as "the whole body of the management of words to the formal purposes of expression" (writing on Karl Shapiro), and Duncan calls "the structure of rime": all relationships within prosodic and connotative patterning. Within Bunting's music, a strong, varied physicality anchors meaning in sensuousness and sensuality. Subdued puns in "pricked," "home," "pebbles" and "Slowworm" are counterpointed into the mason's chiselling, children's bodies, and the weather. Words are relative to this order: "The mason stirs: / Words! / Pens are too light. / Take a chisel to write."

Then the sound changes with the mode of utterance, as the poet comments on this past ideal. True to form, Bunting places pleasure sombrely, within a Sophoclean sobriety: "Every birth a crime, / every sentence life." Shame and blame for "love murdered" charges a narrative which can change nothing: "What can he, changed, tell / her, changed, perhaps dead?" Remorse for unfulfilled responsibilities of love are fused into a classicist sense of doomed life and with the defeat and death of Bloodaxe, the warring, invading king. Beyond tears and the memory of "love laid aside" and "insufferable happiness" lies work to be made. The wheat out of excrement image returns: "Dung will not soil the slowworm's mosaic"—creative fertility makes a timeless object out of time and decay (the mosaic of "Ode 36" returns), but art cannot obliterate remorse: both are hard and resist time. "Amputated years ache after / the bull is beef" fuses images characteristic of Bunting's sense of mutilated manhood. The triple rhythm of the last lines, chiming with "ache," form a hard enclosure which makes guilt and amputation definitive.

But as the opening of Part Two declares, "poet appointed dare not decline" (Bunting's vocation began at the age of five; he remembers telling his grandfather he would be a poet).

As he orders adult experience into the poem, the urban world breaks up the Yorkshire paradisal memory: "self-maimed, self-hating, / obstinate, mating beauty with squalor to beget lines stillborn"—this both describes the materials of much of Bunting's poetry and embodies his stringent self-criticism. It also extends the "ache" sound into lines both fully vital and fully abject. Skills in art are now given as instances of calculating course—bowls and the zodiac, with jack and Sun as centres aimed for; but the centre is also an end made in a work of fifty years which would otherwise be lost in self-doubt. Yet "years at risk" also implies a life energy. Course calculation now becomes the risking navigation of a Norse longboat nearing the northeastern coast—a westward voyage to meet the earlier eastward journey. This kind of objectivity is detailed and condensed (it is what exemplifies that curiously mixed etymology in the axiom "Dichten = condensare" which Pound drew from Bunting), but it is worked as metonymy; nothing is made *to stand for* anything else. The framework of terms, articulating a particular and non-artistic skill, is itself richly ambivalent. For example, "loom" is immediately the shaft of the "sweep" or steering oar, but it carries with it the sense of fabric-weaving machine. "Wake" is both a track and a funeral rite; both refer to the past and a possible future. A "thole-pin" is a gunwhale pin for the oar fulcrum, but "thole" also means to be exposed or subjected to evil, and thence to endure and suffer. "Shrouds" is obviously a double word of support.

The pilotage methods—"blends, balances"—are skills within Norse conquests, but ice is not stone, your name is lost, the voyaging is not to home. The poet reminds himself that the sea, the fells, the tropical seaweed last beyond men. He cries "About ship!" to change the tack of the poem's course—to Italy and southern scenes of sensuousness, music, carving and lust. First, a scene of decadence, empty love on board ship, the wake for flying-fish—an instance of perfect natural control to which poetry might aim: "flexible, unrepetitive line / to sing, not paint," and the familiar Bunting idea of poetry as melodic line in space: "laying the tune on the air, / nimble and easy as a lizard" (taken up from "Laying the tune frankly on the air" in Part One, and related, of course, to "A Statement": "a real sound in air" and "lines of sound drawn in the air"). The slowworm is a lizard, but here the creature is a gecko, "still and sudden." Then the poet suddenly turns course again and obliterates chances of creativity with: "to humiliate love, remember / nothing."

The following set of four quatrains recovers forms of taste (food), sound (Italian), feeling ("submarine Amalfitan kisses") and sight (the shape of work on the page). But art is once again inhibited by guilt: "an unconvinced deserter." The rain, ice and stone elements from Part One re-form in the mountain scene of Carrara, marble cut by a saw, ice, wedge, water and cordite. And again the stone becomes the art of graveyards with their ironically memorial names. But the juxtaposed scene is Lindisfarne, the holy island and its Codex plaited designs. So that the highly condensed image infers loss of Northumbrian origins and ability, as well as "discarded love." The following four lyrical quatrains beautifully condense the conversion of natural lore into chisel edge, but the mason-poet cannot use the tool as he would like to. Yet the passage is exemplary in its use of rhyme and short measures. The poem again changes course and the Bloodaxe elements return: after the mason-poet's yard "littered / with flawed fragments," the flawed king invading under an armour of lies—he is another of Bunting's servicemen, exemplifying weapons in the hands of invading evil and remote from a proper manhood ideal. A finely organized passage on those who perish by the sword consists of clear elements: a chain mail of lies, the rope of life beyond splicing, and the miserable end of life on the enduring fells ("rime on the bent" means hoar frost of frozen mist on reedy grass or sedge, but the application to poetry is included).

From a bitter end in the cold North the poem moves to four six-line stanzas articulating natural with musical forms in the hands of masters, in which Monteverdi's madrigal descant is patterned with the opening of the poem, and is compared to spiral forms of the vulture's flight. But a ruined orchard and sterile hive cannot be "entuned," only scavenged by roe, vixen and rat. Their action, "insolent," "scared" and cringing, gives the resulting "mazurka" a peculiar quality. The rat is "daring," "lithe and alert," daring to thread into the maze of Schoenberg's music: that is, a man-made structure related to spirals, models of natural form imitated in art which recur in Part Three as forms of natural survival (we might recall that Jill Purce subtitles *The Mystic Spiral* "journey of the soul" [London, 1974], and that Bunting carefully praised the *Gurrelieder* in *The Outlook*, February 4, 1928). Schoenberg's forms, like those of Byrd and Monteverdi, are tests of ability to direct energy in sound and space, but they may trap in their spirals (one of the meanings here is the laboratory maze), and in the concluding paragraph the bull and maze elements are transposed away from both Rawthey and Lindisfarne plaited rhymes into the spider's web. And that web is placed in a web of shadows cast by elder trees and the Cretan maze of Daedalus.

This is one of Bunting's most devastating collations of "conditions" from "antiquity." The spider is as "pat" as the "cannibal slug"—exact to its purpose, a destructive and creative force in nature's "contract." But the message is "pat" to the human contract too. The intricate purposes are clear. The avenging sea-god Poseidon made Pasiphae fall in love with a white bull. Daedalus made her a hollow cow form so that the beast could mount her. She gave birth to a bull-man, the grotesque Minotaur, placed at the centre of the labyrinth and later a consumer of human sacrifice. (Bunting refers to a "god-bull," a version of the myth not included in Graves' *The Greek Myths*, Vol. 1, but in any case his classicism has little truck with the Graves or the Kerenyi-Jung interpretations of myth). A monster is created out of lust between unlike entities, another example of lovelessness punished by degradation of spirit and malignant production in Bunting's work. Alma Venus is now a secular woman who manhandles the bull into her own body, and the divine and the sea combine in a malign god whose designs are only augmented by human invention.

As an image of sexual and artistic torment the ideogram is complete. The children of Part One, and the holy Lindisfarne mazings are a remote dream, as far away as the cattle in the 1927 Lucretius invocation:

> In the first days of spring
> when the untrammelled allrenewing southwind blows
> the birds exult in you and herald your coming.
> Then the shy cattle leap and swim the brooks for love.
> Everywhere, through all seas mountains and waterfalls,
> love caresses all hearts and kindles all creatures
> to overmastering lust and ordained renewals.

This ecstatic youthful belief is not fulfilled in Bunting's work, but it is recalled in *Briggflatts*, where its frustration also becomes the theme of great poetry. Radical mistrust of Love and Poetry is neither cancelled nor yielded to, but reconciled with practical achievement. The sense of exile—from idealized community of love and art—is given a sombre, intelligent universality, as it is in Yeats and Pound, during the twentieth century years of continuous combat and emergency. The very vigour and invention of Bunting's poetry challenges its own themes.

Parts Three, Four and Five will have to be summarized here with unfair brevity. Alexander's soldier in the Part Three narrative (leading out of the Cretan materials of Part Two) is, once again, exemplified in a scene of invasion, hunger, fraud, excremental lusts, usury, beggary, disease. The military leader is false; his aspiration to rise from depths invoke Israfel, the Islamic archangel, the angel of death. Ironically, the survivor "squirms" on the earth in Northumbria—the slowworm, no peak-scaler or visionary but a prosperous scavenger, mocks human efforts to grow wheat and make bread. The "eternal forms," the non-human Other, persists. The human equivalent would appear to be a Wordsworthian, low-level existence in which the sexy slowworm had his way. Ambition undermines the experience of pantheistic wholeness. In fact, *Briggflatts* is a major poem of stoic, pacifist regret at having moved from nature, love in nature, and the craft of stone masonry,

into urban society, literature and war. In Part Four, Aneurin, the
Cymric bard who honours dead heroes, is proposed as one way
through the labyrinth of circumstance: a creative life after events—
"the flood's height that has subsided." The Book of Aneurin preserves poems whose main theme is a battle between kings in
Gododdin, territory between Forth and Tyne; it is apparently a
compilation of heroic poetry about North men, some attributed
to Taliesin. Bunting's "skald" is a Scandinavian poet who honours
dead warriors. The poet recalls his own hunting "heroism" and
identifies happily with Aneurin, "being adult male of a merciless
species"; but the binding tone here is fragility of achievement (in
fact the relationship to "Chomei" is clear):

> Today's poets are piles to drive into the quaggy past
> on which impermanent palaces balance.

Contemporary northerners echo the Cymric past—given as a trans-
formation of the web and loom elements from Part Two: from
Norsemen through Columba, Aidan and Cuthbert, the northern
Christians who channelled and developed the cultural inheritance:

> wires of sharp western metal entangled in its soft
> web, many shuttles darting . . .

The value lies in the "splendour" of Northeast culture which has
resisted erosion. The sea-coast life, "mist of spiderlines," dust
whirlwinds, lice fried in a pan, are constant, but men have created
art. And here at last Bunting can movingly make his stand confi-
dently on the instruments of art and love which have not been
reduced by Nature and time, but seem to be part of natural forms
in their lastingness:

> It is time to consider how Domenico Scarlatti
> condensed so much music into so few bars . . .

>   . . . stars and lakes
> echo him and the copse drums out his measure.

In performance, between "the sun rises on an acknowledged
land" and "My love is young but wise," Bunting begins Scarlatti's
B minor sonata (Longo 33), a tender andante which is left playing
after the poet's voice ceases, so that it becomes a bridge to Part
Five. The effect is to provide a dynamic change of pace and tone
impossible to notate in words, and, of course, to amplify the
words "Domenico Scarlatti."* In performance the present tense

---

*In performance, the steady pace of Bunting's carefully inflected voice is contrasted
with the different tempi of the six sonatas used. For example, the presto Longo 25 is
played between Part Two and Three, the allegro Longo 252 between Three & Four, and
the reading ends with a repetition of Longo 33, which acts as a sweet and tender farewell, after the concluding calm cadences.

within the music *is* the poem: "snow peaks are lifted up in moon-light and twilight" and "my love is young but wise." The union dramatized in Part One becomes an "eternal form," and within it spider, web and moth (malign in Part Two) are associated with the girl's love: "hunger" and "lust" are "stayed." The poem's North and South are reconciled: "her blanket comforts my belly like the south." Hard applewood, iced landscape, and stiff clothes on the line, are part of the quiet ecstasy, but also elements of a per-manence in memory which the lyrical verse (with overtones from the "Song of Songs") maintains, and, indeed, if the term is not too strong, memorializes. The metamorphosis proceeds right down to the patterning detail: Part Two's "rime on the bent" becomes "rime is crisp on the bent."

But the navigation changes course again. The boy's "care from dead and undoing" is juxtaposed to the adult poet in "penury, filth, disgust and fury," nervously and irritably "keeping a beat in the dark"—a monotonous stroke and an appointed round —and only fully alert when at bay, like a trapped rat. The present tense love, then and across fifty years to now, recedes, grandly but irrevocably: "stars disperse. We too, / further from neighbours / now the year ages."

Winter continues in Part Five, but in a scenario of dissolu-tion—the initial operative actions are "dilute," "fading," "wrings," and "meeting, parting." But then this becomes the moulding, metamorphic process of mutability in men and nature—neither nostalgia for the bliss of paradises nor the emasculations of earlier work, but a magnificently sustained pleasure in the particularities of music, sea-shore, the fells, and fishing boats on the water at night, in the full knowledge that "God is the dividing sword," that the origin of species is conflict.

Part Five is one of the finest poems in English—richly but clearly orchestrated, the location under complete control as a set of synecdochic instances, the poetic intellect and feeling rhyming experience in lyrical forms whose sounds and movement subsume both Wyatt and Yeats. The vocabulary—"threads flex, slew," "gentles brisk," "pungent weed loudly filtering sand"—is con-stantly particular. The mobility of birds, sea on rock, men fishing, human lights and celestial lights, and the art of sheep-herding is an appreciation without pollution from ambition or war or Venus. The mason and the shore-moulding sea are joint shapers in the universe, and the Bloodaxe element is at least temporarily in abeyance. In "shepherds follow the links" the primary meaning of "links" is the undulating sandy ground near the sea-shore, but it implies both connections (rhymes) and the lights on the sea which control the rest of this section. Beyond the malignant creatures of the rest of the poem, Bunting presents human-trained sheepdogs, "their teeth are white as birch,/slow under black fringe /of silent, accurate lips."

This is an active "peaceable kingdom," "an acknowledged land": "silence by silence sits / and Then is diffused in Now"— and that is the motivating structure of the whole work. Human music "escorts" the lights of Aldebaran, Capella (with its musical as well as long-boat inferences). The hunter-god constellation "strides" over the Farne Islands, present but for the time being undamaging. Sea, heavens, planets and fishing boats are orchestrated into the Earth's nature. The harmonious assemblage of stars links then and now, the fifty years of the love poem. In the context of Bunting's whole work, "I had day enough. / For love uninterrupted night" is an earned affirmation few writers could make, and it draws the reader socially towards a poet's life in a way few poems begin to provide.

But the care for order in natural music and the human sonata—nature and artifice to be part of a single action, a religious experience—is contained in what works as the central passage of the poem, one of those classic articulations of the great commonplace which poetry traditionally presents to us:

> Each spark trills on a tone beyond chronological compass
> yet in a sextant's bubble present and firm
> places a surveyor's stone or steadies a tiller.
> Then is Now. The star you steer by is gone,
> its tremulous thread spun in the hurricane
> spider floss on my cheek; light from the zenith
> spun when the slowworm lay in her lap
> fifty years ago.

The transmutation of the poem's spider's webs to floss and to a girl's hair and then to the concealed thread of the Fates is placed with the technological instruments of mapping, navigation and firm foundations. "Slowworm" understands that he had the time of his life through a metaphysical image of light threads which is as firm as anything in Donne. The poet's book of life can be put aside and then juxtaposed to a combe (a valley, a hive), with an ease which can only be achieved after a lifetime's practice.

The three-stanza coda is, as Bunting says, "carefully arranged as far as vowel sounds go to be very singable, but the stanzas do not repeat themselves exactly" (Dale Reagan, op. cit.). In this lyric, the unknown passage to death is coolly contemplated in a traditional image of the night voyage about to be taken: "Night, float us. . . ." The sea takes both the music and the warring kings; Bloodaxe is recalled but his axe takes on a fatality apart from him —it lasts. The final two rhetorical questions poise the poem in subdued confidence, controlled by the tracery of sounds into last chords without rhetoric—"never a crabbed turn or congested cadence, / never a boast or a see-here!"

The pattern is clear. The travelling man reaches a Quaker self-communing in silence, in the presence of a small community, to whom he offers a poetry as his gift. The urge to epic, present also in Bunting's contemporaries and peers, is never divulged in an arrogance of dogma or ideology. The structural plan is there, but the generalizations are mostly anchored in fact rather than coarsened into abstractions. Northumberland wildness and softness entered Bunting's boyhood, and remained; space between people and the uncongested statement govern his work. Wordsworth's isolated men and women in landscape come to mind, and his dislike of Cambridge and London, and his wariness of political activity (in spite of his engagements in the French Revolution and the Reform Bill). But in Bunting a certain libertarian adventurousness confronts a desire for utter craft: there lies the strengths. Love on the move and waste in lust thematically control much of his poetry, but always within an architectonics which has to be evolved to hold the instabilities of adventure and pacifism in an unstable historical period. *Briggflatts* coheres both adventurous mobility and the need for a home, so that it comes through as a praise for as much paradise, however tenuously grasped, as "an acknowledged land" can afford. In the Reagan interview Bunting says:

> I do believe that there is a possibility of a kind of reverence for
> the whole creation which I feel we ought to have in our bones....
> a kind of pantheism, I suppose . . . .finding out as much as care-
> fully controlled commonsense can find out about the world. In
> so doing, you will be contributing to the histology of God.

At the conclusion of *Briggflatts*, Alma Venus does bring forth "into light" a generative poem. She took her time.

DAVID M. GORDON

THE STRUCTURE OF BUNTING'S SONATAS

I

In considering the sonata form for the structure of a literary work, Bunting would have learned in 1922 from Pound that Joyce supposedly followed the form of a sonata in planning *Ulysses*.[1] And Bunting has remarked that his interest in the sonata finally brought him back to the 18th century composers:

> I got off on the wrong foot trying to imitate Beethoven's sonatas, using extremely violent contrasts in tone and speed which don't actually carry well onto the page, and I had to puzzle about for a while before I discovered it was better to go back to a simpler way of dealing with the two themes and to take the early or mid-eighteenth-century composers—John Christian Bach and Scarlatti —as models to imitate.[2]

As to the 18th century sonata, Pound probably would have suggested Lavignac, who describes the sonata's structure as follows:

Exposition	*First Reprise*	
	Principal Motif.	La major
	(repose in the dominant)	Mi major
	Second motif	
	Second Reprise	
Development	Development	Mi major
	(with modulations	
	in different	
	tonalities)	

---

1. *Polite Essays* (1937; rpt. Freeport, New York: Books For Libraries, 1966), p. 89.
2. Anthony Suter, "Musical Structure in the Poetry of Basil Bunting," *Agenda*, 16:1 (Spring 1978), p. 47.

Recapitu-lation	Return to the principal motif	La major
	(repose on the dominant)	
	Return to the Second motif	
	(coda)[3]	

Lavignac explains this diagram as follows:

Examinons d'abord la première reprise. Après l'exposé du thème qui a bien établi la tonalité principale, un court divertissement conduit à un repose sur la dominante; par équivoque, cette dominante est prise pour une tonique, et dans ce nouveau ton (le ton de la dominante), qui ne sera plus quitté jusqu'à la fin de la reprise, est présenté le deuxième motif; un nouveau divertisse-ment et une courte coda terminent cette reprise. L'usage classique est de la jouer deux fois, probablement pour que l'auditeur se pénètre bien des deux motifs principaux et les case dans sa mémoire.

Passons à la deuxième reprise. Elle débute par le développe-ment; celui-ci peut être conçu de bien des façons; c'est la période où le compositeur peut donner le plus libre essor à son imagina-tion et s'aventurer dans des tonalités éloignées, mais sans perdre de vue qu'il s'agit de ramener le sujet, qui doit être exposé une deuxième fois comme au début et dans le même ton, et aussi aboutissant au même repos, sur la dominante, mais, cette fois, il n'y aura plus équivoque, la dominante restera dominante, et c'est dans le ton principal, qui ne sera plus abandonné, que le deuxième motif fera sa deuxième apparition. . . . (309-310)

[To begin let us examine the first reprise. After the exposé of the theme [or principal motif] which has well established the principal tonality, a short divertimento leads to a repose on the dominant tonality; paradoxically this dominant is taken for a tonic, and in this new tonality (that of the dominant), which will not be departed from until the end of the reprise, is presented the second motif; a new divertimento and a short coda end this reprise. Classical usage generally plays this twice, probably so that the listener can acquaint himself with the main motifs and store them in his memory.

Let us go to the second reprise. It opens with the development; this may be conceived of in the most imaginative fashion. Here is the opportunity for the composer to give the freest soaring to his creative faculties, and to adventure into remote tonalities, but without forgetting that he must return to the subject or principal motif, which must be exposed a second time as at the beginning, and in the same tonality, and also ending on the same repose, on the dominant; but this time there is no feeling of doubt, the dominant will remain dominant, and it is in the principal tonality, which will not be abandoned, that the second motif will make its second appearance. . . .]

---

3. Albert Lavignac, *La Musique et Les Musiciens* (Paris, 1895; rpt. Paris, 1950), p. 310. Cf. *Guide to Kulchur*, p. 136, dedicated in part to B.B. The sonata analyzed by Lavignac is by C.P.E. Bach, and is identical to one of Scarlatti's.

Scarlatti's sonata in C Major offers a very good example of the five parts of the sonata (Longo 104):

The first theme,

The second theme,

The development,

The return to the first theme,

The return to the second theme,

To sum up, we might say that the sonata form develops *two tonally contrasting themes* through *three basic stages:*

I Exposition

The opening theme of the exposition is strongly rooted in the tonic key of the work. Then the second theme of the exposition moves resolutely to a closely related, but distinct key. Thus the exposition sets up an opposition of tonal localities which the development and recapitulation will endeavour to bring to terms.

II Development

The purpose of the development is to discuss and expatiate on the conflicts of tonality and theme that the exposition has introduced; it is a place of tonal change, usually modulating to another key, which key is only remotely related to that of the exposition. The development frequently breaks the principal themes down into smaller units and then places these units into new tonal or contrapuntal relations with each other. Hence, themes or scraps of themes may sound in a new key which may combine to form new melodies, or may be played against each other.

III Recapitulation

Like the beginning of the development, the juncture at which the development passes into recapitulation is one of the most significant psychological instants in the whole sonata structure since this juncture marks the end of the main argument and the commencement of the final synthesis, for which all the prior assertions and arguments have prepared the aural mind. Now the recapitulation presents the themes of the exposition in a new state of equilibrium, usually in the same order as before, but now both themes are in the tonic key—in the exposition the first was in the tonic, but the second in the dominant. As a result of the musical dialectic of the development, the two themes now appear in a new relationship.[4]

II

In just what manner does Bunting avail himself of the sonata form for his poetry? Although it is always hazardous to apply a

---

4. Cf. *Brittanica*, 1973. S.v. *Groves*, ed. Eric Blom (New York: St. Martin's Press, 1955), s.v. William S. Newman, *The Sonata in the Classic Era* (Chapel Hill: U. of N.C.P., 1963), pp. 116ff.

musical analogy to poetry, apparently Bunting continues to do just that as he speaks of his concern about finding "a simpler way of dealing with the two themes."[5] For "the two themes" are specifically the basis of the sonata and its five part structure. Let us look briefly at Bunting's use of the sonata form in his early poems to see how he develops the "two themes."[6] *Villon, Attis,* and *Reich* are all divided into three sections: I corresponds to the exposition of the two themes; II, to the development; and III, to the recapitulation of the two themes. In the case of *Spoils,* Bunting admitted that its structure is musically "lopsided," but it still reveals an interesting use of the sonata form.[7] *Well* is based on an early binary form of the sonata; following the pattern AB, it has only two main sections for the two themes, in which A corresponds to the exposition òf the two themes, and B, to the development and recapitulation of the two themes. Here is a suggested outline of Bunting's early Sonatas:

Villon

I Exposition

First Theme: An illusory vision of beauty of the Emperor and the virgin that does not jibe with the desolation of prison life. "Vision is lies."

Second Theme: The utter transience of life precludes the possibility of the permanence of art. "We are less permanent than thought."

II Development

The powerful seek to wrest life from the flux by imprisoning the artists, Villon and Bunting, who nevertheless attempt to produce art from the ravages of time ("a silk purse from a sow's ear") until they are officially silenced ("a thimble on her tongue"). The violence offered the white bear, the seal, and whale is like that offered to beauty incarnate, Archipiada.

III Recapitulation

Return of the First Theme: The vision is no longer illusory. The

---

5. See previous note 2.
6. The *Sonatas: Attis, Villon, Aus Dem Zweiten Reich, The Well of Lycopolis, The Spoils.*
7. Peter Quartermain and Warren Tallman, *Agenda,* 16, 1, 1978, p. 19. Hereafter, Quartermain-Tallman. (Permanently useful.)

olive trees, the sea, clouds, shrines, the goddess, graveclothes of men—all these are true to life, nature, and the suffering of mankind, "Romans and moderns." In the exposition he could not believe that there was any connection between the apparition of beauty and the horrors of prison, but now in the recapitulation he understands that man has always suffered for the sake of his vision of beauty ("because of the beauty of Helen").

Return of the Second Theme: Art overcomes the transience of life. Art is the "precision clarifying" the vagueness of existence, setting the "boundary to a wilderness of detail." The mind of the poet is the shred of platinum,[8] "the catalytic making whisper and whisper / run together like two drops of quicksilver." Art is more permanent than *rigor mortis*, " stuff that clings / to frigid limbs / more marble hard / than girls imagined by Mantegna." Art is the "factor that resolves / unnoted harmonies."

Attis

I Exposition

First Theme: Attis the eunuch is the prototype of the split-apart soul of modern civilization (with echoes of Bloom of the Lotus-eaters and W. Lewis' *Apes of God*). Attis' mode of being is likened to the tidal drift of an estuary and the serendipity of a fox hunt (The Latin inscription and details seem to be drawn from Catullus' poem on Attis, LXI, with the sea-crossing as Bunting's "salt from all beaches," and the rout up Mt. Ida as Bunting's fox hunt on "Cheviot.")

Second Theme: The traditional superabundance of the earth is scarred by modern civilization (Lucretius, 2, 594 ff).

II Development

The frenetic eunuch type is thematically associated with "a morbid state in which what is naturally repulsive becomes attractive."[9] This description applies to the preview of violence presided over by the furies (*Inf*. ix, 52). And the "morbid" state of the eunuch causes the breakdown of love (echoing the compleynt against pity, Canto XXX), the passivity and lethargy of the poor, and the complacent luxury of a devitalized aristocracy: the furies and Gods

8. T.S. Eliot, "Tradition and the Individual Talent," *Selected Essays* (New York: Harcourt, Brace and Company, 1950), p. 7.
9. "Notes on Dante's Hell" by H. Oelsner in *Dante's Inferno*, "The Temple Classics" (London: Dent, 1902), p. 393. The *Dante* that Pound used.

must therefore *enamel* Attis.

III Recapitulation

Return of the First Theme: Attis intones the apologia for the eunuch's existence in the modern world, and prays to be made whole in Elysium.

Return of the Second Theme: Cybele, Mother Nature, has been defrauded by a schizoid modern poetics.

Reich

I Exposition

First Theme: In modern Germany an automatic soulless, efficient, technology is replacing the evidence of life.

Second Theme: Love becomes stereotyped, meretricious, and trivial in an ambience of mediocrity and insipidity.

II Development

Sexual titillation as a *modus vivendi.*

III Recapitulation

Return of the First Theme: The modern German artist is hollow.

Return of the Second Theme: And beneath its pretence, the culture is sterile.

Well

I

Love, the timeless stuff of poetry (Cf. "Polymnia" and "To Helen Egli," p. 79) must undergo the sufferings and horrors of old age. All that is certain is that beauty will pass.

II

Those who would find love and poetry without paying the cost of suffering, who would attempt to fix the cadence of the sun in stone, but who would not use the "proud, full sail" of love and poetry: these are seeking the surrogates of love.

III

Infamous love: abject poetry; every aspect of disgust, squalor and violence to the senses of love will be equally felt in poetry.

IV

Those who do not love produce no poetry ("Ripped from love's ledger and poetry's"). They passively follow life without ever feeling love for it.

Spoils

I Exposition

First Theme: The traditional qualities of the Seljuks decay in the face of modern civilization.

Second Theme: Redemptive love is also affected by the decay of civilization.

II Development

An apparent resolution is proposed: Bunting will live in Persia with its enduring art and philosophy as a personal affirmation and bulwark against the onslaught of a suspect modernity ("Dread of what's to be / is and has been– / were we not better dead?").

III Recapitulation

Return of the First Theme: The agrarian way of life declines because of the modern dissolution of the traditional folk-culture.

Return of the Second Theme: Modern war is redeemed by a glimpse of transcendent reality in war's midst ("from which heart naked swam / out to the dear unintelligible ocean").

In these early sonatas, each of them dealing in some manner with the deleterious effect of modern civilization upon life, love, and art, Bunting has (except for the variant form of *Well*) used the five part sonata form for an extremely wide gamut of subjects. In each of these sonatas we see that in the exposition the second theme arises out of the first theme; the development takes up some aspect of these two themes and offers a very imaginative and always *impossible* resolution. In the recapitulation, the first and/or second theme offers a true resolution to the first and second theme of the exposition. In these poems we find an overall sense of unity of structure. We also see how Bunting's sonata form has evolved under differing poetic conditions and with different materials. The *Villon* and *Attis* remain among his solidest sonatas.

The later sonatas continue to explore and increase the range of the possibilities of his sonata form.

III

As we move toward *Briggflatts*, we can see Bunting elaborating the sonata form toward a more distinct presentation of the two themes, while at the same time keeping his material within the bounds of his original sonata plan.

From Eliot's work Bunting undoubtedly learned several things, including a new way of playing off the three sections of the sonata (exposition, development, recapitulation) against the five constituent units (first theme, second theme, recapitulation, return of first theme, return of second theme). Kenner has pointed out an exact structural counterpart of *The Waste Land* in the *Quartets*:

> The first movement, like *The Burial of the Dead*, introduces a diversity of themes; the second, like *A Game of Chess*, presents first "poetically," and then with less traditional circumspection the same area of experience; the third, like *The Fire Sermon*, gathers up the central vision of the poem while meditating dispersedly on themes of death; the fourth is a brief lyric; the fifth, a didactic and lyric culmination, concerning itself partly with language, in emulation of the Indo-European roots exploited in *What the Thunder Said*.[10]

Apparently Bunting saw a model for extending the dramatic and meditative range in the development and final sections of the sonata in Eliot's treatment of his third and fifth sections.

Bunting also seems to have learned from Eliot that he must not stray too far from music in constructing his poetry, bearing in mind Pound's axiom that poetry atrophies when it withdraws from music, and that music atrophies when it withdraws from dance.[11] Hence Bunting's iterative caveat, "Poetry, like music, is to be heard."[12] He wants a form for his poetry in which the separate lines and strophes, as well as the entire structure of the two themes, may be effectually retained in the aural imagination. Otherwise the musical form, as such, is utterly pointless: thus Bunting's eschewing of Beethoven's sonatas, and his return to the earlier forms, such as Scarlatti's.

Briggflatts climaxes Bunting's movement toward an increasingly meaningful elaboration of themes and counter-melodies,

10. *The Invisible Poet: T.S. Eliot* (New York: McDowell, Obolensky, 1959), pp. 305-7.
11. *ABC of Reading* (Norfolk: New Directions, 1934), p. 14.
12. Anthony Suter, 46.

toward a greater clarity and distinctness in presentation of themes
and other melodic material in the tonic, dominant, or remote
tonalities, and furthermore towards a larger, organic sense of
underlying unity and wholeness of feeling, which is expressed by
means as close to music as a meaning-bearing medium will allow.

Bunting's diagram of *Briggflatts* as a sequence of five "mountains" helps elucidate the structure of the poem:

In describing how he applied the sonata form to *Briggflatts*,
Bunting says, "You're going to have five parts because it's got to
be an uneven number. So that the central one should be the one
apex, there."[13] That the five parts of *Briggflatts* reflect the structure of the sonata with the development section at the center,
which he describes as "a nightmare or a dream" (Cf. "free fan-
tasia," *Groves* s.v.), is clear in another comment: "But what is
new, the only new thing that I knew of . . . in doing it, was that
instead of having one climax in the other parts you have two."[14]
Here he is pointing in his diagram to the slight elevation of the
right-hand peaks of the two *M*'s as they progress towards the middle figure, and then the lowering of the right-hand peaks as they
descend from the middle. Bunting remarks of these risings and
lowerings, "In the first two the first climax is the less and another
immediately comes out of it when you're not expecting it. So you
have it for those two. In the others the first climax is the greater
and it trails off. . . ."[15] Thus in the two movements before the
development, there will be a rise followed by an abrupt greater
rise; and after the development, a rise followed by a falling off. As
to how these climaxes work, Bunting explains by pointing to the
second section of the poem: ". . . the second part rises up slowly
to a very nice climax with the murder of Eric Bloodaxe, and everybody naturally thinks: this is what—we've had it now—this is the
end of the thing. But then it rises up to a still higher climax which
has to fade almost immediately afterwards. And the same way
with the others, though it's not quite so obvious in the other
ones."[16]

This series of climaxes, as he has diagrammed them, fall within the sonata form of the poem: "The musical structure must be
such that the climaxes happen there and there and there but it's

13. Quartermain-Tallman, p. 9.
14. Ibid.
15. Ibid.
16. Ibid., p. 14.

not a graph of the musical structure. . . ."[17] This puzzling statement seems to mean that he is only diagramming the new ideas he
has brought to *Briggflatts*; as he says, "It is a mere graph of the
climaxes."[18] He has been using the sonata musical structure itself
at least since 1925. And he explains that this musical structure
pre-existed the poem: "I had no idea what was going into the
poem except that the movements would have that shape."[19] The
"five movements"[20] then refer to the sonata form itself, and the
"shape" refers to the series of climaxes.

This handling of climaxes provides a progressive build-up of
the first two themes toward the development, and an unwinding
of the two themes after the development which makes for a more
definite unfolding of the themes in the poem, analogous in musical
terms to "bridge material." And it is precisely this innovative use
of the climaxes that makes *Briggflatts* the most carefully structured of all his sonatas, since these pairs of ascending and de-
scending climaxes provide (as we shall see) a solid footing for the
centrifugal pace of the poem toward the central development
episode, and then, conversely, the centripetal pace away from the
development. Here is Bunting's implementation of the ground-
work of the sonata, since the centrifugal movement flees from
the tonic tonality, and the centripetal movement seeks to return
to tonic home. And now an outline of the poem:

I The First Theme: A Vision that Fades

His subject is a childhood love for a mason's daughter, which
creates a vision of pastoral beauty for him that is symbolized by
the slowworm. But because of some failing that the protagonist
associates with the flaw of Bloodaxe, the love is broken, and as a
result the fabric of his vision begins to worsen: the may, the magic
of the living, resting marble, the speaking mallet, the timing lark,
the singing river Rawthey, the dancing bull, the playing pebbles,
the spelling stone—all decline into a dingy river, a drudge at mallet,
a trashed lark; the sweet tenor bull (the protagonist) becomes
beef, love itself a convenience.

This first section comes to a close as it anticipates section II,
with the beginning of the outward centrifugal movement of the
protagonist, telling in the mason's idiom of his leaving his love,

---

17. Ibid., p. 13.
18. Ibid.
19. Ibid., p. 10.
20. Ibid.

which is connected with the escape of Bloodaxe (who sounds the dominant tonality) to Stainmore, "letter stone to stand / over love laid aside / lest insufferable happiness impede / flight to Stainmore."

II The Second Theme: Life v. Art

Here is the outward movement of the young poet-sailor, agonizing over his laid-aside love, and seeking experience as well as an art that will utter it: the ratio between the Buddha's cheek and a girl's breast. His struggle to acquire a poetic foundation "mates beauty with squalor," or produces a "name cut in ice," or foam written by wind. Northumberland put from mind ("Fells forget him / Fathoms dull the dale") he is only aware of self-hate, -maiming, -sickening; love is a humiliating vapour. He attempts to force experience into four quatrains which he tests with his senses, but finds deficient because he deserted love. Although the memory of the animals plaited in the Lindisfarne initials recurs to him, they stand too near his discarded boyhood love. But in another trial of his ability to shape his life in four more quatrains, he approaches the rock of childhood, becoming himself the reproached and uneasy mason with his still evasive and flawed fragments. But this allows him to make a valid ethical and historical self-discovery as he divulges something of the mystery of the self-hating, -escaping, King Bloodaxe. This momentary synthesis of art and experience manifests to him how essential is the finding of an inherently commensurate musical form for his material. Otherwise he will simply be treating of superficial ornament: "Anemones spite cullers of ornament." In such wise the starfish and poinsettia may be articulated by a galliard, or his experience as a desert soldier by a madrigal. While even the most unpromising compost heap will submit to the labyrinthine intricacies of Schoenberg, all the same his laid-aside love remains intransigently a "bogged orchard," unavailable to his poetry. And centrifugally the protagonist, still in the troubled summer of his life, finds, however violently, the icon for the mating of art with experience, in the coupling of Pasiphaë and the bull.

III The Development: Violence v. Sympathy

This part of the sonata allows the composer the widest soarings of the imagination into tonalities the most foreign from the tonic as he elaborates the possibilities residing in the two themes. And this section of the poem continues the centrifugal movement of the second theme outward into the unknown. The unrelenting intention of the protagonist to push his search for experience to the utmost in order to find a form that will manifest it finds a parallel in the Persian tale of Alexander's trek to the world's end in a disastrous effort to yoke his ambitious ideals with life.

The vertical shape of this climactic section stands above the rest of the sonata in time and place as the roof of the protagonist's life-year, offering an apparent settling of the conflict (like the third act of a drama, or the third section in Eliot's *Quartets*) between art and life.

The primary action is the attempt "to define a road," seemingly the road homewards, but because of his aberrant ambition and pride, the road becomes a phantasmagoria of all that it should have been: "charred hearths," quivering cliffs, a capsizing year, excrement for food, false guides, Corbière-like trenches of corpses, disease, amputees, madness and starvation, culminating in the suicidal scaling of the knife-sharp mountain, and Israfel's readiness to end the world, as the Alexander-protagonist falls.

And now the development, as with a musically foreheard motif, subtly begins the centripetal movement, as the defeated protagonist slowly begins to waken from his fall, recognizes the moss and bracken of Macedonia-Northumberland, and the Red Cross ideal of childhood, the genial slowworm, who cures his pride and ambition by the purity of a simple agrarian life, leading this section finally and carefully back to the tonic tonality of steadfast home.

IV Return to the First Theme: Vision Reconciled in the Modern World

As section I began the centrifugal movement outward, so section IV answers with a centripetal movement back toward his ground, where the tonic tonality is re-established. The first theme is re-presented in the light of the protagonist's development, in which he has unburdened himself of a sentimentalized conception of the Northumberland of his childhood, and replaced it with the reality of the actual land whose beauty he can now esteem in his wiser years: "Today's posts are piles to drive into the quaggy past."

He accepts and rejoices in the very soil itself, its history, its people, its ethos, the war that took it, and the benevolent intelligence that cultured it: King Ida's fight for independence from the British, as sung by the skalds Aneurin and Taliesin (imitating heroic hexameters: Cf. his "Catullus," 131), and the spiritual accomplishment as Christianity enters ("soil shifts vest /

Aidan and Cuthbert put on daylight").

Now as late summer (Sirius) passes into the autumn of his life, his acceptance broadens in looking at the entire design of nature. Who could retrace the paths of the shuttles that wove nature? He realizes that nothing can be left out ("excepting nothing that is"), neither the fox, leech, weevil, nor even the murderous runts. It is only *lice* who despise the world and seek to self-destructively leave it (the Alexander motif).

Scarlatti's music accompanies the sun rising over his "acknowledged land" as the protagonist now consummates the love which he had laid aside in section I.

And as he has come to completely accept ancient Northumbria as his Northumberland, so now in his seasoned years can he accept in himself a rat-like determination to survive the condemnation of a world, hostile to his poetry; without self-hatred he pictures himself, unrecognized, yet sustaining his enduring vision of beauty, even though harassed like a chased rat ("keeping a beat in the dark").

V The Return of the Second Theme: Nature and Art are Reconciled

In his winter of life, a tone of rest and reconciliation follows from section IV, where in a struggle toward a deeper maturity he has recovered his personal vision. Here the second theme of art v. life is brought into the tonic key and to a resolution; the problems of section II as suggested by a *ratio*, a correspondence between life and an ideal ("The Buddha's cheek"), have been clarified by song in this solstitial crescendo.

Where II was anxiously beset with contradictions ("beauty with squalor"), here they are harmonized ("grief turns to carnival. . . . west wind waves to east . . . day is wreathed in what summer lost"). In II the protagonist was the uneasy mason; now he contemplates nature lovingly playing that role: "compos[ing] decay. . . . shaping the shore as a mason / fondles and shapes his stone." Art is like man's ability to constructively mediate between and imitate the infinite structures of nature, as the training of dogs to lead sheep; a complete understanding of the relationships of art and life is ultimately an understanding of oneself in nature.

He then turns to the stars as the archetypes of form, the reckoners of the seasons of his life (Aldebaran, Capella, spring; Sirius, Procyon, summer; Betelgeuse, Rigel, Orion, fall and winter) and as the embodiment of himself as old man winter (his shoulder, Betelgeuse, and his left leg, Rigel, of the constellation Orion).

And now the poem draws to a close, deploying an intense, very condensed, and rapid centripetal movement of the components of the poem. As an older man he gazes at the stars, realizing that they represent the creative soul of the individual ("emphatic fire") in a Platonic sense, and that they are man's connection with the eternal values with which he associates art ("beyond chronological compass"); yet at the same time, the stars control and give finite shape and existence to the actual elements of the *vie vécu* ("places a surveyor's stone or steadies a tiller"). Consequently, in nature the antinomy of art v. life is overcome.

But he also realizes that these stars are the same that he steered by in youth when he was distractedly searching for a meaningful form for the flux of experience in his art. He reflects that although the star Capella has probably long been dead, it rayed out its last light at the moment that he as a child fell in love with the girl who gave him his first vision of beauty, one which he would strive to capture in his poetry ("a light from the zenith / spun when the slowworm lay in her lap"). And this is the same star that led him, as an older man, back to her; thus, without realizing it, this light has given him an inner certainty and an artistic direction ("Then is now").

And so the transcendent value represented by the light of the star has become transformed into an immanent value which has directed his life into a poem: "the sheets are gathered and bound."

Earlier the "heart naked swam / out to the dear unintelligible ocean" (p. 35)—that is, it cast itself outward in a transcendental gesture. But the finale of *Briggflatts* homes unswervingly to its tonic tonality, which returns the whole poem to a greater than anticipated sense of unity, one which reaches back to the beginning. By counter-pointing and -balancing the poem's structure through a rediscovery of the child's world which is far more beautiful than he realized this finale achieves the formidable task of fusing together art and life, by concretely placing the fleshed-out childhood vision of beauty within the arms of the poet, who is now ready for the perpetual night of love after his day of life.

Bunting said that he wanted Scarlatti's B Minor sonata, *fugato*, Longo 33 (see Appendix A) to be played after Section IV and after the coda.[21] In section IV he says, "It is time to consider how Domenico Scarlatti / condensed so much music into so few bars / with never a crabbed turn or congested cadence, / never a

---

21. Ibid., p. 13.

boast or a see-here; and stars and lakes / echo him and the copse drums out his measure." Although this sonata (Longo 33) employs a binary form (like *Well*), having only four parts instead of the five parts of *Briggflatts*, its "fugue style" coincides significantly with the quality that we find in sections IV, V, and the Coda.

The germ of the whole poem (and the first line that Bunting wrote) was the last line of the poem: "For love uninterrupted night."[22] This line is adapted from Catullus' *Nox est perpetua una dormienda*. Of Catullus' line Bunting says, "It is a more complex line than any of the translators has ever got across. The *una* is never given its full value. . . . *Nox est perpetua*: there is an everlasting night. *Una dormienda* doesn't mean one night, it means a night that is all one, that never varies. That is the important point in the Catullus line you see. . . . I think it's probably from that line that the whole train of thought started. . . ."[23] He then adds that Scarlatti's B Minor sonata, *fugato*, was in his mind at the same time as the Catullus.[24] *Fugato* means "in the fugue style but not in strict form" (*OED*), or,

> an irregularly fugued passage or whole movement is called fugato as distinct from a fugue, which though not a settled 'form,' normally adheres to certain structural procedures.[25]

And as to a general idea of the "structural procedures" of a fugue as Bunting quite possibly understood them, Lavignac says,

> Une fugue est un morceau de musique entièrement conçu en contrepoint, et dans lequel tout se rattache, directment ou indirectement, à un motif initial nommé *sujet*; de ce lien résulte l'unité de l'oeuvre; la variété est obtenue au moyen des modulations et des diverses combinations en canon ou en imitation.[26]

> [A fugue is a piece of music conceived entirely in counterpoint, and in which all is fastened directly or indirectly, to an initial motif called the subject; from this bond results the unity of the work; variety is obtained by means of the modulations and the diverse combinations in canon or in imitation.]

Fugato then aptly describes the musical quality of Scarlatti's B Minor sonata, and the *fugato* style precisely answers to the emotional logic of this part of the poem because from section IV to the Coda the childhood vision of love, now consummated, returns as the vital subject that provides a fugue-like coherence and

22. Ibid., p. 10.
23. Ibid., pp. 12-13.
24. Ibid.
25. *Groves*, s.v.
26. Lavignac, p. 299.

continuity with the poem as a whole. Here the older man discovers that the childhood vision is still intact, and completely valid; it is the same land, people, tradition, culture, environing green world, and now he can accept all, even himself. His vision of childhood was, is, and will continue: "Then is diffused in now." A vision fastened to the stars: an ideal resolution to *Briggflatts* because the protagonist has discovered a unity of sensibility within himself that can continue encountering new experience in the manner of a fugue ("trembling phrase fading to pause / then glow"), a vision *that is all one* ("For love uninterrupted night").

SISTER VICTORIA MARIE FORDE, S.C.

THE ODES*

"My excellence, if I have one, isn't new or striking. . . . I'd say I
remember the musical origin of poetry, the singing side of it, better than anybody else except Ezra and Carlos Williams . . ." (L.Z.,
July 6, 1951).**

With a few exceptions in the "Overdrafts" section of his *Collected Poems* and "Chomei at Toyama," the origins of all Bunting's
poems are, in fact, musical. By entitling six of his long poems
"Sonatas," he is immediately identifying this major group in some
sense with music. Half of the translations in the "Overdrafts" section are of Persian poems, originally chanted and accompanied by
music and dancing.[1] The translations of works by Latin poets in
that section together with the forty-five odes in the First and
Second Book of Odes trace their origin, of course, to ancient
Greek drama where the ode was "choral in quality."[2] Accompanied by music, the chorus of Greek singers used the human
voice, "the first, and certainly the most basic, of all musical instruments,"[3] to "express patterns of sustained pitch and rhythm."[4]
By "the musical origin" of poetry, Bunting could be referring to
the idea that the ode, rooted etymologically in the Greek *aoidein*,
"to sing" or "to chant," is defined as "originally . . . a poem intended or adapted to be sung to instrumental accompaniment."[5]

---

*Chapter II of an unpublished dissertation, entitled *Music and Meaning in the Poetry of
Basil Bunting*, by Sister Victoria Marie Forde, Notre Dame, Indiana, 1973. Reprinted
with permission.
**Bunting to Zukofsky letters at Humanities Research Center at University of Texas,
Austin, are cited thus with date in text.
1. Conversations with Jaafar Moghadam and Khosrow Moshtarikhah, Iranian Midshipmen, students at the University of Notre Dame, 1971-1972.
2. William Flint Thrall and Addison Hibbard, *A Handbook of Literature*, 2nd ed. (New
York, 1960), p. 327.
3. Warren D. Anderson, *Ethos and Education in Greek Music: The Evidence of Poetry
and Philosophy* (Cambridge, Mass., 1966), p. 2.
4. *Ibid.*
5. Alex Preminger, ed., "Ode," *Encyclopedia of Poetry and Poetics* (Princeton, N.J.,
1965), p. 585; Joseph T. Shipley, ed., "Ode," *Dictionary of World Literature*, 2nd ed.
(Totowa, N.J., 1966), p. 289.

This of course applies not only to Greek but to most early cultures. In western society it continues to the time of Malherbe who tried unsuccessfully to prevent the dissolution of the "marriage of music and poetry."[6]

Although the odes have definite musical origins, recent definitions have emphasized characteristics which overlook this fact; for example: "In Greek and Latin as in modern poetry, a poem in free verse and structure, frequently addressed to a deity."[7] Bunting's odes with their emphasis on musical origins are marked in some instances by these general characteristics also; Ode 11 has both a formal dedication and a classic address to "Narciss." Generally, however, they do not fit the definition of the formal ode characterized by "public nature, solemn diction, and stately gravity"[8] which omits any connection with music.

A consideration of the two Books of Odes is essential for an appreciation of Bunting's work in its entirety and as a necessary step toward a consideration of his major works, the sonatas. At the outset it must be made clear that these brief odes are not comparable to the poet's longer, more important poems. Some of the odes may have been written, it seems, as technical exercises in which Pound, Zukofsky, and others were involved. Many are stepping stones thematically and technically to later, more mature work. Others are high points in the career of a poet who is never satisfied to remain at a certain stage of development.

To assess Bunting's advancement chronologically through the odes, a reader can simply read each Book in turn, since the odes are arranged according to dates. Bunting himself perfected the chronology in the *Collected Poems*, removing only one ode, "They Say Etna," from the 1950 edition—no great loss. In the Note to the "First Book of Odes" he explains: "I have taken my chance to insert a couplet in the First Book of Odes and promote 'The Orotava Road' from its limbo to its chronological place amongst them, which has obliged me to renumber many" (*C.P.*, 158).*

Since Bunting's chronological development is easily seen through the organization of the odes in the *Collected Poems*, it is more logical to discuss these short poems in a way which leads to the more important discussion of the longer works. In the odes details of craftsmanship are worked out and themes are introduced

---

6. Renee Winegarten, *French Lyric Poetry in the Age of Malherbe* (Manchester, England, 1954), p. 4.
7. Willi Apel, *Harvard Dictionary of Music* (Cambridge, Mass., 1947), p. 503.
8. Thrall and Hibbard, *op. cit.*, p. 328.
*References to *Collected Poems*, 2nd. ed. (London, 1970) are given thus in the text.

which recur with increasing significance in the longer works.

Although, as Bunting insists, the important aspect of his poetry is the music, his subject matter allows him to make a statement about the primacy of human values in life, whether as an individual involved in love and friendship, as a member of society, or as an artist. These thematic concerns become broader and deeper in the sonatas. For discussion purposes, Bunting's odes can be grouped around three themes: love in its broadest sense, society, and art. Only two odes (1 and 4) are not so easily placed in these divisions because of their broader cosmic dimensions, but these two also uphold individual human values above all else. Each of these three topics encompasses a wide range of variations, and at least four odes (12, 34, 37, and 6_2)[9] combine themes.

One of the best love poems and the earliest collected poem in which Bunting analyzes and identifies an emotional state through the depiction of nature is Ode 3 (*C.P.*, 89), "To Peggy Mullett," a poem for which Yeats had a "particular fancy" (L.Z., September 9, 1953):

I am agog for foam. Tumultous come
with teeming sweetness to the bitter shore
tidelong unrinsed and midday parched and numb
with expectation. If the bright sky bore
with endless utterance of a single blue
unphrased, its restless immobility
infects the soul, which must decline into
an anguished and exact sterility
and waste away: then how much more the sea
trembling with alteration must perfect
our loneliness by its hostility.
The dear companionship of its elect
deepens our envy. Its indifference
haunts us to suicide. Strong memories
of sprayblown days exasperate impatience
to brief rebellion and emphasise
the casual impotence we sicken of.
But when mad waves spring, braceletted with foam,
towards us in the angriness of love
crying a strange name, tossing as they come
repeated invitation, in the gay
exuberance of unexplained desire,
we can forget the sad splendour and play
at wilfulness until the gods require
renewed inevitable hopeless calm
and the foam dies and we again subside

---

9. A subscript "2" will be added to the number of the odes from the "Second Book of Odes" to distinguish them from the poems in the "First Book of Odes."

into our catalepsy, dreaming foam,
while the dry shore awaits another tide.

In this poem the movement of all the formal elements such
as rhythm, measure, and sound work together as an intricate unit
to produce a movement paralleling the movement from low tide
to high tide to low tide again. By these means Bunting identifies
all the movements of a fluctuating emotional state with the movements of the sea and the resulting conditions of the shore. Long
periods of cataleptic anticipation and "inevitable hopeless calm"
are mitigated by brief periods of "playing / at wilfulness." Employing a Bergsonian time device, Bunting has the first section
encompassing the period of numb expectancy continue for seventeen lines. Alternating end-rhymes emphasize a rhythmic pulse
imitative of the ebb and flow of the waves and the restless thoughts
of the speaker. Just before this period ends, the rhymes become
imperfect ("indifference"–"impatience"), highlighting the exasperation which "Strong memories of sprayblown days" is urging
to "brief rebellion." An emotionally brief period follows whose
brevity is underlined by its description of only six lines which
reaches the climax of "mad waves . . . braceletted with foam, . . .
tossing as they come / repeated invitations in the gay / exuberance
of unexplained desire." All the elements of the ode then combine
to bring about the lowest point of activity of the sea and of the
mind:

. . . until the gods require
renewed inevitable hopeless calm
and the foam dies and we again subside
into our catalepsy. . . .

But here Bunting moves back to the speaker's actual emotional
condition, the one which began the ode ("dreaming foam"). He
deftly contrasts this with its longed-for opposite in the last line,
"while the dry shore awaits another tide," through the assonance
of "dry" and "tide," two antithetical words which link the two
states. At the same time the duration of "while" and the spondaic
"dry shore" create the slowed life rhythm of the actual state of
the cataleptic persona.

Among the odes concerned with love, Ode 7_2 deserves
special mention [It is discussed in the article on translations elsewhere in this book]. The satire and style of Ode 6, "Personal
Column," mask the sensitiveness revealed in the poignant translation of Hafez's poem, Ode 28, or the mature gentleness revealed
in Ode 3_2, "Birthday Greetings." Ode 29 sings a contemporary
version of the anonymous sixteenth-century song, "O western

wind, when wilt thou blow," and the music of Ode 9 revolves about the skillful use of spondees which underline the power of desires, "summer lightnings," which, "rinsed in cool sleep day will renew." Bunting's note on Ode 33 aptly describes this poem dedicated "To Anne de Silver": "The cool breeze of a pure, uncomprehending rendering of Handel's best known aria" (*C.P.*, 159).

As varied as this sampling proves the love poems to be, those focusing on society as a theme have an even greater variety. Of the two odes in dialect, "Gin the Goodwife Stint," Ode 14, and "The Complaint of the Morpethshire Farmer," Ode 18, the second is so consistently published as representative of Bunting's work that he has exclaimed he is as tired of it as Yeats was of "The Lake Isle of Innisfree" (L.Z., November 10, 1964):

The Complaint of the Morpethshire Farmer

On the up-platform at Morpeth station
in the market-day throng
I overheard a Morpethshire farmer
muttering this song:

Must ye bide, my good stone house,
to keep a townsman dry?
To hear the flurry of the grouse
but not the lowing of the kye?
. . . .
Where are ye, my seven score sheep?
Feeding on other braes!
My brand has faded from your fleece,
another has its place.

The fold beneath the rowan
where ye were dipt before,
its cowpit walls are overgrown,
ye would na heed them more.
. . . .
Canada's a bare land
for the north wind and the snow.
Northumberland's a bare land
for men have made it so.

Sheep and cattle are poor men's food,
grouse is sport for the rich;
heather grows where the sweet grass might grow
for the cost of cleaning the ditch.

A liner lying in the Clyde
will take me to Quebec.
My sons'll see the land I am leaving
as barren as her deck. (*C.P.*, 104-105)

Pound who included these two odes next to selections of E.E. Cummings in his anthology, *From Confucius to Cummings*, comments in his notes:

> The stylistic reform, or the change in language, was a means not an end. After the war of 1914-19 there was definitely an extension of subject matter. This anthology cannot analyze the results, it is a lead up, but the poetry of the last forty years definitely breeds a discontent with a great deal that had been accepted in 1900. Of the poets who appeared in the 1920's it has been asserted that Cummings and Bunting show a deeper concern with basic human problems in relating to the state of the times..., Bunting in more glum sobriety.[10]

These early odes of Bunting's in the Northumberland dialect are comparable to the early poems of D.H. Lawrence in the Midland dialect which Pound praised highly.[11] Although both D.H. Lawrence and Bunting are faithful to local speech patterns, Bunting's dialect poems seem closer to the traditional form and compressed language of the ballad. Kenneth Cox, for one, sees in the "sparseness and purity of Mr. Bunting's line, especially manifest in his earlier work, the tempered and taciturn spirit of the border ballads," and he regards his compression of language as a compression of emotion, "as of speech through compressed lips." In this way, he believes, Bunting keeps his poetry close "to the feeling which engendered it and to the object described." Cox sees not only these "ballads," but all Bunting's poetry "in the stark tradition he adorns, close to the state of inarticulateness."[12]

Cox supplies the doctrine and poetry of Wordsworth as an interesting connection between the border ballads in their northern tradition and Bunting's poetry. This is strengthened by Bunting's acknowledgement of Wordsworth's influence. Cox makes the Wordsworthian doctrine explained in the Preface to the second edition of the *Lyrical Ballads* a link in this "stark tradition": ". . . choose incidents and situations from common life, . . . relate or describe them, . . . in a selection of language really used by men. . . ."[13] In a casual sketch of his background entitled "the Education of X," Bunting credits Wordsworth for showing him when he was "a small kid . . . what [poetry] was" (L.Z., August 6, 1953), and the "Lucy" poems, remarkable for their simplicity and their ballad qualities,[14] seem to be favorites of his:

10. Ezra Pound and Marcella Spann, eds. (New York, 1958), pp. 315-316.
11. "D.H. Lawrence," *Literary Essays of Ezra Pound*, ed. T.S. Eliot, 2nd. ed. (London, 1960), p. 387.
12. Kenneth Cox, "The Aesthetic of Basil Bunting," *Agenda*, IV (Autumn, 1966), 22.
13. *Ibid.*
14. Martin S. Day, *History of English Literature: 1660-1837* (New York, 1963), p. 342.

> [Wordsworth] attempted in Lucy, etc. the simplicity which is
> commonly recommended as the nearest road to the sublime, and
> sometimes came within sight of the distant peak: and he attempted
> the Lucretian manner, not without successful pages.
>
> (L.Z., November 3, 1948)

Bunting unfalteringly approaches the simplicity he admires
in Wordsworth as "the nearest road to the sublime," not only by
means of the compression of speech in the dialect poems, but in
the simple colloquial utterance he strives for in all his poetry. This
ability to condense real speech into simple, naturally rhythmic
patterns in his poetry is the result of a lifetime's work.

To some extent like Wordsworth, and to a greater extent like
D.H. Lawrence, Bunting sees the radical dichotomy between urban
and rural life. Like his contemporary, he blames a materialistic
society for changing lives which need to be in touch with the soil
at least to some degree in order to be in touch truthfully with
life.[15]

However, although he expresses these values in his poetry,
he never attempts primarily to reform society through his art.[16]
Bunting's stance toward those trapped in an urban culture is
usually that of an observer, as in Ode 25. This is true even when he
speaks in the first person through a persona, for example, in
Ode 26.

In the strong eighteen-line Ode 31 (*C.P.*, 116), Bunting uses
Latin in an epigraph to root the present situation in the past as
part of the universal situation of men in society: "*O ubi campi.*"
Unlike the ruined Morpethshire farmer headed for Winnipeg, the
alternative for the farmer addressed in this ode is "a city job or
relief—or doss-and-grub." The ironic tone seems directed not so
much toward the farmer as toward those responsible for the man's
plight:

> The soil sandy and the plow light, neither
> virgin land nor near by the market town,
> cropping one staple without forethought, steer
> stedfastly ruinward year in year out,
> grudging the labour and cost of manure,

---

15. As a twenty-seven year old journalist in London, he wrote an article, "Squares and
Gardens," *Outlook*, LIX (May 7, 1927), 542, reviewing the pamphlet, *London's Squares
and How to Save Them*, in which he vigorously defended their inestimable value.

16. Bunting wrote to Harriet Monroe, May 1, 1931, *Poetry Magazine* Papers, University
of Chicago Library, about a "repulsive" letter published in *Poetry*: "Will people never
learn that the business of poetry is poetry, and not social reform nor setting up the
damaged selfesteem of diffident nations?" Forty years later he refused to contribute to a
"Special Issue" of *Poetry*, CXX (September, 1972), "Against the War": "Poetry does
not seem to me to have any business with politics. . . . We are experts on nothing but
arrangements and patterns of vowels and consonants. . ." (362).

drudging not for gain but fewer dollars loss
yet certain to make a bad bargain by
misjudging the run of prices. How glad
you will be when the state takes your farm for
arrears of taxes! No more cold daybreaks
saffron under the barbed wire the east wind
thrums, nor wet noons, nor starpinned nights! The choir
of gnats is near a full-close. The windward
copse stops muttering inwardly its prose
bucolics. You will find a city job
or relief—or doss-and-grub—resigned to
anything except your own numb toil, the
seasonal plod to spoil the land, alone.

This ode is interesting technically as a study in the use of Horatian contrasts in mood, vocabulary, and description.

Through the influence of Pound, but more from Bunting's own travels, society as a theme broadly includes farflung cultures; for example, the Far East in "Vestiges," Ode 20, the Near East in the Samangan Ode, 32,[17] and in Ode 5_2, and Spanish culture in "The Orotava Road," Ode 30, and in Ode 8_2. Each has a music and form to fit its meaning and mood. Among these, "Vestiges," important as a transition to the article on translation and adaptations, will be discussed in detail at the end of this article.

One of the most outstanding poems about society is Ode 35 (*C.P.*, 120). Not specific geographically, it belongs to any place or people whose suffering awakens the same kind of guilt and compassion Bunting describes:

Search under every veil
for the pale eyes, pale
lips of a sick child,
in each doorway glimpse
her reluctant limbs
for whom no kindness is,
to who caress and kiss
come nightly more amiss,
whose hand no gentle hand
touches, whose eyes withstand
compassion. Say: Done, past
help, preordained waste.
Say: We know by the dead
they mourn, their bloodshed,
the maimed who are the free.
We willed it, we.
Say: Who am I to doubt?
But every vein cries out.

---

17. "Let them remember Samangan" with "Mesh Cast for Mackerel" (Ode 22) are recorded by Bunting on *The Poet Speaks*, Argo Record PLP 1087.

Bunting comments on this poem in a letter to Zukofsky:

> . . . the change of weight in the middle of "Search under every veil" is very deliberate: up till then I have only a stock sentimental poem which I attempt to raise suddenly onto another level altogether. The fact that you don't grumble at the sentimental beginning is quite possibly due to what is thus reflected back from the end, which I think I couldn't have got in the same light movement. (July 28, 1949)

A link between the odes concerned with society and those concerned with art are the few that combine themes. Many of those about society and all those with combined themes carry graded tones of irony which at least two critics see as characteristic of the ode in the twentieth century.[18] Whether the use of irony is especially modern is debatable, but it is a characteristic means Bunting uses to express his vision of the relationship of the poet and society, and at times his views of society. One example is the bitingly satiric Ode 23, "The Passport Officer," (*C.P.*, 109), in which the impersonal official is compared to a dog who "scrutinizes the lamppost," "sets his seal on it," and "moves on to the next." In Ode 11, "To a Poet who advised me to preserve my fragments and false starts," (*C.P.*, 97), the controlled disdain is a match for Alexander Pope's "Sporus." The dignified tone coupled with the less than elegant diction of

> . . . in the damp dustbins amongst the peel
> tobacco-ash and ends spittoon lickings litter
> of labels dry corks breakages and a great deal
>
> of miscellaneous garbage. . . .

is reminiscent of Yeat's

> A mound of refuse or the sweepings of a street,
> Old kettles, old bottles, and a broken can,
> Old iron, old bones, old rags.[19]

Through a montage technique Ode 12 depicts with ironic humor the decline of a poet who is finally "cadging for drinks at the streetcorners." Its tone is much less sarcastic than Ode 6_2, "What the Chairman Told Tom," an ode Bunting labelled a joke.[20] Although "Tom" is most probably Tom Pickard, Bunting's Northumbrian disciple, the character represents any unrecognized poet struggling against insensitive àcademics.

---

18. Thrall and Hibbard, *op. cit.*, p. 328.
19. *The Collected Poems of W.B. Yeats*, 2nd ed. (London, 1950), p. 392.
20. Bunting to John Matthias, March 23, 1970.

These poems, however, do not reach the level of bitterness that Ode 37 (*C.P.*, 122) does. Whether or not it is because of its intensity, this ode ranks among his best:

On the Fly-Leaf of Pound's Cantos

There are the Alps. What is there to say about them?
They don't make sense. Fatal glaciers, crags cranks climb,
jumbled boulder and weed, pasture and boulder, scree,
et l'on entend, maybe, *le refrain joyeux et leger*.
Who knows what the ice will have scraped on the rock it is smoothing?
There they are, you will have to go a long way round
if you want to avoid them.
It takes some getting used to. There are the Alps,
fools! Sit down and wait for them to crumble!

Without the title, the ode is simply a lively commentary on the Alps; with it the poem is one of the greatest compliments from one contemporary poet to another. The date on the ode, "1949," that is, during the time of Pound's commitment to St. Elizabeths Hospital, makes the tribute all the more valuable and explains somewhat the exasperation of the last line. The forthrightness and indignation echoes Pound's tone, heard so often in his letters and in some of his writings.

Both this ode and Ode 3 use the same opening device, a stark four-word sentence, to gain the reader's attention: "I am agog for foam" and "There are the Alps." In the ode, however, this blunt statement occurs in some form three times, as if, unbelievably, he must point out the obvious and unavoidable fact before the viewer.

Besides the interest which the tone and the balance of short and long sentences provide, there are the unexpected areas of ono-matopoetic dissonance in phrases such as "crags cranks climb" and in the contrast of sound and meaning of verbs within the whole movement of "Who knows what the ice will have scraped on the rock it is smoothing?"

Bunting's few odes concerned with art have a singular beauty none of the others have. Ode 15 (*C.P.*, 101), published in *Poetry*[21] as "The Word" with Ode 16 (*C.P.*, 102) as "Appendix: Iron," was described by Zukofsky as an "adaptation of classical quantitative measure to English."[22] Since this topic will be discussed in my translation article, it is enough here to call attention to the basic pattern in the five-line strophes of 5-10-6-4-4 syllables seen, with a slight exception, in such lines as:

---

21. *Poetry*, XXXVII (February, 1931), 260-261.
22. Louis Zukofsky, "Correspondence," *Poetry*, XXXVIII (April, 1931), 56.

```
Celebrate man's craft                              5
and the word spoken in shapeless night, the       10
sharp tool paring away                             6
waste and the forms                               4
cut out of mystery!                                6
```

Further, the strong stresses and even the alliteration in some lines echo the Anglo-Saxon verse:

and hewn hills and bristling forest,
steadfast corn in its season

More than any other, this ode looks forward to *Briggflatts* in tone, theme, and technique.

Ode 16, separated now from "The Word," is an instance of a modern poet's effective use of industrial imagery:

Molten pool, incandescent spilth of
deep cauldrons—and brighter nothing is—
cast and cold, your blazes extinct and
no turmoil nor peril left you,
rusty ingot, bleak paralysed blob!

Bunting's Note to Ode 36 clears up any misconceptions about the meaning of the poem:

A friend's misunderstanding obliges me to declare that the implausible optics of this poem are not intended as an argument for the existence of God, but only suggest that the result of a successful work of art is more than the sum of its meanings and differs from them in kind. (*C.P.*, 159)

It is evident why Thomas Cole spoke of the ode as "Yeatsian"[23] and perhaps just as easy to see the influence of the Book of Revelation and St. John's Gospel:

See! Their verses are laid
as mosaic gold to gold
gold to lapiz lazuli
white marble to porphery
stone shouldering stone, the dice
polished alike, there is
no cement seen and no gap
between stones as the frieze strides
to the impending apse:
the rays of many glories
forced to its focus forming
a glory neither of stone
nor metal, neither of words
nor verses, but of the light
shining upon no substance;

---

23. Thomas Cole, "Bunting: Formal Aspects," *Poetry*, XLLVIII (September, 1951), 368.

a glory not made
for which all else was made. (*C.P.*, 121)

After Zukofsky had read this, Bunting answered his comments:

> The words that bother you in "See their verses are laid": "im-
> pending" is weak, but I couldn't find what's wanted—what's the
> word for quarter of the solid formed by the rotation of an elipse
> on its axis, and has it an adjective? "shouldering" probably has for
> you moral echoes which haven't worried me. I meant it physically,
> in which sense it is exact. Neatness: the civil service air of an em-
> bassy overcoming my natural untidiness? Energy? Of a kind. Both
> ["Search under every veil" and "See! Their verses are laid"] are
> attempts to concentrate a lot of weight behind one punch. The
> first is artful—makes a feint to deceive the reader: the other
> "comes out fighting." There's nothing more to it. One could
> easily have said as much in a page and a half. (July 28, 1949)

Needless to say, whatever "one could easily have said" would have
completely lost the powerful impact of this brief ode.

Ode 34 combines all three themes of love, society, and art in
a poem which Cole as early as 1951 singled out as "an excellent
example of Bunting's lyric quality."[24]

To Violet, with prewar poems.

> These tracings from a world that's dead
> take for my dust-smothered pyramid.
> Count the sharp study and long toil
> as pavements laid for worms to soil.
> You without knowing it might tread
> the grass where my foundation's laid,
> your, or another's, house be built
> where my weathered stones lie spilt,
> and this unread memento be
> the only lasting part of me. (*C.P.*, 119)

Cole's comment that in Ode 34 "rime is used to fine advantage,
making one wish that Bunting had used it more often"[25] over-
looks the deeper influence of Malherbe, after Horace, Bunting's
"other first spur" (L.Z., "June the New Moonth, 1953").[26] To
Bunting Malherbe was

> the man who never forgot music for a moment and who, for all
> his determination to eat more toads than the next fellow, ate 'em
> with such a clean melody and so little mumbo-jumbo that he

24. *Ibid.*, 366.
25. *Ibid.*
26. Bunting wrote to Zukofsky: "I've been thinking . . . about how and where I got
whatever I know and feel about poetry, and the more I think the bigger Malherbe's part
in it seems. . . . Malherbe produced all I afterwards found in Ezra's writing except what
I'd already got from Horace" (August 6, 1953).

stands inspection still without any allowances for period, etc.
(L.Z., August 6, 1953)

This French poet who tried to preserve "the marriage of music and poetry"[27] by writing his odes always within a musical framework recognized a musical foundation as inseparable from the ode. "From the welter of metrical forms, Malherbe chose the ten-line strophe of 5-syllable lines, . . . and by increasing the number of syllables to eight, Malherbe transformed it into an instrument of incomparable harmony."[28] By using Malherbe's ode form, Bunting achieves a degree of this harmony in Ode 34.

When Ode 34 was published, Bunting made a comparison between a gun and a work of art which points out qualities he was striving to incorporate in his odes:

> What do I "feel with a machine-gun?" Well, it depends on the gun. I criticise a machine by nearly the same criteria as I do a work of art. A Lee-Enfield rifle, a Hotchkiss machine-gun, have nothing superfluous nor fussy about them. They are utterly simple—having reached that simplicity via complication and sophistication galore. The kind of people who, if they had literary minds at all, would like Euphuism or trickiness, prefer Lewis guns or Remington or Ross rifles. My machine-gun is a Hotchkiss and I feel toward it something similar in kind to what I feel for Egyptian sculpture. . . . I think Holbein or Bach or Praxiteles, as well as Alexander, would have appreciated a Hotchkiss gun; whereas a lot of our machines might *merely* have astonished them.
> (September 22, 1941)

This kind of simplicity which he holds out as a goal to himself is the outstanding quality of Ode 20. As an "adaptation" this poem could easily be grouped with those in my translation article. However, its brevity, its unique source, and Bunting's own categorization suggest its discussion here where it can also serve as a transition to the poems in "Translations and Adaptations of Basil Bunting" [See elsewhere in this book].

Like Eliot's notes for *The Waste Land*, Bunting's note about "Vestiges," Ode 20 (*C.P.*, 106-107), is presumably written tongue-in-cheek for all those who wish to chase after the references and allusions which he scorns in his "Statement" on poetry.[29] Nevertheless, the information about the Jengiz Khan-Chang Chun correspondence in E. Bretschneider's *Medieval Researches from Eastern Asiatic Sources*[30] deepens the reader's awareness of the poet's

---

27. Winegarten, *op. cit.*, p. 4.
28. *Ibid.*, p. 21.
29. *Descant on Rawthey's Madrigal*, ed. Jonathan Williams (Lexington, Ky., 1968).
30. (London, 1887), I, 9-24, 35-108.

background and is valuable for a full appreciation of the poem. From pages of details in Bretschneider's book and from his own imagination and background, Bunting has chosen single items which he piles up to create a realistic montage of "vestiges."

Part I balances Part II with an almost oriental simplicity. In Part I (*C.P.*, 106) the personae of the poem describe in pithy phrases their present poor conditions, shifting to remembrances of the past which impinge on the present:

> Salt grass silent of hooves, the lake stinks,
> we take a few small fish from the streams,
> our children are scabby, chivvied by flies,
> we cannot read the tombs in the eastern prairie,
>   who slew the Franks, who
>   swam the Yellow River.

> The lice have left Temuchin's tent. His ghost
> cries under northwind, having spent
> strength in life: life lost, lacks means of death,
> voice-tost; the horde indistinguishable;
> worn name weak in fool's jaws.

> We built no temples. Our cities' woven hair
> mildewed and frayed. Records of Islam and Chin,
> battles, swift riders, ambush,
> tale of the slain, and the name Jengiz.

Between the mention of "the name Jengiz" and the introduction of tall Chutsai, sitting under a tree, Bunting builds a bridge between present and past with a one-line stanza, "Wild geese of Yen, peacocks of the Windy Shore." The scene of ancient Peking is suggested with oriental simplicity by means of two details which reveal the strength, pride, and grandeur of that ancient civilization.

In the next stanza Bunting vitalizes what is essential in Bretschneider's history about Chutsai, "an ingenious statesman" recognized by his height and "splendid beard," a former prisoner who rose to the highest position in the empire. In this vignette Chutsai, who administered the taxes on the land north of the Yellow River, calculates wisely a specific business deal, underlining the ageless greed of men and the regard of a wise administrator for the people.[31] The simplicity of the ending parallels that same quality in ancient governing:

> Tall Chutsai sat under the phoenix tree.
> —That Baghdad banker contracts to

---

31. *Ibid.*, 10-12.

double the revenue, him collecting.
Four times might be exacted, but
such taxation impoverishes the people.

No litigation. The laws were simple.

Bretschneider admires the correspondence between Jengiz and Chang Chun for creditable reasons:

> The translation of these letters will enable the reader to form a judgment of the character and mode of thought of those illustrious men. Chinghiz, in his simplicity, professes such sound principles of governing people, and his words express such profound truths, that they would be valid even in our days and for our countries in Europe. On the other side, Ch'ang Ch'un inspires sympathy by his modesty, candour, and sincerity. He seems to have been endowed with high intelligence, knowing well his time and human nature.[32]

In Part II (*C.P.*, 107) of the ode the vestiges of this correspondence are as strong and yet as delicate as calligraphic writing. Bunting strips down pages of the letters, written in formal, classical Chinese style, to their utmost simplicity:

Jengiz to Chang Chun: China
is fat, but I am lean
eating soldier's food,
lacking learning.
In seven years
I brought most of the world under one law.
The Lords of Cathay
hesitate and fall.
Amidst these disorders
I distrust my talents.
To cross a river
boats and rudders,
to keep the empire in order
poets and sages,
but I have not found nine for a cabinet,
not three.
I have fasted and washed. Come.

Chang: I am old
not wise nor virtuous,
nor likely to be much use.
My appearance is parched, my body weak.
I set out at once.

From all the details about Liu Chung Lu and the escort of twenty Mongols for the three-year journey, the golden tablet with

---

32. *Ibid.*, 36-37.

the Khan's order that the Taoist master should be treated as the
Emperor himself, and finally Chang's reluctance to travel with
girls for the Khan's harem, Bunting chooses only the telling few:

> And to Liu Chung Lu, Jengiz:
> Get an escort and a good cart,
> and the girls can be sent on
> separately if he insists.

By selecting details and arranging them within a broad historical framework, Bunting creates a double and even a triple perspective in Part I. He shifts this perspective to focus on the close-
up of specific details in the correspondence in Part II. The chronological time of the first three stanzas of the poem is so indefinite
that it can include both eras immediately following the Jengiz
Khan Empire and the present when "litigation" is all-important
and laws are anything but "simple." This multiple perspective enlarges Bunting's theme beyond the limits of the documentation of
his source.

Poetically, Bunting reinforces the contrasts of vestiges of the
past and the present by speaking in at least three voices in Part I,
and then contrasting these with the extreme simplicity of the two
voices of the correspondents in Part II. Speaking in the first person plural, the reminiscing voice of the persona of the first three
stanzas describes matter-of-factly, yet with an overtone of sadness,
the present conditions. The past quickly intrudes in his description
in the restless form of the "life lost," "voice-tost" ghost of Temuchin. Bunting underscores the mournful tone through long vowels
and diphthongs and open syllables ("hooves," "tomb," "few,"
"who," "who slew," "who," "cries," "flies," "prairie") which
lengthen the lines:

> we cannot read the tombs in the eastern prairie,
> who slew the Franks, who
> swam the Yellow River.

Bunting counterpoints the slower movement with a quickened
rhythm suggestive of the restlessness of Temuchin's ghost, paralleling in the present the restlessness of the poverty-stricken descen-
dants of his people. The internal rhyme of "name"—"slain" neces-
sitates a dramatic pause before the word "Jengiz," the signal for
the shift to the perspective of the more distant past.

The voice of an anonymous narrator bridges the eras in the
one-line stanza already commented on and then in a more ordinary tone sets the stage for the new scene: "Tall Chutsai sat under
the phoenix tree." The interesting detail of the phoenix tree which

Iranians assure me is well known as an actual tree and as a metaphor places Chutsai in the Near East as definitely as does his comment about the "Baghdad banker." Its metaphorical meaning, "a
single time," "a unique time," elevates the period of the Jengiz
Khan Empire to a unique era of government.[33]

The thoughts of Chutsai in a third voice record in direct,
economical terms a proposed tax plan, its possible extension, and
its logical bad outcome. By leaving the counselor's judgment implicit, Bunting underlines its obvious justice at the same time that
he furthers the economy of the poetry.

With his single line, "No litigation. The laws were simple,"
the anonymous commentator provides, first, a smooth distancing
to bring the reader back to himself to encourage a personal judgment; second, a finished ending to Part I; and third, a dramatic
transition to Part II. The chief voices in the second half of the
poem are, of course, those of the two correspondents. Bunting's
choice of details outlines the uncomplicated wisdom and way of
life of the two men, representatives of different kinds of power:
one with the soldier's talents to create a new empire, another
with the poet's and sage's power to help keep the empire in
order. In a few rhythmic phrases Bunting delineates the essential
character of each man. Neither downplays his worth with a false
humility, yet each knows his limitations. Without embellishment
Bunting has Jengiz summarize his successes:

> In seven years
> I brought most of the world under one law.

Perhaps it is too much to expect the reader to recognize the
writing of Chutsai in the Khan's letters, though the simple rhythm
of his brief statements and his straightforward manner of speech
echo Chutsai's style in Part I. Bunting more easily brings out the
basis for Jengiz Khan's powerful leadership through each detail
he selects to represent the lengthy correspondence. Further,
through his selecting of only a few details from his letters and
Chang's, Bunting has as his purpose not to rewrite the historical
prose correspondence as poetry, but to create vestiges of it which
fit into the whole structure of his poem:

> Jengiz to Chang Chun: China
> is fat, but I am lean
> eating soldier's food,
> lacking learning.

---

33. Conversations with Khosrow Moshtarikhah and Jaafar Moghadam, Iranian students
at the University of Notre Dame, 1971-1972.

In seven years
I brought most of the world under one law.
The Lords of Cathay
hesitate and fall.
Amidst these disorders
I distrust my talents.
To cross a river
boats and rudders,
to keep the empire in order
poets and sages,
but I have not found nine for a cabinet,
not three.
I have fasted and washed. Come.

The culmination of the section, the single word, "Come," is at once inviting and commanding. Bunting balances Chang's courteously humble description of himself by the simple, composed acceptance of the "invitation-command": "I set out at once." Whether or not the reader knows that his acceptance cost three years of arduous travel is not important for Bunting's purpose, to point up the basic simplicity and order in this flourishing culture. Again, according to his poetic intent, he has transformed the historical correspondence into telling vestiges of a past civilization:

Chang: I am old
not wise nor virtuous,
nor likely to be of much use.
My appearance is parched, my body weak.
I set out at once.

Finally, in four short lines, Bunting rounds out the picture of the wise ruler who gives indisputable orders to subordinates, yet leaves them free to arrange details methodically and expeditiously:

And to Liu Chung Lu, Jengiz:
Get an escort and a good cart,
and the girls can be sent on
separately if he insists.

Although Bunting insists that the poet remain anonymous in the poem,[34] . . . the details he has chosen to include in "Vestiges" and the structuring of the parts to emphasize their interdependent meanings make this not simply an artifact which, as an artifact, is independent of its sources, but a poem with a highly personal vision. Bunting has incorporated historical and imagined details within a broad perspective to create an independent artifact which has its own original structure and which presents its own

---

34. See three strong statements in letters to Zukofsky, March 5, 1949; December 31, 1950; May 10, 1953.

special vision. The vestiges of the Jengiz-Chang correspondence point to the essential factors in a civilization strong enough to last, as is known from history, through Jengiz Khan's lifetime and even after his grandson's, Kublai Khan's. The poet creates his poem with indivisible form and content which highlight the essential factors which made this possible—simplicity and disciplined order. Deliberately, Bunting has contrasted the strength and human appeal of even the vestiges of this ancient civilization with the poverty and degradation of succeeding ones which could include the present. He suggests this contrast through a montage of details which in their turn become vestiges of a different sort from those of the correspondence; the single details combine to suggest all that is left of this civilization much later through the neglect of values which made it great: "grass silent of hooves," stinking lake, scabby children "chivvied by flies," lice and "cities' woven hair mildewed and frayed." Restless ghosts of former times and undecipherable legends on tombs are the only vestiges these people in their turn can faintly recognize. The interlocking parts of the poem—contrasting perspectives and voices, rhythms and images—reinforce the interlocking structure of vestiges in this profound poem.

Through the odes Bunting demonstrates his idea that "Poetry is a craft which you learn by trying. . . . Unless you work very hard for it you won't get anywhere."[35] Although the overall quality of the odes is uneven, the chronological development is steady, as the difference between Ode I (1924) and an uncollected ode published in 1970 proves:[36]

Stones trip Coquet burn.
Grass trails, tickles
till her glass thrills.

The breeze she wears
lifts and falls back.
Where beast cool

in midgy shimmer
she dares me chase
under a bridge,

---

35. Anthea Hall, "Basil Bunting Explains How a Poet Works," *Newcastle Journal*, July 17, 1965.
36. 1970 ode, untitled, *Georgia Straight Writing Supplement*, VI, November 18-24, 1970.

    giggle, ceramic
    huddle of notes,
    darts from gorse

    and I follow, fooled.
    She must rest, surely;
    some steep pool

    to plodge or dip
    and silent taste
    with all my skin.

The themes throughout are generally "what men experience in common life."[37] Bunting strongly believes "you can't write about anything unless you've experienced it; you're either confused in your subject matter or else you get it all wrong." However, Bunting has not set out to make a poem of his experience in each ode: "You set out to make a shape of sounds: musical sounds. You set out to make something that is agreeable to have around."[38] Through the odes and also through the translations and adaptations he is continuously refining his ability to create agreeable musical shapes which he combines to their best advantage in the sonatas.

---

37. "The Northerners," *The Listener,* LXXXIV (October 8, 1970), 484.
38. Hall, *op. cit.*

PETER QUARTERMAIN

"TO MAKE GLAD THE HEART OF MAN":
BUNTING, POUND AND WHITMAN[1]

> the only tokens of history continually
> available to our senses are the desirable
> things made by men.
>
> *George Kubler*[2]

A poem is a desirable thing. And made by man. I cannot see, else, how it might last, like say Sappho even in fragments, or even as William Carlos Williams, without Greek, translates:[3]

> That man is peer of the gods who
> face to face sits listening
> to your sweet speech and lovely
>   laughter.
>
> It is this that rouses a tumult
> in my breast. At mere sight of you
> my voice falters, my tongue
>   is broken.
>
> Straightway, a delicate fire runs in
> my limbs; my eyes
> are blinded and my ears
>   thunder.
>
> Sweat pours out: a trembling hunts
> me down. I grow
> paler than grass and lack little
>   of dying.

1. Pound calls poetry "an art originally intended to make glad the heart of man" in *ABC of Reading* (New York, New Directions, 1960), p. 13. In the following, I refer to conversations with Bunting and to stories he told. From September to December 1970 he taught at the University of British Columbia, Vancouver, B.C., and from September 1971 to April 1972 at the University of Victoria, Victoria, B.C. During these two periods we saw a great deal of each other, and talked a lot.
2. George Kubler, *The Shape of Time: Remarks on the History of Things* (New Haven, Yale University Press, 1962), p. 1.
3. William Carlos Williams, *Sappho* (San Francisco, *Poems in Folio*, 1957). A somewhat different version of the text is in *Paterson* V, part 2.

I too lack Greek, so cannot say how distant this is from the original.

But that original is only putative—like, say, the world "out there." I do not *think* Sappho can be translated. Or Catullus. Or, who can know, Propertius. The text that history has transmitted is uncertain—a fragment, or a muddled pastiche—but our relation with the past is tenuous at best, and only an antiquarian might want the "real thing." Some learn Greek so that they might read Homer "in the original," but who knows *what* it is they read. We need not, of course, step so far afield: we guess the text of *Pericles, Prince of Tyre* even as we guess its author. We argue over the texts of Whitman, preferring one to another. William Carlos Williams was so careless of his manuscripts that even *he* seems not to have "known" what his text was—but he, unlike Bunting and Zukofsky, resisted the definitive. We have no clear text of Pound's *Homage to Sextus Propertius*, though at least one scholar claims to have established it. There is much we *never* knew.

We have forgotten much, by choice, by necessity, by accident. And there is, still, what we *know*: the poem.

> Under molde hi leggeth colde
> And faleweth so doth medewe gras.

(That is Thomas Hales, who was a Franciscan, writing before 1240.) A desirable thing. How else would it survive these seven hundred and more years—or this, say, for the next how many:

> AN ERA
> ANY TIME
> OF YEAR

To be printed as a two-inch square, said Zukofsky. Nine vowels. Nine Consonants. An E; Any; Y. Ambiguous Y. Playful repeats and variations. So simple as to be cheeky and daring—like the astonishing opening line (Bunting's),

> A thrush in the syringa sings.

An extraordinary lyrical grace and beauty. It is an opening line anyone might covet, yet few would dare think or write, so fine is the path it treads.

If it cannot be translated (and what poem can?), assuredly it cannot be explicated—nor need it be. "Understanding" is only one kind of perception, and "explanation" is not one at all. One can only point—and the deaf, who cannot hear the music of the poem, nevertheless have to be sung to, while the moving finger points. And in pointing, I would distinguish (though George Kubler does not) between the desirable and the useful object; indeed I would oppose them. The desirable object is self-sufficient in a way in which the useful object is not, for the useful always gestures towards its purpose, points away from itself. Occasionally we find tools whose purpose we no longer know, and it is then we are struck by their beauty. The tool is anthropocentric, for it serves man. But the poem does not. "A drunken soldier singing 'Eskimo Nell,'" Basil Bunting once said to me, "is serving God, while a parson preaching temperance and thrift is serving only man." Or words to that effect. Children hop, skip, dance on their way to school; a thrush in the syringa sings. "O gay thrush!"

For much of his career Ezra Pound struggled with the notion that poetry should be useful. He seems to say with Eliot that its purpose is to ennoble the language, to purify the dialect of the tribe. His incursions into Confucius propose in part at least that the poem is therapeutic for the State if not for the poet, for it will put the language in order, and the heart, and the house. Such need for the poet to justify himself, to defend his craft and art, should surprise no reader of *Mauberley*, say, or of Margaret Anderson's and Harriet Monroe's autobiographies. *My Thirty Years' War* sounds more accurate a note than *A Poet's Life*, and that note is not, one might add, at all peculiar to the opening decades of this century, and in North America. Matthew Arnold's *Culture and Anarchy* of 1869 elaborates in specifically aesthetic and literary terms on what Dickens had fifteen years earlier said in *Hard Times*, and asserts a function for art. When Basil Bunting sailed from Italy to the Canaries in autumn 1933, penniless though he was, he was treated royally by the officers and crew (moved to a better cabin, even) because he was "*poeta!*"; when he was in Persia (and perhaps still, for all I know) Firdosi's epic was recited serially on national radio every morning. At such times and in such places, the poet needs no defence, and need not pretend to be of use. But in a culture which places man at the centre, whose "humanism" demands the greatest happiness for the greatest number, and which sees "that which ministers to the material needs of man" as good (the words are Franklin's, I think), then everything is thought of in terms of that end, in terms of "use," use is thought of as the only good, and all is subservient to some "human" end. (Our notion of "human" is as fuzzy as our notion of what we call, or used to call, "God.") Good, and virtue, become quantifiable, and the word *measure* as an arithmetical rather than a musical term begins to creep into discussions of poetry.

Hard Times is a plea for the imagination, but Dickens' great insight (following Swift, I suspect) is into *fact*, which reduces the world to the verifiable. Verification rests on the appearance of things, and on the rather curious assumption of constancy or stasis in the universe, that events can repeat themselves, that conditions or circumstances can be—let us say—replicated. Words thus become counters which are used to record the appearance of things in propositions which must be verifiable. If the real can be described, then it can be verified, and the test of reality comes to lie in how far it can be reduced to discourse in the language of the senses. Reality is not, then, a matter of experience and feeling, but of observation and record. The known and indeed the knowable becomes what can be verbalised. And words, *then*, point to and somehow correlate to observable reality and can—in the case of someone like Bitzer—be wholly mistaken for it. What is a horse?

> "Quadruped. Graminivorous. Forty teeth, namely twenty-four grinders, four eye-teeth, and twelve incisive. Sheds coat in the spring; in marshy countries, sheds hoofs, too. Hoofs hard, but requiring to be shod with iron. Age known by marks in mouth."
> Thus (and much more) Bitzer.[4]

—and *now*, Gradgrind tells the unfortunate horse-rider's daughter, "You know what a horse is." The real is experienced or perceived, "understood" let us say, only through words used as counters, in the language of definition. We demand our language be precise, as though there could be an absolute correspondence between the words we use and the things we refer to—yet the only precise languages are of mathematics and logic, both of which, *outside their own systems*, are sterile.

Hence Eliot, not at all unlike Arnold, can talk of seeking to lift the language *out of* the realm of the verifiable—the world we call "mere"—but does so by talking of the *use* of poetry and the *use* of criticism. Bunting is a dissenter (he is a Quaker), and to my knowledge, he never has. In a much-quoted remark he has said that there is no excuse for literary criticism. (William Carlos Williams, one might note in passing, took a somewhat different tack, and talked of lifting things to the imagination.) Poetry does not make language more precise, though Eliot fondly hoped that it did, and "use" is a sign of man's rapacity. Zukofsky called it "predatory." Pound resisted poetry as useful, among other ways by relieving *The Waste Land* of much that was more or less directly

---

4. Charles Dickens, *Hard Times*, edited by David Craig (Harmondsworth, Middlesex, Penguin Books, 1969), p. 50.

(Pope-ishly) satiric, and it is quite clear that the early drafts of that poem are the product of a writer who has something he wants to say: as though the poem had a *use*, as though he had a use for the poem. It is not wholly an accident, surely, that through such rigorous editing as Pound gave it *The Waste Land* acquired a more or less clear musical structure (Bunting once commented to me that if you remove section four it sounds like a sonata). And with the exception of *The Pisan Cantos* and perhaps such early work as say *A Lume Spento*, the least "useful" of all Pound's poems is also one of his best, *Homage to Sextus Propertius*, which Bunting in a 1932 essay called "the most important poem of our time, superseding alike 'Mauberley' and 'The Waste Land.' "[5]

If the point of translation is to make available in one culture a work produced in another, undoubtedly *Homage* fails: it is not, that is to say, very useful for the purposes of "cultural transmission" (whatever *that* might be). If the point of translation is to provide in one language a work which is in some sense equivalent to one originally written in another, then *Homage* fails, if only on the grounds that Propertius, as Pound's critics and commentators never tire of saying, was neither as mocking nor as satiric as Pound's work implies. Even the poem's staunchest admirers, such as Sullivan or Richardson, point to what they consider weaknesses —though I must say right now that these only look like weaknesses if you expect the poem to be *doing* something. *Homage* is not, indeed, a useful translation. Richardson thinks it is addressed to the reader who, knowing Latin, reads the text with Propertius at his side, or *en face*, so that he can appreciate "the value of possibilities that appear in the Latin itself as it strikes the eye, imagination, and wit"[6] of the translator who, writing *Homage*, gives us a poem which records the processes of translation. (Such a reading strikes me as somewhat far-fetched. Pound becomes an elaborate navel-gazer.) Sullivan complains of inaccuracies left in for the sake of the sound, and of interpolations—especially in Section IV— which "have no connection at all" with the poem, but are there for the sake of "*mere* word-play and phrase-mongering."[7] Sullivan assumes, however, that "as living poetry the classics *can* only exist in translation" (p. 22), which not only immediately ascribes a purpose (use) to *Homage* but also, in its notion of "classic,"

5. Basil Bunting, "Mr Ezra Pound," *New English Weekly*, I (26 May 1932), 138.
6. Lawrence Richardson, "Ezra Pound's Homage to Propertius," *Yale Poetry Review*, No. 6 (1947), 23.
7. J.P. Sullivan, *Ezra Pound and Sextus Propertius: A Study in Creative Translation* (Austin, Texas, Univ. of Texas Press, 1964), pp. 57, 23 (emphasis added). Further references parenthetically documented in my text.

suffers from the archeological fallacy that the experience the original audience had of the poem can be replicated (after, of course, it
has been somehow discerned). In so doing, he completely misses
the skill and beauty of Section IV of *Homage*, which he finds
"very obscure"(p. 56), and indeed misses the poem altogether,
since he demands that it have a "point," be *about* something. And
if *Homage* is satire, as many readers have claimed, then certainly it
can hardly be successful (useful) if critics and readers are still
arguing (as they are) over who or what exactly is being satirised.
The value of the poem– what makes it a desirable object–lies
elsewhere. It is a *tour de force* of voice, of tones of voice: "weary
with historical data," says the opening section of the poem, "they
will turn to my / dance tune." There is a deflation in that "dance
tune," and what follows is, as many readers have noticed, a series
of verses of great skill and diversity, of a freedom and range and
tone; a collection of more or less complex tunes. Which Eliot
called "a most interesting study in versification."

In his obituary notice of Ezra Pound, "Prince of Poets,"
which appeared in the (London) *Sunday Times*, 12 November
1972, Basil Bunting wrote that Pound

> said in the Thirties that Eliot had got stuck because he could not
> understand Propertius, and all the rest had got stuck a few books
> earlier still. I think he excepted Louis Zukofsky and myself.

I find it interesting that Eliot excluded *Homage* but not *Mauberley*
from the *Selected Poems*. *Mauberley*, like *The Waste Land*, has
been taken as a poem of some use because it is, identifiably, saying
something, and perhaps saying something that matters. *Homage*, I
suspect, has been spared the classroom because, though skilled
and painstaking, it looks naive and facile. It also looks more book-
ish than it is. Bunting tells the story that when Zukofsky was
staying with him in Rapallo in August 1933 (which is when Eliot,
that is to say, was seeing *The Use of Poetry and the Use of Criticism* through the press), the conversation turned to the *sound* of
poetry, and to *Homage* which they got Ezra to read. They were
surprised at his orotund declamation, and so remonstrated, where-
upon Pound got Zukofsky to read first, then Bunting. Instead of
reading *Homage*, Bunting read Whitman, "Out of the Cradle Endlessly Rocking"–and to his astonishment heard Pound reciting it by
heart along with him. Eliot, I recall, called Whitman a writer of
prose, and a writer of bad prose at that.

That Bunting should have turned to Whitman, and to "Out of
the Cradle," in such a context is not perhaps too surprising. "Out of
the Cradle" is indeed one of Whitman's more obviously "musical"

pieces, almost a set piece in fact, not only rhythmically (as in the patterning of -uu -u -uu -u, almost onomatopoeic, of "out of the cradle, endlessly rocking," patterned with such things as the spondees of "out of the ninth-month midnight": -uu - - -u, where the tone almost completely suppresses the accentual nature of the verse, pushing it towards quantitative measures so that "midnight" is *in duration* a spondee); not only rhythmically, then, but also in the activity of the vowels and consonants and the patterns they make, and in its movement from line to line. "It's a matter of making the rhythms," Bunting told Jonathan Williams and Tom Meyer, "develop and shift around themselves."[8] One might recall that when he was fifteen years old Bunting was sought out by Whitman's friend Edward Carpenter, on the strength of a prize essay he had written on Whitman, "a more or less national prize—a national prize for Quaker schools."[9]

Bunting is a dissenter, I have said. He is also a progressivist: he demands of his verse that it do something no-one else *quite* did before. Hence Ode 36 of the *First Book of Odes*, "See! Their verses are laid," is an extension of Yeats. And a progression can be discerned from Whitman through Pound to Bunting. This is a conscious working, I believe, but it is *not* to say that Bunting draws on, "uses"(!), all of Pound (what poet could? "There are the Alps, / fools"). Nor is it to say that he is wholly derivative (if, indeed, at all!). It is to point to a progression. It is to say that there are clear similarities between "Out of the Cradle," *Homage*, and *Briggflatts* (if not indeed *all* of Bunting, for of the three Bunting is the most insistently and consistently "musical"). Comparing them, we see a movement progressively further and further away from the movement of blank verse (and, incidentally, from the long blank-verse poem and *its* organisation), progressively further from the stressed language of accentual verse, and especially the iambic. Whitman's rhythms only *seem* largely accentual, and Bunting's, one is tempted to say, are not at all. Much has been written about Whitman's "prosody," in terms of stress-patterns; so too of Pound, and of *Homage* in particular, as "rhythm." What I seek to do in the next few pages is examine various patterns other than the crudely rhythmic ("stress"), which occur in three short passages, fragments indeed, from these three writers. Naturally it would be helpful if the reader kept the larger context of

8. Jonathan Williams and Tom Meyer, "A Conversation with Basil Bunting (1976)," *Poetry Information*, No. 19 (Autumn, 1978), p. 38.
9. Eric Mottram, "Conversation with Basil Bunting on the occasion of his Seventy-fifth Birthday," *Poetry Information*, No. 19 (Autumn, 1978), p. 6. It would be interesting indeed to read that essay.

each passage in mind (I discuss only a part, for example, of a sentence by Whitman). What I have to say will certainly be clearer if the passages I discuss—and the discussion itself—were *read aloud*, voiced.

Whitman, Pound, and Bunting. I believe, though I shall not try to show it here, that these patterns are of a kind which do not occur in English writers before Whitman (or if they do, they occur only rarely, as in Campion, say, or the sadly neglected William Barnes), and that they are not to be found in writers like say Eliot, who I think got stuck somehow in the iambic. Whitman brought something new into English verse (and it has to do with the cadences of English prose—or, better, speech), and Pound and Bunting picked it up, refined it. What Whitman brought is a new kind of noise, a new kind of song if you will. It has to do, that newness, with the organisation of the verse—and that, obviously, cannot be entirely divorced from what the verse says. The quantity of vowels, for example, has to do with the *tones* of words, and tone is related to syntax and diction. Fuzzy thought gives a fuzzy voice.

That should be obvious. Here are the passages:[10]

I. Walt Whitman: "Out of the Cradle." 1891 "Deathbed edition," lines 1-4. Hereafter called *Whitman*.

> Out of the cradle endlessly rocking,
> Out of the mocking-bird's throat, the musical shuttle,
> Out of the Ninth-month midnight,
> Over the sterile sands and the fields beyond, where the child
>   leaving his bed wander'd alone, bareheaded, barefoot,

II. Ezra Pound: *Homage to Sextus Propertius*, VI. 1926 *Personae* text, lines 1-6. Hereafter called *Pound*.

> When, when, and whenever death closes
>   our eyelids,
>
> Moving naked over Acheron
> Upon the one raft, victor and conquered together,
> Marius and Jugurtha together,
>   one tangle of shadows.

III. Basil Bunting: *Briggflatts*, Canto IV. Oxford University Press edition of *Collected Poems*, 1978, lines 1-7. Hereafter called *Bunting*.

---

10. I wish to thank Meredith Yearsley, whose analysis of these passages helped me very much.

> Grass caught in willow tells the flood's height that has subsided;
> overfalls sketch a ledge to be bared tomorrow.
> No angler homes with empty creel though mist dims day.
> I hear Aneurin number the dead, his nipped voice.
> Slight moon limps after the sun. A closing door
> stirs smoke's flow above the grate. Jangle
> to skald, battle, journey; to priest Latin is bland.

I shall also, at times, point to lines following these. What I hope to hint at—for who can *definitively* show it? (who could *want* to?)—is the way in which each line indeed *grows* out of its predecessor, so that the two make a kind of figure of their own, and each is linked to each in a kind of perpetually altering pattern, occasionally stabilised by a recurrence—of rhythm perhaps, or of image, but *usually of a sound* of some sort, so that the stability, the framework if you will (such verse as this, however, always threatens to overbalance), establishes itself through variation and repetition. Establishes *itself*. Recurrencies. It all has to do with what the voice can carry and what the *ear* remembers—more or less arbitrarily I'd say the ear remembers up to some seven or eight lines. Each passage preserves the word order of speech.

If we look at sentence length, there is at first sight little similarity at all between the three passages. Whitman's opening sentence is 208 words (some 22 lines) long; Pound's is 28 words (6 lines); and Bunting's 19 words (2 lines). In 7 lines Bunting gets 5 sentences of roughly 12 words each, but two of those sentences are compound or compound-complex, making them look, syntactically, like 7 sentences. (I might note in passing, however, that Bunting's sixth sentence, beginning on line 8, is 38 words—4 lines—long.) Yet there are indeed close similarities, for all three passages proceed in a cumulative way, piling phrase upon phrase or (in Bunting's case) sentence upon sentence paratactically, a lyric catalogue. There is hardly any subordination at all: in his whole opening sentence Whitman has three subordinations (in lines 4, 6, and 10); in his first eleven lines, Bunting has three (in lines 1, 3, and 10); in his opening sentence, Pound has none. Pound is interesting because the opening "When" (with its repeats) leads us to expect a subordinate adverbial clause, and what we get is a fragmentary sentence—though we do not recognise it as fragmentary until the last line of the sentence. The effect of piling these phrases, one upon the other, within an apparently subordinate clause, is to resolve the whole pile in "*one* tangle of shadows," and this comes about through the curious suspense or suspension of the breath at or just before that "one," as the eye runs ahead of the voice to the period at the line's end. The suspense involved

—and resolved—is not unlike that in Whitman's larger and indeed looser strategy, where the cumulative delay through prepositional phrase after prepositional phrase comes to a head and is nicely resolved, compacted, in that "I" at the beginning of line 20, which invites us—sandwiched as it is between two commas—to expend a good part of a whole breath on it.

The Bunting moves somewhat differently, for the element of suspense has been (comparatively) suppressed and, where Whitman and Pound both move in what might be called a periodic sentence (the predication held till the very end), Bunting moves through a series of comparatively straightforward, rather short, more-or-less expository sentences. The connecting thread between them is not at all obvious (this is the source of the suspense, where Whitman and Pound use syntax), and they move to a generalisation towards which they did not seem to point, for they did not seem to point anywhere:

> Today's posts are piles to drive into the quaggy past
> on which impermanent palaces balance.

The generalisation itself, however, rounds out the progression and balancing (the stabilising of the pattern) of "I hear Aneurin," and at the same time signals a shift and the start of a new progression, announced in the next line's "I see Aneurin's. . . ." That series of sentences, moreover, comparatively straightforward though they may be, is nevertheless noticeably interrupted by the syntactic variation and surprise (we have been led to expect something else) of line seven:

> to skald, battle, journey; to priest Latin is bland.

An apparently simple syntactical repeat or progression (to skald, to priest) gives us pause as we wonder whether "priest" is a verb or a noun, while the "is" comes as a surprise since the first half of the sentence (before the semi-colon) has no verb at all, though we may feel one is implied. The effect is not unlike that in Pound. All three passages move somewhat paratactically: the reader is given few signposts whereby to organise the data.

Within this rather general and crudely sketched over-all pattern there are a number of elements common to all three passages, which serve to tie the lines together, and presumably to engender them, to engender repetition. Let me simply list them:

1. *Repetition of phrases and words.* This is obvious indeed in Whitman and Pound, subtler in Bunting. "Out of the . . . ," and "when, when, and whenever"; Whitman, with his greater expansiveness,

plays the variations of "Down from," "Up from," and so on as well. Bunting: "I hear Aneurin number the dead," "I hear Aneurin number the dead" and "I see Aneurin's. . . ." And, Whitman to Bunting, very clearly, the variation on this: "Out of the cradle," "Out of the mocking-bird's," and so on, and "number the dead, his nipped voice," "number the dead and rejoice"; "I see Aneurin's pectoral muscle swell"—and one hears the "s . . ll" of "*mus-cle*" and "*swell*," which is another kind of repeat and variation. Pound, I might add, repeats "together," rhymes (if that is the word) "cl*o*ses" and "shad*o*ws," and half-rhymes "Jugurtha" and "together"—a device to which I shall return (No. 3, below).

2. *Repetition of vowel-vowel, vowel-consonant, and consonant-consonant sequences* (and variation). Bunting is so dense in this that it is hard to know where to start. I have already mentioned "muscle/swell." There is also the more or less continual chime of the *a* of "gr*a*ss . . . th*a*t h*a*s . . . b*a*red . . . *a*ngler" and the variants (of which "b*a*red" is one) which push toward the *e* of "ledge," the length of "d*e*ad," and so on. Variation of vowels (i.e. lengthening) leads to a transformation into another vowel. There is also such a sequence as "*mist dims day*," which is a lovely interweaving utterly characteristic of a writer like Whitman ("*shower'd halo*" "*play of shadows*"—which also, incidentally, involves an inversion), and this too points toward No. 3 below. It is precisely this kind of interplay which largely holds Pound together, both tonally and rhythmically: the sequence "vowel-r-vowel," for example: "*our eye . . . over Acheron . . . victor and . . . together,/one.*" It is worth noting that the "w" of "one" is in turn a repeat (and variation) of the opening "when," and that the slight juncture between "one" and "raft" echoes this pattern, as does the minuscule pause between "tangle" and "of." Pound, like Whitman, is astonishing in his use of vowels.

There are interlockings, too: Whitman's "*ninth-month mid-night*" (the pacing here is important, too), Pound's "m*o*ving n*a*ked *o*ver *Ach*eron"—which also patterns "moving naked over Acheron" (one might also notice Pound's use of *n* in these six lines), Bunting's "*mist dims day*." The difficulty with all three passages is that as soon as you start noticing such patterns, repetitions, variations, at all, you tend to be overwhelmed by them: there is a subtle shift, for example, in the *dl* of "cra*dl*e" and "en*dl*ess" in Whitman (who rhymes "rocking" and "mocking" to draw your attention to the sound patterns—note the play of "the" and "throat"). One can endlessly point, when all one need do is hear.

3. *Shift from voiced to unvoiced* (or the reverse). Again, prominent in Bunting, but present in all three. "*The* nin*th*-mon*th* midnight" also shifts *d* and *t*—with interweaving. "Mis*t d*ims *d*ay" (again!) also weaves *s* and *z*; and "vic*t*or conquere*d t*oge*th*er . . . Jugur*th*a *t*oge*th*er" also weaves *k* and *g*, while the *v* is a voicing of the *f* of "raft." In Bunting there is the astonishing and lovely "ske*tch* a le*dge*"—and, in a clause hard to understand, "Jan*gl*e/ to ska*l*d." I note simply that unvoiced to voiced shift is *t* to *d*, *s* to *z*, *f* to *v*, *k* to *g*, among others. The shift from *p* to *b* is only *apparently* rare in all three: in *Song of Myself* Whitman "*b*ends an arm on an im*p*al*p*a*b*le certain rest" (which is unusually fine); I have already quoted Bunting's "im*p*ermanent *p*alaces *b*alance." And I notice, too, that in Pound the *k* occurs only in the first four lines, and *g* (overlapping a shade) in the last three.

4. *Consonant clusters and juncture (pause).* All the devices I list (and others) affect the pace and rhythm of the verse; not only do consonant clusters have the most clearly audible effect upon pace and rhythm, however; they have a profound effect upon stress, and push the verse towards quantity. All three passages are rich, here, and once again, Bunting most. The only sensible way I can see to show this is simply to copy out, once again, each passage, italicising the consonant clusters which force a pause, and indicating the pause with a slant /.

Whitman:

> Out of the cradle endlessly rocking,
> Out of the mockin*g*/*b*ird*'s*/*thr*oat,/*th*e musical shuttle,
> Out of the Nin*th*/*m*on*th*/*m*i*dn*ight,
> Over the sterile s*ands*/*a*nd the fie*lds*/*b*eyond, where the chi*ld*/
>   *l*eaving his be*d*/*w*ander'd alo*ne*,/*b*areheade*d*,/*b*arefoot,

Pound:

> Whe*n*,/*w*hen, and whenever dea*th*/*cl*oses
>   our eyeli*ds*,/
> *M*ovin*g*/*n*aked over Acheron
> Upon the o*ne*/*r*a*ft*,/*v*ictor a*nd*/*c*onquere*d*/*t*ogether,
> Marius a*nd*/*J*ugurtha together,
>   o*ne*/*t*angle of shadows.

Bunting:

> Gra*ss*/*c*aught i*n*/*w*illow te*lls*/*th*e floo*d's*/*h*eight/*th*at/*h*a*s*/*s*ubsided;
> overfa*lls*/*s*ketch a le*dge*/*t*o be bare*d*/*t*omorrow.

No angle*r*/*h*ome*s*/*w*ith empty cree*l*/*th*ough mi*st*/*d*im*s*/*d*ay.
I hear Aneuri*n*/*n*umber the dea*d*,/*h*i*s*/*n*i*pp*ed/*v*oice./
*S*light/*m*oon/*l*imps after the sun. A closing/*d*oor
stir*s*/*s*moke'*s*/*ff*low abo*v*e/*t*he gra*t*e./*J*angle
to ska*ld*,/*b*a*tt*le,/*j*ourney; to prie*st*/*L*atin i*s*/*b*land.

It is, perhaps, worth remarking that the pause resulting from
consonant cluster is occasionally emphasised by punctuation
(usually a comma) or a line-break. It is also worth noting that a
similar kind of quantitative pause occurs when a slur from consonant to vowel might lead to confusion (closes / our, for example). If we read "priest" in line 7 of Bunting as verb, the quantity
and tone are changed, because stress is changed. Bunting uses a
great deal of aspirate *h*. His verse tends to be more turbulent than
Whitman and Pound.

5. *Shift from front to back vowels, or the reverse.* I am not at all
sure about this. Each poet exhibits a movement towards back
(open) vowels, which we associate with the noise of *song*.[11] The
problem here is that the English language seems to exhibit a tendency to *middle* its vowels—we drift, that is to say, towards *schwa*.
It is easy, at any rate, to confuse the two movements. But there
are, nevertheless, interesting variations and interlacings. I point to
two, both Bunting, both vowel transforms: "slight moon limps
after the sun." Here the diphthong of *slight* (front lower *a* to front
upper *i*) becomes the *i* of *limp*—a kind of clarification I suppose—
whilst back upper *moon* becomes middle *sun*—though the value of
the *u* will shift if you pronounce it Northumbrian, which shifts
down and is perhaps more voiced. But there is an interweaving, I
think. A similar shift seems to occur—this is all very tentative—in
"*a closing door stirs smoke's flow*," which is more clearly a move
towards roundness and the full-voiced open-throated noise of
song. A similar shift, perhaps, occurs in from "when" to "one" in
Pound, and even in "*Out of the cradle endlessly rocking*" (quite
complex).

This is very impressionistic, but I think all this means that as
you move from Whitman through Pound to Bunting your mouth
has to work a great deal more, moving around all those vowels,
voicing all those consonants. Bunting seems to be fighting against
the centering tendency of the language (he uses back/front/back
moves a great deal). All writers, however, seem consciously to be

---

11. This is a very difficult area indeed, where one must in the long run rely on intuition.
There is a *vast* literature, but a good introduction, for those who wish to follow it up, is
Roman Jakobson: "Why 'Mama' and 'Papa'?," *Selected Writings, I: Phonological
Studies* (The Hague, Mouton, 1962), pp. 538-545.

forcing certain kinds of articulation: as the voice moves towards middle, towards *schwa*, it moves towards *slur*; words begin to blend together, and the noise of speech begins to be fuzzy and vague.

Which is to say, what? NOT that Bunting, Pound and Whitman see poetry as a way to keep the speech muscular. But that they push for the *variety* of sounds that make our speech, and seek weavings and patternings that make for what we think of as song. It would be interesting indeed to examine the work of Eliot in this way, for I suspect (and indeed hear, though I have not worked it out) that his intent on the *use* of poetry has locked him into iambics, and into a very limited range of sound indeed; so, too, one might look at/listen to Zukofsky, for *he* I suspect (and indeed hear) is pushing for the full range of the voice, in song. The four of them, Whitman, Pound, Bunting, Zukofsky, provide I think a resource for the poet in a way in which say Eliot (my whipping post in this note) does not. It may indeed be that *Homage* outlined a door; Bunting, I believe, tells us where it might lead. Words as song.

A BRIGGFLATTS SYMPOSIUM

DONALD DAVIE

ONE WAY TO MISREAD BRIGGFLATTS

Briggflatts opens thus:

Brag, sweet tenor bull,
descant on Rawthey's madrigal,
each pebble its part
for the fells' late spring.
Dance tiptoe, bull,
black against may.
Ridiculous and lovely
chase hurdling shadows
morning into noon.
May on the bull's hide
and through the dale
furrows fill with may,
paving the slowworm's way.

A mason times his mallet
to a lark's twitter,
listening while the marble rests,
lays his rule
at a letter's edge,
fingertips checking,
till the stone spells a name
naming none,
a man abolished.
Painful lark, labouring to rise!
The solemn mallet says:
In the grave's slot
he lies. We rot.

Decay thrusts the blade,
wheat stands in excrement
trembling. Rawthey trembles.
Tongue stumbles, ears err
for fear of spring.
Rub the stone with sand,
wet sandstone rending

roughness away. Fingers
ache on the rubbing stone.
The mason says: Rocks
happen by chance.
No one here bolts the door,
love is so sore.

Stone smooth as skin,
cold as the dead they load
on a low lorry by night.
The moon sits on the fell
but it will rain.
Under sacks on the stone
two children lie,
hear the horse stale,
the mason whistle,
harness mutter to shaft,
felloe to axle squeak,
rut thud the rim,
crushed grit.

Stocking to stocking, jersey to jersey,
head to a hard arm,
they kiss under the rain,
bruised by their marble bed.
In Garsdale, dawn;
at Hawes, tea from the can.
Rain stops, sacks
steam in the sun, they sit up.
Copper-wire moustache,
sea-reflecting eyes
and Baltic plainsong speech
declare: By such rocks
men killed Bloodaxe.

Fierce blood throbs in his tongue,
lean words.
Skulls cropped for steel caps
huddle round Stainmore.
Their becks ring on limestone,
whisper to peat.
The clogged cart pushes the horse downhill.
In such soft air
they trudge and sing,
laying the tune frankly on the air.
All sounds fall still,
fellside bleat,
hide-and-seek peewit.

Her pulse their pace,
palm countering palm,

till a trench is filled,
stone white as cheese
jeers at the dale.
Knotty wood, hard to rive,
smoulders to ash;
smell of October apples.
The road again,
at a trot.
Wetter, warmed, they watch
the mason meditate
on name and date.

Rain rinses the road,
the bull streams and laments.
Sour rye porridge from the hob
with cream and black tea,
meat, crust and crumb.
Her parents in bed
the children dry their clothes.
He has untied the tape
of her striped flannel drawers
before the range. Naked
on the pricked rag mat
his fingers comb
thatch of his manhood's home.

On this long passage a recent commentary, designed (no doubt shrewdly) to reach the greatest number of Bunting's countrymen,[1] reads as follows:

> *Briggflatts* is subtitled 'An Autobiography'. We are warned not to read it as literal autobiography. In the first section Bunting peoples a Northumbrian landscape with images and then skilfully coordinates them. We meet the lively bull, Rawthey, and the less lively tombstone maker, reading his new inscription with his fingertips. Life, passion and 'music' are embodied in Rawthey, while death is embodied in the mason. Against the backdrop of these images, two lovers come, watch 'the mason meditate / on name and date', and generally appreciate what they see. They go home and make love before the fire, in a passage where Bunting's rhetoric gets the better of him and he produces banal effects. The lover unties 'tape / of her striped flannel drawers' and at last 'on the pricked rag mat / his fingers comb / thatch of his manhood's home'. The unfortunate rhyme and conceit, the academic poise, are totally out of keeping with the poem.

The verse and the commentary thus bleakly juxtaposed, what are we to do about it? It is too late, I think, for the strategy already time-honoured, of holding the philistine up to ridicule, and trusting the common reader in time to see his way around him. We should

---

1. Michael Schmidt, *An Introduction to Fifty Modern British Poets.* Pan Literature Guides, 1979.

have learned by now that the common reader has neither the as-
surance nor the resources to see his way around the knowledgeable
philistine, least of all when that philistine is his professor, as nowa-
days he often is. And in this case the commentator, Michael
Schmidt, has as it happens deserved rather well of the British public, in his capacities as editor and publisher. He is not a philistine,
in any simple sense; but rather a man who has been extensively
educated (first at Harvard, I think, and thereafter at Oxford—so
the blame is shared across the Atlantic) into a frame of mind towards poetry, and a set of assumptions about it, out of which, and
in terms of which, it is impossible for him to engage with what is
going on in any page of *Briggflatts*. We will merely note in passing
that the Rawthey is a river not the bull. We must surely deny ourselves the rhetorical pleasures of derision and invective, applying
ourselves instead to discovering patiently just what unformulated
and doubtless unconscious assumptions in the commentator have
impelled him so wide of the mark.

   And we must deny ourselves, except in passing, the pleasure
of asking Michael Schmidt whether striped flannel drawers are
normal underwear amid his female acquaintances, since the word
"banal" seems to imply that they are. But we can certainly ask
him what circumlocution for pubic hair he would prefer to
Bunting's, which he finds so "unfortunate." Is he of those who
would call a spade a spade, and hair, "hair"? And if he is not, how
can he deny that "thatch of his manhood's home" is a circumlocution at once accurate and elegantly ingenious, compact and yet
tender? I fear that the words "elegant" and "ingenious" will
point for others besides him to what he calls "academic poise"—
perhaps the unkindest cut of all, from Bunting's own point of view.
And it is true that circumlocution has been in bad odour, as a
poetic resource, ever since the Preface to *Lyrical Ballads*. But
what we have here is a *kenning*, as in Old English; that is to say,
a sort of circumlocution that is, as a poetic form, very ancient and
primitive indeed, being only a special version of that most primitive of forms, the riddle. *Briggflatts* is full of such "kennings";
and if we applaud them as elegant and ingenious, that implies only
that elegance and ingenuity were as much valued by the Anglo-
saxon- or Cymric-speaking Briton of the allegedly Dark Ages, as
by us heirs of Laforgue.

   We can hardly fail to note, in this passage as in the phrase
"out of keeping," how the spectre of neo-classical decorum hovers
over Michael Schmidt's responses. However, we can with more
profit, to ourselves as well as to him, dwell on his observation that

"Life, passion and 'music' are embodied in Rawthey, while death is embodied in the mason." This comment in fact takes us back to the origins of the Modern Movement, in *Bouvard et Pécuchet*, where Flaubert's couple of sublime and touching idiots are side-tracked time and again—by their readings in popularized science as by popularized aesthetics—into disregarding the infinitely various and satisfying surface of things, probing *through* that surface to arrive at significances allegedly "deeper," and certainly much simpler. Rather than let the bull be a bull, and the mason a mason, Michael Schmidt, like Bouvard or Pécuchet, asks that each of them "stand in for" (the currently acceptable term is "embody" or "incarnate," though there is always the maid-of-all-work, "symbolize") some large abstraction like "life" or "death." If we object that for Bunting as for Flaubert a bull is a bull is a bull, and a mason is a mason is a mason, Schmidt will be provoked to unhelpful thoughts about Gertrude Stein. Yet so it is: in literature or out of it, a mason is a man who pursues one particular trade, and if that trade commits him to trafficking with the dead, that traffic does not define him so as to scant the living variety of him, in his other capacities. That variety Bunting honours, even in the relatively few verses we have quoted. But for his commentator, that variety is unmanageable; and so he subscribes instead to what E.A. Burtt called (in his *Metaphysical Foundations of Modern Physical Science*) "the postulate of an impoverished reality"; that is to say, to the unargued assumption that Nature is simpler and less bounteous than she seems. This is to suppose that Nature "puts up a good show," or "keeps up a splendid front"; but that her entertainments, which seem so unflaggingly novel, are really variations on a very few basic themes, and similarly her furnishings, which seem so various, are in fact only cunningly disguised variants on a strictly limited wardrobe. But of course it is possible to believe, as Bunting seems to do, that Nature (*human* nature included) is just as inexhaustibly various, as copiously inventive for good and ill, as she seems to be. For instance she knows and provides for many ways of "making love," from the shy caress, and the shining look exchanged, through to various sorts of copulation. And so the commentator's blunt assertion that "they" (two children, though he doesn't say so) "make love before the fire," quite brutally over-rides the range of possibilities that Bunting with quiet delicacy leaves open. Undoubtedly a sexual passage of some sort happens between the girl and the boy; but to say that they "make love," appealing necessarily to what we usually understand by that expression, is to define just what Bunting tactfully leaves indefinite. And so it seems we must say that the reader who finds "striped flannel drawers" indecorous is unable to recognize decorum when his author observes it on a matter rather more important.

It's from this point of view that we can see what Michael Schmidt means by calling the striped flannel drawers "banal." He means that, try as he may, he can't make these words symbolize anything beyond themselves. The words stubbornly point to that which they name, and to nothing else, to nothing "beneath" or "above" or "beyond." And we should not delude ourselves; thousands of readers besides Michael Schmidt believe that in poetry words must always do something other than this, something "more." These are the readers for whom it would make no sense to say that Flaubert is a very *poetic* novelist. Seventy years after Ford told Pound that today's poet must compete not only with the great poets of the past but with Stendhal and Flaubert also (and Pound passed the word to Eliot, and both Eliot and he began preaching that same gospel), Ford's lesson has not been heard in most influential circles, or else, if heard, it has not been understood.

The most baleful word in Schmidt's account is "coordinates":

> . . . Bunting peoples a Northumbrian landscape with images and
> then skilfully coordinates them . . .

It is not beside the point to remark that "coordinate," as a noun, has a special and specially privileged place in the language of mathematicians. What Schmidt seems to mean by it is something like this: that the reader (and, for all we are told to the contrary, writer also) sets up in his mind two columns, one headed "Life" and the other "Death"; and that whatever images thereafter present themselves (blessedly vague word, that "images") must be entered in the one column or in the other. How inadequate and obfuscating such a procedure is, as regards *Briggflatts*, will appear if we extend by a few verses our quotation from the first section of the poem:

> Gentle generous voices weave
> over bare night
> words to confirm or delight
> till bird dawn.
> Rainwater from the butt
> she fetches and flannel
> to wash him inch by inch,
> kissing the pebbles.
> Shining slowworm part of the marvel.
> The mason stirs:

    Words!
    Pens are too light.
    Take a chisel to write.

The slowworm has here become the boy's penis, but without scanting in the least the literal meaning that it has had at the very start of the poem, which it will later have again—as (O.E.D.) "A small harmless scincoid lizard, *Anguis Fragilis*, native to most parts of Europe"; and the "pebbles" have become the boy's testicles, without however in the least diminishing their status as (O.E.D.) small stones "worn and rounded by the action of water." When we reflect that, as small stones, pebbles are units of that material which the mason shapes and incises so as to honour the dead, this kenning forces us to realise how hopeless it is to approach this poem by way of sorting its images into "lively" and "deathly." The life is *in* the death, and *vice-versa*; as the poem itself has told us, quite explicitly:

    Decay thrusts the blade,
    wheat stands in excrement
    trembling. Rawthey trembles.

What Rawthey trembles at isn't fear of death; he trembles with erotic excitement, sparked to it precisely by the "deathly" images of decay and excrement. And yet that isn't quite right, either: fear of death is part of erotic excitement, and *vice-versa*. Once we take "lively" and "deathly" as mutually exclusive categories, we have closed our minds in advance to just the perceptions that this poem is designed to explore and enforce.

Our purpose—let us remind ourselves—is not to score points, nor to exercise a facile and self-serving derision. The purpose is diagnosis—of a condition like Michael Schmidt's, from which it is impossible to engage with one of the great poems of our time. It's in this spirit that one enquires how Schmidt came to entertain a set of assumptions that so conclusively shut him off from Bunting's poem. And the answer, I believe, comes on the next page of his commentary, when he is commenting on a phrase from the second section of Bunting's poem, "Schoenberg's Maze," and on the allusion to the Minotaur in the last lines of that section:

    The image of the labyrinth—Muir's image for the mind—comes
    into play.

Why this abrupt invocation of a poet surely as unlike Bunting as it is possible to imagine? I think the answer is plain: Edwin Muir is one poet with a respectable reputation from Bunting's lifetime who certainly did subscribe to "the postulate of an impoverished reality." His use of symbols like the labyrinth (*fixed* symbols, at the opposite pole from the fluid and provisional symbols of the *symbolistes*) can only make sense on that postulate. And to some of us—for at this point one has to take sides—it is precisely this in Muir which makes him a poet of the second order at best. It is unfortunate that one cannot make the case that needs to be made for Bunting without, at least in the present context, denigrating Muir, who was a harmless and amiable man and indeed something more, for it was he, collaborating with his wife, who introduced the English-speaking world to Kafka. (That Kafka's world, the world of German expressionism, was Muir's point of departure, doubtless helps to explain how he could for his own purposes afford to ignore the Flaubertian French challenge thrown down by Ford Madox Ford. Another less readily explicable puzzle is how Eliot, as elderly poet-publisher, came to sponsor Muir.) At any rate a reader who trusts or admires Muir's platonic or platonizing intelligence, who thinks that that is the characteristically *poetic* intelligence (and there are many who do think so—Kathleen Raine for one) will, like Michael Schmidt, just not *see* how a poetic intelligence like Bunting's moves through and among his images. What will baffle them is that Bunting's images are always of particulars—"striped flannel drawers," "pricked rag mat"; and that they have to be so because only in that way can the poet relish and celebrate the inexhaustible plentitude of particulars *in nature*. By the same token (since Muir is enough of a poet to be all of a piece) the ear which takes as a poetic norm the deliberate iambic mellifluousness of Muir's verses just can not *hear* the sharper notes of Bunting, and his more dancing transitions from sound to sound; will indeed, as I'm afraid Michael Schmidt does, hear one of the loveliest sequences in *Briggflatts* as "near doggerel."

And the conclusion? Perhaps only this: that the resistance to Bunting's poetry, on both sides of the Atlantic but particularly in England, is not always and in every case the product of obtuseness and/or bad faith. The obstruction may be, and in some cases is, philosophical. Which doesn't in the least absolve us, who champion Bunting, from asserting that the philosophy which would debar him is false, and below what the plentitude of nature deserves and demands.

JOHN PECK

BARDIC BRIGGFLATTS

Basil Bunting would have us say nothing *about* his poetry. To be sure, the best honor we can do any poetry is to read it, and attest to its durability in our ears.

Bunting's best lines are durable indeed. And the "music" which he defends against expositors of meaning does not reinstate *symbolisme*. It does take us toward an older region, but at first let us be concrete. Whatever musical patterns have guided Bunting in composing *Briggflatts*, in general effect they come down to a pair of principles declared in the last two sections: "never a boast or a see-here" (in praise of Scarlatti) and "Then is diffused in Now." With those twin claves, through repetition and variation of phrase, the patterns weave around his recollection of a "love murdered" and "laid aside" in adolescence. Motif and ritornello around bitter-sweet memory: it is a Wordsworthian poem in a Poundian arrangement, its feeling coherent in ways that a mention of Pound does not suggest.

That coherence also has little to do with Bunting's explicit gestures toward music. When he names a composer, or when he orchestrates the starlight of his last section with harp, horn, and flute, he more loudly sweeps the string after having already sounded the real harmonies of feeling. That feeling is Romantic and northern, winding materials both heroically harsh and elegiac around a delicately sentimental armature. And in those windings not only does Then become Now, but also There becomes Here, with sea, Italy, and the desert impelling a northlander's homecoming. In no small way the language navigates a homecoming as well.

It is this last dimension that I wish to think more *about*, if Mr. Bunting will forgive me, for with his moving central recollection of a love he once stifled ("it is easier to die than to remember") comes a language whose finding enlarges that moving effect, for he finds it in the history which comes home to him as he lets memory supervene. Neither is that finding of language an easier thing, for the archaic traditions of northern heroic and elegiac poetry, when they inform the writing, press in upon Bunting. The old bardic forms compel him to use them; he may not even be happy about the fact, for in that part of the writing they are chiefly, in ways that must remain partly obscure, all that he has.

Why compelled to use them? Because the impulses of his experience take their patterns. "I hear Aneurin number the dead and rejoice," he writes in the fourth section, "being adult male of a merciless species"—with the figure named by those last two verbs being both men, given the fluid syntax. The murdered affection of Bunting's adolescence lies among those dead; and likewise the archaic northern male pattern, in its heroic function, stands over against the soft feminine thing it may abandon but which it never forgets. Indeed, the tenacity of its fixation on that feeling both distinguishes and limits this heroic type. Ibsen satirizes Norwegian failings in the figure of Peer Gynt, but holds to the pattern: the hero betrays his first love, then as a melancholy wanderer discovers its value, making it the object of reference and longing. (*Peer Gynt* strangely anticipates Bunting's own wanderings as those enter his poem, south and then into the desert before turning home again.)

When experience takes this pattern, the longing which it creates makes the present thrall to the past. The wrong or violence once done to feeling gets feeling stuck—with the consequence that no intensity emerges which does not get colored by the fixation, acknowledged or not. "He lies with one to long for another, / sick, self-maimed, self-hating, / obstinate, . . ."[1] Then and Now become one, but in a struggle for resolution of feeling. Bunting's "autobiography" of feeling surely reaches resolution. Psychologizing is not my aim, but instead an accounting for a necessity in his form, which appears in the poem's bardic aspect, in the apparent inescapability of heroic and elegiac writing for the homecoming to feeling and its past.

We describe both an individual psychology and a cultural tradition when we observe that in northern heroic and elegiac poetry the prevailing sense is an unmediated one: an important thing no sooner happens than it gets captured by the past, seized by the template of the Old Songs. And within those songs the same thing holds: between the fated warrior and the carrion crow

---

1. Section two of the poem, in *Collected Poems* (Oxford, 1978), p. 43. Further page-references in parentheses.

there stands no middle term.

Although Bunting's poem recovers a tender and traduced eros, it is the unmediated pattern of heroic lament which grips him as he makes that recovery. King Eric Bloodaxe, a screen for part of Bunting's own nature, dies at Stainmore, "Spine / picked bare by ravens"—to be followed by a gallery of delicately etched creatures, one of them a rat; and it is the rat, two sections later, that occasions a pointed confession of identity.

> Where rats go go I,
> accustomed to penury,
> filth, disgust and fury;
> evasive to persist,
> reject the bait
> yet gnaw the best.
> My bony feet
> sully shelf and dresser,
> keeping a beat in the dark, . . . (55)

This bestiary entry is not simply personal; it also touches the poem's bite on language, for in the Bloodaxe section the inaugural passage on vocation describes the poet in this way:

> Secret, solitary, a spy, he gauges
> lines of a Flemish horse
> hauling beer, the angle, obtuse,
> a slut's blouse draws on her chest,
> counts beat against beat, bus conductor
> against engine against wheels against
> the pedal, . . . (43)

A Villon in the post-Baudelarian city, this poet is a kind of sharp-eyed and sharp-eared scavenger. And to this same poet comes the counterpoint not only of urban impressions but, by the poem's evidence, also of the heroic laments and the sagas. The rat of the later section keeps his beat in solitude not far distant from Aneurin and Taliesin as they preside over Bunting's communion with his dead. To repeat: in the Old Songs nothing stands between doomed warrior and clacking raven; and Bunting's poem offers singular testimony to the power of that configuration over strong feeling within a modern form. Eliot's Thames-side rats scavenged near the sites of vulgar trysts to the tune of strains from Spenser's *Epithalamion*. But literary irony of that sort is not the Sign over Bunting's rodents. In finding the bardic hero as one necessary projection for himself in *Briggflatts*, Bunting found immediately that the scavenging beast was another. And finding that his own language needed partly to reflect the archaic poems and their feeling, he found that the lowly tenacity of the modern poet in his gritty landscape cast himself as the scavenger upon that tradition—a survivor in genuine need of it, but keeping his beat in darkness.

The verbal music of *Briggflatts*, particularly when it rings of chisel and stone and bitter seas, supplements this relationship, but it derives as much from the relation as it contributes in turn. Bunting's invocations of Monteverdi and Scarlatti, among others, hearken to a southern music crammed with present motion and empty of see-heres. Yet might not his own reliance on motif-and-variation in the poem's phrasing, given the tenor of feeling and theme, more plausibly suggest analogies with the Ceol Mor, the heroic pibroch laments? When at the poem's end starlight comes in with flute, horn, and harp, one of the stars appears as a Viking longboat; that is to say, light from a star now consumed, the love laid aside, and the music with them, have arrived intact from a particular configuration of the past. And that, not surprisingly, is a northern one.

† † † † †

Because topography shapes much of *Briggflatts* it is difficult to overestimate the degree to which its journeys quicken the root meaning of *nostalgia*. Eric Bloodaxe's seafaring in the second section joins with Bunting's own sojurns in Italy; in the third, Alexander's legendary journey to Gog and Magog inflects into a Northumbrian idyll. Both sections come round upon *nostos* or homecoming.

The poem's language performs a parallel action, returning to ancestral springs. In the fourth section, where Bunting stations himself at the seventh-century battlefield of Cattraeth, overhearing a farmer take stock of flood-damage, he stands in the presence of Welsh warrior-poets and Celtic missionary-saints (types of an inner opposition), but also in the presence of part of his poem's speech, or of access to it. By excerpting from the passage we isolate this second presence:

> I hear Aneurin number the dead, his nipped voice.
> Slight moon limps after the sun. A closing door
> stirs smoke's flow above the grate. Jangle
> to skald, battle, journey; to priest Latin is bland.
>   . . . . .
> I hear Aneurin number the dead and rejoice,
> being adult male of a merciless species.
> Today's posts are piles to drive into the quaggy past
> on which impermanent palaces balance.
>   . . . . .
> Clear Cymric voices carry well this autumn night,
> Aneurin and Taliesin, cruel owls

for whom it is never altogether dark, crying
before the rules made poetry a pedant's game.
Columba, Columbanus, as the soil shifts its vest,
Aidan and Cuthbert put on daylight,
wires of sharp western metal entangled in its soft
web, many shuttles as midges darting;
not for bodily welfare nor pauper theorems
but splendour to splendour, excepting nothing that is.
Let the fox have his fill, . . . (53)

Aidan and St. Cuthbert, bishops of Lindisfarne, anchored the swirl of Northumbrian Christianity, which swept over the Angles who had conquered with western metal. It began with the Irish St. Columba's astonishing missions (of royal blood, he was known as Crimthann or the Fox), his vigor trumped only by St. Columbanus, who left place-names through England, France, and Italy. Both of course left Latin hymns. Bunting's transitions move not only from skald and bard to chanting priest but also from these figures to owl and fox, with a side-glance at the medieval and post-Fabian commonwealths: "not for bodily welfare nor pauper theorems." Glory and hierarchy of spirit, in the face of defeat, emerge from Bunting's weaving of these figures. Skaldic tradition and apostolic succession converge for him here, even across his region's shift of its historical vesture. They converge in respect of song, and from that convergence he derives a strength that detours around impermanence and that also counterpoints native *jangle* to Latin *blandus*, the smoothly pleasing. (That counterpoint is everywhere Bunting's own: "The bull streams and laments.")

The depredations which Bunting lists a few lines later do not gainsay the continuity which he senses as he numbers his dead. This continuity is not the memorable or even the commemorative so much as the memorious; it is continuity as lament and hymn, grim and fluent. The poet we hear speaking in the fourth section of *Briggflatts* posts his song unquaggily in that ground, through which the bards and wandering clerics reach him because, directly but also mysteriously, he has come home to the whole of that ground. The relationship between his song and theirs, although it quickens inoperative hierarchies of the memorious, neither mystifies nor mythifies the function of song, for Bunting here fabricates no smokey auras around that web of transmissibility and affinity which it is the peculiar work of poetry to weave. Very little writing from any one period goes about that work. The opening half of the fourth section of *Briggflatts* goes into it as well.

Nostos in this poem brings home *anamnesis*, an access to language as well as to time. Herbert Read hears Chaucer behind the

opening notes and Anglo-Saxon rhythms throughout, Kenneth
Cox the King James Old Testament behind the portrayal of country life. But resonance bears most pointedly on the authenticity
particular to Bunting's language with the tone most clearly borrowed by him, in the heroic-elegiac writing. For there his service
to personal memory exercises the tone most remote from its occasion. We paraphrase some of the poem's peculiar coherence if
we say that its Wordsworthian fusion of times requires the attendance of heroic elegy. And that attendance also corrects narrow
appreciations of Bunting's own analogies for his tone—whether in
the "Lindisfarne plaited lines" of illumination or the "Flexible,
unrepetitive line" of sound laid frankly on the air.

† † † † †

  The poem's largest allegorical screen for autobiography is
Eric Bloodaxe, whose seafaring and death at the battle of Stainmore dominate the second section. This ninth-century Norwegian
king, granted Northumbria by Athelstan, nonetheless "had little
land and many followers" and so "he grew short of money. For
this reason he spent the summers a-harrying,"[2] as the *Orkneyinga
Saga* has it. "No tilled acre, gold scarce" (44), writes Bunting, himself an inveterate sailor who has spent whole seasons on a small
boat and frequently made do with little. Eric's circuits through
the Orkneys, to Dublin, and back to Northumbria, receive the
following imagining from Bunting (in the inset following), in
which the terse itemization of skaldic verse compresses time—
"scurvy gnaws, steading smell, hearth's crackle"—and telescopes
murderous process—"brawn brine, bone grit." That last line lodges
bardic alliteration within a short formal epitaph and tests, if anything in the poem will, the status of the bardic note: flourish or
something more?
  Bunting inscribes this epitaph not only over King Eric and
his kind but also over himself—for Bunting has already made the
tombstone-carving mason a pivotal figure (who points out Stainmore to the young lovers) and made headstones another armature
for the second section. The northern-sea epitaph is no ornament
because his mason has chiselled the occasion and his embittered
sea-harrier has supplied both travel and travail. Both figures compose a self which commands rather than dabbles with the epitaph's
archaic tone, to crystallize rather than chronicle autobiography.

---

2. The translation by Alexander Burt Taylor (Edinburgh and London, 1938), p. 144.

Thole-pins shred where the oar leans,
grommets renewed, tallowed;
halliards frapped to the shrouds.
Crew grunt and gasp. Nothing he sees
they see, but hate and serve. Unscarred ocean,
day's swerve, swell's poise, pursuit,
he blends, balances, drawing leagues under the keel
to raise cold cliffs where tides
knot fringes of weed.
No tilled acre, gold scarce,
walrus tusk, whalebone, white bear's liver.
Scurvy gnaws, steading smell, hearth's crackle.
Crabs, shingle, seracs on the icefall.
Summer is bergs and fogs, lichen on rocks.
Who cares to remember a name cut in ice
or be remembered?
Wind writes in foam on the sea:

Who sang, sea takes,
brawn brine, bone grit.
Keener the kittiwake.
Fells forget him.
Fathoms dull the dale,
Gulfweed voices . . . (44)

The next lines abruptly turn the northern sea-lord toward Italy, insisting with that gesture on the figure's subservience to poetic rather than historical meaning.

About ship! Sweat in the south. Go bare
because the soil is adorned, . . .

To be sure, Bunting's own history of sojourn in Italy informs that meaning, sensuously so, "with the half-sweet white wine of Orvieto / on scanty grass under great trees / where the ramparts cuddle Lucca." But Eric's legendary history and Bunting's personal history converge, as north and south do in a composite topography, under signs which neither alone wholly dictates. It is the bardic hero who makes the anomalous turn toward Bunting's Italy, just as it is Bunting's remorse over "love laid aside" which goes with Eric to his hapless death at Stainmore (a motive nowhere suggested in the sagas and chronicles). And so, should we be tempted novelistically to psychologize from Bunting's own occasions, it is just there, any knowledge that we might have from his interviews notwithstanding,[3] that we are returned to composite pattern in the writing. For so, I take it, the strong conclusion of the second section returns us, with northern sailors "driven by

---

3. *Descant on Rawthey's Madrigal*: Conversations with Basil Bunting by Jonathan Williams (Gnomon Press, 1968).

storm fret" inexplicably reminded of Cretan Pasiphae and the
godly bull:

> nor did flesh flinch
> distended by the brute
> nor loaded spirit sink
> till it had gloried in unlike creation. (48)

The shock of this ending reaches back through the yoked and unlike figures and their spliced topographies. The skaldic epitaph and
love-lorn death, with which a fate flinched and sank, "Spine /
picked bare by ravens," find their counter-measure here.

† † † † †

The third and middle section of the poem, a retelling of Alexander's legendary ascent of a mountain in the range of Gog and
Magog at world's end, in Bunting's mind stood as "the central
moment of the poem, from the very start."[4] As Alexander's soldiers tell it in Bunting's narrative, they could not follow him to
the forbidding peak. Bunting's own war-years in the Near East in
some way prepared him to acknowledge the centrality of this
moment, one which turns to homecoming for Alexander, and
which Bunting echoes with a visionary homecoming of his own.
Another skaldic form, the riddle, plays its part in this doubling
of the *nostos*—but in the idyllic rather than the heroic portion of
the section.

Having journeyed through abominations to the falls of the
dead, the soldiers long for return to Macedonia. Through their
eyes we see a Dantesque allegory of the world's business: turd-
mongers and purveyors. Though his exhausted men had lost the
will to go on, Alexander scornfully pushed upward through icy
night

> till the morning star reflected
> in the glazed crag
> and other light not of the sun
> dawning from above
> lit feathers sweeping snow
> and the limbs of Israfel,
> trumpet in hand, intent on the east,
> cheeks swollen to blow,
> whose sigh is cirrus: Yet delay!
> When will the signal come
> to summon man to his clay?

---

4. "Basil Bunting Talks About *Briggflatts*," *Agenda* 16.1 (Spring 1978), p. 10.

Heart slow, nerves numb and memory, he lay
on glistening moss by a spring;
as a woodman dazed by an adder's sting
barely within recall
tests the rebate tossed to him, so he
ascertained moss and bracken,
a cold squirm snaking his flank
and breath leaked to his ear:
I am neither snake nor lizard,
I am the slowworm. (51)

In the legend, Alexander's brush with apocalypse sent him top-
pling from the peak; he came to his senses and returned to Macedonia. Bunting shifts, however, into recovery from a dream-vision,
whose anonymous third-person dreamer answers the summons to
"man" and also transmutes Alexander as seer of the nearly fatal.

The transition through this figure seems to me one of the
most English moments in the poem, incorporating Blake or
Vaughan's "innocence," the medieval *swevyn*, and the even older
riddle. The harmless slowworm, observed also by Sir Thomas
Browne and Tennyson, is of course not fatal; Bunting had made
him the phallic totem of spring in section one. He returns here
with harvest, his unique eyelids (which have earned him the by-
name Blindworm) part of the mystery which Bunting has him
retain. Perhaps that mystery requires him, even after he has identified himself, to speak in the archaic riddle form:

Ripe wheat is my lodging. I polish
my side on pillars of its transept,
gleam in its occasional light.
Its swaying
copies my gait.

Vaults stored with slugs to relish,
my quilt a litter of husks, I prosper
lying low, little concerned.
My eyes sharpen
when I blink. (51)

The elemental bed and temple couch a psychic transformation,
which Bunting stages after an intervening sequence of reaping,
autumn gale, and first snow, closing the central part of the poem
with his figure now a revenant.

Swaggering, shimmering fall,
drench and towel us all!

So he rose and led home silently through clean woodland
where every bough repeated the slowworm's song. (52)

I cannot read this close without seeing certain pastoral and vision-ary watercolors and etchings by Samuel Palmer.

Between Eric Bloodaxe, Aneurin and Taliesin, and Aidan and St. Cuthbert, Bunting has framed elements of self-recognition. The legend of Alexander and the dream-vision which Bunting makes of it, then, rest at the center of a duality which it becomes the poem's central impulse to focus. The vision sets at the focus of *Briggflatts* a transformation of violence into peace, and of one kind of dream-ing into another, apocalypse into *swevyn*, in which the riddling speech of the worm anchors consciousness. Even with waking and self-recollection, contact is still maintained with the beneficent dream and its speech. With Bunting's pacifism in World War One and his desert duty in World War Two, we have one version of the duality imaged here, but even without such knowledge we must take the thrust of this section somewhat as I have paraphrased it here. However modernist the pedigree of its modulations, there is little mistaking its meaning.

† † † † †

To be even blunter: the heroic and elegiac writing in *Brigg-flatts* must be defended against claustration within discussions of music and tone, so that its edge can be felt. Feeling it, we can face the music of certain literary comparisons, both then and now.

Returning to the fourth section's setting at Cattraeth, I con-front the justification for everything which I have noted so far.

> Grass caught in willow tells the flood's height that has subsided;
> overfalls sketch a ledge to be bared tomorrow.
> No angler homes with empty creel though mist dims day.
> I hear Aneurin number the dead, his nipped voice.
> Slight moon limps after the sun. A closing door
> stirs smoke's flow above the grate. Jangle
> to skald, battle, journey; to priest Latin is bland.
> Rats have left no potatoes fit to roast, the gamey tang
> recalls ibex guts steaming under a cold ridge,
> tomcat stink of a leopard dying while I stood
> easing the bolt to dwell on a round's shining rim.
> I hear Aneurin number the dead and rejoice,
> being adult male of a merciless species.
> Today's posts are piles to drive into the quaggy past
> on which impermanent palaces balance.
> I see Aneurin's pectoral muscle swell under his shirt,
> pacing between the game Ida left to rat and raven,
> young men, tall yesterday, with cabled thighs.
> Red deer move less warily since their bows dropped.
> Girls in Teesdale and Wensleydale wake discontent.

> Clear Cymric voices carry well this autumn night,
> Aneurin and Taliesin, cruel owls
> for whom it is never altogether dark, crying
> before the rules made poetry a pedant's game.
> Columba, Columbanus, as the soil shifts its vest, . . . (53)

Moments from Bunting's desert years, the tenor and cadence of Aneurin's *The Gododdin*, "cabled thighs" for lordly lament and homely details from the landscape of the Dales, history's accountings and poetry's, and one man's own stock-taking, all congregate with authority. The poem's bardic strain here has become its means of observation, necessary both to these interpenetrating presences and to the man who is alive to them. Necessary, and also bardic with neither a boast nor a see-here: the modern poetry I know does not show its like (with the exception of several poems by Sorley Maclean in a different mode).

Perhaps Auden comes to mind, in his earliest poems and plays, or in the poem of the early thirties which he later titled "The Wanderer." But, Auden's deep attachment to the Sagas and Anglo-Saxon poems notwithstanding, that poem's invention sustains itself at the level of glancing pastiche and adroit manipulation.

> But ever that man goes
> Through place-keepers, through forest trees,
> A stranger to strangers over undried sea,
> Houses for fishes, suffocating water,
> Or lonely on fell as chat, . . .

Robert Lowell expressed gratitude to Auden for "the sad Anglo-Saxon alliteration of his beginnings."[5] Necessary though Auden's needs were to experiment with ellipsis and other features of "The Wanderer," that writing came to be, in his own development, dispensable, a manner along the way rather than a matter at which he later came to arrive.

If Auden comes to mind, then certainly too does the Pound of Cantos I and II. Before rearranging the early cantos, he printed an "Eighth Canto" in *The Dial* for 1922 which began with the Tyro, Neptune, Eleanor, Helen, and Homer now lodged in Canto II, but before that with a figure now found in Canto VII's telescoped history of epic, a figure amusingly rhymed with the epic muse:

> Dido choked up with tears for dead Sichaeus;
> And the weeping Muse, weeping, widowed, and willing,
> The weeping Muse
>   Mourns Homer,

---

5. The Auden issue of *Shenandoah* (Winter 1967).

Mourns the days of long song,
Mourns for the breath of the singers,
Winds stretching out, seas pulling to eastward,
Heaving breath of the oarsmen,
            triremes under Cyprus,
The long course of the seas,
The words woven in wind-wrack,
            salt-spray over voices.[6]

As the *Odyssey* heaves into view, so do Roman Imperial triremes
(one of which brought the dying Virgil with his poem to Brun-
disium). It takes no straining to hear Pound, in this introit to the
cancelled eighth canto, jibing at those who contended "that no
long poem" (the quotation appears in drafts of Canto V) could be
fashioned paratactically from constellations of images. And so
"long song" comes in for a drubbing, at the expense of those who
hold exclusive notions of epic length. "Heaving breath of the oarsmen. . . ." But these mariners are not straw-sailors only, for Pound
also shades them toward Anglo-Saxon measure—"The words
woven in wind-wrack, / salt spray over voices"—even as later
(shifted to Canto II) he infuses the tale of Acoetes with Anglo-
Saxon compounds, beginning with shorebird notations from *The
Wanderer*:

Quiet sun-tawny sand-stretch,
The gulls broad out their wings,
            nipping between the splay feathers.

The uses to Pound of Anglo-Saxon, polemical in the cancelled
eighth canto and critical in Cantos I and II (equations for Homer
and for Ovid's source, the Homeric Hymn to Dionysos), were diag-
nostic, inaugural discriminations in a series that came to include,
among many others, Homer again in Canto XX's dangerously
"ringing, keen song" of the sirens, *ligur'aoide*, and in Canto
LXXIV's "sound ever moving / in diminutive poluphloisbois / in
the stillness outlasting all wars." From the full scale of notes in
Homer, Pound was reminding us, our own heroic tradition reso-
nated with several (harried wandering and loss of comrades). Diag-
nostic and demonstrative, this equation became personal in *The
Pisan Cantos*: "Lordly men are to earth o'ergiven." By that point
any polemical intent had receded; other proof had come home,
upon the breath of the oarsman, and it moves us accordingly.

Near the end of *Briggflatts*, as Bunting tallies the rising of
the principal stars over the Northumbrian shore, he sees among
them a longboat:

---

6. *The Dial* LXXII (May 1922), 505.

> Capella floats from the north
> with shields hung on his gunwale.

In Auriga or the Charioteer, Capella (Pliny's "rainy Goat-Starre") trails three lesser stars in close tow: Bunting's glimpse is exact. But this moment also caps Bunting's reaction to heroic elegy in the poem. This quiet processional cadence for the bardic in *Briggflatts* rises as Sign over the thorough keeping which he has managed, all the while that he has kept his scavenging rodent's beat in darkness: the arriving starlight is thirty-five years old, and the Viking aura more than thirty-five generations. More than Pound, and more, certainly, than Auden, Bunting has brought to his scavenging among the bones a need that was his own, while acknowledging their antiquity and the distance across which the light has made its way to us.

The occasional American who squints at the poems of W.S. Merwin or Galway Kinnell and dubiously mutters, "bardic," of course applies that term in the only way his circumstances allow. For along with the poems whose manner he resists, he too inhabits a civilization that withers traditional culture. His resistance, then, to whispers or intonations of a darkly primal fundamental whose wisdom may be a style of saying, acquires an anomalous character: his pejorative term is itself a former casualty on the side of the resistance. In this style his critique looks as curious, in its way, as Kinnell's donning of bloody bearskins or Merwin's riddling with the ozone in sepulchres. Given the pitfalls of such usage, it may seem startling to recognize that the work of the Scots-Gaelic poet Sorley Maclean still lends precise meaning to the term, in poems such as "Hallaig," or the elegy for Calum I. Maclean, or "Heroes" from the desert campaign in Egypt (although of course Gaelic culture stands gravely threatened). And *Briggflatts* in quite another way, more narrowly but still authentically, restores to the term its meaning.

Auden, in the early poems which adapt Anglo-Saxon, projects an heroic-elegiac fantasy onto an engineered diction and phrasing. Subtly, his motive was psychologistic; a temporary rhetoric for a fledging heroic self was his need, beyond which the poems did not need to go. Lowell, like Auden intrigued by the control and dispersal of a personal tone, of course found this invention remarkable. By contrast, the need which Bunting brought to a comparable language in *Briggflatts* was not simply dramatic and personal, for he also sought what his fourth section secured: initiation into time and a hierarchy of language with no sacrifice of objective perception. That endeavor sets Bunting alive among his antecedents in a way which American poets, for all of our romantic apostrophes to the wraith of rootedness, have not managed for ourselves.

† † † † †

Were Edwin Muir to have read Bunting's poem, he would have commented, I believe, not only on its Wordsworthian access to time but also on the Fable to which its interlinked Stories implicitly bear witness. The presiding genius of the poem is music; the love laid aside, or murdered, returns with the redemption of Then in Now; and the dualities of Bunting's own nature, projected into the poem's range of figures and its composite topography, sound the entire vertical scale, from Alexander's glimpse of Israfel, horn at the ready, down to identity with the rat who rummages through "Schoenberg's maze." These themes and interpenetrating worlds, with the announced music, fill out a Fable which is not announced: that of Orpheus.

Pressed too far this claim becomes merely ingenious. But also in a way it must be acknowledged. To the extent that we acknowledge it we set the poem's bardic features on their most archaic ground.

The third and final stanza of the poem's "Coda" places in question the historical connectedness which the poem's moments of communion have conjured. These final words serve as a ritual disenchantment from the spells woven by "strong song"—and they work powerfully to reinstate a sensible scepticism which, looking backward and then forward along time's tunnel, echoes the fourth section's counsel: "Follow the clue patiently and you will understand nothing."

> Where we are who knows
> of kings who sup
> while day fails? Who,
> swinging his axe
> to fell kings, guesses
> where we go? (59)

The poem's own lopped kingly head, of course, belongs to Eric Bloodaxe; axe falls to axe, spell to dispelling. But even as this coda breaks the spell, it reminds us that the conjuring had joined Bunting's profile with Bloodaxe's.

Reverting from this coda to the poem's climaxes, then, we more consciously enter the spell. And the death of Bloodaxe in the second section leads into a sequence surprisingly Orphic in connotation. After the beheading and scavenging of the corpse there follow discrete stanzas on creatures of the shoreline, the desert, and an English bog-orchard in summer: starfish, crab, vulture, roe, vixen, rat, and wind-lofted spider. Some of these creatures rhyme with music (Monteverdi, Schoenberg, the mazurka). The sequence seems a pleasant descriptive modulation away from Bloodaxe's beheading into Pasiphae's coupling, an exquisite bestiary gallery. But even in outline this modulation suggests more. After the severed head comes a stream of animals tallied with strains of music, ending with a god-animal in the heat of love (the minotaur will be its issue). In part this sequence suggests the animals and music of the slain Orpheus, and in part something else of "unlike creation."

These suggestions only hover, for the composition compels them to. But the effect remains remarkable. I think of Muir's comment on the imagery for another severed head in Hölderlin's "Patmos":

Two separate aspects of time appear to be fused in the lines

> *and the plucked head*
> *Of the Baptist was like unfading script*
> *Visible on the unscathed dish.*

This image is static, in spite of its violent fusion of strange elements, but beneath its surface an unknown mode of change seems to be working, so that the effect is both of rest and motion.[7]

That "unknown mode of change" also seems to work beneath the surface of Bunting's second section, or in his third section's passage from Alexander to the slowworm and anonymous revenant. My warrant for attaching this power as Muir has phrased it to the Orphic Fable derives from that myth's redemptive struggle with the orders of both nature and time. Muir's description of Hölderlin could fit that struggle. Oddly coincident with part of Muir's phrasing is the title of a poem by Richard Pevear, "Motion and Rest," in which the head of Orpheus, as it floats down the Hebrus, sings every feature of his story, the animal enchantments of course among them.

> the head of
> Orpheus, singing
>
> Toward Lesbos, held out in a constant moment
> All that he was. . . .[8]

---

7. *Essays on Literature and Society*, rev. and enl. edition (Cambridge, 1967), pp. 97-98.
8. *Night Talk* and Other Poems (Princeton, 1977), p. 18.

Such is the Fable. Sighting back from it along Hölderlin's lines about St. John the Baptist, we can see one thing: only the power of song, or of the unfading script, can contain that unknown mode of change which so strangely brings the coordinates of time, place, and identity into transformed relation. It would be surprising after all if the music in Bunting's second section had nothing to do with this other music, neither galliard nor lament.

If the sceptic pulls back, of course he still has the warrant of Bunting's "Coda." But that coda needs to resolve Then and Now back into historical time, precisely because the poem has fused aspects of time into sequences through which "an unknown mode of change seems to be working." That working produces a quality from which even the sceptic will not withdraw, however: observation of a whole and continuous way of life, the communal form of the "constant moment." That is another way of describing the bardic function, and the most concrete way, proved upon the homeliest qualities of continuity. If times fuse within such observation, they do so only through what has been kept truly at hand. This observation comes when Bunting thinks of the dead at Cattraeth: "Girls in Teesdale and Wensleydale wake discontent." It forms the tenor of Sorley Maclean's "Hallaig" (these stanzas are his own prose versions):

> I will wait for the birch wood
> until it comes up by the cairn,
> until the whole ridge from Beinn na Lice
> will be under its shade.
>
> If it does not, I will go down to Hallaig,
> to the Sabbath of the dead,
> where the people are frequenting,
> every single generation gone.
>   . . . . .
> The men lying on the green
> at the end of every house that was,
> the girls a wood of birches,
> straight their backs, bent their heads.[9]

It brings each register of Orkney life into the "Sea Orpheus" of George Mackay Brown (to whom Palsson and Edwards dedicate their 1978 translation of the *Orkneyinga Saga*). Both island farmers and fishermen enter the poem's beginning, in the undersea realm of a drowning:

---

9. *Spring Tide and Neap Tide: Selected Poems 1932-72* (Edinburgh, 1977), pp. 142-4.

A plough and barley fiddle
For one tide-raped girl
Sang in the looms of the sea.
Driftwood red as lashes
Scored the strings, seals
Clustered around (old salts
They swig shanties like ale,
They shine like bottles).
           The fiddle
Stretched one thin strand across
The warp of the ebb.[10]

The affinity of such lines with passages in *Briggflatts*, though the Orkneys will never come to Northumbria, seems to me no chance harmony.

The affinity shows even when Bunting's inweaving refers to his poem's elements first of all, rather than immediately to the life of his region. These lines from the last section chime against earlier motifs (adorned Italy, Pasiphae's pungent sweat, bone grit, the mason) and at the same time give us the Northumbrian shore. As the features of Orkney life weave through Mackay Brown's lines, so Bunting's motifs do through these, natively and firmly.

           Sing,
strewing the notes on the air
as ripples skip in a shallow. Go
bare, the shore is adorned
with pungent weed loudly
filtering sand and sea.
Silver blades of surf
fall crisp on rustling grit,
shaping the shore as a mason
fondles and shapes his stone. (56-7)

It happens that Bunting has known what it means to rub down a gravestone with his own hands. But even without that knowledge we can see that the poem's earlier epitaph, cut into ice and strewn over waves, here is supplanted by a sturdier one, cut in the poem's landscape by the poem's seas.

Both this passage and Mackay Brown's, with the features of the continuously known, construct that double aspect which Muir elucidates in Hölderlin, the motion and rest which meet in the Orphic Fable and its images. "Orphic" we may or may not choose to say; but such images amount to what some men call music even as they read them as stories, held. as they are between both qualities in the singleness of their experience. And to that music bardic *Briggflatts* attunes itself.

---

10. *Poems New and Selected* (New York, 1973), p. 20.

M. L. ROSENTHAL

STREAMS OF TONALITY IN BUNTING'S BRIGGFLATTS

Briggflatts came to us in Ezra's long wake, a gathering of Basil Bunting's finest possibilities after what seemed a long poetic slumber. The affinities and derivations are clear. *Briggflatts* even has its hell-canto: Part III, with the requisite scatological smell. In general, the sequence presents the usual Poundian mixture of tonalities that has influenced so many other works as well—the affirmations amidst bitter alienation, the rhetorical fulminations against the evils of modern urban culture, the moments of sharpest observation or dancing fantasy or passionate memory, the flash of ironic or exalted insight connecting the real or mythical past with the present instant, and the devout aestheticism that yet does not blur an essential harsh clarity and even fatalism about life as it is.

Bunting has neither the master's scope and copiousness nor his powerful originality. Yet within the Poundian shell he has made a small, pure creation of his own: a living stream of verse that makes its way from beginning to end, disappearing from sight at times when the urge to bluster and convince takes over or the voices of other poets (not only Pound but a chorus of others from Tennyson to Austin Clarke and Auden) create a kind of static. Or one should say, rather, that certain streams of tonality combine to form an essentially elegiac poem compounded of lyrically celebratory elements and tormenting personal memories of young love and the hard but wholesome life of artisans—memories betrayed by the poet's abandonment of the provincial world of his youth. This is the world of Northumbria and its Anglo-Saxon past, evoked by direct historical reference and by the recurrent use of a starkly alliterative, compressed line. The evocation of a more primitive native culture, with its axe-swinging warriors, earthy basic language, and immersion in raw contact with resistant nature, is a parallel stream of tonality intermingling with the others. It contributes an insistent melancholy to the sequence and reinforces the idealized memory of the stone-mason at the center of the poet's nostalgia for his youthful past. The stonemason's materials and cutting skills were exercised against the same resistant nature with which ancient folk contended. To have left his tutelage, and the love of his daughter, is identified with turning one's back on the life and language and history of the region.

Part I of *Briggflatts* is the heart of the sequence and its most fully successful section. Its dozen thirteen-line stanzas, each ending in a rhyming couplet, combine Anglo-Saxon with modern versification in flexible units allowing for complex development and for many shifts of feeling and intensity. The exquisite opening stanza is at once sheer song, charming comedy, and ominous vision; it is saturated with a sense of local place and with the mixture of elated spirits and near-lugubriousness characteristic of the whole work:

> Brag, sweet tenor bull,
> descant on Rawthey's madrigal,
> each pebble its part
> for the fells' late spring.
> Dance tiptoe, bull,
> black against may.
> Ridiculous and lovely
> chase hurdling shadows
> morning into noon.
> May on the bull's hide
> and through the dale
> furrows fill with may,
> paving the slowworm's way.

The familiar linking of vital sexuality with the death-principle is implicit here, but held at a distance by the sheer delightful buffoonery of the first half of the stanza. We have been charmed into the dominant tonal realm of the sequence, where currents of buoyancy and power and decay and fatality constantly flow together in varying proportions. Then, in the second stanza, the mingling of opposites (spring and fertility, intractable reality and death) continues in a grimmer key; notice how much more emphatic the final couplet is here:

> A mason times his mallet
> to a lark's twitter,
> listening while the marble rests,
> lays his rule
> at a letter's edge,
> fingertips checking,
> till the stone spells a name
> naming none,

a man abolished.
Painful lark, labouring to rise!
The solemn mallet says:
In the grave's slot
he lies. We rot.

The middle stanzas (5-9) of this opening poem center on the
very young (pubescent?) lovers. The fifth stanza, especially, evokes
the homespun passion and magic of that remembered time, placing
it within its context of a world of hardworking folk whose speech
and history are vividly related to their everyday life. We see the
"children" in their astringent Eden, lying together in the horse-
drawn lorry the mason uses to fetch marble for his trade:

> Stocking to stocking, jersey to jersey,
> head to a hard arm,
> they kiss under the rain,
> bruised by their marble bed.
> In Garsdale, dawn;
> at Hawes, tea from the can.
> Rain stops, sacks
> steam in the sun, they sit up.
> Copper-wire moustache,
> sea-reflecting eyes
> and Baltic plainsong speech
> declare: By such rocks
> men killed Bloodaxe.

Apart from the fey lyricism of the poem's opening lines,
Bunting's great achievement in this first movement of *Briggflatts* is
his recovery of a lost world of reality: its decisive sensuous detail,
the body of its physical presence. Thus, two stanzas further on,
the journeyers are home again.

> Rain rinses the road,
> the bull streams and laments.
> Sour rye porridge from the hob
> with cream and black tea,
> meat, crust and crumb.
> Her parents in bed
> the children dry their clothes.
> He has untied the tape
> of her striped flannel drawers
> before the range. Naked
> on the pricked rag mat
> his fingers comb
> thatch of his manhood's home.

The nostalgia here may be too pungent, the baby-sexuality
recalled may seem at once sentimental and a little brackish, but
the atmosphere summoned up in this stanza and in the quotation

preceding it has the authority of deeply significant memory. The authority is reinforced by the more impersonal memory imbedded in the older regional language throughout this section: "Their becks ring on limestone," "fellside bleat," "fog on fells"—and with it the heavy stresses and echoes of an ancient poetry. Neither the historical nor the impersonal past can be restored: "No hope of going back." Even the recovery in words alone is painfully difficult, like the mason's work: "It is easier to die than to remember." And yet the opening poem *has* remembered, in the face of a debilitating depression that rides almost every stanza and that controls the whole sequence except in certain limited respects.

The four remaining sections of *Briggflatts* cope with the work's prevailing depressive perspective in various ways. One way is the exaltation of disciplined workmanship with intractable materials: "No worn tool / whittles stone." The axe swung by fighting forebears, and their language that was a sharp, rock-splitting weapon in its own right, were tools for a different kind of stone-masonry. So the work presents a staunch ideal, although the imagery of cultural defeat is pervasive. In Part II, the inevitable defeat of the axe-wielders is presented in terms suggesting a cultural betrayal comparable to the Poundian view of the modern world:

> Loaded with mail of linked lies,
> what weapon can the king lift to fight
> when chance-met enemies employ sly
> sword and shoulder-piercing pike,
> pressed into the mire,
> trampled and hewn till a knife
> —in whose hand?—severs tight
> neck cords? Axe rusts . . .

In the same section, music and mythology are mobilized as sources of morale for the poem. The struggle of the defeated king in the lines just quoted finds a curious parallel in men's efforts to encompass natural process in the organic structures of music and the myth of Pasiphaë. The musical theme is developed in four subtly unfolding sexains that take us from a simple, pleasant equation—

> Starfish, poinsettia on a half-tide crag,
> a galliard by Byrd—

to the more complex, deliberately unattractive proposition that a

> rat, grey, rummaging
> behind the compost heap has daring
> to thread, lithe and alert, Schoenberg's maze.

The mythical motif is introduced in the concluding, and climactic, stanza of the section. This stanza reinforces the impression created in Part I of the sequence that the most intense notes of affirmation in *Briggflatts* will have an almost pornographic glow of erotic transport. Now Part II ends with the lines on Pasiphaë—who, we are told,

> heard the god-bull's feet
> scattering sand,
> breathed byre stink, yet stood
> with expectant hand
> to guide his seed to its soil;
> nor did flesh flinch
> distended by the brute
> nor loaded spirit sink
> till it had gloried in unlike creation.

Part II has a rather wandering movement. It begins with the language of utter desolation, in a familiar, even trite, poetic mode. The alienated poet walks through London's streets, disheartened by the same things that have disheartened Blake, Wordsworth, and Eliot before him. (One difference, however, is the sexual obsessiveness that colors his sense of, and participation in, metropolitan squalor.) Then the poem turns away from the city with its available "sluts" and consequent opportunities for the poet to grow "sick, self-maimed, self-hating." Suddenly a language of self-questioning is introduced that lifts the poem's sensibility out of the romantically autobiographical morass.

And suddenly, again, we are in the midst of a fantasy-voyage in cold northern seas, its context that of the Anglo-Saxon "Wanderer." The shift of poetic focus culminates in a fatalistic intoning endemic to such verse. And after this passage, once more abruptly and arbitrarily, we are borne toward the appealingly sensual south—escape to Italy and lush experience, with the language reminiscent of Browning's "The Englishman in Italy." This mood, too, alters. It is too easy and free for Anglo-Saxon conscience to bear, a desertion of the worlds of chisel and mallet and rime-cold sea and the ever-presence of deprivation and uneaseful death: "wind, sun, sea upbraid / justly an unconvinced deserter."

So Italy is left behind. With its "white marble stained like a urinal" and its innumerable teeming dead, it is no genuine salvation. The poem must return to the true ground of its being. It must face directly into the challenge, despite near-hopelessness and a sense of helpless corruption, of certain native realities: the region of one's birth and early life and inherited history, the cultivation of a somehow indigenous art despite cosmopolitan seductions, and the repossession, sweatily and experientially, of certain mythical events—a repossession like Ovid's but at greater risk because crucial personal commitment is at stake. The events (Pasiphaë and the bull) are conceived as projections of agonizing, probably destructive elementary choices entailing an oddly hard-pressed ecstasy.

From here on the sequence strikes various balances in the long struggle with a profoundly depressive state. Part III is the "hell-canto" of *Briggflatts*, seeing modern man as reduced to dung-selling in the marketplace. Only the cleansing rhythms of nature can purge away the vision of sheer foulness that presides over this section. Parts IV and V, after the drop of III into the abyss of total revulsion, settle into something like release through acceptance of life's meanness and living within one's emotional means. Part IV finds sources of energy in the candor and death-preoccupation of Cymric poetry. The poet accepts poverty, a new and very earthy love, the plainest satisfactions, along with his irrevocable separation from the stonemason's world. Separation nevertheless breaks the heart permanently:

> Stars disperse. We too,
> further from neighbours
> now the year ages.

These lines, at the end of IV, make a transition to the very lyrical Part V, which in many ways approaches Part I in its formal character. There is no rhetoric to mar the melody of this movement, which begins with winter-images rather than the images of spring in the opening stanza of I. The sequence has returned home, finding sufficient calm and an entrancement with the winter landscape that together make for a special music of sheer perception, even when what is perceived is chill and barren:

> Light lifts from the water.
> Frost has put rowan down,
> a russet blotch of bracken
> tousled about the trunk.
> Bleached sky. Cirrus
> reflects sun that has left
> nothing to badger eyes.

Because it is in part a reprise of earlier sections, and because it also moves into a wider, cosmic frame of reference, Section V is slightly overextended. Otherwise, however, its precise conversion of feeling into a distanced, impersonal language of impressionistic nature-description is as effective as it is surprising at this critical point in the sequence. Bunting chose to end, not with a bang *or* a whimper, but with a straightforward yet elegantly controlled movement whose reverberations are at once joyous and cool until a few notes of loss and regret chime in at the very last. Of course, the "Coda" that follows plunges the work into the sea of primordial despondency again. So be it. Bunting's real reputation will surely hang on *Briggflatts*. It is his one masterpiece of affective balancing, despite the problems I have suggested.

L. S. DEMBO

BUNTING'S BRIGGFLATTS: *A Strong Song to Tow Us*

Put off by Bunting's insistence that his major poem, *Briggflatts*, is to be listened to for its music alone and that the "attempt to find any meaning in it would be manifestly absurd," Peter Dale, with Coleridge as authority, has argued that poetry is (of course) "not a matter of mere sound," but an "infinitely intricate balance of paired opposites, including sound and sense; reason and emotion." Bunting, he asserts, "massively contradicts himself in that meaning is easy enough to detect in *Briggflatts*."[1] Dale is not entirely unconvincing, especially since he is able to give a synopsis in which that meaning is clear. Thus, he explains,

> the poem is divided into five movements and the overall plan is Spring, Summer, Autumn, Winter, with an interlude of what Bunting has called a dream or nightmare inserted in the middle. The bull, of the opening passage, recurs as the theme of nature's fecundity and renewal at various points; the male principle seems to be echoed again in the slowworm's behaviour. This theme is reflected in the human sphere by what seems a reminiscence of a love affair with a mason's daughter and the mature reflections and lyrics on love that occur later. The theme of the mason carving a headstone introduces the subject of writing which forms another motif running through the poem. . . . The theme of music also recurs intermittently in references to Schoenberg, Domenico Scarlatti, and others, tenor bulls and flutes. . . . These references and the writing-theme make it yet another of those modern works whose subject is self-reference and the problems of the writer. Bloodaxe and Cuthbert provide the standard touch of history. (57)

This description is precisely what Dale implied that it was: an account of the "meaning" that is easily detectable in the poem; indeed his perfunctory tone confirms that Dale experienced no

---

1. "Basil Bunting and the Quonk and Groggle School of Poetry," *Agenda*, 16, No. 1 (1978), 55-65.

joy of discovery (as it were) when this meaning emerged. Nor was
he any more impressed when it came to the "music" itself, which
in his estimation turns out to be "primitive" and simplistic, certainly no advance in the "musical tradition." "Both in its use of
sound and its gesture toward musical structure," he tells us, *Briggflatts* "is rather obvious and not a little contrived." "The poem is
tediously dominated by the simple sentence, extended by apposi-
tional developments to subject and object." "Syntactical boredom" is only one of a number of effects mentioned by Dale that
we need not go into here.

I have spent this much time presenting Dale's view because
it is sufficiently persuasive, in its apparent common sense, to require a response by anyone who does not believe that Bunting
should be relegated once and for all to the ranks of the obscure
from which he only recently, after decades of neglect, arose. I
admit that Bunting's remarks about *Briggflatts*, as well as about
those who would "analyze" it, are less than encouraging; nonetheless, I am convinced that any view that judges this poem, in
its music or meaning, to be primitive and simplistic is itself guilty
of those very sins.

It was John Crowe Ransom who pointed out that the sound
(meter) meaning relationship was not simply the untroubled one
in which, as in say onomatopoeia, sense is reflected in sound.
Rather he argued just the opposite: when one element was determined, the other became indeterminate. That is to say, if the poet
has a rhythm in his head, he will seek those words in which the
rhythm is expressed and any number of meanings are possible,
just so long as they go with words that manifest the rhythm.
Conversely, when a specific meaning is uppermost in the poet's
mind, the sound becomes indeterminate, insofar as the words
expressing that meaning can be arranged according to any number
of sound-patterns. Thus for Ransom all poems contain a dialec-
tical process in which opposites are brought to a resolution.

This theory is instructive if for no other reason than that it
discredits once and for all that simplistic view in which one assumes that sound is a "mirror" of sense, no more, no less. This
does not, however, end all discussion of the subject. When it
comes to "musical structure," the aspect of the sound-sense problem that has preoccupied Bunting throughout a lifetime, does the
same situation pertain? Does Bunting's infatuation with the sonata
in fact make all his themes "indeterminate" and therefore secondary? So he would have us believe. In this he is like that other
poet-musician, Louis Zukofsky, who also made sound-patterns

his primary consideration.

Now it is no accident that Bunting and Zukofsky (as Pound and Eliot) have all, at one time or another, explicitly or indirectly, expressed an aversion to revealing details about their personal lives, especially in poetry. Neither poet will admit to being *merely* autobiographical in his "autobiographical" long-poem. While Zukofsky, for instance, asserts that *"A"* is in "a sense autobiography," he quickly makes it clear that he is using this term in a special way: "The words are my life;" he says and continues: "The form of the poem is organic—that is, involved in history and a life that has found by contrast to history something like perfection in the music of J.S. Bach."[2] What Bach is to Zukofsky, Scarlatti is to Bunting:

> It is time to consider how Domenico Scarlatti
> condensed so much music into so few bars
> with never a crabbed turn or congested cadence,
> never a boast or a see-here; and stars and lakes
> echo him and the copse drums out his measure,
> snow peaks are lifted up in moonlight and twilight
> and the sun rises on an acknowledged land. (*Briggflatts* IV)[3]

Not only does an ideal of music (the Scarlatti sonata) here serve as a model for poetry and implicitly for a way of life, it also appears to be taken as a means for imposing an order on nature in the manner of Wallace Stevens (whose singing woman "measured to the hour its solitude" and indirectly "mastered the night and portioned out the sea / . . . Arranging, deepening, enchanting night").

This passage is typical of Bunting in its movement, without transitions, from one level of meaning to another. What might begin as mere description, in *Briggflatts*, frequently becomes evocative lyric or part of a "musical structure" in which various elements, images, motifs, symbols, or associations are integrated. It is just such integration that thematically and formally is the aim of the poet-lover-speaker of *Briggflatts*, as it is indeed of Bunting, who, like Zukofsky, is seeking to transform "autobiography" into the perfection of music. Accordingly, the sense of disintegration in all its many forms becomes a primary source of emotion. Like *The Waste Land*, that model of the highly unified poem that proclaims universal disunity, *Briggflatts* in fact achieves an integration on the level of form that belies one of its principal themes:

---

2. Statement made for dust cover of *"A" 1-12* (London: Jonathan Cape, 1966).
3. I have used the 1968 edition of *The Collected Poems* (London: Fulcrum). Since *Briggflatts* is divided into fairly short parts, I have given only the section number for the quotations.

> No worn tool
>   whittles stone;
> but a reproached
>   uneasy mason
>
> shaping evasive
>   ornament
> litters his yard
>   with flawed fragments. (II)

Flawed fragments? A heap of broken images? Perhaps.

In taking the mason and masonry as a metaphor for the poet and poetry, Bunting is actually seeking a form or "shape" for his own (literally autobiographical) experiences. On this point he is most explicit:

> I've rubbed down gravestones and that's how I know how it feels to rub down a gravestone. And how your fingers ache on the damn job . . . and so on. I take care not to write anything that I don't bloody well know. And that is something that is different I think from a lot of poets who write. If I write about how it feels rubbing down a gravestone, well I have rubbed down a bloody gravestone. . . . If I write nautical technicalities, they're those of a guy who's sailed a lot, and so on. . . .[4]

Conversely, the pains of actual masonry are, by metaphor, transmuted into those of the poet-narrator:

> Brief words are hard to find,
> shapes to carve and discard
>
> . . . .
>
> Take no notice of tears;
> letter the stone to stand (I)

But the point is that these lines are a refutation of the very statement they make: "Brief words are hard to find. . . ." are themselves the brief words that Bunting has found to express his theme. Hence his description of Eric Bloodaxe, a tenth-century Northumbrian warrior-king, who is taken to be both an appropriate subject for the Northumbrian "bard" (for example, the poet-narrator) and also as a metaphor for the poet-figure himself. (Bloodaxe, "king of York, / king of Dublin, king of Orkney," was supposedly assassinated at Stainmore.) In this passage Bunting, still dealing with autobiographical material, suggests that the distractions of a love-affair must be renounced if the epic poet is to fulfill his mission:

> Take no notice of tears;   [hers, no doubt]
> letter the stone to stand

---

4. "Basil Bunting Talks about *Briggflatts*," *Agenda*, 16, No. 1 (1978), 12.

over love laid aside lest   [a tombstone to commemo-
insufferable happiness impede   rate a love that has been laid
flight to Stainmore,   aside]
to trace
lark, mallet,   ["A mason times his mallet /
becks, flocks   to a lark's twitter"]
and axe knocks.

An earlier passage had already presented this image of the epic poet:

Copper-wire moustache,
sea-reflecting eyes
and Baltic plainsong speech
declare: By such rocks
men killed Bloodaxe.

Fierce blood throbs in his tongue,
lean words.

But this ideal of poetic utterance, stone carving, with its claims to permanence and immortality both for itself and its subject, is counterpointed with this assertion on the harsh realities of life:

Dung will not soil the slowworm's [the *slay* worm, so-called be-
mosaic. Breathless lark   cause of its poisonous sting.]
drops to nest in sodden trash;
. . . .
Drudge at the mallet, the may is down,
fog on fells. . . .
. . . .
It is easier to die than to remember.
Name and date
split in soft slate
a few months obliterate. (I)

That it "is easier to die than to remember" is the crux of the matter; it is the chief cause of the poet's failure to create the work that will commemorate lost love or legendary past. "To humiliate love, remember / nothing."

Ironically, the poet is never more articulate than when he is lamenting his incapacity. Describing the murder of Bloodaxe in the passage immediately following the "flawed fragments" lines, Bunting displays his linguistic virtuosity. Since one easily misses the forest because of the trees, I take the liberty of directing attention to the sound pattern created by the last word in each line:

Loaded with mail of linked lies,
what weapon can the king lift to fight
when chance-met enemies employ sly
sword and shoulder-piercing pike,

> pressed into the mire,
> trampled and hewn till a knife
> —in whose hand?—severs tight
> neck cords? Axe rusts. Spine
> picked bare by ravens, agile
> maggots devour the slack side
> and inert brain, never wise.
> What witnesses he had life,
> ravelled and worn past splice,
> yarns falling to staple? Rime
> on the bent, the beck ice,
> there will be nothing on Stainmore to hide
> void, no sable to disguise
> what he wore under the lies,
> king of Orkney, king of Dublin, twice
> king of York, where the tide
> stopped till long flight
> from who knows what smile,
> scowl, disgust or delight
> ended in bale on the fellside. (II)

Not only does every line conclude with a word containing a long *i*, but the last dozen or so lines have a rhyme scheme, which, though slightly irregular, points toward a kind of unity and harmony. This is to say nothing of the alliterations that pervade the whole passage. Thematically, Bloodaxe is here associated with the failed poet; just as the mason has no tool, Bloodaxe has no weapon, and is weighted down with his own chain mail (here explicitly equated with "lies"—or language abused). Anthony Suter has suggested that Bloodaxe symbolizes the vainglorious poet and one cannot but agree;[5] but this figure also represents the way in which Bunting sees himself.

In any case, this passage, written in the "brief words hard to find" that mark ideal poetry, is no less a monument, a memorial etched on stone, an epitaph, given form by the sound pattern that is its "music." Peter Dale's complaint that Bunting wrote only simple sentences and was guilty of inspiring only "syntactical boredom" surely misses the point.

Certain exotic things, Bunting tells us, have their (musical) form. Thus "Starfish, poinsettia on a half-tide crag," are like a galliard by the pre-Bach English composer, William Byrd. And anemones, which "spite" mere "cullers ·of ornament" ("flawed fragments"), "design the pool / to their grouping." "The hermit crab," says Bunting, referring to Hermit crabs and solitary poets, "is no grotesque in such company." And the "Asian vulture" or

---

5. "Art and Experience: Basil Bunting's Ideal of Poetry," *Durham University Journal* 66, 307-14.

"desert ass" "figures sudden flight of the descant / on a madrigal by Monteverdi." Unfortunately, these are not the *materia poetica* with which Bunting's poet must deal; rather it is

> a bogged orchard,
> its blossom gone,
> fruit unformed, where hunger and
> damp hush the hive. . . .
> A disappointed July full of codling
> moth and ragged lettuces. . . .

Yet even this blighted land has its "musical forms":

> roe are there, rise to the fence, insolent;
> a scared vixen cringes
> red against privet stems as a mazurka;
> and rat, grey, rummaging
> behind the compost heap has daring
> to thread, lithe and alert, Schoenberg's maze.

"Schoenberg's maze" apparently leads Bunting to think of another maze, the labyrinth of Crete, and the bull that first appeared in the opening lines ("sweet tenor bull") as an image of poetry, and implicitly of rebirth and immortality, set against the slowworm of death, now reemerges in the legend of Pasiphae, who gave birth to the minotaur after having had intercourse with a sacred bull. Pasiphae's passion for the bull, at least in one version of the myth, was satisfied by an artificial cow made for her by Daedalus. This would scarcely do, however, for a poet celebrating the violent drama of spring, death, rebirth, and creation:

> men
> driven by storm fret,
> reminded of sweltering Crete
> and Pasiphae's pungent sweat,
> who heard the god-bull's feet
> scattering sand,
> . . . yet stood
> with expectant hand
> to guide his seed to its soil;
> nor did flesh flinch
> distended by the brute
> nor loaded spirit sink
> till it had gloried in unlike creation.

This event is but the mythic variation of the activity that opens the poem. The "sweet tenor bull," here shown in a mating dance, is associated both with the poet-singer and poet-lover: "Dance tiptoe, bull, / black against may. / Ridiculous and lovely / chase hurdling shadows / morning into noon."

My quarrel with Peter Dale is not that he has failed to see the "meaning" in *Briggflatts*; to the contrary, I have already suggested that his description of the themes and motifs is, as far as it goes, accurate enough. The trouble is that, perhaps taking Bunting at his word, Dale seems to view these elements as "flawed fragments" and to be content with merely listing them, whereas I believe that Bunting is working toward an integration of them so complete as to justify his regarding the poem as a form of music.

If any single passage can be said to provide an insight into the overall conception of *Briggflatts*, it is the one that appears toward the end of Part V, in which Bunting deals mainly with the Northumbrian coast in winter and the constellations visible during this season:

> Furthest, fairest things, stars, free of our humbug,
> each his own, the longer known the more alone,
> wrapt in emphatic fire roaring out to a black flue.
> Each spark trills on a tone beyond chronological compass,
> yet in a sextant's bubble present and firm
> places a surveyor's stone or steadies a tiller.
> Then is Now. The star you steer by is gone,
> its tremulous thread spun in the hurricane
> spider floss on my cheek; light from the zenith
> spun when the slowworm lay in her lap
> fifty years ago. (V)

The stars belong to an order of reality that "beyond chronological compass" is ultimately beyond analysis ("our humbug"). In this, they are akin to poems in general or even to the present poem in particular. This notion had been presented in Part IV in a somewhat different form:

> Let the fox have his fill, patient leech and weevil,
> cattle refer the rising of Sirius to their hedge horizon,
> runts murder the sacred calves of the sea by rule
> heedless of herring gull, surf and the text carved by waves
> on the skerry.

The text carved by the waves on the skerry is beyond human intellect, with its rules and measures; perhaps only a poet or musician could begin to "comprehend" it:

> Can you trace shuttles thrown
> like drops from a fountain, spray, mist of spiderlines
> bearing the rainbow, quoits round the draped moon;
> shuttles like random dust desert whirlwinds hoy at their
>   tormenting sun?
> Follow the clue patiently and you will understand nothing.

Those who patiently follow clues—scholars, critics, and all others who would probe the unprobeable—are like lice, who, discontent

with the small dimensions of the world they inhabit (the seams of
a jacket),

> crawl with toil to glimpse
> from its shoulder wall of flame which could they reach
> they'd crackle like popcorn in a skillet.

The image here is apparently that of a jacket, no doubt the poet's
own, hung up to dry beside the fireplace during a storm. And we
learn shortly thereafter the literal source of this metaphor:

> My love is young but wise. Oak, applewood,
> her fire is banked with ashes till day.
> The fells reek of her hearth's scent,
> her girdle [griddle, skillet] is greased with lard;
> hunger is stayed on her settle, lust in her bed.
> Light as spider floss her hair on my cheek which a puff
> scatters.

Just as the flame (Reality) is to be associated with the stars ("wrapt
in emphatic firing roaring out to a black flue") in Part V, so the
spider floss will again evoke memories of the lady, even though
this time it, too, is associated with the stars ("the star you steer by
is gone / its tremulous thread spun in the hurricane / spider floss
on my cheek.")

Both the lady and the star have long since been "gone." Yet
through its light, the latter can still serve as a point of reference
("in a sextant's bubble present and firm, [it] places a surveyor's
stone or steadies a tiller."). The lady, identified with the star
Capella, accordingly serves through memory as a point of reference for the poet; she is "light from Zenith / spun . . . fifty years
ago," a light by which Then becomes Now, and the past is re-
captured.

A solitary adrift in the squalid world of the present, ("where
rats go go I, / accustomed to penury, / filth, disgust and fury")
the poet seeks to turn his memories, both personal and cultural,
into song, monument, or sonata, for herein lies what orientation
or salvation is possible in a trackless universe governed only by
entropy ("Stars disperse. We too."). In such a world the slowworm's song of death and disintegration is everywhere:

> O, writhe to its measure!
> Dust swirling scans pleasure.
> Thorns prance in a gale.
> In air snow flickers,
> . . . .
> So he rose and led home silently through clean woodland
> where every bough repeated the slowworm's song. (III)

And, for Bunting, this is the song that prevails:

> A strong song tows
> us, long earsick.
> Blind, we follow
> rain slant, spray flick
> to fields we do not know. (Coda)

All connection with the past is severed:

> Where we are who knows
> of kings who sup
> while day fails? Who,
> swinging his axe
> to fell kings, guesses
> where we go?

On this inconclusive note *Briggflatts* ends.

There is, of course, nothing remarkable about this conclusion —not when we think of the many other modern quest poems that ended with the poet's doubt about the outcome of his quest and despair over his inability to see the ideal realized in the modern world. "What's lost, what's left?" is a question asked by the authors of *The Waste Land, The Bridge, Paterson, The Maximus Poems*, as well as of *Briggflatts*. Their readers know what is left: the poem itself; and for some of them at least that is an even stronger song than the one that tows us to nowhere.

ANTHONY SUTER

BRIGGFLATTS *AND THE RESURRECTION OF*
BASIL BUNTING

It is now nearly thirty years since Hugh Kenner (in a review
of *Poems 1950* in *Poetry*) called Basil Bunting a "resurrected
poet," but Bunting's "resurrection" came in the sixties. *Poems
1950* and *The Spoils* (1951) made no deep impression on a fifties'
England that was turning its back on a European tradition and
"foreign influences" that Bunting's work firmly espoused. However, resurrection in the sixties does not imply total eclipse in the
fifties. Bunting's poetry continued to be read by a select few: by
Gael Turnbull, who found in it a model of economy for his own
verse, by Bunting's own near-contemporaries, David Jones and
Hugh MacDiarmid, and part of a small public that kept interest
alive. It was Gael Turnbull, who republished *The Spoils* and who
introduced Bunting to Stuart Montgomery of the Fulcrum Press,
who was responsible for bringing out *Loquitur, First Book of
Odes*, *Briggflatts* and *Collected Poems*.
  There is a paradox in Bunting's critical reception in the
sixties. The long neglect could, for another poet, be interpreted
as the sign of the precursor of a literary movement, but in
Bunting's case it shows a writer whose aim is always to be entirely
true to himself. Although he has helped young writers, such as
Tom Pickard, another who participated in arousing new interest
in his work, his help, like Ezra Pound's, has always had a liberating
effect. (The parallel with Pound is also important because
Bunting's resurrection coincides with his former mentor's critical
rehabilitation.) Bunting is neither the founder nor the member of
a movement. While some of his subject matter and language make
him a "Northern" poet, there is no Northern school around him.
In this he is similar to Hugh MacDiarmid, a recalcitrant outsider
and anti-conformist like Bunting, who is himself only just beginning to be appreciated at his true value. MacDiarmid is only superficially just a "Scots" poet, for Scots was a means he adopted to

escape from English insularity. His preoccupations, such as the long poem as a vehicle for ideas and the cosmic significance of the materiality of Man's existence (which we shall notice in a parallel I make with Bunting later in this essay), place him on a different plane.

If Bunting can be classed with Eliot and Pound as a European poet, as my comparison of *Briggflatts* with *Four Quartets* and St.-John Perse's *Anabase* will reveal, and a defender of tradition in literature, he is nonetheless one who defends with a personal voice that remains distinct from much of the rest of artistic expression in the sixties, whether it be the watered down sentiment of hangovers from the Movement or the experiments in "Concrete" poetry of such writers as Edwin Morgan. Bunting's poetry has a hardness and a permanence which stand against both these extremes. It rises above the mawkish and the trivial with a grandeur that also mocks the built-in self-destruction of re-arranged sculpture and aleatory music, continuing what George Steiner has recently called the classical "gamble on transcendence."

Bunting's art contains nothing "new" to be linked with current aesthetic trends. Its success goes against all the odds, but has a complete inevitability that is one of the major features marked by *Briggflatts*, the logical outcome of all Bunting's previous poetry. It was *the* poem required to assure Bunting's success. Without *Briggflatts* there would never have been a sustained new interest in the rest of the work. *Briggflatts*, with its dialogue on permanence, is a monument to art's indifference to time. Bunting's poetry could have been "resurrected"—if "resurrected" it ever was—at any moment, because it could afford to stand outside time, the time that does not exist for the *summum* of the "oeuvre," *Briggflatts*.

The title of the poem, *Briggflatts*, is indicative of a poetic career that has its roots in early childhood. Briggflatts, the Quaker hamlet in Cumbria that Basil Bunting knew as a boy, is the starting point for the poet's latest and greatest work. Briggflatts, Bunting has said,[1] is not just the touchstone for childhood memories. Far more significant is the fact that the Quaker meeting house breathes an essence similar to the essence of poetry as Basil Bunting has come to see it. He describes Briggflatts as a meeting house put together by the hard work of poor people, not to show off their skill, but as a place in which to meet God. The poem is

---

1. In a B.B.C. 2 "Release" feature on his poetry, 23rd November, 1968. I am grateful to Francis Gladstone, producer of the programme, for specially showing it to me at a later date and for lending me the tape-recordings from which the sound track was made.

not exactly that, not exactly theological; but the description presents the spirit in which the work of art must be viewed (one could almost say "entered"). The meeting house is an appropriate symbol of what the poem should be to the reader.

One must consider also the sub-title, "An Autobiography," a misleading term, for, as Richard Hoggart has pointed out,[2] the poem follows no continuous line of narrative; there is no story to it. "Autobiography" is also misleading in the sense that it would be wrong to explain the poem by making specific references to Basil Bunting's life. Emphasis should be put on the indefinite article, "an." This is *any* artist's autobiography, and the experience presented in it has *general* human significance rather than the quality of personal revelations. The poem is a presentation of a protagonist's journey through the wilderness of life, just as St.-John Perse's *Anabase* describes a spiritual "journey into the interior." This is achieved by the order which the poem creates out of the chaos of imprecision of feeling and experience. Like the Quaker meeting house where the worshippers wait to be moved to speak, *Briggflatts* is a structure where one can meet different kinds of experience. The important and immutable thing is the structure. Whereas the experiences can be re-interpreted by each reader according to his own life, the structure cannot. The structure is what belongs to the poem and to the poem alone.

In fact, the poem came to Bunting as a shape, a shape to be filled with appropriate experiences.[3] *Briggflatts*, more than any other poem by Bunting, is an attempt to create a musical pattern of themes. What Bunting had particularly in mind as he was conceiving the poem was the early eighteenth century sonata form of Scarlatti; but in reality the structure of the poem, as we shall see, is more complex than this. Also, at the beginning of composition, the poet was conscious of the sort of mood he wished to create in each section of the work. Each movement has a different pattern, but each takes up again some or all of the basic ideas which are put before us in Part I. The musical pattern invites immediate comparison with the *Four Quartets*, and, to a lesser extent, with St.-John Perse's *Anabase*. This is not to say that what Bunting is doing is derivative or imitative, but rather to measure the stature of his achievement with that of these great and *acknowledged* poets.

In Eliot, each quartet has five sections, all of which, apart

2. Richard Hoggart interviewed Basil Bunting on B.B.C. 2. I should like to thank Professor Hoggart for permission to quote from his comments.
3. As he said on B.B.C. 2.

from the fourth, are divided into two basic parts. This makes nine sections in all, which can be labelled as follows:

1.   a) An experience in horizontal (clock) time
       b) Vision of plenitude

2.   a) (lyrical) The emotional impact of the vision
       b) Awareness of the present moment

3.   a) Ordinary experience
       b) Withdrawal from ordinary experience

4.   a) (lyrical) Dark night vision

5.   a) Art and experience
       b) Final resolution in the tonality of the first section[4]

Eliot presents various ideas, some of them similar to those in Bunting (the moments of ordinary experience, the relationship of art to life, for example) and then reveals their different nuances by passing them through four parallel structures. Not only does each quartet resolve itself by a restatement of its opening tonality, but also the four structures, seen as a whole, have a cyclic form. "Little Gidding" ends with the rose garden with which "Burnt Norton" began. However, this is more than a mere repetition, because the opening theme, after the modulations through which it passes, has gained a host of meanings and associations that are implied in the final resolution.

These complex details show a tightly knit structure. *Briggflatts* is at once looser and more complex. Its shape must be seen as a total design which cannot be broken down into parallel sections. Each part of *Briggflatts* can be seen as having a similar relationship with the other parts as a single part of an Eliot quartet relates to its other parts but with much more intricate detail. *Briggflatts* approaches in genre the freer form of *Anabase*, which combines passages of narrative with lyrical sections, but which does not really have a linear structure. Framed by two "chansons," indicating "my end is in my beginning," *Anabase* passes under review a whole range of themes, such as justice, sexual love, and salt as a symbol of life force. The themes are presented in ten sections which represent different moods and moments in time:

---

4. I have followed the basic pattern indicated by Northrop Frye in his book in the Writers and Critics Series, *T.S. Eliot* (New York: Oliver and Boyd, 1963), p. 78.

1. Arrival of the conqueror on the site of the city he is to found.

2. Marking out of its boundary walls.

3. Consultation of the augurs.

4. Founding of the city.

5. Longing for new worlds to conquer.

6. Plans for establishment and for filling the coffers.

7. Decision to undertake fresh expedition.

8. The march through desert wastes.

9. The arrival at borders of a great land.

10. The warrior prince, received with honours and celebrations, who rests for a spell but is soon yearning to be on his way again, this time with the navigator.[5]

Although not as epic in scope as *Anabase*, *Briggflatts* does go beyond the somewhat limiting term "sonata." The elements of the classical sonata (statement of theme, development and recapitulation) are certainly present. However, there is something more, an element which has (to continue the musical analogy) more affinity with the modern symphony as composed by Sibelius. Whole themes are not stated, but rather, fragments which build into themes as the work progresses.[6]

Part I, which sets out the themes or fragments of themes of the whole of *Briggflatts* begins immediately with a musical image— that of a bull singing an air against the accompaniment provided by the river Rawthey. Not only is the reference of the first paragraph musical, but also its structure is polyphonic in that it weaves several strands of theme together—the bull's song, the bull's dance, various elements of nature, and, especially important because it recurs later, the slowworm:[7]

5. Quoted in T.S. Eliot's preface to his translation, *Anabasis*, French and English parallel texts (London: Faber and Faber, 1959), p. 11.
6. I am thinking in particular of the Symphony No. 5 in E flat major, Opus 82.
7. Here the slowworm has the mystery of, for example, the appearances of the blind beggar in *Madame Bovary*.

Brag, sweet tenor bull,
descant on Rawthey's madrigal,
each pebble its part
for the fells' late spring.
Dance tiptoe, bull,
black against may.
Ridiculous and lovely
chase hurdling shadows
morning into noon.
May on the bull's hide
and through the dale
furrows fill with may,
paving the slowworm's way.

This technique of interweaving themes is one which Bunting often uses in the poem. Whereas in the early long (sonata) poems, such as "Attis, or: Something Missing" (1932) and "The Well of Lycopolis" (1935), he strains towards this effect and sometimes only arrives at congestion and obscurity; here he achieves purity and complexity at the same time. Each strand of meaning maintains its individual character, but the sum total of the parts creates something new in addition, no doubt because the technical experience of the *Odes* failed to make itself felt in *The Spoils*. Here in *Briggflatts* Bunting's lyrical gifts are employed to the full within the framework of a long poem.

Another aspect, again seen for the most part only in the *Odes*, is revealed in the first paragraph: Basil Bunting the poet of nature. Although the presentation of the material is highly intellectual, the material itself gives the impression of having derived from acute observation of the countryside. This is an impression which will stay with us throughout *Briggflatts*, and at this point in the poem it is already an indication that his subject matter is less "literary" than in most of the earlier works. In giving pointers to recurring features of the poem, we can also note the extreme simplicity of diction and the predominance of monosyllabic words.

The nature poet tells us it is spring, but in relation to this information the next paragraph introduces a paradox which is once more part of the fabric of the whole of the poem: in the midst of spring dwells death. A mason carving on a tombstone provides the drone bass of death against which the living lark sings.

A mason times his mallet
to a lark's twitter,
listening while the marble rests,
lays his rule
at a letter's edge,
fingertips checking,
till the stone spells a name

> naming none,
> a man abolished.
> Painful lark, labouring to rise!
> The solemn mallet says:
> In the grave's slot
> he lies. We rot.

Paradox is enclosed within paradox, for a monument is being erected to signify that which no longer exists. But the position of the living is even more paradoxical than that of the dead. The last two lines quoted imply less permanence for those living (i.c. moving towards death) than for those who are dead (i.e. in a fixed state).

Bunting then develops this idea of life and death in nature, stating the cyclic processes in progress:

> Decay thrusts the blade,
> wheat stands in excrement
> trembling. Rawthey trembles.
> Tongue stumbles, ears err
> for fear of spring.
> Rub the stone with sand,
> wet sandstone rending
> roughness away. Fingers
> ache on the rubbing stone.
> The mason says: Rocks
> happen by chance.
> No one here bolts the door,
> love is so sore.

Everything is part of a process, and no part has greater importance than another. In being interviewed, Bunting has said that, to speak in theological terms, all creatures spend their time praising God by living the life they were intended for.[8] To use Wordsworth's phrase, everything is:

> Rolled round in earth's diurnal course
> With rocks and stones and trees.[9]

The parallel ideas in Bunting and Wordsworth are also echoed in a poet he particularly admires, Hugh MacDiarmid. Taking the image of rock or stone, employed by both Bunting and Wordsworth, MacDiarmid, in "On a Raised Beach," finds in it the ground and being of the universe, saying that all things "come back to the likeness of stone. . . ." A preoccupation similar to Bunting's is revealed:

---

8. B.B.C. 2.
9. Wordsworth, *Poetical Works*, Oxford, 1959, p. 149.

> Every stone in the world
> Covers infinite death, beyond the reach
> Of the dead it hides; [10]

Bunting associates with stone the actual bodies of the dead:

> Stone smooth as skin,
> cold as the dead they load
> on a low lorry by night.

Human flesh is part of the great physical universe.

These are the opening lines to a paragraph which introduces two human figures onto the scene. (One is almost tempted to say the *first* human figures, for the mason, associated with death and the art which tries to build something permanent out of death, is weird and dehumanised.):

> The moon sits on the fell
> but it will rain.
> Under sacks on the stone
> two children lie,
> hear the horse stale,
> the mason whistle,
> harness mutter to shaft,
> felloe to axle squeak,
> rut thud the rim,
> crushed grit.

(We can note again here the sound verbs.)

In this scene of death and nature are placed two children in love. (We must remember that the season is spring.):

> Stocking to stocking, jersey to jersey,
> head to hard arm,
> they kiss under the rain,
> bruised by their marble bed.
> In Garsdale, dawn;
> at Hawes, tea from the can.
> Rain stops, sacks
> steam in the sun, they sit up.
> Copper-wire moustache,
> sea-reflecting eyes
> and Baltic plainsong speech
> declare: By such rocks
> men killed Bloodaxe.

The latter part of this section indicates not only that the future (ironically a future of eventual death) is being made by these children, but also that they contain the deep roots of the past of

---

10. "On A Raised Beach," pp. 163-176 in *Longer Contemporary Poems*, Penguin, 1966. Quotations from pp. 166 and 175.

their race. Later on the poet will say more specifically that past
and future are merged in the present. At this point occurs only a
first, brief reference to Bloodaxe,[11] who becomes more important
later in the poem, and his significance is the link with the past.

Bunting develops this idea in a further paragraph (with more
sound imagery) before resuming the story of the two children,
first employing nature imagery to give them, as a background, the
life of the world that decays ("knotty wood" burning to ash,
"October apples") and then putting them directly in the presence
of death once more:

>   they watch
>   the mason meditate
>   on name and date.

We follow the children home, and in a passage of utter simplicity
and realism, Bunting describes their love-making:

>   He has untied the tape
>   of her striped flannel drawers
>   before the range. Naked
>   on the pricked rag mat
>   his fingers comb
>   thatch of his manhood's home.

Love, that night, is like a comforting music that pervades all. She
washes his body. Here the slowworm is used as a phallic symbol:

>   Shining slowworm part of the marvel.

But its mysterious presence signals a transition to the mason, as
when it first appeared in the poem. The idea of art implicit in the
first reference to the mason is made clearer here:

>   The mason stirs:
>   Words!
>   Pens are too light.
>   Take a chisel to write.

---

11. Eric Bloodaxe is mentioned in the *Anglo-Saxon Chronicle*, but for a more complete
view of his career, as Bunting himself says in a note to *Briggflatts*, it is necessary to look
at the Orkneyinga Saga and the *Heimskringla*. King Harald of Norway gave his throne to
his son, Eric Bloodaxe, in 934. Because of the jealousy of Harald's other sons, Bloodaxe
had difficulties in keeping control of his kingdom. As he was rapidly losing support in
Norway, he set off in 937 raiding, first in the Orkneys, then in Scotland and finally in
Northern England. King Athelstan, in order to keep the peace, gave him Northumbria. It
is difficult to piece the rest of the story together because of conflicting accounts and
conflicting dates, but it would appear that Eric Bloodaxe was twice King of Northumbria.
He was driven out in 939 by King Edmund, the brother of Athelstan, and spent several
years harrying in the Orkneys, the Hebrides, Ireland and Wales before returning to England, to re-establish himself at York when he had gathered enough strength. After
reigning at York for a further two years, he was killed through the treachery of an Earl
Osulf by a certain Macon or Maccus in (?) 950.

These lines begin a series of general reflections by the poet on life, death, art, mutability and the guilt associated with love. It is as if the writer, after living in the beautiful evocation of young, innocent love in the past that he has created, suddenly wakes up and says: What is the use, since death is the result of everything? Tombstones are the only works of art that are true to life. There is no going back. Life once lived cannot be retrieved, and even if the poem tries to represent, to render immutable in art a past experience, it cannot dominate the experience sufficiently to do so:

> shame deflects the pen.
> Love murdered neither bleeds nor stifles
> but jogs the draughtman's elbow.

Only, paradoxically, human guilt achieves the permanence towards which art strives:

> What can he, changed, tell
> her, changed, perhaps dead?
> Delight dwindles. Blame
> stays the same.

Here we have the first of several discussions in the poem of art in relation to life.[12] Although at this point the poet is dispirited about the powers of art, he presents his *ideal* of what a writer *should* do. Form and expression are difficult, but what is more difficult is the domination of experience which, undominated, can ruin the poetic utterance:

> Take no notice of tears;
> letter the stone to stand
> over love laid aside. . . .

The way in which Bunting associates Bloodaxe and his flight to Stainmore, where he was killed by his enemies, with the difficult art of writing poetry is significant as the first of several references to the failure of poetry linked with the downfall of the proud and ambitious king.

Pessimism concerning the artistic cause is extended to the last lines of Part I, where the death of Bloodaxe is paralleled by the "death" of spring in the coming of summer. The change in nature echoes the changes in human life and experiences. More painful than death is the transformation from a period of unrealised hope to the disappointment of realisation:

---

12. Richard Hoggart (B.B.C. 2) noticed this as one of the very important features of *Briggflatts*. It is one of the themes that recur throughout Bunting's poetry. With reference to *Briggflatts*, the poet replied to Richard Hoggart that the importance of the theme lies in the fact that "it is there all the time."

> Guilty of spring
> and spring's ending
> amputated years ache after
> the bull is beef, love a convenience.
> It is easier to die than to remember.

The ambiguity of "amputated years ache after / the bull is beef" parallels in verbal terms breakdown and decay. We have even lost the notion of the cycle of life and death in nature. Even the part of art which seemed the most permanent is subject to the same forces:

> Name and date
> split in soft slate
> a few months obliterate.

The theme of art and life dominates Part II. Linked with the reference to Bloodaxe, whose name Bunting put to this movement as the emotion fixing tag when planning the poem, it binds the whole together. The theme moves from the picture of the poet, "sick, self-maimed, self-hating," in an even darker despair than at the end of Part I, through the impossibility of expressing nature in art and the description of the fall of Bloodaxe, to a kind of forced reconciliation between art and life in the remarkable image of Pasiphaë's rape by the bull.

The texture of the movement is far more complex than this outline suggests. The theme of the poetic ideal plunging the aspiring poet into despair is effective for its sordid, urban setting this time. The poet is surrounded by cheap tricksters. His stock of imagery comes from the common sights around him ("bus conductor . . . Tottenham Court Road . . ." etc.), a contrast with the nature imagery of the beginning of the first part. The poet retains his ideal, but is forced to reconcile himself with sordid reality. Gone is the innocent, young love of Part I, except in memory:

> He lies with one to long for another,
> sick, self-maimed, self-hating,
> obstinate, mating
> beauty with squalor to beget lines still-born.

Bunting uses at this point an image associated with the course of life, that of bowls rolling towards the jack. Continuing the pessimistic note, the protagonist finds himself subject to exterior forces:

> What twist can counter the force
> that holds back
> woods I roll?

Even the scientist ("You who elucidate the disc / hubbed by the sun,") cannot calculate the course of an individual human life.

Here the scene switches, suddenly, cinematographically. A series of nautical passages follows, all the more effective for being placed after the urban imagery. The sea passages express the hard struggle against the elements; they rise to their highest pitch in lines and words that have an Anglo-Saxon brevity and dourness and express the same kind of grim resolution as does the Anglo-Saxon:

> Who sang, sea takes,
> brawn brine, bone grit.
> Keener the kittiwake.
> Fells forget him.
> Fathoms dull the dale,
> gulfweed voices . . .

Here we have one of many sea images in Bunting's poetry where the sea is often associated with forces hostile to the protagonist. In counterpoint to the maritime descriptions are the two main themes already stated in the movement, art and love. Here is no stone to carve. The ever-changing sea mocks man's efforts to immortalise himself in art:

> Who cares to remember a name cut in ice
> or be remembered?
> Wind writes in foam on the sea . . .

The sea, expressive of eternity in its vastness, seems for the protagonist to point to the transience of human love:

> Love is a vapour, we're soon through it.

Flying fish are content to follow their graceful course in the water and not strain after a life other than their own. The present dominates. And

> to humiliate love, remember nothing.

The scene shifts once again, this time to Italy. The senses, taste, hearing, touch, appreciate the Italian landscape. They grasp its immediacy as art never can. The poet's insistence on the inadequacy of his art returns:

> It looks well on the page, but never
> well enough. Something is lost
> when wind, sun, sea upbraid
> justly an unconvinced deserter.

However, although the artist may be a "deserter," this does not prevent his materials from being of the very stuff of nature. The memorial stones (a recurrence of the tombstone/mason theme) which line the road are made of marble that once formed part of a mountain. And nature seems associated with art, with music, be it only hillside fiddlers apparently sheltered by nature; or, more profoundly, the patterns and harmonies created by birds and beasts. They

> punctuate a text whose initial,
> lost in Lindisfarne plaited lines,
> stands for discarded love.

This is the essential paradox. All the real, the natural elements are there; they are lost (the lost element being represented by past experience of love and the familiar guilt) in the artistic form, the shaping of the work of art which conceals the original experience.

Bunting describes the difficult technique of art in terms reminiscent of Théophile Gautier, because the difficulty is likened to that of the sculptor, in the guise of the mason. However carefully his tools are made, the mason/poet

> litters his yard
>   with flawed fragments.

This artistic failure is placed next to a passage which describes in greater detail than before the death of Bloodaxe. (Therefore, the theme of death is specifically linked with the poet.) Bloodaxe is not merely struck down from without; he is corrupted within himself, "Loaded with mail of linked lies. . . ." The image expresses a failing in a character paralleled in the poem by the mason and the poet, and is itself parallel to the "Lindisfarne plaited lines."

This section links with what Basil Bunting has also stated about the poet:

> The poet who tries too hard is lost. It's no use insisting upon
> being a poet.[13]

The poet must let the association between art and life form naturally. For the human mind, or the *poet's* mind, can find parallels between art and aspects of the natural world: starfish and "a galliarde by Byrd," the flight of Asian vultures and "a madrigal by Monteverdi," the movement of a rat and "Schoenberg's maze." Although art cannot arrange nature ("entune a bogged orchard"), parallels of harmony can be established.

The poet begins a reconciliation between art and life, or at least an acceptance of experience. The concluding passage of Part II is a description of Pasiphaë being raped by the bull. In relation to this image, Bunting has said that the poet should work as Pasiphaë did to get a new creation, accepting what happens to

---

13. B.B.C. 2.

him.[14] Richard Hoggart said that the image of Pasiphaë was   one
of the most striking he had read, especially the description of the
girl guiding the phallus into her and the horrifying idea of her
being willingly distended by the act:[15]

> and Pasiphaë's pungent sweat,
> who heard the god-bull's feet
> scattering sand,
> breathed byre stink, yet stood
> with expectant hand
> to guide his seed to its soil;
> nor did flesh flinch
> distended by the brute
> nor loaded spirit sink
> till it had gloried in unlike creation.

Part III stands somewhat apart from the rest of the poem.
Bunting indicates that in one sense it is a simplified version of the
whole of *Briggflatts*.[16]

The imagery seems at first similar to that associated with the
journeyings in *Anabase* ("glimmer of ancient arms," "horses,
barley pancakes"), and there is further temptation to see a parallel
with this poem, since it evokes the journey of a great conqueror,
Alexander. In fact, the subject is not the same at all. In St.-John
Perse, the journey and the striving after fresh fields to conquer
matter. In Bunting the subject is failure. Alexander's journey may
be a civilising mission but it can have no civilising effect because
the human condition is past remedy. Humanity is seen at its basest.
Its representatives here are the cheating turd-bakers:

> scavengers
> whose palms scoop droppings to mould
> cakes for hungry towns.
>
> Leave given
> we would have slaughtered the turd-bakers
> but neither whip nor knife
> can welt their hide.

Against this is set Alexander's heroic persistence, despite
the reluctance of his followers:

> But we desired Macedonia,
> the rocky meadows, horses, barley pancakes,
> incest and familiar games,
> to end in our own place by our own wars,
> and deemed the peak unscalable; but he

---

14. Ibid.
15. Ibid.
16. Ibid.

reached to a crack in the rock
with some scorn, resolute though in doubt,

However, all is futile, for the angel Israfel[17] is waiting to blow the last trumpet. He has merely scorn for the endeavours of mankind as he impatiently awaits the signal for the end of the world:

Israfel,
trumpet in hand, intent on the east,
cheeks swollen to blow,
whose sigh is cirrus: Yet delay!
When will the signal come
to summon man to his clay?

Here a remarkable transition and change of tone follows. Instead of man in all his strength, we see a human being, poisoned by an adder's sting, man at his very weakest, because he is conscious of the possibility of death. Only in the face of death is there reality. Onto this scene comes the slowworm. When asked what the slowworm suggests, Bunting replied that he could not "figure it out" precisely himself, except that it represents "the quietest attitude."[18]

This is the impression given by the slowworm's song, beginning:

Ripe wheat is my lodging. I polish
my sides on pillars of its transept,
gleam in its occasional light.
Its swaying
copies my gait.

The slowworm is a creature which, like the flying fish of Part II, is content to sing its humble song of praise and submit itself to what nature offers:

Sycamore seed twirling,
O, writhe to its measure!
Dust swirling trims pleasure.
Thorns prance in a gale.
In air snow flickers,
twigs tap,
elms drip.

Swaggering, shimmering fall,
drench and towel us all!

The tone of the poem then becomes hushed and religious, as if the protagonist (Man) were chastened by his experience of the nearness of death and by the slowworm's example:

---

17. Israfel: the Islamic archangel.
18. B.B.C. 2.

> So he rose and led home silently through clean woodland
> where every bough repeated the slowworm's song.

Thus, Part III of *Briggflatts* ends in peace and resignation.

Part IV opens simply with a short description of men returning from a profitable day's fishing. There has been a flood. The
catch is good:

> Grass caught in willow tells the flood's height that has subsided;
> overfalls sketch a ledge to be bared tomorrow.
> No angler homes with empty creel though mist dims day.

But fishing, an apparently innocent activity, reveals essentially
man's killer instinct, the same instinct that is in the hunter standing mercilessly over the leopard he has shot. The same instinct
leads man to kill in war. The heroic dead are celebrated by Aneurin and Taliesin.[19]

> I hear Aneurin number the dead, his nipped voice.
>
> I hear Aneurin number the dead and rejoice,
> being adult male of a merciless species.

They can at least render the dead permanent in their poetry:

> Aneurin and Taliesin, cruel owls
> for whom it is never altogether dark, crying
> before the rules made poetry a pedant's game.

Art is seen as the only force for permanence against a background of mutability:

> Today's poets are piles to drive into the quaggy past
> on which impermanent palaces balance.

Poetry, together with Columba, Columbanus, Aidan and Cuthbert, whom Bunting evokes in this section and who can be said to
represent universal love, are the side of man's being that strains
towards eternity. But this does not tell us anything, *our* poet
seems to say. The representatives of universal love are at one with
nature, clothed in daylight:

> Columba, Columbanus, as the soil shifts its vest,
> Aidan and Cuthbert put on daylight,
> wires of sharp western metal entangled in its soft
> web, many shuttles as midges darting. . . .

In contrast, the artist cannot see the structure and texture of the
light:

---

19. Aneurin and Taliesin: two Brittonic poets of the sixth century.

> Can you trace shuttles thrown
> like drops from a fountain, spray, mist of spiderlines
> bearing the rainbow, quoits round the draped moon;
> shuttles like random dust desert whirlwinds hoy at their tormenting sun?
> Follow the clue patiently and you will understand nothing.

(Note the Eliot-like tone of the last line.)

Death, the past, the impossibility of reducing nature to anything other than itself, the role of poetry: Bunting passes some of his main themes under review and gives, up to this point, an impression of the futility of the attempt to order experience in art. (Remember that Aneurin and Taliesin only *record*.) The secret, however, is in an unassuming art, the great ideal shown by Scarlatti:

> It is time to consider how Domenico Scarlatti
> condensed so much music into so few bars
> with never a crabbed turn or a congested cadence,
> never a boast or a see-here. . . .

Although it is not usually pertinent to attribute the attitude of the poetic protagonist in *Briggflatts* to the poet himself, one cannot help noticing that this ideal of unpretentious skill is one that Bunting himself professes. The harmony is so perfect that it seems in accord with nature:

> and stars and lakes
> echo him and copse drums out his measure,
> snow peaks are lifted up in moonlight and twilight
> and the sun rises on an acknowledged land.

(We remember the parallels between aspects of nature and various musical forms in Part II.)

The ideal of art is juxtaposed with a section expressive of the ideal of love. However, whereas perfect musical harmony is in tune with the processes of nature, love is drowned in the rest of human activity. After a night of passion, the hero must leave and plunge into the ordinary course of life again. The sheer limpid, distilled beauty of the lines recalls the scene of young, innocent love in Part I and is reminiscent of Pound's love poems in *Cathay*:

> My love is young but wise. Oak, applewood,
> her fire is banked with ashes till day.
> The fells reek of her hearth's scent,
> her girdle is greased with lard;
> hunger is stayed on her settle, lust in her bed.
> Light as spider floss her hair on my cheek which a puff scatters,
> light as a moth her fingers on my thigh.
> We have eaten and loved and the sun is up,
> we have only to sing before parting:
> Goodbye, dear love.

> Her scones are greased with fat of fried bacon,
> her blanket comforts my belly like the south.
> We have eaten and loved and the sun is up.
> Goodbye.[20]

The atmosphere is quiet and resigned (although not untinged with nostalgia) as the slowworm passage at the end of Part III. Parting is necessary.

However, acceptance is never complete. Bunting develops the slight nostalgia on the love passage into a reflection of the passing nature of existence:

> Cobweb hair on the morning,
> a puff would blow it away.

The image derives from the spider floss of hair in the love passage; but whereas the earlier form of the image emphasizes the intense beauty of a moment that will pass, the variant is more despairing; indeed, it forms part of a passage in which the protagonist describes his bitterness and loneliness:

> Shamble, cold, content with beer and pickles,
> towards a taciturn lodging among strangers.

The situation of the poet-hero (again we remember that of Bloodaxe) is presented as the death of a rat in a trap. He has to face the hostility of the rest of humanity who do not accept his role as seer. The earlier mood of reconciliation is gone; and this would be the final tone, were it not for three short lines which stand apart from the rest of the movement:

> Stars disperse. We too,
> further from neighbours
> now the year ages.

These lines introduce a cosmic dimension to what has gone before and proclaim what will come later in the poem: the parting of individual human beings parallels the changes of the stars. Time separates us from those we have known.

In Part V, it is winter. The seasons have run their course in the poem. Once again we can note Bunting's wonderful observation of nature in a section which is the equivalent of the "spring song" at the beginning of Part I.

> Winter wrings pigment
> from petal and slough
> but thin light lays
> white next red on sea-crow wing,
> gruff sole cormorant
> whose grief turns carnival.

---

20. On B.B.C. 2, Basil Bunting read this passage against the musical background of Scarlatti's Sonata in B minor, L. 33.

There is the usual music imagery too:

> a flute clarifies song,
> trembling phrase fading to pause
> then glow. Solstice past,
> years end crescendo.

and a continuation of the descriptions of nature in terms of art:

> Even a bangle of birds
> to bind sleeve to wrist
> as west wind waves to east
> a just perceptible greeting . . .
>
> Mist sets lace of frost
> on rock for the tide to mangle.[21]

Part of the harmony is in the dance of maggots which

> group a nosegay
> jostling on cast flesh,
> frisk and compose decay.

This is a beauty that extends to all creation.

Because it is winter, these parallels can only lead us into memories of the past, which swiftly, briefly, come and go:

> Sing,
> strewing the notes on the air
> as ripples skip in a shallow. Go
> bare, the shore adorned
> with pungent weed loudly
> filtering sand and sea.
> Silver blades of surf
> fall crisp on rustling grit,
> shaping the shore as a mason
> fondles and shapes his stone.

All these images have appeared earlier in the poem.

They lead further to an evocation of Northumberland and of a scene that could belong equally to past or present:

> Shepherds follow the links,
> sweet turf studded with thrift;
> fell-born men of precise instep
> leading demure dogs
> from Tweed and Till and Teviotdale,
> with hair combed back from the muzzle,
> dogs from Redesdale and Coquetdale

The scene has the deep roots of silence. Horizontal time seems no longer to exist:

---

21. R.S. Woof in a study of *Briggflatts* suggests that this image may be derived from Lindisfarne designs. "Basil Bunting's Poetry," *Stand*, 8, No. 2, p. 34.

silence by silence sits
and Then is diffused in Now.

The lines possess the profound stillness associated with the slow-worm's song, although now the mood is not of resignation before impermanence or death, but is linked with the conquest of time. The light is the very last light, that reflected by cirrus, the "sigh" of the angel Israfel in Part III.

After a further beautiful "rappel" of winter description, music imagery comes in with a tutti:

Young flutes, harps touched by a breeze,
drums and horns escort
Aldebaran, low in the clear east, . . .

Great strings next the post of the harp
clang, the horn has majesty,
flutes flicker in the draft and flare.

This is the music of the spheres: Aldebaran, Capella, Betelgeuse, Rigel, Orion, Procyon, the names of the stars Bunting deliberately links with music, give us a sense of the panorama of the whole of creation. The stars tracking the magnitude of the skies (Capella like a Viking ship "with shields hung on his gunwale," for the stars have their past too). Boats sailing the shifting vastness of the seas. The poet's imagery links the above and the below, the world of men and the space beyond:

That is no dinghy's lantern
occulted by the swell — Betelgeuse,
calling behind him to Rigel.
Starlight is almost flesh.

The tonalities in the poem define themselves, after the shifting modulations. "Then is Now." Even that vastness and the light of stars which lie beyond this world are relative:

Then is Now. The star you steer by is gone,
its tremulous thread spun in the hurricane
spider floss on my cheek; light from the zenith
spun when the slowworm lay in her lap
fifty years ago.

The sheets are gathered and bound,
the volume indexed and shelved,
dust on its marbled leaves.
Lofty, an empty combe,
silent but for bees.
Finger tips touched and were still
fifty years ago.
Sirius is too young to remember.

> Sirius glows in the wind. Sparks on ripples
> mark his line, lures for spent fish.
>
> Fifty years a letter unanswered;
> a visit postponed for fifty years.
>
> She has been with me fifty years.
>
> Starlight quivers. I had day enough.
> For love uninterrupted night.

The poet can create his own eternity. This is the triumph of his integrity.

Stars, time, eternity, art, the experience of love, the slow-worm and the mason images are rolled into one whole, bound together in one volume. Bunting achieves a remarkable parallel between what he says as "meaning" in these lines, and his expression (pattern of themes, images, words and lines). This is not only true of the passage under discussion, but of the whole poem, which we come to see clearly in this way in the light of the final passage.

Bunting has maintained an ambiguity, or at least a kind of uncertainty about art, throughout his poem, at the same time accepting the idea of art in the act of writing. Now he positively states his faith in art. We see the work of art as something wrought out of the chaos of life but standing outside time. Bunting adds a Coda to *Briggflatts* which points to the presence of past influences, to the forces that move those who are open to experience across the uncharted seas and wastes of life towards an unseen future:

> A strong song tows
> us, long earsick.
> Blind, we follow
> rain slant, spray flick
> to fields we do not know.
>
> Night, float us.
> Offshore wind, shout,
> ask the sea
> what's lost, what's left,
> what horn sunk,
> what crown adrift.
>
> Where we are who knows
> of kings who sup
> while day fails? Who,
> swinging his axe
> to fell kings, guesses
> where we go?

Nothing is certain in life, except the work of art.

THE THINKER

Photograph by Hugh Kenner, Durham, 1979

DALE REAGAN

BASIL BUNTING
obiter dicta

Introductory Note

Bunting has spent a lifetime educating himself in the art of poetry. This process has generated, by the way, a significant body of observations on the nature, function, and techniques of his craft, the practice of his fellow artists and his relation to contemporary society.

To date, there has been no attempt to gather together these *obiter dicta* from the articles and reviews, prefaces, lectures, interviews and letters where they were recorded. Access has been limited to the enthusiast who has had time and funding to compile his own collection from widely scattered sources.

What follows is a preliminary attempt to remedy this situation. Considerations of space have made it necessary to set aside many passages that would have a place in a fully representative survey. The selections below, however, should be sufficient to acquaint the reader with Bunting's basic critical attitudes and standards and to suggest his qualities as a critic.

Each passage is followed by a brief notation indicating when the remarks were made and whether they have been drawn from a public statement, an interview, or a letter. These coordinates should be kept in view as the passages are considered.

The Origins and Nature of Poetry

I suspect that most poets have never made up their minds what poetry is, or what they are doing with it. *Ad hoc* definitions and amendments get nowhere. What a lot of people have called poetry for a long time can't be left out of account: that is to say, history is the road that might conceivably lead somewhere, not abstract cogitation.

("A Letter," *Agenda*, 1972)

† † † † † † †

Poetry and music are both patterns of sound drawn on a background of time. That is their origin and their essence. Whatever else they may become, whatever purpose they may sometimes serve, is secondary. They can do without it in case of necessity. Whatever refinements and subtleties they may introduce, if they lose touch altogether with the simplicity of the dance, with the motions of the human body and the sounds natural to a man exerting himself, people will no longer feel them as music and poetry. They will respond to the meaning no doubt, but not with the exhilaration that dancing brings. They will not think of them as human concerns. They will find them tedious. I think that is what happened to poetry a good deal in the last century. A lot of Victorian poetry and a lot of the poetry contemporary with it in France and other countries lost touch with music and with the simplicity of bodily movement and became merely a rather puzzling way of setting down facts on the page, whereas it really has no fundamental connection with facts at all. . . .

("The Art of Poetry," a lecture, 1970)

† † † † † † †

Religions and philosophies simplify life and err. Science often fails to keep method in its place and elevates a handy tool into a prime condition of the universe. . . . Poets, makers, know, if they reflect at all, the complexity of things made. They offer no easy explanations.

The minimum requirement of a poem is that it should trim some known thought to a greater precision, or note comprehensively and communicably some previously unknown thought.

(from *The Cantos of Ezra Pound: Some testimonials. . .*, 1933)

† † † † † † †

. . . you have read Wittgenstein; you have pondered the limits that language imposes on thought. You know *damn well* that the function of poetry is to enlarge those limits, to make new thoughts possible, to . . . specify what was vague, to render understandable what was not. In brief, to preserve in good condition, intact and faultless, the most necessary of all instruments for social life. This is a practical and indispensable role. The *direction* does not matter at all. All directions lead rapidly to the circumference of thought and of already existing language: without trying to claim that the new propositions are true, either scientifically, religiously, or in any other manner, or that they have any forseeable use. They are simply rendered accessible. *Wovon man nicht sprechen kann, darüber muss man schweigen.* (What cannot be spoken about must be consigned to silence.)

The aim of poetry is to diminish that desert of obligatory silence. This is a long undertaking, an interminable undertaking.

No art for art's sake, Mr. Mangan, we beg you! This is a game for avoiding the fatigue of thinking. Art for the love of the continued and not the disintegrated existence of man, or rather if it is by chance an Eliot, art for the sacred love of God.

("Lettera aperta a Sherry Mangan, Esquire," 1932, translated from the original Italian)

† † † † † † † †

One of the uses of poetry is to give a design to things the gods have left lying about in slovenly piles—to take a director's hand in the business of creating the world. It is not, I believe, its chief utility but it is an important one. Whether the Americans like it or not Williams has been tracing patterns their children will have to fill in. He is like Yeats a national and nation-making poet. *Nazim* (Arabic) one who sets things in order, a poet or the governor of a province.

("Carlos Williams's Recent Poetry," *The Westminster Magazine*, 1934)

† † † † † † † †

And supposing a poem is neither a tool nor a vessel nor a remedy for anything but only and just a poem: for at any rate that's what it survives by—we don't read Lucretius for a concourse of atoms, no fear! nor even Dante for catholic philosophy though he did it so well that he's still usable by converts, I'm told; and I'm damned if I really know what the "Ode on the Intimations of Immortality" is driving at, but I can still get a lot of pleasure from it. OK. Haven't we all, poets, been riding much too high a horse for a long time? A bit of the Yeatsian Grecian goldsmith or just plain potter (not for teacups though) or the guy who paints the Sicilian carts and British canal boats. Without anonymity you can't have a healthy art nicht wahr. Nobody's tripes are daubed on the circus caravans, nobody knows who tiled the Masjed-e Shah, Durham cathedral exhorts nobody. Sure, we've all said it repeatedly: but we haven't drawn the conclusion. Poets still act as though they thought they had some special claim. A skill worth preserving, with possibly some rather tenuous uses from the economic-social point of view: but if nobody buys my pots I don't accuse the customers of anything worse than poor taste, if nobody buys my poems what's the difference? The old millionaire ferryman at Baghdad earned his living weaving baskets when he was viceroy of Syria for the Emir-ol-Momenin, and the shepherds make their pipes for the fun of it. The fowler could get a better living in another occupation. Poetry is overrun with guys who want to tickle their own vanity, and I don't like it Louis! That's what falsifies everything. If we'd had the sense to be anonymous amongst these, when you were Objectivisting, and to stay anonymous, maybe we'd have had more effect so that more people would have had pleasure in reading us and more people would have written in a way to give them pleasure.

Reverting to the West has made me more convinced than before that we've got to learn almost everything from the East (which, to the measure of my limited experience is the lands of Islam) before there's a chance of any peace of mind or dignity for most of us. And that's a way of saying To hell with material welfare, and, logically, of all the laws and reforms and adages designed to procure it.

(Letter to Zukofsky, 1953)

† † † † † † †

The effect of literature does not depend on its content. Its function is not propaganda, any more than the function of an analytical chemist is propaganda. Neither is its function to amuse the public. It is to explore the resources of language and make language available for all existing or potential thoughts. In so doing it must constantly bring into sight new thoughts whose relation to the immediate political and economic situation is so remote that no mind can trace it, and which do not depend for their truth or falsity upon the truth or falsity, usefulness or uselessness, of the sentiments they may incidentally inspire in a reader not a professional poet.

I do not think a political-economic paper has any need of a literary section, but I am certain that a literary section subordinated to a general editor chosen on political-economic grounds is certain to be a bad literary section, and to discredit the paper not only with those who understand literature but with those whose minds are sensitive enough to feel literary falseness or validity without understanding what it consists of. If it is considered advisable for a paper to have a literary section at all, it should be an absolutely autonomous section, edited by a man chosen for his literary skill and knowledge without reference to his politics and conducted according to literary criteria only. If the Communist Party cannot trust literature to do its own work (which is not political nor economic propaganda) in its own way (which disregards politics and economics, whether they are included in the 'content' or not) it had better have nothing to do with literature at all.

("Observations on Leftwing Papers,"
unpublished manuscript, 1935)

† † † † † † † †

Doesn't he [the poet] do all his own bit for progress (or the maintenance of the world) by purely linguistic exercises? Public spirit is abused when people try to do what isn't in or pretty close to their own speciality. Ain't that Confucian? You and I and Zuk have to keep the language alive, and damn difficult as it is, as I am finding more and more, and we don't do any appreciable good by turning aside to propagate the worthiest causes in economics or politics or patent medicines or quack religions or other subjects we've only a secondary interest in. I don't propose to limit a man's subject matter, but to limit the critic's right to judge him on it.

(Letter to Pound, 1935)

† † † † † † † †

No art depends principally or even very largely on its appeal to the intellect, and in the Age of Reason itself Pope was preferred to Young for melody, not for sense; Voltaire's style gained him more admirers than his doctrines, and Chardin was appreciated not for the realism of his rabbits but for the nobility of his rhythm and design.

("Criticism and Music," The Outlook, 1928)

The Art of Poetry

I think that a man who wants to write in the twentieth century makes a great mistake if he doesn't begin by reading *The Origin of Species* where he will find the most magnificent example of the building up and testing of hypothesis.

(Interview, Poetry Information, 1978)

† † † † † † † †

Science teaches a respect for fact that no one concerned with making an honest report on things can be without. It's just as important for a poet as it is for a scientist to have an expert's knowledge of his world and I think that just such a detailed acquaintance with things is what many poets lack.

(Unpublished interview, 1977)

† † † † † † † †

Perhaps I am too hopeful in imagining that the impulse of Northumbrian culture may not yet quite have vanished from the North. I think that our best hope of an art or a literature of our own doesn't lie in imitating what has come to us from Rome or Europe or from the south of England, but in trying to discern what is our own and to develop it. . . . It will be a very complex art, a difficult one, but I think its results need not be difficult to the beholder or the reader. It's not easy, first to simplify detail til only the barest essentials of the detail are left; second to weave an enormous number of such details into an intricate pattern which yet keeps perfect balance and proportion; and thirdly to set your central theme with infinite care in just the right place . . . and to leave it there without drawing attention to it, leave it there for the reader to discover for himself.

("The Art of Poetry," a lecture, 1970)

† † † † † † † †

I have never supposed a poem to be organic at all. I don't think the thing grows, it's built and put together by a craftsman. Of course the ideas in the minds of craftsmen vary but it's usual for anybody of the sort to begin with some idea of what he's going to do. It need not be a very definite and exact idea, but he'll have some general pattern in mind. You don't take a block and start making a woodcut without some notion of what you're going to put on that woodcut, even if it's only that you mean to leave this corner blank and fill up the other corner with something. What the something is may not yet be in your head, but you'll have a general notion of what it's going to be like. Well, in the same way a poet starting off should I think surely have some notion of the shape his poem is going to be. It may be that when he gets going he spoils a corner and has to chop that off or he finds that he's got a whole lot of stuff that he's bound to say, or feels he's bound to say, and squashes it in and it puts the thing out of shape. That kind of thing does happen undoubtedly. But the nearer you can stick to the plan you've started with the more likely the poem is to have a real balance, an effective kind of architecture.

(Interview, *Montemora*, 1977)

† † † † † † † †

I don't feel that poetry offers a means of discovery or a way of clarifying perception. If I have a perception, I can write it down. If not, I can't. I won't discover it while writing. All you'll get is a bad poem.

(Unpublished interview, 1976)

† † † † † † † †

Interest in technical experiment tempts writers to over-estimate the importance and instructiveness of French movements. The French relied too much and too long on the dictionary, and are now driven to exaggerate (for purposes of exploration) the properties of words not in immediate connection with a meaning. But what is their antidote is the poison that has kept English back. A disproportionate idea of the power of words in themselves, from the Elizabethan dramatists to Lewis Carroll and from Latimer to the author of Anna Livia Plurabelle has regularly played into the hands of enemies of literature. The Brittanic appetite for soufflés and cream puffs has been overindulged continually. Cummings is presumably unable to see that the non-farcical part of Cummings is just Keats and Swinburne over again.

English needs a treatment quite other than that now being administered (still, after a century) to French: needs stress on the intelligible meaning, the intelligent purpose of words. Don't, please, understand "intelligible to William Ellery Leonard or Carl Van Doren" but "intelligible to any reasonably quick mind that *hasn't* been subverted by a literary education."

Carlos Williams usually fills the bill. It isn't, fortunately, required that one should agree with him, or be convinced. Indeed, he knows too much to let his mystical Americanism do more than dictate the matter to be treated. That settled, his extraordinary technical virtuosity is used to ensure that the matter shall be matter and not opinion. Writing without motive turns pretty and goes sour in print. But any motive (not "pretext") married to an adequate technique will beget clear, solid and musical verse.

("Carlos Williams's Recent Poetry,"
The Westminster Magazine, 1934)

† † † † † † † †

Every revivification of poetry has taken the same route, towards the language of the streets and the cadences of song or bodily movement.

(Literary review, *The Criterion*, 1938)

† † † † † † † †

The main thing is the notion of setting side by side statements or names, the names of objects, and leaving them to suggest everything, without ever making a moral or abstract statement of your own, allowing merely the accumulation of things, things you can touch, things you can hear, things you can see, to do all the suggesting. It is of course closely connected with the kind of idea on which Eliot touched when he wrote about what he called the "objective correlative" by which he meant something concrete which will convey the emotions or the feelings or the ideas which you want to convey, without betraying you into abstract treatment of things.

(from Open University program on
Ezra Pound, BBC 2, 1975)

There are two kinds of concision. One involves a paucity of words. The second kind, which is much neglected, involves the habit of leaving *things* out. You get on with the matter in hand, leaving out what the reader can supply for himself.

(Unpublished interview, 1976)

I suppose I really got going when I started playing about with quantity. I don't mean direct imitations of Greek quantity. That won't do. English is another language. English is full of long syllables and there is hardly one of the classical metres that you can adapt into English without making your syntax totally impossible. So you've got to invent new metres in quantity if you want to do anything with them. You'll see that in the Elizabethans who tried it. Sidney and Spenser and Campion are very rarely using classical metres. They are using metres that they have adapted and altered and put in rather more long syllables to make it possible in English. . . . Very few poems in modern times have been written in quantity. They are written instead in stress patterns copied from the quantity patterns of the ancient Greeks. All this Victorian stuff, Victorian hexametres and so on, they are written really by stress and not by quantity.

(Comments made during a reading, 1970)

There are exceptions, but I think that most good work, whether in poetry or in music or in drawing, is a matter of condensation as far as the immediate technique is concerned. There are different levels of technique. Prose is very difficult to do properly; if you study Swift you get some notion of how it's done. Swift manages to sound as though he were a man speaking unpremeditated speech and yet in sentences so perfectly articulated that they will last two or three pages before they come to end, and which have got enough in them to fill out four chapters of an average novel. All serious writers ought to read *Gulliver's Travels* and *The Tale of the Tub* every year. Organisation of some sort has got to be there or music fails to function. There's a repetitiveness which distinguishes music from noise, to that extent order is necessary; but there can be a great deal of what most people would regard at first sight as disorder.

(Interview, *meantime*, 1977)

† † † † † † †

You have to have the factors working correctly. The first one is
the music and they've all got to be subordinate to that. If you can
also get words which are exact and current, something that might
happen in conversation, that helps. The words which come out of
dictionaries I don't like; much of the time I have no idea what
most of the critics are writing about. If finally you can have something to say which hasn't been said before, that helps too. But
there's more than craft to it, as you can see if you look at composers. You find composers of great learning, great skill, extremely
deft, but whose work has no life in it; and so it is with poetry too.
You can find people who are very handy at putting words together,
but what is missing is not a prose meaning or something that you
could paraphrase, what is missing is something in the actual tune
itself, so to speak.

(Interview, *meantime*, 1977)

† † † † † † †

Re sonnets: nobody objects to sonnets per se, except as a
form that has been overdone and got boring. There are other
forms as symmetrical and much more satisfactory as accomplishments of technique. They are harder to produce, only because
onc's ear isn't so full of echoes of them. If I were you, feeling, I
presume, the need for a pattern, I'd see what could be done in the
way of adapting Greek quantitative patterns into English. It wants
doing, our knowledge of English quantities is slight, though a good
third of the respectable poets since Spenser have tried their hand
at it. You know—

> Unhappie verse, the witnesse of my unhappie state,
> Make thy selfe fluttering wings of thy fast flying
> Thought, etc.—

I suppose, though, the dons don't like it and leave it out of as
many editions of Spenser as they can. Latin's the strictest and
least satisfactory—though you can get a lot of fun out of Catullus
and Horace's measures. The Greeks took more liberties, and the
Persians have a superior system of measuring. But even if quantity
worries you, there are plenty of forms attractive in themselves.
It's the sonnet, Miltonic blank verse, and the later mishaps of the
Spenserian stanza, that have so monopolised English poetastry
that it's difficult not to fall into their traps. Try Burns's admirable

and difficult stanza. Or ballades, or better, ballatas: or the madrigal (Drummond of Hawthornden, dull everywhere else, strikes a little smouldering fire out of the madrigal).

But whatever pattern you choose, for heaven's sake don't assume it's going to tie you to it forever. The desire for it seems to me probably a good thing, indicating dissatisfaction with the sloppiness a great many writers indulge in under cover of "experimenting." Maybe after a while of the appreciable labour of filling in the blanks in a rhyme scheme, it will be easier to see how to set about filing down an exuberant mass of improvisation into a formed free verse poem. I mean, you may discover that you can do without quite a lot that seems very essential at the improvising stage.

But nobody is going to get any good out of sonnets, or sapphics, or any other system fixed in advance, if they begin with a scheme, say, four lines long and fill it out to match. If you begin with fifty lines and get them down into fourteen, well, I don't see one need then bother so very much about the rhymes. Especially rain-pain.

Pound will tell you whatever is good for you, I have no doubt. He does me, and the rest of us. He has some sonnets in his Personae, and he once wrote a hell of a lot of them not for publication but to get a control of mere words. And no one has said more about the futility of runnin' dahn the road. Your sonnet in the same number as Chomei doesn't strike me as good poetry nor as a promise of anything better in that line. If I were you, I'd change the line; but if you really want to go on writing sonnets, let me try to indicate a few things that you must somehow avoid.

First, inventing unspeakable syntax to permit an extra monosyllable for filling out a line. People say "set a boat drifting," not "set it to drifting," which suggests "set it to music." One can't treat the language as though it were one's private property. If you want to omit a lot of particles that people think they say, but usually swallow while speaking, that's all right, no one will miss them but the grammarbook writers: but if you want to add extra particles, then I suggest you erase the line and start afresh. Second, inverted idioms like "the steel that is my heart." "He had a heart of gold" by all means, but only an orator or a perverse ironist would talk about the gold that was his heart. Thirdly, inversions of the common sentence. They are rarely justified, never when they go the miltonic lengths of your third sentence. Fourthly, literary language. Wordsworth said all that need be said on that subject. It is possible to write well in literary language, but damn difficult. A Racine doesn't ransom all the thousands of bad poets you can find in any French anthology, and even a Racine becomes rather hard to appreciate when the fashion in phraseology changes. Hence the history of his declining reputation not in England only, but also, more slowly, in France.

In short, it's not the sonnet one objects to, but the sins it invites writers to commit against language. Language is speech first and last, it is only a set of written symbols in between whiles. And the speech of one epoch (the renaissance, chiefly, in the sonnet's case) changes before the next. When you write a sonnet before first thoroughly revising the sonnet and bringing it up to date, when you write a sonnet in sonnetty language and apparently in a sonnetty frame of mind, you are doing the same as what-you-may-call-im who wrote a lot of moving elegies in latin about the year 1800. They are the admiration of scholars, but a mere reader who happens on the volume is left stone cold. Tibullus doesn't leave me cold. Or you are doing what Chatterton did and will doubtless come to a bad end.

If you will write a few sonnets without twisting or diluting the English of A.D. 1934, Tennessee, you will displease the school-masters, but maybe do something worth the trouble, and learn a lot about writing incidentally. But if you keep on writing them like a Petrarch who has learned his English out of books, you will, I am afraid, do as you fear and lapse, and lapse and lapse.

(Letter to George Marion O'Donnell, 1934)

The Role of Criticism

Criticism, especially my own, is painful to me. Presumably the poet knows what he meant to do. The detection of fraud and adulteration is necessary policework, but must keep within the rules of evidence: fact, not hearsay; history, not speculation; all the exhibits there alongside their expert analysis.

There is a purpose in the showcase too; select samples with a sufficient but succinct and unobtrusive ticket, as in "quality" shop-windows. I have very much admired your skill at that job. But:

If I buy a hat I am content that it should fit, be impermeable of good texture, and of colour and cut not outrageously out of fashion. If I am a hatmaker I seek instruction in a series of limited practical operations ending in the production of a good hat with the least possible waste of effort and expense. I NEVER want a philosophy of hats, a metaphysical idea of Hat in the abstract, nor in any case a great deal of talk about hats.

The uses of hats are few, definite and practical. Let a doctor call attention to them from time to time for the conversion of the Hatless Brigade, the rest of us will take them for granted.

This is what I would understand by Objectivism, if the word were mine. It seems to me that one passage in your admirable "Recencies" essay in the Objectivist anthology oversteps the limits of useful criticism.

For the reader, an expert's certificate of precision, concision and general goodworkmanship; or a warning of their absence. For the state, now and then, a reiteration of the known, definite, limited, practical necessity of poetry. For the poet, technical information as from one good craftsman to another; such as doctors exchange in the medical papers.

For this last, Pound's three items quoted by you are a model (Direct treatment: to use no word that does not contribute to the presentation: to compose in the sequence of the musical phrase, not in the sequence of the metronome) His wellknown 'Don'ts' are as explicit and concrete.

Johnson understood the value of minute examination: there is more to be learned from his Notes on Shakespear and the critical parts of Lives of the Poets than from almost all the rest of English criticism put together. You have yourself used a similar method both in public and privately correcting my poems, and it has been valuable. Your version of Rexroth's Prolegomena, compared with his original, is likewise instructive. I think this is what criticism should be.

But these definitions of A Poem! You are not content to swab up Eliot's mess.

We have a pretty good working notion of a poem. Its marks? They can be recorded in a purely scientific spirit. A naturalist can define a tiger, but his definition fits a wretched, mangy, undergrown, pitiful specimen as well as a Blakean super-tyger. He counts its teeth and vertebrae, measures its skull, observes the structure and disposition of its organs. He does not mention ferocity, barely strength; nothing we un-experts commonly associate with tigers.

I distrust your page 15. "A poem. . . . perfect rest. . . . the desire for what is objectively perfect. . . . the desire for inclusiveness. . ." (I select what I like least). There is discrimination; but whether the things discriminated between have any bearing on poetry I doubt. If they have, it is remote.

The aspirations of the hatmaker can only faintly affect the hat. The psychology of the poet is not the critic's business.

Psychology has become as insidious a nuisance to our age as ethics was to the last or theology to an older one. People are constantly committing psychology without knowing it. I have nothing against psychology in its proper orbit (restricted); nor against, ethics, nor theology.

The value of Pound's preaching of Confucius does not lie in Confucius, whose wisdom seems to me to be mixed with the usual quantity of bunk, some of it quite as unpleasant as anything in St. Paul: but in the fact that Pound has not isolated a set of precepts, but developed a pervading stress on the immediate, the particular, the concrete; distrust of abstractions; shrinking from even the suspicion of verbalism; from the puns and polyvalencies in which mystics delight. It is not unspeculative but skeptical. It will build with facts, but declines to soar with inevitably unsteady words. All this is as important to criticism (or any other department of knowledge or action) as it is to poetry.

I have always supposed you to have a greater care for facts than almost any critic now living; a greater partiality for the particular, for the "very words." But these paragraphs about poetry look to me like flights into darkness, away from ascertained and reascertainable fact to speculative mysticism, to a region I think void of anything permanently valuable.

The mystic purchases a moment of exhilaration with a lifetime of confusion; and the exhilaration is incommunicable but the confusion infectious and destructive. It is confusing and destructive to try and explain anything in terms of anything else, poetry in terms of psychology. And in fact the inclusion of Rexroth's vast vagueness in your anthology is, I think, traceable to the importation of an extraneous standard into your judgement of poetry.

I have no alternative *principle*. I do not think anything can be simplified. We can only be content to begin at the beginning and to remain very near the beginning all our lifetime.

We cannot afford to let a subtle monism obscure the lucidity you have often brought to bear on specific poems, as in your study of the "Cantos." A movement, a religion, is no substitute for clearsight, even if it be a much better religion than those recently current amongst writers.

Criticism is to poetry what anatomy, histology, physiology are to the living body. You quote Pound's triple distinction: melopoeia, phanopoeia, logopoeia: a contribution to the science. Criticism is concerned with what is written, not with the mind of the writer, as anatomy with man's body, not with the unguessable intentions of an unlikely Creator.

("Open Letter to Louis Zukofsky," 1932)

† † † † † † † †

As to criticism, let it be written only in latin; the mixed language of latin and english usually employed is too confusing.

(Letter to Harriet Monroe, 1931)

† † † † † † † †

It distracts attention from the work almost always. There are, of course, exceptions. One overstates things as a rule. But there are not very many exceptions. I think that a man who will read *De Vulgari Eloquentia* will have got most of the literary criticism he's ever going to require.

(Interview, *Poetry Information*, 1978)

Critical Views

I like the common eye, cleared, maybe, and very sharp, much better than the inward one or the lens-aided dissecting eye. Hence on the one hand the Illiadic Homer and the Shahnamehic Ferdosi (rather than Odyssey and Yusuf, old man's work, skill above the matter), and on the other the makers of something not altogether drawn from the life: the enamelled flora, alcoholic crescendo, goldleaved erudition, with which Manuchehri surrounds simplicities and gives them overwhelming power. (There are fitful glimpses of the kind of thing in Catullus and Villon.)

(Letter to Pound, 1954)

Manuchehri? . . . . If one puts Homer and Firdosi carefully in one place and then looks for the three or four greatest poets remaining I don't see how anyone who has had the luck to read him can omit Manuchehri. His variety is enormous and everything he did he did better than anyone else. You want the directness of some Catullus? Go to Manuchehri. You want the swiftness of Anacreon? Manuchehri. The elaborate music of Spenser? Manuchehri. The formal fulldress ode with every circumstance of solemnity and splendour? Not Pindar, Manuchehri. Satire direct and overwhelming, Manuchehri all alone—no competitor.

(Letter to Zukofsky, 1949)

† † † † † † † †

. . . there were various characteristics of Northumbrian art which I find repeat themselves through the centuries now and again when you get Northumbrians who are at all sensitive doing anything in the way of the arts. The first great achievement, of course, of the peculiar mixture which grew there, which I suppose must have been two-thirds Celtic and one-third Anglic, the *Codex Lindisfarnensis*, the big famous pages and some of the initials in it, are amongst the major achievements of Western art. And how it is that they aren't in most of the art books—though they are in a few—I cannot understand. What you have there is an extreme intricacy of pattern. There's no underlining. Each of those big, so-called carpet pages has as its theme the cross, but in at least two of them you've got to look a long time before you see it. It's only gradually that it emerges from this wonderfully rich pattern. This lack of underlining and intricacy of pattern are two things which I see in other Northumbrian work, also a combination of terseness and limpidity, which can be seen also in "The Dream of the Rood." All this sort of thing is there permanently; you may be unaware of it, but it's there.

(Interview with Duncan Bush and
Paul Merchant, 1976)

† † † † † † † †

In Tudor music composers were fond of beginning a note just before where we now place the bar and carrying it on over the bar. The technical term for this is syncopation. The effect is to displace a stress or lose it altogether. Wyatt uses this principle very often. If you read carefully, you'll find it used in some of Shakespeare's songs and here and there in other Elizabethan songwriters. . . . But it vanished from music, or at least became less prominent in music, particularly popular music, soon after Elizabethan times and did not revive until this century in verse, except amongst a few highly sophisticated writers. I don't think you really find it used deliberately in verse except perhaps—though he wouldn't have given it that name—in Hopkins, until, very gingerly and only in refrains and such, William Butler Yeats tried his hand at it within my lifetime.

(Lecture, 1974)

††††††††

English poets are too often on their dignity, they strive too constantly to be sublime and end by becoming monotonous and empty of lifegiving detail, like hymn-tunes. They have often been the slaves rather than the masters of their metres. (The sonnet exploited Wordsworth, not he the sonnet.) This is partly because they have neglected the music of Byrd and Dowland so much more supple rhythmically than English poetry or than the music of the classical masters until recently most in favour.

English poets are commonly too much of a piece to be anything but fragmentary, for life is not of a piece. Their movement, their vowel-successions, their alliterations, have been too commonly splendiferous, until verbal splendour has lost its virtue in English: and when, as recently, they frequently fail because they will not devote sufficient care and labour to anything much below the sublime; because they do not understand that cacophony is at least as intricate an art as harmony; because they despise or patronise jazz and other popular music; because, I might add, they do not value or study Dickens, from whom they could, if they would, learn more about poetry than from Milton, Wordsworth, Baudelaire and Rimbaud rolled into one.

In their debauch of easy magnificence—for it has become more difficult to avoid than to achieve the over-rich—English poets have hazed over sharp outlines and made too free a use of translucent but comparatively empty passives and intransitives, forgetting that the world of daylight and full consciousness is, above all, opaque and complex. They have sought yet remoter abstractions even by forced adjectives, and conceits, like some of Mr. Eliot's, painful to follow. They have often thought more carefully about the impression made by their own personality than about that made by the ostensible object of their verse.

Ash Wednesday might serve to demonstrate any of these errors.

Our greatest are not free of these faults. Few have resolutely "kept their eye on the object" (in Wordsworth's phrase), but these few have saved our literature from being merely a series of Marlowes, Miltons, Keatses. I would mention Burns, the last of Dryden, the first of Wordsworth, the author of "Arden of Feversham," possibly Denham and Crabbe, as the few just men for whose sake

Sodom may be spared. I do not imply that these were the best
endowed of our writers: obviously not: but that they were those
who best maintained their poetic integrity. Equally important has
been the example of the series of great prose writers captained by
Swift, Samuel Butler, Wycherley and Dickens.

Shakespeare's talents were much greater than those of any
other north European writer, yet he who reads both Shakespeare
and Dante must notice how Shakespeare makes three or four casts
at an object, three or four approximations, by comparing which
we arrive at his exact meaning. Often the multiplicity is disguised
by deft dovetailing of metaphors; nevertheless the drawing, however marvellous its design, is blurred. Whereas Dante says a thing
once and exactly. His outlines are sharp and precise.

Similarly he who reads Shakespeare and Homer or Firdusi
must notice how Shakespeare fits his cadence to the mood of the
speaker (to some extent—often he is careless). Almost all his cadences are in some sense subjective. The epic music, on the other
hand, belongs to the object, the matter in hand. Shakespeare's
method is admirably suited to the theatre, where actions and physical things are visible and where it is precisely the mood of the
speaker that needs to be created, verbally and by dramatic gesture: but it has been applied imitatively and abusively by other
poets to kinds far different to the infinite damage of literature.

("The Lion and the Lizard,"
unpublished manuscript, 1935)

† † † † † † †

I wrote in a letter a few years ago: "All Ford's biographers
miss the point: what's it matter if he told lies? He was a writer of
fiction. What does matter is his kindness to young men and men in
distress, his readiness to talk to them at length, without being patronising or pedantic, his willingness to consider everything, the
tolerance in his frivolity, his care for living English, his generosity, his fun. Ford did a great deal of good one way and another
and has never been given full credit for it. He was a good poet and
a good novelist too. To dwell on what was comical or exasperating
in him is to mislead a generation that cannot meet him."

Among the young men who owed Ford thanks, few owed
more than Ernest Hemingway: early publication, a chance to edit
in part *the transatlantic review*, or at least to influence its editing,
some introductions, some knowledge of the town, or of that part
of the town Hemingway was least likely to see for himself, gossip

no doubt, and perhaps some notions about the structure of novels. Hemingway too was a writer of fiction, entitled to his lies, and to live them as vividly as he dared, for a novelist must inhabit the people he invents to make them convincing. His chronic fantasy was unusually vulgar, the dream so popular with women and womanish men of a magnanimous bully. It brought him readers and prosperity though it obliged him to write what is really the same book over and over again. He had a right to it.

But his sketch of Ford in *A Moveable Feast* is another sort of lie, one deliberately assembled to damage the reputation of a dead man who had left no skilled close friend to take vengeance; a lie cunningly adjusted to seem plausible to simple people who had never known either Ford or Hemingway and to load his memory with qualities disgusting to all men and despicable to most; yet so false that I, for instance, who knew them both, would never have guessed the unlaughable caricature was meant for Ford if Hemingway had not named it.

Before I heard of *A Moveable Feast* Hemingway was protected by his own grave from what might have been said about him.

("Preface," *Selected Poems:*
Ford Madox Ford, 1971)

† † † † † † †

I HATE a niggard. Let works be vast and artists giving to the limit of their nature. Who, that could build St. Paul's, would potter at bungalows in the outer suburbs? Who, that could write Iliads, would waste his time on triolets? Who, having it in him to write "Gurrelieder," would trifle with dance suites, Brigg Fairs, London Symphonies or any of the other ingenuities and pretty-pretties that fill our ears during nine months of the year whenever we are dragged away from the classics? The true artist is a prodigal who spends all that he has to entertain the Muse, his mistress. Some, even, in emulation of the rich and great, spend more than they have and grow hopelessly insolvent and threadbare, the snobs of Parnassus, representing themselves as symphonists when they are only Elgars. But this age has such a horror of giving itself away (which detestable state of funk it dissembles under the innocent names of modesty, irony and hatred of pretence—as though its irony and modesty were not themselves ridiculous pretensions) that we are in more danger of seeing a man do less than his best, for fear that he should be thought to claim too much, than of having to rebuff one for making claims out of proportion to his abilities.

Yet amplitude and nobility are heart's-demands. The sublime still towers magnificently over the merely beautiful. If we are grateful to Mr. Delius for his polished manners and charming tunes and have no wish to see him leave Brigg Fair to jostle heroes in Valhalla, it is only because we suspect that his idea of the sublime would be as commonplace as Mrs. Todgers' notion of a wooden leg, which nobody except Mr. Pecksniff—and drunk, too—ever desired to see. Contrarily, we forgive the overweening Wagner his frequent bombast, because he walked with gods as well as men and gave us the terrible delight of hearing them speak. We scoff at Wagner as we scoff at Wordsworth, on the plane of the Absolute. We praise Mr. Delius as we praise Mr. Shaw, by reference to the undistinguished mass of his contemporaries.

Alas! We ask for Thucydides and are given—Strachey! We search for Rubens and find—Grant! We listen for an echo of Beethoven and hear—Bax! Clever men, restrained and chaste, working well within what they conceive to be their powers; unemphatic, *gentlemen*; and barren as rock! Beethoven was no gentleman. Good manners are incompatible with the sublime. This glut of polished poverty, this bourgeois habit of husbanding resources, this old-wives' wisdom of never putting all your eggs into one basket, makes us clutch at anything ambitious and full with an eagerness that arches the eyebrows of the prevailing, precious sect.

("Gurrelieder," *The Outlook*, 1928)

† † † † † † † †

There is no poetry in England, none with any relation to the life of the country, or of any considerable section of it. . . . the rulers of England for a generation or more have never been indifferent to literature, they have been actively hostile. They have even set up and encouraged the frivolous imbecilities of cat-poetry, bird-poetry, flower-poetry; country-house Jorrocks-cum-clipper-ship poetry (as Mr. Masefield does it); and innumerable other devices for obscuring any work that smells of that objectionable quality, truth.

There is no need for complete suppression. If the price of poetry is high, or books hard to get by smuggling; and if education is managed so as to represent Rupert Brooke as the romantic high-light of the last generation, Humbert Wolfe as the delightful drawing-room poet of this, the divorce between literature and the British subject is complete. The gulf is unpassable. The intelligent reader in England is the frequenter of two small public-houses in Bloomsbury, plus a few isolated idiosyncratic scholars in the provinces.

When they see what is given out publicly as poetry, men of good but not specifically literary intelligence conceive a contempt for poetry similar to that traditional amongst the army and hunting people, and still fostered in the schools. The readers of Mr. Squire, Mr. Shanks, and so forth, are the school-teachers.

Poetry withdraws into itself. It can reach but a small audience, small enough to have special learning and, as it were, passwords; too small to hope to influence even a corner of the national culture, so that, proposing no end but the exercise of its special knowledge, it delights more and more in approximations to the acrostic, less and less in true concision, which implies force and clarity as well as paucity of words. The cure?—I can see nothing for it but patience.

("English Poetry Today," Poetry [Chicago], 1932)

[Mary Butts] knows one milieu well, that of the rich or almost-rich dilletantes of bohemian art and life. These are the chosen few who condescend to write or to paint in the quiet, comfortable, rich squares of Bloomsbury and who do not seem to notice that the sweet, drippy, unbearable smell of decadence which has recently pervaded every English product, comes precisely from Bloomsbury. Mary Butts, however, does not satirize that dung heap believed to be a bed of lillies. She does not even consider it from a comic perspective. Rather, she sanctifies and worships it, the stubborn rear-guard of a dying golden age in which the servants were servile and even the well-off tradesmen prudently bowed to Birth and Education. This attitude does not help the author understand the servants and tradesmen. A parallel to this perhaps could not be found in modern times outside of England or pre-revolution Russia.

(Literary review, Il Mare, 1933,
translated from the original Italian)

The world doesn't spend all its time reading books, and we all assumed that they do. We have far too many references to things.

There we tumbled below Yeats. Yeats is very careful. He produces very few references to previous literature. His references are those you can find in the life around you, and that is much easier, and much better, and more provident, especially where literary fashions change. Eliot above all, of course, is using other literature all the time. Pound, to a considerable extent; Zukofsky, to some extent; me also—and that will weigh against us as the century goes on.

(Interview, *St. Andrews Review*, 1977)

† † † † † † † †

The public is genuinely anxious to do what it has been told is its duty by men of genius, but at the same time it wants, and quite reasonably, to be able to understand what it pays for. It is not able to understand the really serious poet, but it can notice his mannerisms, and when it sees these mannerisms reproduced over and around a content it can with care get the hang of, it thinks it has found a genius it can honour and you get those bubble reputations that the next age finds so extraordinarily puzzling.

(Letter to Leippert, 1932)

† † † † † † † †

Ezra asked in a previous number [of *Poetry*] : Whose judgment would one trust next to one's own? I think he meant the question seriously, so here's my list.

Ezra Pound, Carlos Williams, Louis Zukofsky, W.B. Yeats, Marianne Moore, Mina Loy, and Eliot. In that order.

Some of these have opinions very different from mine, but for one reason or another worth serious consideration. Two of them would probably exclude my work from any list they might make of decent poetry.

(Letter to Morton Dauwen Zabel, 1933)

† † † † † † † †

The young are apt to say that Yeats was an old square, or even a fascist beast. Such criticism may be irrelevant to poetry— I think it is—but it is as well to get it out of the way if possible. There were plenty of other fascist beasts about in the thirties, and among the poets, Yeats's close friend Ezra Pound is the most obvious. Eliot is another, the more insidious for being disguised as an English gentleman. What these poets and many other writers really had in common was a love of order. With order in society it matters little whether you are rich or poor, you will not be harassed by perpetual changes of fortune, you can plan your life's work within known limits, not felt as limits because they are as unavoidable as the limits imposed by our physique or the duration of human life. Whether an orderly society ever really existed or could exist is beside the point. Plato planned one, in our own day the socialists have proposed half a dozen different models for one, and in Yeats's youth William Morris had imagined yet another Utopia and made a great impression with *News from Nowhere*. Yeats went further than the rest when he called for ceremony, manners as elaborate as those he imagined in the Byzantine court. All such fancies assume tacitly that the regulations and ceremonies are made by extremely wise and perfectly unselfish rulers, not by Stalin or Hitler or even Mussolini, and none of their proponents, not Plato himself, pauses to consider where and how such rulers are to be found. The maxims given to guide the wise rulers are plausible and disastrous. You are told how blessed the ruler is who will make two blades of grass grow where one grew before, but never reminded that the people may not give a damn about blades of grass. They may, like the Arabs in Libya and in Palestine, prefer a desert, and there may be good reasons for preferring a desert. Abdulaziz Ibn Saud might have listed them. The blades of grass maxim is the standard excuse for imperialism, and I think Yeats would never have used it; but it lurks under all utopian dreams of order.

Weighing this up, if it is worth weighing at all, you must of course allow for my own conviction that "God is the dividing sword," and that order is no more than a rather unfortunate accident that sometimes hampers civilization. But my purpose is only to remind some critics that Yeats's love of order is something he shared with Dante and Shakespeare and probably far more than half of the world's great poets, as well as with nearly all the philosophers and historians. His way of expressing it was his own; he took his instances largely from the world around him, that of the Anglo-Irish gentry, which differs in personnel from the hierarchy of the church or of business management or of the civil service, but does not differ from them in principle. He was much nearer to Bernard Shaw than he would have liked to think.

Still, if Yeats's political thought hardly differed at bottom from what was current all around him, if his philosophic, theosophic, magical quasi-religion was trivial and by origin insincere, politics and religion were not his business except in the sense in which they are everyone's business. He was a poet. It is true that he loaded his conception of being a poet with all manner of lofty moral responsibilities, which seemed to claim authority in politics and religion. He wrapped an invisible bardic cloak around him whenever he uttered a line of anyone's verse. His determination that poetry should be noble rather starved his own of the humour which was part of his conversation. But for him, at least in middle-age, poetry needed no formal thought, no logical theory. It was in him. Just as we say some painter thinks with his brush, so Yeats thought with his pen, and if his pen ever misled him on purely poetical matters, it was so rarely that I cannot think of an instance, though perhaps a search through his volume might bring a few to light. I don't suppose that he was born that way. So far as my experience goes, poetry is a craft hard to learn and only acquired by long apprenticeship. In these days, of course, there is no one for a man to be apprenticed to except himself, so that diligence is more necessary than ever. Yeats was diligent. He must have taught his ear to attend to rhythm and vowel sequence and what the Welsh have codified but the rest of us grope for to hold the sounds of our verse together, yet he learnt all these so early that people who are content with inaccurate phrases would say he was born with them.

("Yeats Recollected," Agenda, 1974)

† † † † † † †

Ezra Pound came to England some years before the War, wearing the mantle of Browning with a difference: with its redundant folds excised and the rest reshaped aesthetically. Mathews was his publisher.

He was welcome. His poetry at that time offended nobody because it seemed to deal with remote, picturesquely historical themes, while its beauty of rhythmic texture, not unakin to early Yeats, was in itself pleasing.

He was heard of as a scholar, explaining the "Spirit of Romance," the poets of Provence and Tuscany, the French and Spanish epics. He translated Bertran de Born, Arnaut Daniel, Guido Cavalcanti, the Anglo-Saxon "Seafarer." He interested himself in every branch of the technique of verse, rhymed, rhymeless, accentual, quantitative, alliterative, as strict as the ballade and altogether free. He wrote Sapphics successfully in English, and a Sestina stronger than, and almost as musical as, Spenser's. He made himself, early in his career, one of the most consummate masters of the technique of versification that our literature has ever seen.

He excluded from his poetry the arbitrary inversions then, as still, common; the mechanical adjectives sought not because the sense needed them but out of habit or to fill up a line; all unnecessary explanation or elaboration; everything that impeded the swift, direct movement of a poem. He knew how widely the yardstick metric of the pedants differs from the metric of the ear, and explored the difference more and more boldly.

The troubadours wrote to be sung; all lyric poetry was written to be sung down to the time when Racan lamented that Malherbe was handicapped by his inability to finger the lute, in the middle of the XVIIth century. Pound felt poetry to be aural and at all times made the ear the arbiter of what was admissible. Not all, not very many of the poets of our time have perceived that fact or dare trust themselves to it.

Pound's announcement of the results of his years of technical research (which had, as they went on, flowered in several volumes of very delicately beautiful verse) was the whole life of Imagism. But he was not content to rest there. While the other Imagists were attempting with varying success to live up to his list of "Dont's," he had turned with the same energy and thoroughness to other matters. His apprenticeship was over, he could begin to record the modern scene.

His apprenticeship was over, but not his researches. His studies of modern French poetry, amongst the first in England, had considerable repercussions. He reconsidered Catullus and Propertius. He studied and translated Japanese Noh and Chinese classical poetry—his volume "Cathay" has given every subsequent translator a method and a model; and as Fenollosa's literary executor he published that scholar's "Essay on the Chinese Written Character," which, though still little known, must eventually have a far-reaching influence on Western literature. He has quite recently deepened his study of Guido Cavalcanti and edited the monumental edition of that poet published by Marsano of Genoa.

(It is worth noting in passing how differently Eliot underwent the discipline of Gautier: making the enamel brighter, harder, more rigid than ever; phrases for posters. Compare "The Hippopotamus" and the Sweeney poems with "Mauberley," and both with "Emaux et Camées.")

It is impossible to understand why Eliot should have excluded the "Propertius" from his selection of Pound's work. The plea of its difficulty will not hold, for as a consummation is always simpler than a beginning, the "Propertius" is certainly much simpler than some of Pound's short earlier works whose content is sometimes elusive, tenuous, evanescent. London or Rome, does the name, the ostensible date, much signify? We are amongst contemporaries, listening to a contemporary, the difficulties are the difficulties of our own lives. We are not going to be confused by the use of a mythology that is common enough in all our poets. If we are cornered by it, a classical dictionary will help us out.

The question of the relation of Pound's poem with the book of Propertius's elegies does not arise, except for the literary historian. There is no claim that this is a translation. The correspondence, the interpenetration of ancient and modern is Pound's, not Propertius's. There is an implicit criticism of Propertius, a deep and intimate study of him, but that does not concern the reader unless he wants it to.

The beautiful step of the verse, the cogent movement of thought and feeling throughout, the sensitive perception of the little balanced in the great and their mutual dependence, the extraordinary directness, here and there quite naked, achieved in spite of the complexity of the whole conception; a poem that is a society and an age, that of Rome as well as that of London. It certainly earned Thomas Hardy's esteem. Or say, London with a veil of Rome, softening the brutality of contemporary fact; today as a man sees it, who knows what has been as well as what is, knows, that is to say, a good deal of our future as well as our present, sees the age with a background of the ages as in "Mauberley" he sees the poet with a background of the age.

In my considered opinion, "Propertius" was the most important poem of our times, surpassing alike "Mauberley" and "The Waste Land." . . . Since leaving England after the publication of "Mauberley," Pound has published "Thirty Cantos" of a poem "of some length." . . .

The method explored in "Homage to Propertius" is here enormously expanded. A whole world, it seems, is to be built up, all ages, or all that present any features to the purpose, interpenetrating and corresponding. The parallel with Dante is obvious, and obviously in the poet's mind. The Divine Comedy is a world built up of thousands of individual instances classified and correlated. The "Cantos" take their matter here and there, at first it seems haphazardly: but order is beginning to show in the great conglomeration. The fact of correlation is already clear, if not yet the principle it is based on. To illustrate, comment, contrast, organise, the Good Life is presumably the object of the poem, as of Dante's. Here, however, the unseen organiser of the framework is not St. Thomas, but, if anybody, Confucius, whose "Ta Hio" Pound has translated. . . . The best equipped poet of our time is here grappling with the greatest task that poetry can present. Success or failure, the effort is one that speakers of our language have reason to be proud of and to applaud.

He first publicly recognised the talents of Joyce, Eliot and others: and a good deal of later criticism has been merely, in effect, repetitions of Pound's very early perceptions. His interest in the musical element in poetry led, naturally, to the study of music itself: two years' concert criticism for the "New Age"; a book on Antheil; a logical and convincing extension of the theory of harmony; and the opera "Villon," recently performed by the B.B.C.

The pamphlet "How to Read," recently published by Desmond Harmsworth, conveniently epitomises his criticism and rounds off the cycle begun with "The Spirit of Romance."

"Lustra," in 1915, surveyed London by items, by epigrams. Soon after the War appeared the two long poems of modern life, "Mauberley" and "Homage to Propertius."

In "Mauberley" Pound desired to do in short compass for 1920 what Henry James had repeatedly done, a couple of volumes at a time, for the '80's. Its metrical system may have been derived in part from Gautier. Pound's own personality is too vivid to allow this derivation to show. "Mauberley" was, in the result, a work of the highest originality. A man, not quite Pound himself, living and moving in a whole environment, expressing himself in verses more supple, less glittering than Gautier's. The gnaw of the century's indifference and incomprehension recorded without being heightened, as Eliot later heightened it in "The Waste Land," into tragedy.

("Mr. Ezra Pound," *The New English Weekly*, 1932)

Dante made his samplings of all previous ages known to him superficially plausible by the device of his journey made through the other world. Mr. Pound has dispensed with the allegory. We may be glad to be spared the kind of allegory that is like a message in code. Examples make their own point without the need of any sermons by riddles. What comment the author deems

indispensable is supplied by the arrangement and occasionally by
the hint of a cross-reference, . . . echoes and anticipations. . . .

(from *The Cantos of Ezra Pound:*
Some Testimonials . . . , 1933)

† † † † † † †

A short poem or a short piece of music can exist and endure
mainly by its texture, the sound of a few lines, or a few lines at a
time. Even so, you usually have something more general, a shape
that begins with the poem or the piece and doesn't complete itself satisfactorily til the poem is finished. We're all used to that
idea in music where we specify a piece by the name of the particular shape, sequence, symmetry, or whatever it has: fugue or
minuet, toccata or symphony or sonata, or whatnot. And add to
that where necessary its key and its number amongst the composer's works, and so on. Some poetical forms are equally familiar: sonnet, rondeau, hokku, but others are less definite, at least
they've got no name, a lot of them.

In the last century Browning invented something that we've
taken to calling the 'persona', but it's hardly really a form. A
persona is a mask, that is the meaning of the word, and Browning's
form has been imitated by Kipling, by Ezra Pound and T.S. Eliot,
and some other people, but as I say, it's not really a form at all in
the sense I'm speaking of. It is merely the poet imagining some
other person speaking, and that person's words are the poem. . . .
the words just go on falling out til everything has been said without necessarily being shaped by anything more than the poet's
taste.

Now, a poem of any length whose parts are not related to
each other by something much more precise than taste is apt to
sag or lose proportion. One or two poets before and after 1920
who had understood the notion of modifying and combining
rhythmic themes the way Whitman had sometimes done and
Pound did in his "Propertius" and who found that a satisfactory
way of conducting the verse from line to line or over a few pages,
began to wonder whether music could furnish them with an overall shape as well as with a tissue or texture or whatever you might
call the local shape of the verse.

Eliot in "The Waste Land" stumbled by sheer accident on
something very closely analogous to the form that musicians call
the sonata but he was surprisingly slow to realize what he had
done—though in the end he proclaims it in the title of the "Four

Quartets," a quartet being normally a sonata written for violins, viola and a cello. Pound, however, and Zukofsky after him, was fascinated by the close texture of the fugue and by its somewhat spurious air of logicality. They wanted to know whether the design of the fugue could be transferred to poetry. A short but incomplete answer to that is that it can't. A fugue is essentially contrapuntal, several voices imitating each other, yet free of each other, all talking simultaneously, whereas poetry is written for one voice at a time or, at most, for voices in unison. But Bach had set an example. He wrote at least two fugues for unaccompanied violin. Of course they are not really fugues. No amount of double stopping can get three or more voices to sing simultaneously on the violin. The entries in Bach's unaccompanied violin fugues wait til the last entry is done or nearly done before they start. Yet he manages to convey a rather teasing sensation of a fugue, never really satisfied. Similar sequences of notes are thrown up time and again, but they never mesh together as those of a true fugue do.

Zukofsky wrote a fugue of this sort for unaccompanied voice. It's Part 7 of his long poem *"A."* It is not a fugue, but it does suggest one, suggests it very strongly. But Pound, thinking out his *Cantos* a full decade before Zukofsky was not looking for a form that fulfils itself in a page or two. Whatever suggestion he took from fugal writing must be capable of being sustained through 120 Cantos, some of which proved to be very long. "Canto 72," I think it is, lasts for about an hour and a half. Obviously Pound was going to need many themes, not just one or two or three or four. He was going to involve himself in a polyphony far beyond anything that Bach contemplated or even the great Flemish composers of the fifteenth century who occasionally have as many as forty parts going at a time. And yet it could never be a true polyphony because poetry has only one line at a time. Pound wanted something that would carry on a theme, a sequence, in the hearer's mind since he couldn't provide it actually in his ear. And so he had to go beyond the musical elements of poetry and rely on ideas or images. That's what he did. *The Cantos* are so long and were written over such a long time—more than fifty years—that they are not wholly consistent, but right through them there are images and ideas that perpetually recur, combine and recombine, and that stay in the reader's mind, half-noticed, while some other idea or image is being announced, making a huge, polyphonic pattern of images. Polyphonic is obviously the wrong word since we are no longer speaking of sound, but ideas. But I didn't know what word I could invent to take its place. This is quite consistent with composing the actual words according to the rhythmical notions he had derived through Whitman from nineteenth century music.

Moreover, this use of images fell in with ideas he'd picked up from Fenollosa's theory of the Chinese written character. I am told that Ernest Fenollosa was wrong as a philologist, but his notion was certainly fruitful for poetry and criticism. He thought that by putting together two or more very simple images you could show, graphically, a meaning different from either of them which they added up to. A picture of the sun set behind a picture of a tree makes a Chinese character, evidently the sun shining through the branches which, in a normal countryside, must be either sunrise or sunset and that is the meaning of the character. A man standing beside a mouth with something issuing from it must be a man standing by his word, keeping his promise, therefore faithful, trustworthy, and all that sort of meaning. In poetry, men commonly put two images together, either explicitly or implicitly, and it's called metaphor. From each metaphor the hearer can get something more than what is meant by either image alone, or even by both of them if they were not presented together. That's a great gain in concision.

Of course this is a very old practice and a very old commonplace of criticism, but Pound enlarged it enormously. He found it possible to leave out far more than is usually left out between the separate images which combine together to produce a meaning. He deals not so much in single images set against one another as in whole families of images. For him Helen of Troy whose beauty caused wars ties up at once with Eleanor of Aquitaine whose similar beauty caused similar war and with certain less celebrated ladies of Provence and with a President's wife who caused political dissension and with a whole array of goddesses. After all, Helene is the Attic form of the older Greek Selene, a goddess, goddess of the moon, Artemis, Diana, Latona—who presides over childbirth—and several other goddesses, all tying up with the moon, with each other and with Helen. Diana caused Actaeon to be chased by his own hounds, and a certain Provencal lady caused, accidentally, her poet-lover to be chased by dogs too. There is no end to the ramifications of image of which Helen, Eleanor, Artemis, and so on, are all facets.

Now, he has many such bundles of images and it's these great bundles that Pound plays with, and the bundles are not permanently tied together. He can always take a few sticks from one faggot and a few from another to make yet a third, so that there's an extraordinarily complex system of related images, changing as fluidly as the data of life and thought themselves, and yet never losing touch with each other. I suppose that's what baffles critics who are used to rigid systems in which one image always implies another, but not to one in which the relationships are so multiple that before you reach the end of the poem you may be inclined to think that each image implies all the rest. That was no doubt what Pound intended. I think he falls short of it, but he comes near enough to make a most wonderfully intricate work of art which I think will keep the scholars busy for generations and delight readers more and more as the principles on which it is composed become more familiar to them, as the little part you happen to be reading more and more seems to imply the whole poem.

And that's probably all I have to say about *The Cantos* that hasn't been said by others. A good many people have had a go at explaining them but all of them seem to be thinking rather of what *The Cantos* say than of how they say it. That's a mistake because all art, poetry particularly, is concerned with form and what the form encloses is always secondary, sometimes entirely negligible. A partial exception among these critics is Hugh Kenner, the Canadian critic, who is also the most readable contemporary critic. He conducts his investigations rather like a combination of Sherlock Holmes, Maigret, and Hercule Poirot, and it's just as easy and fascinating to read as the chronicles of those illustrious detectives. If you get interested in *The Cantos*, don't neglect to read Kenner's books. But you don't *need* to. The sound alone will carry you through a great deal of the poem and nearly all the matter, though it may seem obscure at first, clarifies itself bit by bit as the poem procedes and as it takes up its relationship to all the other bits of matter in it.

However, Kenner has written very acutely about the first Canto as a program for the whole. I don't think he notices, or at any rate, brings out very clearly, the fact that the second Canto is also part of this program with which he sets out. I'll tell you very briefly what these two Cantos seem to imply. . . .

The first Canto takes an episode from Homer's *Odyssey* which seems, on the face of it, to be Homer's refashioning of something very ancient indeed, the passage in which Odysseus visits the underworld to consult the dead seer Tiresias about his own future. They call this passage the Nekuia. To find out the future of course you must interrogate the past and that's what Odysseus is doing and this is part of what Pound intends to do in his poem. The ghosts that Odysseus meets can only talk when they have been fed with fresh blood from the sacrifice and this may be taken as a symbol of the severe labour and research. Odysseus has to drive away his own mother, Anticlea, to keep the blood of the sacrifice for Tiresias—as a poet must drive away his own intimate emotions to keep faithful to the form of his poem as a whole. And when Tiresias comes he says something that is not in Homer. He says, "A second time? why?" Odysseus only went to hell once. The second visitor is Pound in the character of Odysseus. Now, to underline things still further, Pound shows that he is not translating directly from Homer, but from a Latin translation made by Andreas Divus in 1538, so that what we are getting is Pound's view of Divus' view of Homer's view of the pre-historic Nekuia, and that's the best that history can ever do for us. Hardly any of history's evidence is even second-hand. In the last two lines of the Canto Pound seems to identify Circe with Aphrodite. All this, except the last few lines, is done in a metre, or—metre is hardly the word—in a system which Pound first elaborated to re-produce what he felt to be, not the form, but the feeling of Old English verse, thus to ram home the notion that we are dealing with something very remote, archaic and fundamental. And so we are to interrogate the past.

But that's not all. We go on to the second Canto and he be-gins by complaining of Browning's romanticization of the Italian troubador Sordello, about whom the real evidence is scanty and not very illuminating. The Sordellos come from Mantua—as the item which Pound uses for the purpose—and a certain Chinese sage, So-shu, is discovered churning in the sea, as it might be Pound churning the inchoate mass of the past and its records. Now, if you churn milk, it turns into butter, so if you churn the sea, presumably it turns into dry land, with an identifiable shape, and if you churn history industriously enough, it too will take on a shape. A lot of people in the early part of this century expected to find laws of history like laws of nature—Spengler and Toynbee, for example. But if you are going to get results of the kind they hoped for, you will need more than merely interrogating the dead and churning in the sea of facts.

There follows in the Canto a series of metamorphoses such as Ovid wrote about, that is, stories of how human beings were sud-denly changed by the gods into trees, animals, all sorts of things, so that they became visible under a totally new aspect, just as by a sudden insight. Within the frame of reference set up by the first Canto, a metamorphosis can only mean the means by which we do suddenly see men and things under a new aspect—what are called modes of vision, whether we're talking about the abrupt formation of a new scientific hypothesis or the abrupt contact with god which mystics claim, or merely the insight that comes from a combination of study and natural sympathy. The identification of Eleanor with Helen by applying to her the famous Homeric tag, "destroyer of ships, destroyer of cities," and following with the words of the old men on the wall when they looked at Helen is almost a metamorphosis in itself. And then there are two sea metamorphoses, divided by the main part of the Canto which consists of a very free version of Ovid's story of how Acoetes warned King Pentheus against showing contempt for Dionysus, the god of wine, by telling about the ship and sailors which were trying to kidnap the young god which he, when he discovered what they were up to, changed suddenly into rocks, vegetation and fishes. And, by the way, besides its function of showing the kind of thing that you are afterwards to expect in the poem, the sudden insight, this story had contemporary significance because it was elaborated at the moment when, against the will of Woodrow Wilson, Congress committed America to try Prohibition, a contempt for Dionysus which was, ultimately, thoroughly avenged. . . .

By way of curiosity and to show you how carefully all the details are selected in this enormous mass of stuff, there is a name there, "Illeuthyeria," and in the heavy work of reference that's been concocted to tell you what's what all through *The Cantos*, they find no explanation for Illeuthyeria. She's not in Ovid, she's not one of the usual metamorphoses about the place, but a few months ago I happened to read what I think is very rarely read except by professed classical scholars, the facts of the Homeridae, and there in one of the followers of Homer, in a fragment saved by some dictionary makers, there's Illeuthyeria alright, doing just what Pound said she did. He had read all these obscure things to make sure he got things right.

("Ezra Pound," a lecture, 1974)

Mr. Eliot's *Criterion* is an international disaster, since he began to love his gloom, and regretfully, resignedly, to set about perpetuating the causes of it—kings, religion and formalism. From the announcement of his back-to-Madame-de-Maintenon program dates his acceptance by the English weeklies. *The Criterion* has gone about the business of blunting the English intelligence as systematically as the quarterlies of a century ago, but less crudely; disclaiming any intention of stoning budding Keatses, even occasionally printing work of candidates for pages in the literary histories of the next century.

Mr. Eliot's intelligence, turned to the work of drugging intelligence (having first, let's charitably suppose, drugged itself), can do much more havoc in England than in America; for kings, priests and academies are not living issues in the States. Mr. Yeats, almost single-handed, made modern Ireland, God forgive him; and Mr. Eliot, given a little more energy, might manage to keep England wallowing in its present misery a few more years by administering bromides and soporifics to the—well, intelligentsia. The deadly influence of London on sensitive Americans might have been noted before Henry James, but James lauded a confessedly ended system of stultification, while Eliot seems rather to desire to inaugurate a new one. I have nothing to say against his poetry, amongst the finest of the age; but against his influence on the poetry of others, the involuntary extinguisher he applies to every little light, while professing, maybe truly, to hate the dark.

("English Poetry Today," *Poetry* [Chicago], 1932)

† † † † † † † †

. . . when one attacked Eliot that didn't mean one didn't value Eliot; it meant that one felt he ought to be up and doing with the same sort of vigour and uncompromisingness of Pound, Zukofsky and Carlos Williams.

(Interview, *meantime*, 1977)

† † † † † † † †

"The Waste Land's" reputation is secure. It stands with Pound's "Propertius" at the head of modern English poetry. It has had an enormous influence; greater than Pound's, partly because its surface aspect is simpler, almost bare of mythological or historical names; partly because it is easy for a generation in love with earnestness, not to say solemnity, to overlook, if it chooses, the sardonic humour of "The Waste Land," whereas Pound's sceptical humour is all-pervading and will not let the reader rest satisfied with the importance of his own nostalgias; and finally, because the notes invite the great brigade of acrosticians, pedants, commentators, more numerous now than for centuries.

"The Waste Land" should be read without the notes. It needs no explaining that is not contained in its own lines. Every reference is a red-herring to drag the reader away to hunt the "meaning" of the poem anywhere but in the poem itself. And as for the poet's intention, intention and achievement are two things.

Structure: not the typical tragedy of a creature pitted against fate, nor yet the Hamlet-tragedy of uncertainties. The protagonist, having foreseen the end, having appraised his own strength and reckoned it inadequate, refuses the combat, not with resignation, since one can only be resigned to something known whereas what fate has in store is unknown, but with nervous suspense, waiting for an indefinitely terrible event; and with no better hope than that of saving a few pitifully inadequate scraps of what has been found good. "These fragments I have shored against my ruins": thus he announces his despair with a sneer at himself—and at us, the world, that has not known how to provide better comfort than these half-dozen phrases.

It is not easy to remake in durable verse a mood of intense emotion, common enough to be checked by a great many men, and yet which has almost no contact with tangible, definite *things*; or rather, which has such multifarious contacts that no one or no few of them will serve to define it. That the emotions are simple in themselves and popular—nothing arouses such enthusiasm as despair—help only thus far: that the reader is ready to take a hint. Rats and bones, slightly ridiculous, decidedly hackneyed, will serve to point his emotions where to go and he will not be too critical of these fingerposts if the road is otherwise satisfactory. Eliot mobilised all the devices he had practised in his earlier poems: and the sumptuous rhythms native to him could be allowed to display their full splendour often.

The reader will recognise the persistent beat, the precision of phrase (now with scarcely a trace of preciousness), parody, emotional states doubled by or entrusted wholly to the rhythm, the heightening of a splendour by setting amongst shabby lines (here, however, reminding one of Rembrandt rather than of Horace), the abrupt transitions. The humour must be underlined because it is usually passed over in silence. It is oftenest a sneer, very often a sneer at the protagonist: but the Stetson episode; "When Lil's husband got demobbed"; and the parody of Elizabethan profusion in part II, seem to me a freer mirth, more like the gaiety underlying "Prufrock," and such as I am sorry Eliot should, apparently, have lost. It is a gaiety without philosophic implications, compatible with tragedy, leaving no afterthought; and, I should have thought, better to shore against the ruins than "Le Prince d'Aquitaine à la tour abolie." Besides, it is a safeguard against tripping over from the impressive to the foolish, a danger which Eliot has sometimes barely avoided ("a broken Coriolanus" and the later centenarian pose, beside the rats). Its use in a tragic poem is, of course, Elizabethan, though an extension of Flaubertian theories of contrast could also have led to it.

Eliot has investigated jazz as a medium for tragedy. It is not such a very far call from the strong beat on which his earlier work is based to the still stronger, exaggerated beat of jazz, and some of the other devices used in his poems have a parallel in common dance-music. It is astonishing that the tentative fragment "Wanna go Home, Baby?" has never been followed up either by Eliot or by his imitators.

A much greater modification of his earlier methods was needed to fit them to a "devotional" content. Two carols, written with at least as much skill as his other work, remained tepid and a little stodgy. Subtle rhythms, with no remaining trace of the trap-drum; a more complex metrical system, substituting a visibly controlled intricacy of pattern for the opulent simplicity of blank verse; and a vocabulary of ascetic simplicity; besides, naturally, the abandonment of all parody and irony, were clearly needed. Accordingly, they appear: first in "The Hollow Men," harshly, as though there had been not a development so much as a forcible break with the earlier manner: then, more graciously and much more consummately in "Ash Wednesday," "restoring with a new verse the ancient rhyme." Considered as a technical feat, "Ash Wednesday" easily surpasses "The Waste Land," or would surpass it if it were not marred several times by the intrusion of verses alien to the rest, such as the earlier manner would have tolerated but which are here repugnant to their context: "Enchanted the may-time with an antique flute"; and by two or three bad verses, bad in any context: ("Why should the agèd eagle stretch its wings?") or again, the one about the agèd shark; where the adjective is affected as well as gratuitous. If John Collier had retouched the poem to turn it into a caricature, he could not have insinuated any line more to his purpose.

The alleged anachronism of Pound consists in assuming a reader better acquainted with history and literature than readers usually are. Eliot's, in his devotional verse, is more fundamental. He writes as though from conditions that have vanished, as a contemporary of George Herbert. He has his reward. What is antique enough is notoriously harmless, is supine, and the ruling powers can encourage its circulation without uneasiness.

("Mr. T.S. Eliot," *The New English Weekly*, 1932)

. . . though the *Four Quartets* were written with great skill and have been very carefully thought out, are patterned exactly on *The Waste Land* which had already made its success, somehow there remains something very contrived about the *Four Quartets*. Even the best passages in them seem more like exceedingly good pastiche rather than like something that had forced itself on Mr. Eliot. I think it arises from the fact that he is, not himself, but as the author of those poems, claiming a direct mystical experience which he hasn't got. It is in fact forged out of the English mystics and St. John of the Cross, and so forth.

(Interview with Duncan Bush and
Paul Merchant, 1976)

. . . for some people whose writing we see, we lower the hurdles on the course and applaud a race which is all very well for that class of runner; but . . . in dealing with some other people, of whom Ezra is one and you yourself another, we say "This chap means business: he is entered without a handicap against Dante and Lucretius, against Villon and Horace," and we make no allowances at all and if he is beaten we say so: but there is perhaps more credit in coming even almost last in such a race than in winning the other: at any rate to make a good show in it, to be taken seriously in it, whether you break your neck on the hurdles or not, is nothing discreditable. At least for my part I'd rather have somebody who is thinking of Horace call my poems bloody bad than hear them praised by somebody who is thinking of— who? of—Dylan Thomas.

(Letter to Zukofsky, 1949)

† † † † † † † †

A large part of his *"A"* is almost confessedly a diary from the beginning. It's not a scheme to show the entire world as Spenser

tried, as Pound tried, as Dante succeeded in doing. Zukofsky is
simply portraying Zukofsky's own progress through the world—
which is, of course, very interesting in itself, but it's certainly an
easier scheme to carry out. Any change, any inconsistency is ac-
counted for by the passage of life. As with Wordsworth's "Prelude."

(Interview, *St. Andrews Review*, 1977)

† † † † † † † †

You have a singing voice that floats off most of the odd syntactical things you often do: a deeper voice than the others one hears:
and an absence of moral fervour which is refreshing. As the years
go on I find my Zukofsky far more in these lyrics than in the
larger more ambitious stuff which seems to claim importance for
people and ideas I don't find important and sometimes for tor-
tuous metricalities which aren't necessary because you have the
slight of hand to dispense with them—which would lighten the
product.

(Letter to Zukofsky, 1953)

† † † † † † † †

There is a difference . . . between myself and Zukofsky, and
. . . that is partly a result of his having been all his life a professional poet and practically nothing else, whereas I have produced
very little. It always was my idea, when I was a youngster, that
there were a certain number of things which every man ought
to do, to experience, without which he would hardly be whole,
and my notion was that somebody like Sir Walter Raleigh was
such a person one ought to be; he did a mass variety of things, did
them all well, some of them supremely well. And so, though Zukofsky is full of praise of eyes, writes *Bottom: on Shakespeare* to
tell you that eyes are what matter, and so forth, in fact he hasn't
got any, so to speak. I'm exaggerating there. He is a New York
Cockney, and though he has very sharp eyes, when he uses them,
Louis has spent most of his life confined to his room getting things
out of books and ideas out of his head, and out of books, rather
than seeing things. Now that always tends towards a degree of
abstraction, and abstraction is the enemy of poetry at all times,
the enemy of other kinds of writing too, it's not a peculiarly
poetical thing. Whereas I believe that I have always had my eyes
very wide open, have always lived out and away from books, and

so things seen fit very well as matter to fill up the form. And that has an advantage in that, to most people, things seen, things noticed for the first time especially, are particularly vivid, they come over much better to the reader than any abstraction. It is an advantage which I share to a considerable extent with Pound. Though Pound also tied himself a good deal to books he had extremely sharp eyes which were always at work all about him, and at any rate once he got out of London there was all that material to use. The lights drifting out to sea in the festival at Rapallo he does beautifully; I was the first to do that but my poem was too bad and I tore it up.

(Interview, *meantime*, 1977)

[Like MacDiarmid] Pound and Zukofsky have sought a poetry of facts . . . , but neither, I think, has ever quite separated facts from metaphysics. MacDiarmid has his mysticism; and no doubt science itself is founded on undefined faith; but MacDiarmid sees things washed clean of irrelevancies as Darwin did. Suckling poets should be fed on Darwin till they are filled with the elegance of things seen or heard or touched. Words cannot come near it, though they name things. *Their* elegance is part precision, more music. . . .

For MacDiarmid all knowledge is organised by art and centres round it. He has written much about art, mainly about poetry itself, seen oftenest in the light of complex music. Sometimes his writing seems to be largely an attempt to persuade people muddled by economics and politics, enthralled by feats of technology, that their safety lies at last in poetry and music, poetry as music, words that name facts dancing together.

Thus there is no gulf between the great series of MacDiarmid's didactic and polemical poems—*The Kind of Poetry I Want* for example—and the lyrics, ballads and meditations in Lowlands Scots which are nearer to types less literate ears can recognise and some of them well on the way already to being as much loved as the best of Burns. In these, the sound is the sense, whatever a man with a dictionary may make of it, as it is in the best of the songs we inherited from Tudor poets as much musicians as poets. It is not for the likes of me to hamper with comments. They are for ears. Read them aloud. They are not all modulations on folk-tunes; but if you can follow a pibroch or disentangle a fugue none will fail to reach you.

To say that MacDiarmid reinvented a nation when he wrote *A Drunk Man looks at the Thistle* is not a very flagrant exaggeration; by now it is almost commonplace. Since, he has enriched that nation not only in poems which broaden the original theme, such as *The Island Funeral* or *Lament for the Great Music*, but with others perhaps less accessible but no less valuable based on interests astonishingly wide which have led him to chase knowledge in many sciences and many languages. He has been fertile and generous.

("Thanks to the Guinea Worm," *Agenda*, 1970)

✝ ✝ ✝ ✝ ✝ ✝ ✝

I've been thinking . . . about how and where I got whatever I know and feel about poetry, and the more I think the bigger Malherbe's part in it seems. Wordsworth, when I was a small kid, showed me what it was; Rossetti's translations from the Dolce Stil people, in my teens, and Whitman at the same time, enlarged the scope. Horace gave the first inkling of how it was done (odes). Malherbe produced all I afterwards found in Ez's writing except what I'd already got from Horace. Ez and Spenser, great galleries of technical accomplishment. Lucretius. Dante. And after that, Hafez for what I got from Horace (and Ez from Chinese,) only more, taken further: Manuchehri, greater and more splendid gallery than Ez and Spenser: Wyat: the Mu'allaqat: and for sheer pleasure, when I am not out to learn or have my mind fixed, for diversion, for mere living, Homer and Ferdosi. Could one make a kind of "Education of X?" out of these reflections, I wonder?

(Letter to Zukofsky, 1953)

My excellence, if I have one, isn't new or striking. I suppose that's what TSE misses. I'd say I remember the musical origin of poetry, the singing side of it, better than anybody except Ezra and Carlos Williams; and that the process of association or contrast or what you will that I think I derive from Horace, Hafez, and the symphonic composers, differs from Ez's "ideogram" or the Waste Land manner, being at once less arbitrary and more under control . . . but if so, that won't be perceived in this generation. I've added nothing much. But I think I've done the job quite well. . . .

(Letter to Zukofsky, 1951)

Music has suggested certain forms and certain details to me, but I have not tried to be consistent about it. Rather, I've felt the spirit of a form, or of a procedure, without trying to reproduce it in any way that could be demonstrated on a blackboard. (There's no one-one relationship between my movements and any of Scarlatti's). You could say the same about the detail of sound. Eliot—and Kipling—show prodigious skill in fitting words to a prearranged pattern, very admirable: yet they don't do it without losing some suppleness. . . . Critical notions are in control from the outside so that the poem is constrained to fit them, as though it had never been conceived in the form it wears. . . . My matter is born of the form—or the form of the matter, if you care to think that I just conceive things musically. There's no fitting, at least consciously. Whatever you think I am saying is something I could not have said in any other way.

(Letter to Sister Victoria Marie Forde,
Music and Meaning in the Poetry of Basil Bunting, 1972)

Mallarmé would begin with a mood and then look for an objective correlative to suit it. For me, the thing itself has to provoke the mood; it has to carry its own implications. I don't go hunting for objective correlatives.

(Unpublished interview, 1976)

The Symbolist notions of sound, of poetry *as* sound, went further than Pound was prepared to go and were nearer to what I had in mind. I think that I have always been more concerned with the autonomy of the poem than any of the others—Pound, Williams or Zukofsky.

(Unpublished interview, 1976)

† † † † † † † †

I think people see that one has taken care to write about things one knows about, or to make damned sure they are correct, and so forth, even if one has thereupon afterwards twisted them and altered them, as Pound twisted and altered things that he knew perfectly well what the exact thing was. I take care, for instance, if I say that a certain star is rising over the Farne Islands, at the moment in question that star is rising and the other stars will correspond in their positions, and so forth. I take care for that kind of thing, then people proceed to use words which I would never use about it at all. If you draw a map you get out a pair of dividers and see the distances are right for the place you are putting down on the map; if you draw a picture you check the pencil; you take care, that's all there is to it. It's that in writing anything you must be as careful as a painter is in drawing or a composer in composing; it's no bloody use just slopping; that's all, full stop. . . . You know, there's a great deal to be said for a medical training; I think that a great many of Carlos Williams' advantages come from the fact that he had been trained so many years, taught to look for symptoms, taught to observe them correctly and report them correctly. And he did the same with other things besides symptoms; if he sees a flower he doesn't see just a smudge of colour; he's been careful about that flower.

(Interview, *meantime*, 1977)

Values and Beliefs

Zukofsky has always had a very warm spot for philosophers; I have nothing but the coldest dislike for the most part. My philosophy is English eclecticism—Locke, and Hume who proved that they all knew nothing; in fact one could say the same almost of Wittgenstein's *Tractatus*, which I read when it was first published and was immensely struck by.

(Interview, *meantime*, 1977)

Forgive the anarchico who believes nothing because he can't, not because there are no pleasing or even useful beliefs to choose from. I'd like to be a catholic, but can't swallow it even by re-in-re-interpreting the symbols of symbols. The pretty paganism Ezra has made up for himself (the real thing would horrify him), these ladies' school lynxes which don't eat children, no it's too childish: yet he made excellent poetry out of it. Others profess science (usually without noticing that it requires an act of faith), but Hume stands in my way, or what Hume stands for does.

(Letter to Zukofsky, 1951)

✝ ✝ ✝ ✝ ✝ ✝ ✝

Yeats? His Platonism respects Plotinus as yours does Spinoza or Ezra's his misunderstanding of Scotus. All three abominations to my empiricism.

(Letter to Zukofsky, 1951)

✝ ✝ ✝ ✝ ✝ ✝ ✝

I am fundamentally averse to acts of faith. Faith being belief contrary to the available evidence.

(Letter to Zukofsky, 1939)

✝ ✝ ✝ ✝ ✝ ✝ ✝

I'm a Quaker by upbringing, and fortunately it is a religion with no dogma at all—and consequently there's very little you can quarrel with, and I don't have to believe this or that or the other. I think that the real essence of the Quaker business is exactly as it was at the beginning: if you sit in silence, if you empty your head of all the things you usually waste your brain thinking about, there is some faint hope that something, no doubt out of the unconscious or where you will, will appear—just as George Fox would have called it, the voice of God; and that will bring you, if not nearer God, at any rate nearer your own in-built certainties.

(Interview, *Poetry Information*, 1978)

✝ ✝ ✝ ✝ ✝ ✝ ✝

I have no use for religion conceived as church forms or as believing as historical fact what are ancient parables, but I do believe that there is a possibility of a kind of reverence for the whole creation which I feel we all ought to have in our bones if we don't, a kind of pantheism, I suppose. If the word "God" is to have any use it must include everything. The only way to know anything is to consider yourself a student of histology, finding out as much as carefully controlled commonsense can find out about the world. In so doing, you will be contributing to the histology of God.

(Interview, *Montemora*, 1977)

✝ ✝ ✝ ✝ ✝ ✝ ✝

Quakerism is a form of mysticism no doubt, in that it doesn't put forward any logical justification whatever, only the justification of experience.

(Interview, *meantime*, 1977)

† † † † † † † †

I began with a wish to limit my aims (abolish the protection of "game" in England to extend the range of black-faced sheep), and they were still too abstract and ambitious to do anything but harm if I'd persisted. I haven't, and after my first twenties I never have had any idea of setting all or most things to rights by some scheme —usually it is one disguise or another of inflation—because I am sure that any scheme, anything extensive or uniform, must put more and always more men under the mortmain of "administration"; and our only hope for our children is to destroy uniformity, centralisation, big states and big cities and big factories and give men a chance to vary and live without more interference than it is in the nature of their individual neighbours to insist on.

(Letter to Pound, 1953)

† † † † † † † †

All the attempts to better the world by constraint that ever I heard of have ended in worsening it, and most of those that wanted to better it by nothing more lethal than precept were nearly as objectionable. Still, Jesus and Spinoza and so on have done less direct damage than lawgivers.

(Letter to Zukofsky, 1953)

† † † † † † † †

More I've seen of govts and the people who run them, more certain I've become that ANY govt is evil and only to be tolerated when the other evils it can obviate are absolutely proved by long trial of them to be of perfectly satanic dimensions. There would be very few laws in my Utopia and hardly any govt to enforce them. Sure, we'd have to pay dearly for freedom: but we pay even more dearly for daily petty oppression. The most tolerable habitats I've surveyed are those where the govt is least efficient. Which give most scandal to the moralist—any systematic moralist, not just the kind lately in fashion. The desert Arab, the Afghan, the Persian provincial, get on pretty comfortably where govt consists solely in extracting bribes from those who can afford them. The usurers of Golpaygan who oppress the Fereidani peasant are subject to unavenged murder. (By the way, they are mostly Georgians like Papa Stalin, not Jews). It works pretty well. If the usurers weren't there the peasants would be oppressed by land-lords instead, better able to avoid knives and hammers.

(Letter to Pound, 1953)

† † † † † † †

. . . the thirst for power, the envy of power, that is, the root of what the newspapers call democracy, begins to seem to me almost as idle as the thirst for money. I doubt if it has any satisfactions comparable to those your father and his like find in submission to their god, or the peasant peoples in submission to the toil of their agriculture. It's an old enough notion, and very out of fashion; but I begin to hate reformers, they so rarely learn anything except how to give service to lies in order to profit by lies. The wilderness may be a better place than Pharoah's Egypt, so that we ought to envy the Children of Israel their desert instead of despising it. I used to think that I put up with my own wilderness out of forti-tude, and that something ought to be done about it, if not by some Moses, then by me. But I see now that I loved my desert. . . .

St. Francis was no fool for wooing poverty. He got his free-dom that way. And if we could multiply our power over nature many times, if there were truth in the old nonsense about an age of plenty, we would be the fools to accept that power and plenty at the price we are already paying for the instalment we did ac-cept. I mean, the slavery that began by extending the costly no-tion of respectability to the masses, and that has, in my lifetime, become a system of documents and regulations that immobilise the bodies of most of us and the minds of nearly all.

I think of the huge armies of teachers (no disrespect to you!) engaged in making whole encyclopedias of statements seem self-evident axioms, to go unquestioned and un-found-out for the future. The fresh discovery a man makes is examined and has meaning: what he learns at school has only purpose, not his own purpose either. The newspapers, the popularisers of all degrees— hateful in their usefulness. You cannot be useful and retain posses-sion of your own mind.

In short, isn't Society a fallacy? Whatever is shared that is worth having is shared amongst a few, because only a few have retained any freedom. What is worthless is doled out by the slaves of power in the name of equality, at the expense—which they count so small—of cutting off men from the essence of their manhood, their mind and soul and freewill.

(Letter to Zukofsky, 1947)

"Civic sense" as you mean it, stifles me. The more the epidemic of it spreads, the beastlier the world becomes. England is grunting with the weight of 50 million civic consciences, which have tied everybody hand and foot.

Freedom is so expensive that every people that has been allowed to have its way has abolished it in the interest of all the hard cases which arouse their civic sense. I prefer freedom to the security thrust on me, which feels like prison bars and tastes like skilly. I am a hard case myself now, but I'd put up with worse to get rid of some of the order and control, which I detest when I feel them myself and which I believe prevent the Pounds and Dantes and what-have-you's from *making* things which do, really, not illusorily, improve the world.

(Letter to Pound, 1955)

But I will try to insinuate here and there [into the *New English Weekly*] that the workingman might have some look in other than what amounts to a larger dole: including the man who works at writing poetry, and even though the life said workingman wants is incompatible with nearly every law in the country and certainly with all those Lord Bankerville and Lady Whatshername want to bolster. I'd rather have a revolution, blood and skulls, but since Stalin has reduced himself to a larger Hitler and pretty good imitation of someone else, I doubt whether I could work with communists except for exceedingly strictly limited objects: and there's no other revolutionary party in sight.

(Letter to Pound, 1936)

WILLIAM S. MILNE

BASIL BUNTING'S PROSE AND CRITICISM

> No art is worth the effort it costs nor the con-
> sequent renunciation of many pleasurable things,
> at least if it does not propose to perform func-
> tions which nothing else can.
>
> Bunting, "Diagnoses," 1932

The unusual feature of Bunting's prose and criticism is that it has
been critically consistent over the years. From his first printed
essay of 1924 (a review of Joseph Conrad's *The Rover, The Transatlantic Review*, July 1924) to his last printed critical essay
("Yeats Recollected" in *Agenda*, Summer 1974) his views on
poetry over that period of fifty years have changed remarkably
little. This reflects in part his classical outlook on both life and art
and suggests a steady, life-long dedication to a central cluster of
important ideas. To illustrate this view I have listed his more important preoccupations and quoted in each instance from three
essays from widely disparate periods of his life.

As a necessary qualification it should be said that Bunting
views poetry in a wider light than such discrete ideas may suggest
to the reader. It should be borne in mind that the following areas
of Bunting's critical interest are all subsumed under the wider
aegis of his concern as a poet with poetry as a force which recon-
ciles emotional and physical fact with moral and intellectual
truth. The following list therefore should not be regarded as exhaustive of Bunting's theoretical statements regarding the nature
of poetry. In addition, of course, many of the separate areas of
interest must be seen as overlapping each other:

Poetry as Fact

1. The detection of fraud and adulteration is necessary policework, but must keep within the rules of evidence: fact, not

hearsay; history, not speculation. . . . Poetry will build with facts, but declines to soar with inevitably unsteady words.

"Open Letter to Louis Zukofsky," 1932

2. Philosophy and fact seem to be mutually repugnant. America however is an agglomeration of facts. What Williams thinks about it he has said in prose elsewhere. In his verse he arranges a mosaic of facts, American facts even if most of them are also cosmopolitan.

"Carlos Williams's Recent Poetry," 1934

3. Pound and Zukofsky have sought a poetry of facts . . . but neither, I think, has ever quite separated facts from metaphysics. . . . Abstract words hide and corrode the facts. The matter (of the poem) must have a physiological analogy which can dispell the fog for one bright, definite moment.

(Review of) "More Collected Poems" and
"A Clyack-Sheaf" by Hugh MacDiarmid, 1970

Poetry as Music

1. He [Pound] knew how widely the yardstick metric of the pedants differs from the metric of the ear, and explored the difference more and more boldly. The troubadours wrote to be sung; all lyric poetry was written to be sung. . . . Pound felt poetry to be aural and at all times made the ear the arbiter of what was admissible. Not all, not very many of the poets of our time have perceived that fact or dare trust themselves to it.

"Mr Ezra Pound," 1932

2. No art depends principally or even very largely on its appeal to the intellect, and in the Age of Reason itself Pope was preferred to Young for melody, not for sense. . . . It may be due to the deficiency of my intellect that it gets but little more from one art than from another. If music speaks first to the emotions, so, it seems to me, do poetry, sculpture, painting, architecture, even drama or the novel. All arts are of a party against the intellect, and if music does outrun the others it is by a very short lead.

"Criticism and Music," 1928

3. Poetry, like music, is to be heard. It deals in sound—long sounds and short sounds, heavy beats and light beats, the tone relations of vowels, the relations of consonants to one another which are like instrumental colour in music. Poetry lies dead on the page, until some voice brings it to life, just as music, on the stave, is no more than instructions to the player. A skilled musician can imagine the sound, more or less, and a skilled reader can try to hear, mentally, what his eyes see in print; but nothing will satisfy either of them till his ears hear it as real sound in the air. Poetry must be read aloud.

"The Poet's Point of View," 1966

Poetry and Substance

1. Mr Cummings has no real subject matter. Instead he sets up symbols which symbolise nothing. . . . He makes a verbal surface but there is next to nothing beneath it. It is Swinburne's error repeated in another key.

"Directory of Current English Authors," 1931

2. Depth cannot be achieved by tricks of form alone.

"English Poetry Today," 1932

3. Suckling poets should be fed on Darwin till they are filled with the elegance of things seen or heard or touched.

MacDiarmid review, 1970

Poetry and Exactitude

1. But many new sciences as exact as physics must be invented before it becomes possible to write with accuracy on a whole subject.

"Some Limitations of English," 1932

2. For the reader, an expert's certificate of precision, concision and general good workmanship; or a warning of their absence. . . . For the poet, technical information as from one good craftsman to another; such as doctors exchange in the medical papers.

"Open Letter to Louis Zukofsky," 1932

3. Words that name facts dancing together.

MacDiarmid review, 1970

Poetry and Objectivity

1. Of the English language:
   A more concrete word . . . would be valid to people less given
   to splitting ideas, chipping off *I* from *am*, etc. . . . . We sacrifice
   in language the sharp differentiation which we observe in life.
   Impersonal utterance is increasingly difficult.

"Some Limitations of English," 1932

2. If I buy a hat I am content that it should fit, be impermeable,
   of good texture, and of colour and cut not outrageously out
   of fashion. If I am a hatmaker I seek instruction in a series of
   limited practical operations ending in the production of a good
   hat with the least possible waste of effort and expense. I
   NEVER want a philosophy of hats, a metaphysical idea of Hat
   in the abstract, nor in any case a great deal of talk about
   hats. . . . This is what I would understand by Objectivism, if
   the word were mine.

"Open Letter to Louis Zukofsky," 1932

3. Of the Modernist poets:
   What these poets and many other writers really had in common was a love of order. With order in society it matters little
   whether you are rich or poor, you will not be harassed by perpetual changes of fortune, you can plan your life's work within known limits, not felt as limits because they are as unavoidable as the limits imposed by our physique or the duration
   of human life.

"Yeats Recollected," 1974

Poetry as Intellectual Illumination

1. The precise function of literature is to augment the accessible
   quantity of communicable thought.

"Diagnoses," 1932

2. The separate chunks of fact in each [Carlos Williams] poem
   project a foreseen design; the separate poems, or nearly all of

them, are ready to unite at the right focus into the unfinished
and unfinishable design of their common theme, America.

"Carlos Williams's Recent Poetry," 1934

3. There is no need of any theory for what gives pleasure through
the ear, music or poetry. The theoreticians will follow the
artist and fail to explain him.

"The Poet's Point of View," 1966

Poetry and Compression

1. He [Pound] excluded from his poetry the arbitrary inversions
then, as still, common; the mechanical adjectives sought not
because the sense needed them but out of habit or to fill up
a line; all unnecessary explanation or elaboration; everything
that impeded the swift, direct movement of a poem.

"Mr Ezra Pound," 1932

2. The minimum requirement of a poem is that it should trim
some known thought to a greater precision, or note compre-
hensibly and communicably some previously unknown
thought.

Bunting's essay on Pound in
The Cantos of Ezra Pound: Some Testimonies, 1933

3. Beware of adjectives; they bleed nouns.

"I Suggest," 1966

Poetry as Transfigured Prose

1. (a) Yet grant every harsh interpretation envy can apply, without questioning its coherence or its compatability.

A review of Muggeridge's *The Earnest Atheist:
A Study of Samuel Butler*, 1936

(b) Search under every veil
for the pale eyes, pale
lips of a sick child. . .
Say: We know by the dead
they mourn, their bloodshed,

the maimed who are the free.
We willed it, we.
Say: Who am I to doubt?
But every vein cries out.

Odes I: 35, 1947

2. (a) We are modified even more by our temporal than by our
spatial environment, for our contacts extend further in
time. It is a common error for 'realists' or 'moderns' to
ignore or deliberately flout this fact. Pound has made it
contribute to poetry, not for the first time, but perhaps
for the first time consciously. His Now is so interpene-
trated by Then it is sometimes hard to separate them; and
this is as it is in life for all of us.

Bunting's essay on *The Cantos*, 1933

(b) Snow lies bright on Hedgehope
and tacky mud about Till
where the fells have stepped aside
and the river praises itself,
silence by silence sits
and Then is diffused in Now.

Briggflatts, 1965

3. (a) Of Pound's *Propertius*:
London or Rome, does the name, the ostensible date,
much signify? We are amongst contemporaries, listening to
a contemporary, the difficulties are the difficulties of our
own lives.

"Mr Ezra Pound," 1932

(b) Ten or ten thousand, does it much signify, Helen, how we
date fantasmal events, London or Troy? Let Polyhymnia
strong with cadence multiply song, voices enmeshed by music respond bringing the savour of our sadness or delight
again.

Odes I: 5, 1927

Poetry and Translation

1. One realizes that the corner of the known universe expressible
in any language is small. A fusion of all existing and all dead

languages would be needed to express human experience at all fully and there would still remain the mass of the known-but-hitherto-unexpressed-in-any-language.

"Some Limitations of English," 1932

2. On Pound's *Propertius*:
    He selects from Propertius and points his irony with anachronisms. By an effort of understanding such as we must constantly make with living men but few attempt with the dead we feel the Roman, the foreigner, not in the decor only but in the manner, for, from the point of view of perfection, it is not enough to be idiomatic in language: there is also an idiom in the sequence of ideas.

"Modern Translation," 1936

[This is Bunting's model of translation not only in the "Over-drafts" but also in Chomei at Toyama *and* Villon.*]*

3. If ever I learned the trick of it, it was mostly from poets long dead whose names are obvious: Wordsworth, Dante, Horace, Wyat and Malherbe, Manuchehri and Ferdosi, Villon, Whitman, Edmund Spenser.

Preface to *Collected Poems*, 1968

Poetry and Rhythm

1. The everlasting sea . . . in all its change and monotony.

Review of *The Rover*, 1924

2. Writing of Eliot's "Portrait of a Lady":
    The words floating on the full lift of the wave.

"Mr T.S. Eliot," 1932

3. Vary rhythm enough to stir the emotion you want but not so as to lose impetus.

"I Suggest," 1966

Poetry and Dance

1. The hardest of all graces to be recorded is that of motion.

"Lydia Sokolova," 1927

2. He [Herbert Read] juggles with ideas, playing them together and against each other, deriving from their contrasts and changes a flickering beauty, a kind of abstract dance.

"What About Herbert Read?", 1969

3. To me it seems that history points to an origin that poetry and music share, in the dance that seems to be a part of the make up of *homo sapiens*, and needs no more justification or conscious control than breathing. The further poetry and music get from the dance and from each other, the less satisfactory they seem.

"A Letter" on Rhythm, 1972

Poetry and History

1. Everything living is full of the past, fuller, maybe, of the past than of the present, conditioned alike by the acts of the dead and by the material and spiritual memorials they have left.

Essay on Pound's *Cantos*, 1933

2. Art for the love of the continued and not the disintegrated existence of man.

"Open Letter to Sherry Mangan," 1932

3. On Lord Redcliffe-Maude's report on the Arts Council of Great Britain: Lord Redcliffe-Maude's report has been accepted by the Arts Council and I believe by most of the regional associations, though it seems to me as crude as his redrawing of our county boundaries without regard to history, or sentiment or anything whatever except economics—the convenience of administrators.

"Presidential Addresses," 1976-77

Poetry as Relationship and Organisation

1. Of Pound's *Cantos*:
   To illustrate, comment, contrast, organise, the Good Life is presumably the object of the poem, as of Dante's.

"Mr Ezra Pound," 1932

2. Neither the forms of induction nor those of the syllogism can

make a false proposition true, nor will the rhyme relations of a sonnet turn nonsense into a poem. The unity of any work is the sum of innumerable relations that exist between its minutest parts. Though any particular thread may be hard to trace, though many, perhaps even most threads still dangle their loose ends . . . no one of any sensibility can read more than a few pages without feeling the texture, satisfactorily thick and opaque.

Essay on Pound's Cantos, 1933

3. Ford and Conrad talked too much about Flaubert but did not waste much time playing hide-and-seek with the precise word. They surrounded their meaning with successive approximations instead, and so repeated in the texture of prose the pattern by which their narrative captured their theme. It is a circuitous technique, prodigal of paper. For sure, Flaubert would not have recognised it: yet nebulosities and imprecisions are much of our landscape without or within, and worth reproducing.

Preface to Ford Madox Ford's Selected Poems, 1971

Poetry and Syntax

1. Syntax is almost the only element of our grammar that seems to admit the interdependence of ideas.

"Some Limitations of English," 1932

2. Sometimes a long, even syntax provides continuity, carries the eye through without the effort of focussing. Maybe even such a syntax could be made suppler, more continuous without losing the muscle of common speech that keeps the sentence from going flat or dragging.

"Carlos Williams's Recent Poetry," 1934

3. Skipsey was too ready to confuse his syntax in order to keep the stresses on the theoretical beat of the metre, not knowing, or not noticing, how one syllable drawn out beyond the metrical limit can keep the swing of the rhythm yet introduce an expressive change of pace.

Preface to Joseph Skipsey's Selected Poems, 1976

Poetry and Justice

1. La même justesse d'esprit qui nous fait écrire de bonnes choses nous fait appréhender qu'elles ne le soient pas assez pour mériter d'être lues.

    Preface to *Redimiculum Matellarum*, 1930

2. Mr Lawrence [D.H.] is ready at any time to sacrifice truth for force, to forgo the just epithet in favour of the momentarily more effective one.

    Letter to *The Nation And Athenaeum*, 1927

3. Writing of Yeats's political beliefs and symbols:
    All such fancies assume tacitly that the regulations and ceremonies are made by extremely wise and perfectly unselfish rulers, not by Stalin or Hitler or Mussolini, and none of their proponents, not Plato himself, pauses to consider where and how such rulers are to be found. . . . Politics and religion were not his business except in the sense in which they are everyone's business. He was a poet. . . . Either a work of art is its own justification or art crumbles to propaganda and advertisement.

    "Yeats Recollected," 1974

[The ideas here recollect those of two earlier articles by Bunting: firstly in his review of Allied Propaganda and the Collapse of the German Empire, *by George C. Bruntz of July 1939 and secondly in his long article "The Roots of The Spanish Revolt," July 1936, where Bunting's concern for justice can be discerned in his conclusion: "The problem of government in Spain is to feed the people. The peasants are half-starved and half-clothed, yet it has always been impossible to get a quorum in the Cortes for any economic debate."]*

Poetry and Difficulty

1. (a) I do not think anything can be simplified. . . .

    "Open Letter to Louis Zukofsky," 1932

    (b) Simultaneity, interdependence, continuous crossreference and absence of simplification are characteristic of all fact, whether physical or mental or emotional.

"Some Limitations of English," 1932

2. (a) It takes knowledge amounting to character to subordinate readymade inspirations from the unconscious to what is constructed by acquired skill to produce an effect gauged and willed in advance. . . . English needs stress on the intelligible meaning, the intelligent purpose of words.

    "Carlos Williams's Recent Poetry," 1934

    (b) Poets, makers, know if they reflect at all the complexity of things made. They offer no easy explanations.

    Piece on Pound's *Cantos*, 1933

3. Talking about the composition of *Briggflatts*:
    One little notebook, two little notebooks, completely full both sides of each page, with the cuttings out and so forth. And I reckon roughly twenty-thousand lines, to get my seven hundred.

    "Basil Bunting Talks About *Briggflatts*," 1970

Poetry and Synthesis

1. (a) But we have lost the benefit of a whole view, a unified conception, concentration, intensity. It is comparable to the breakup of craftsmanship with its complex of deft motions which are not separated from one another in the mind of the craftsman into a series of simpler motions which can each be performed by a separate man and of these into still simpler motions which a machine can do. We lose contact with whole things and deal with items instead: and these items have a thinness of meaning, an absence of associations by comparison with the thing as a whole.

    "Some Limitations of English," 1932

    (b) There is no poetry in England, none with any relation to the life of the country, or of any considerable section of it.

    "English Poetry Today," 1932

2. A word is much more animated and resistant than a number

since it derives its life and adaptability from use . . . use not by a single man in a single book but by thousands of generations of millions of men speaking. . . . A word is at the same time a fact and an action, not a pokerchip that has no value other than what the player gives it before beginning the game.

"To Define Our Terms," 1932

3. The world will be no richer when all the tents are folded.

Bunting on Persia: "In pursuit of a pattern," 1973

[This piece is similar to one entitled "Mirage and Men" of September 1936.]

Poetry and Form

1. It is arguable that no particular purpose is served by the enunciation of points of view which are not resolved into some wider vision. The spirit of the age is, of course, diverse enough. But this postulates all the more necessity for some centralizing control.

A review of *Aspects of Modernism* by Janko Lavrin, 1936

2. Every revivification of poetry has taken the same route, towards the language of the streets and the cadences of song or bodily movement.

A review of *Chinese Lyrics*, trans. Ch'u Ta-Kao, 1938

3. Pound has provided a box of tools, as abundant for this generation as those that Spenser provided for the Elizabethans, and a man who is not influenced by Pound, in the sense of trying to use at least some of those tools, is simply not living in his own century.

Bunting in conversation with Eric Mottram, 1975

Poetry and Sonata-Form

1. (a) Bunting's own definition of sonata-form:
   The marriage of two contradictory spirits who both insist on talking stormily at the same time.

"Chamber Orchestras," 1927

(b) Writing of a Scarlatti sonata:
Its themes are living things, not specimens pinned down
for dissection . . . the development is as spontaneous as the
movement of a beautiful living body. It is intricate as life
is intricate: intricate but not involved. It is concise with
something approaching the concision of life.

"Recent Fiddlers," 1928

2. (a) Writing of *The Waste Land*:
Eliot succeeded in bringing together under one glaze the
extravagant vocabulary of parody and lines of the most
august and authentic elevation, with abrupt transition or
none, yet without cracking the surface or startling the
reader.

"Mr T.S. Eliot," 1932

(b) In Villon and in Corbière sublimities and atrocities are
made to rub shoulders in consecutive lines, but with a very
different effect. They do, deliberately, crack the surface,
jar the reader. They have a quite personal poignancy, they
make claims.

"Mr T.S. Eliot," 1932

*[These two quotations shed considerable light on Bunting's
working-methods in all of his* Sonatas.*]*

3. It is time to consider how Dominico Scarlatti
condensed so much music into so few bars
with never a crabbed turn or congested cadence,
never a boast or a see-here; and stars and lakes
echo him and the copse drums out his measure,
snow peaks are lifted up in moonlight and twilight
and the sun rises on an acknowledged land.

Briggflatts, 1965

Poetry and Influences

1. Style is something that must be learned by pains and practice. . . . A man first follows the fashion and then varies it to
suit his own taste. . . . He cannot have too much practice and
experience and knowledge of precedents and he dare neglect

no opportunity of checking his own results by those of others.

"Some Limitations of English," 1932

2. In his [Liszt's] early life he went ... to other musicians, first as pianist, then as composer, exercising his technical gift and his deep understanding of other men's music . . . arranging fantasias on themes from their operas. . . . Later he found his stimulus in literature or philosophy or religion.

"Liszt," 1927

3. Sooner or later we must absorb Islam if our culture is not to die of anaemia.

Preface to *Arabic and Persian Poems in English*, 1970

Poetry as Artifact

1. Cut cleanly and exactly.

"English Poetry Today," 1932

2. (a) It seems to me of less importance that some of Pound's matter has echoes and anticipations distributed here and there in the poem than that where the words occur, be they echo or anticipation, or self-sufficient phrase, they are all in their place.

Essay on Pound's *Cantos*, 1933

(b) Of Williams's poetry:
On inspection the separate stones are very distinct, the cement undissimulated . . . that is, there is confessed cement or no cement at all, the cohesion of a perfect fit.

"Carlos Williams's Recent Poetry," 1934

3. A work of art is something constructed, something made in the same way that a potter makes a bowl. A bowl may be useful but it may be there only because the potter liked that shape, and it's a beautiful thing. The attempt to find any meaning in it would be manifestly absurd.

"Package 3," Newcastle upon Tyne, 1969

Poetry and Mystery

1. Writing of his experience of reading Conrad's *Romance* in prison: In that emptiness, where no new thing ever enters, it
   took possession of my ears and eyes. My cell grew full of aro-
   matic bales, fading into the shadows of Don Ramon's ware-
   house; Thomas Castro walked with me around the patch of
   rotting cabbage-stalks that was our exercise ground; even Seraphina visited me occasionally, keeping modestly to the dark
   places, an indistinct but sympathetic form.

   Review of Conrad's The Rover, 1924

   *[I think that one can detect here the "dark embryo" of Villon:
   it is perhaps not too fanciful to see a link between the characters
   of Seraphina and Archipiada.]*

2. I think that the real essence of the Quaker business is exactly
   as it was at the beginning: if you sit in silence . . . there is some
   faint hope that something, no doubt out of the unconscious
   or where you will, will appear—just as George Fox would have
   called it, the voice of God; and that will bring you, if not nearer
   God, at any rate nearer your own built-in certainties.

   Bunting in conversation with Eric Mottram, 1975

3. (a)   . . . . but of the light
            shining upon no substance;
            a glory not made
            for which all else was made.

   Odes: I: 36, 1948

   (b) Yet for a little longer here
       stone and oak shelter
       silence while we ask nothing
       but silence.

   "At Briggflatts meetinghouse," 1975

THE TRANSLATOR

CID CORMAN

EARWORK

> . . . the result of a successful work of
> art is more than the sum of its mean-
> ings and differs from them in kind.

When Basil Bunting chose to "do" his friend Zukofsky's "In
that this happening" lyric into Latin—it was clearly not as a mere
exercise or even as a compliment. If it were either—it would not
have been retained—in the *Collected Poems*.

And it is of no great consequence to judge it as some classical
scholar might—in terms of its Latin correctness. It is best sounded
as an analogue of the "original" to catch the originality of the
translator's ear and awareness of the Zukofskian music.

Bunting titles the work: "Verse and Version."

In that this happening
    is not unkind
it put to
    shame every kindness

mind, mouths, their words,
    people, put sorrow
        on
    its body

before sorrow it came
    and before every kindness,
happening for every sorrow
    before every kindness

        (Louis Zukofsky)

quia id quod accidit
    non est immitis
pudebat omnia
    mitiora.

```
mens, ora, dicta horum,
        hominesque, tristitiam
superimponunt
        eius membra.

prius quam tristitia accidit,
        omnisque prius quam mitiora;
accidit pro omnibus tristitiis
        prius quam omnia mitiora.
```

(Basil Bunting)

Characteristic of Bunting is the fact that nothing committed to print fails to reveal excellence of musical detail—clarity and care.

Is it only incidental that his collected work should—apart from CHOMEI AT TOYAMA—be listed under the headings of SONATAS and ODES and OVERDRAFTS? There is a sense both of Horace— classical music—and Arabic (Persian) lyricism running over and under and through the entire oeuvre. It is impossible to read Bunting's work (just as that of Shakespeare or Zukofsky or Dante) without wanting to "say" the words—to get the weight and substance and sense of them on the tongue—via breath and mouth. Words are shaped for meaning in utterance in this body of work.

Even without much knowledge of Latin one can *feel* the translator had made his version "in his head" first—before committing it to paper. The brevity of the English and the composition of meaning *as* utterance clearly grabbed Bunting and compelled an attempt—feeling too the classical balance and play of the original.

(Not uninteresting would be to compare this rendition with the Latin versions of Shakespeare songs that Hopkins did.)

Translation in our time—in English poetry at least—has been a key factor in the quality and richness of the poetry that has accrued. Pound's translations cannot be excised from the core of his work—nor can Zukofsky's. Even more central is translation to Bunting's achievement.

Let me take two short versions of Horace—works from 1931 —to demonstrate both how "acute" (to quote Kenneth Cox) the man's ear is and how—though he has learned from Ezra—he has gone beyond him and sets the way for a Zukofskian Catullus.

The first one in Latin reads (Book 3, #12):

```
Miserarum est neque amori dare ludum neque dulci
mala vino lavere, aut exanimari metuentes
        patruae verbera linguae.
```

tibi qualum Cythereae puer ales, tibi telas
operosaeque Minervae studium aufert, Neobule,
    Liparaei nitor Hebri,

simul unctos Tiberinis umeros lavit in undis,
eques ipso melior Bellerophonte, neque pugno
    neque segni pede victus;

catus idem per apertum fugientes agitato
grege cervos iaculari et celer alto latitantem
    fruticeto excipere aprum.

The prose version of this (by C.E. Bennett) in the Loeb Library edition goes: (*Neobule's Soliloquy*)

> Wretched the maids who may not give play to love nor drown their cares in sweet wine, or who lose heart, fearing the lash of uncle's tongue.//From thee, O Neobule, Cytherea's winged child snatches away thy wool-basket, thy web, and thy devotion to busy Minerva, so soon as radiant Liparean Hebrus//has bathed his well-annointed shoulders in Tiber's flood, a rider better even than Bellerophon, never defeated for fault of fist or foot,//clever too to spear the stags flying in startled herd over the open plain, and quick to meet the wild boar lurking in the thick-set copse.

In Horace's very balanced verses with their strategic turns and inner play of music and irony—you feel a strong societal wit working. A poem for a cultivated circle and no doubt with specific innuendo. T.E. Page (back in the 19th century) commented: "A soliloquy in which Neobule (=one with new ideas), a dissatisfied and love-sick maiden, laments her lot."

The Bunting version (with anachronistic updating in EP fashion) is full of surprises—but it stays Horatian while—in a way Walter Benjamin would have been the first to appreciate—it brings over into English some of the Latin possibility (almost without our realizing it—it seems so natural):

> Yes, it's slow, docked of amours,
>   docked of the doubtless efficacious
> bottled makeshift, gin; but who'd risk being bored stiff
> every night listening to father's silly sarcasms?
>
> If your workbox is mislaid
>   blame Cytherea's lad . . . Minerva
> 's not at all pleased that your seam's dropped for a fair
>   sight
> of that goodlooking athlete's glistening wet shoulders
>
> when he's been swimming and stands
>   towelling himself in full view
> of the house. Ah! but you should see him on horseback!
> or in track-shorts! He's a first-class middleweight pug.

He can shoot straight from the butts,
　　　straight from precarious cover, waistdeep
in the damp sedge, having stayed motionless daylong
when the driven tiger appears suddenly at arms'-length.

It is perhaps worth noting from the start that Bunting himself has remarked that "It would be gratuitous to assume that a mistranslation is unintentional."

The fact that the scholars call it a soliloquy is at once misleading. Horace leaves that open. It *can* be read as such—but need not be. And Bunting wisely leaves it at that too. I mean: it could be Horace—or the poet—speaking—in imagination—to the beleaguered young woman. Bunting makes no attempt to imitate the metrical structure—yet he has maintained an analogous pace in the phrasing.

What one feels keenly in Horace here—and generally—is an unusual felicity and exactitude in word placement and the concatenation of syllabic motion and music. Every turn is drawn to maximum sense: it is hard to conceive of a more total poetry of language. There is an economy of means that accomplishes an unusual richness of meaning. And it is this that Bunting so effectively brings off.

At no point could you guess the development of word to word and line to line that Bunting manages and does so persuasively. This can only have come about through painstaking effort —hearing each word out. The version has all the freshness of the original and provides the same variety and surprise throughout with equal wit.

The young man—Sicilian Hebrus—anonymous in Bunting— seems a young Hemingway—presciently so—and comes on in a way decidedly nearer us in time. The classical references almost seem out of place in the context—but are there precisely to maintain the source and cut out any pretense of being *not* a translation.

There are many fine points in this version that could be scored—from the initial "Yes" picking up the weight of "Mis..." to the final startling image—made even sharper by a tiger at close range—for the closing "aprum" (wild boar).

What engages us most perhaps is Bunting's unflagging attention at every point—so that we—as with the Latin—are kept with it—convinced only as each word and turn establishes itself as the poetic fact.

Interestingly the next poem—and I suspect both poems were done almost simultaneously—introduces the name "Dulcie" out of seemingly nowhere—but you can see how it was probably suggested by the "dulci" in the Latin of the previous poem's first line. This one (I: 13) reads in the Latin:

Cum tu, Lydia, Telephi
cervicem roseam, cerea Telephi
    laudas brachia, vae meum
fervens difficili bile tumet iecur.
    tum nec mens mihi nec color
certa sede manet, umor et in genas
    furtim labitur, arguens
quam lentis penitus macerer ignibus.
    uror, seu tibi candidos
turparunt umeros immodicae mero
    rixae, sive puer furens
impressit memorem dente labris notam.
    non, si me satis audias,
speres perpetuum, dulcia barbare
    laedentem oscula, quae Venus
quinta parte sui nectaris imbuit.
    felices ter et amplius,
quos irrupta tenet copula nec malis
    divolsus querimoniis
suprema citius solvet amor die.

As you can see the "dulci" finds its resonance here too in "dulcia." And here Bunting has preferred to move away from the classical immediacy—though the "thrice blest" of his version is suggestive.

The idea of jealousy—which the Loeb translator adds as a title he seems—as before—to have picked up from the notations of Page. The literal Englishing is:

When thou, O Lydia, praisest Telephus' rosy neck, Telephus' waxen arms, alas! my burning heart swells with angry passion.// Then my senses abide no more in their firm seat, nor does my color remain unchanged, and the tear glides stealthily down my cheek, proving with what lingering fires I am (inwardly) devoured. //I kindle with anger whether a quarrel waxing hot with wine has harmed thy gleaming shoulders, or the frenzied lad has with his teeth imprinted a lasting mark upon thy lips.//Didst thou but give heed to me, thou wouldst not hope for constancy in him who savagely profanes the sweet lips that Venus has imbued with the quintessence of her own nectar.//Thrice happy and more are they whom an unbroken bond unites and whom no sundering of love by wretched quarrels shall separate before life's final day.

This is somewhat of an Horatian set piece—but—as always—well-made: the words sparse and telling—while sensually full and phrasing candid.

Bunting strikes for center—keeping the poetic action alive:

Please stop gushing about his pink
neck smooth arms and so forth, Dulcie; it makes me sick,
badtempered, silly: makes me blush.
Dribbling sweat on my chops proves I'm on tenterhooks.
—White skin bruised in a boozing bout,
ungovernable cub certain to bite out a
permanent memorandum on
those lips. Take my advice, better not count on your
tough guy's mumbling your pretty mouth
always. Only the thrice blest are in love for life,
we others are divorced at heart
soon, soon torn apart by wretched bickerings.

This version cuts and emends and in ways that —without
altering the feeling of the original—brings the whole thing directly
home to us. Literality is by no manner of means in Bunting's
effort: you can readily see how freely he moves—yet he moves
always in consort with Horace. And one feels Horace would have
enjoyed this.

Bunting's work makes an ideal threshold for the Zukofsky
Catullus. Sometimes I believe that Zukofsky enjoyed vying with
his best contemporaries—trying to show how he could surpass
them at their own best. But Bunting's translations lead on to
"The Spoils" and *Briggflatts.*

For me—however—the ultimate critique of Bunting's Horatian versions—and in a way also of his entire oeuvre is the 1971
(40 years later) version of the famed "Eheu fugaces, Postume,
Postume"—which adheres more closely to the original but reverts
to a simpler—and more profoundly realized—poetry—that pene-
trates Horace tremblingly. Look to the Latin for yourself—for we
have an enduring English of it now:

You can't grip years, Postume,
that ripple away nor hold back
wrinkles and, soon now, age,
nor can you tame death

not if you paid three hundred
bulls every day that goes by
to Pluto, who has no tears,
who has dyked up

giants where we'll go aboard,
we who feed on the soil,
to cross, kings some, some
penniless plowmen.

> For nothing we keep out of war
> or from screaming spindrift
> or wrap ourselves against autumn,
> for nothing, seeing
>
> we must stare at that dark, slow
> drift and watch the damned
> toil, while all they build
> tumbles back on them.
>
> we must let earth go and home,
> wives too, and your trim trees,
> yours for a moment, save one
> sprig of black cypress.
>
> Better men will empty
> bottles we locked away,
> wine puddle our table,
> fit wine for a pope.

This is no exercise; this is poetry to engage those who are involved in the making of poetry for a long time yet.

SISTER VICTORIA MARIE FORDE, S.C.

THE TRANSLATIONS AND ADAPTATIONS
OF
BASIL BUNTING*

"If ever I learned the trick of writing poetry, it was mostly from poets long dead whose names are obvious. . ." (*C.P.*, 9).** One method Bunting used to learn the "trick" of it was writing translations and adaptations. He groups most of these in "Overdrafts," an appendix to his *Collected Poems*, although he includes the best in the main sections of the book. The variety (works of Latin, Italian, Persian, Chinese, and Japanese writers) witnesses to his background and interests.

Bunting clearly learned from Pound's advice to young poets about translating. As early as 1913 Pound had advocated a training program for prospective poets which included reading poetry, "preferably in a foreign language," to "fill the candidate's mind with the finest cadences he can discover" and translating this poetry: "Translating is likewise good training, if you find that your original matter 'wobbles' when you try to rewrite it. The meaning of the poem to be translated can not 'wobble.' "[1] In 1912 Pound had written "As for 'adaptations'; one finds that all the old masters of painting recommend to their pupils that they begin by copying masterwork, and proceed to their own composition."[2] Through his early translations Bunting was embarking on just such a program. His exasperated ending of Catullus' lyric poem, LXIV, indicates he was translating this more as an exercise than anything else: "—and why Catullus bothered to write pages and pages of this drivel mystifies me" (*C.P.*, 139).

In even the most exact paraphrase of a foreign work, Bunting

---

*Chapter III of an unpublished dissertation, entitled *Music and Meaning in the Poetry of Basil Bunting*, by Sister Victoria Marie Forde, Notre Dame, Indiana, 1973. Reprinted with permission. The section on Latin translations is scheduled for publication in the October issue of *Classical and Modern Literature*, Terre Haute, Indiana.
**References to *Collected Poems*, 2nd ed. (London, 1970) are given thus in the text.
1. Ezra Pound, "A Retrospect," *Literary Essays*, T.S. Eliot, ed. (London, 1954), p. 7.
2. *Ibid.*, p. 10.

creates something more than a literal translation. Pound's ideas in "A Retrospect" throw light on Bunting's goals:

> My pawing over the ancients and semi-ancients has been one struggle to find out what has been done, once for all, . . . and to find out what remains for us to do, and plenty does remain, for if we still feel the same emotions as those which launched the thousand ships, it is quite certain that we come on these feelings differently, through different nuances, by different intellectual gradations. . . . No good poetry is ever written in a manner twenty years old, for to write in such a manner shows conclusively that the writer thinks from books, convention and *cliché*, and not from life, yet a man feeling the divorce of life and his art may naturally try to resurrect a forgotten mode if he finds in that mode some leaven, or if he thinks he sees in it some element lacking in contemporary art which might unite that art again to its sustenance, life.[3]

From this struggle to discover the best way to "unite that art again to its sustenance, life" Bunting's translations emerge.

During the mid-thirties Pound from Rapallo kept "nagging"[4] W.H.D. Rouse in letter after letter about his translation of Homer. This correspondence has a close connection with Bunting. In March, 1935, Pound wrote to T.S. Eliot: "Re translatin': ole Rouse is getting stubborn, won't even pay any attention to Aurora's manicuring or Telemachus' feet. Damn. And he might have been a useful stimulus to Bunt. and Bin. [Binyon]."[5] What Pound was trying to convince Rouse to work for, Bunting too was trying to accomplish in his translations:

1.   Real speech *in* the English version.
2.   Fidelity to the original
     a. meaning
     b. atmosphere
No need of keeping verbal literality for phrases which sing and run naturally in the original.[6]

As important as this background is to understanding Bunting's poetry, the most essential ideas regarding his translations are his own. In the *Criterion* review of E. Stuart Bates's *Modern Translation*, Bunting unequivocally states his position. He deals with *Modern Translation* in one succinct paragraph which concludes: "Closing Mr. Bates's book, one may repeat his introductory statement: the subject of modern translation 'does not appear to

3. *Ibid.*, p. 11.
4. Ezra Pound to W.H.D. Rouse, Rapallo, March 23, 1935. D.D. Paige, ed., *The Letters of Ezra Pound: 1907-1941* (New York, 1950), p. 274.
5. Ezra Pound to T.S. Eliot, Rapallo, March 28, 1935. *Ibid.*, p. 272.
6. Ezra Pound to W.H.D. Rouse, Rapallo, April, 1935. *Ibid.*, p. 273.

have yet been dealt with.'"[7] He discusses his own position by first
tracing Dryden's idea that

[some] translations [are] meant to stand by themselves, works
in their own language equivalent to their original but not compelled to lean on its authority, claiming the independence and accepting the responsibility inseparable from a life of their own.[8]

Bunting then distinguishes among a crib, which translates "sentence by sentence; Dryden, effect by effect"; and Chaucer who
"translates nothing less than the whole poem." He backs his
preference for Chaucer's model by holding that the greatest poems
result from that kind of translating which "long and deeply influence literature and are therefore best worth discussing." In this
line he places the translations of Fitzgerald and Pound, explaining
their merits in detail and comparing their methods. He admires not
only an idiomatic language, but "an idiom in sequence of ideas,"
something he believes Pound lacks, and "*familiar* comprehen-
sion" rather than "academic lucidity."[9] "As to the morality of
tampering with texts," Bunting claims that "the question does
not arise when the main purpose is to make an English poem, not
to explain a foreign one: and between these two aims no middle
course seems to prosper."[10]

Latin Poems

The only hint outside the poems themselves that Bunting
gives his reader to this background of ideas is his note to the "Overdrafts": "It would be gratuitous to assume that a mistranslation is
unintentional" (*C.P.*, 160). Besides his general ideas about translation, his meticulous concern for technique would preclude any
such assumption in this regard. The painstaking care with which
he translated Zukofsky's tribute to Pound into Latin is an index
of his concern for precision. However, even here in "Verse and
Version," if he must choose between clarity of meaning and
sound, his choice is a foregone conclusion:

First your poem: I am no hand at Italian and intended sending it
to Monotti, but in the meantime tried what I could do with it in
Latin, which seemed to me more suited than modern Italian (not
Dante's) to the monumental terseness, especially when dealing in
relatives without antecedents—this? Italian reader inquires Which?

---

7. *Criterion*, XV (July, 1936), 715.
8. *Ibid.*
9. *Ibid.*
10. *Ibid.*, 716.

So I showed my poem to Ezra and he seems to intend to print it, and that will be all right, . . . provided I haven't made any egregious errors, which is quite possible, and I am not certain Ezra would detect them though he knows more Latin than I do.

But since Latin is in some ways more precise than our own lingo, there were places where I was in doubt and may have got your meaning a few shades out, shades not delicate as the difference of pale pink and paler, but properly Cimmerian catastrophic indigoes. In the second stanza, what tense is *put*? I have made it present, rejecting past or perfect not from any ability to penetrate the ambiguity of English, but because *superimponunt* sounds better than *superimponebant* or *superimposuerunt*. And in the last line of the poem is *every kindness* object or subject? Before happening for every kindness happens? I have made it nominative. If ablative, then '*prius quam pro omnibus mitioris.*' Or maybe omitting '*pro*' . . . .

As for the difference of *verba* and *dicta*, *tristitiam* and *maestitiam*, I chose by the noise they make; though I rejected *luctus* as being too definitely funereal. *Dicta* perhaps connects with *mens* as well as *ora*. *Id* for *this* rather than *istud* because I conceived you to be avoiding rather than courting emphasis on the pronoun: the *horum* of line 15 being plural is not likely to cause confusion. *Its* in line 8 may refer either to *sorrow* or to *this*: so might *eius*, though I think it would be more natural to take it with *id*. The dislocation of *omnia* in line 10 avoids the ugliness of *-que quam* and of course is not, in Latin, an inversion, that is, a *per*version. The only other liberty with your word order is *tristitiam* before *superimponunt*, which is more natural in Latin, makes a better rhythm, and avoids the possible ambiguity that might arise from setting *tristitiam* and *eius* together. Punctuation supplied, concession to the deadness of the dead language. (September ?th, 1932)*

The completed poem (*C.P.*, 138) shows the results of this careful attention to details:

In that this happening	quia id quod accidit
is not unkind	non est immitis
it put to	pudebat omnia
shame every kindness	mitiora.
mind, mouths, their words,	mens, ora, dicta horum,
people, put sorrow	hominesque, tristitiam
on	superimponunt
its body	eius membra.
before sorrow it came	prius quam tristitia accidit,
and before every kindness	omnisque prius quam mitiora;
happening for every sorrow	accidit pro omnibus tristitiis
before every kindness	prius quam omnia mitiora.
(Louis Zukofsky)	(Basil Bunting)

---

*Bunting to Zukofsky Letters at Humanities Research Center at University of Texas, Austin, are cited thus with date in text.

Bunting's attention to technique has precedent in the writings of the Latin poets themselves. Commenting at length on the "Law of Iambic Shortening" operative in Lucretius, an editor of *De Rerum Natura* concludes that "metrical convenience or necessity is the determining factor."[11] Bunting's modern translation of Lucretius' invocation to Venus, the opening lines of *De Rerum Natura* (*C.P.*, 139), follows this principle of musical necessity overriding all else. This is more easily seen in a comparison of Bunting's work with those of others. In this comparison other factors just discussed as important to Bunting are highlighted also. For example, even though one translator prefaces his work with strong statements against the "mechanical and pedantic accuracy of grammar and syntax,"[12] and argues for "the throbbing reality of the great living Roman," and for the "higher accuracy: the accuracy of the imagination, at once interpretative and creative,"[13] in the final analysis he is describing Bunting's work better than his own. In Bunting's version twenty-five lines of the original are condensed to eighteen. Phrases translated as "Makest to teem the many voyaged main / And fruitful lands,"[14] Bunting with simple directness translates as "you fill rich earth and buoyant sea with your presence." The difference in diction makes it difficult to believe these translations were made within a few years of each other.

In a translation ten years later than Bunting's, lines are rendered unmusically and archaically; for example, "Each kind of living creature is conceived / Then riseth and beholdeth the sun's light."[15] Bunting translates this as "for every living thing achieves its life through you, / rises and sees the sun." Instead of such a translation as "Before thee, Goddess, and thy coming on, / Flee stormy wind and massy cloud away,"[16] Bunting writes directly, "For you the sky is clear, / the tempests still." Years of work will eliminate such congestions as the "-ts st-" in "Tempests still" and the heaviness of "untrammelled all-renewing southwind." With these exceptions the invocation is smooth and rhythmical, reminiscent both in tone and content of Chaucer's "Prologue" to *The Canterbury Tales*.

11. William Ellery Leonard and Stanley Barney Smith, eds. *De Rerum Natura: Libri Sex*, T. Lucreti Cari (Madison, Wisconsin, 1942), p. 199.
12. William Ellery Leonard, *Lucretius: On the Nature of Things: A Metrical Translation* (London, 1921), p. x.
13. *Ibid.*, p. xi.
14. *Ibid.*, p. 3.
15. R.C. Trevelyan, trans., *Lucretius* (Cambridge, 1951), p. 116.
16. Leonard, *op. cit.*, p. 3.

Besides the translation of Lucretius' invocation, Bunting made at least one attempt to translate Catullus which he thought worth preserving, LXIV. The classical scholar, L.P. Wilkinson, notes that Catullus wrote this epyllion, "the Peleus and Thetis," under the influence of late Greek poets and that, peculiarly, this influence marked a period of decadence in Roman poetry before its period of maturity.[17] Bunting, like Catullus, may have wished to try his hand at "a poem distinctly epic in character, partly as giving scope to a greater variety of powers,"[18] since this was written about the same time that Bunting was working on the Persian epic, Firdosi's *Shahnamah*, which both Pound and Bunting were trying to get published.[19] Whatever may have been the reason, Bunting did manage to capture the predominant alliteration of "p's" in the first line of Catullus' poem, "s's" in the second, and "f's" in the third:

> Peliaco quondam prognatae vertice pinus
> dicuntur liquidas Neptuni nasse per undas
> Phasidos ad fluctus et fines Aeeteos,[20]

> Once, so they say, pinetrees seeded on Pelion's peak swam
> over the clear sea waves to the surf on the beaches of Phasis
> when the gamesome fleece-filchers, pith of Argos, picked for a foray,
>   (*C.P.*, 139)

In fact, by transferring "Phasis" from the third to the second line, he was able to reproduce the "as" sound repeated three times in the original second line. It does not seem that Bunting was attempting the quantitative Latin verse in the hexameters of the original, so difficult to approach in English, but rather to translate the excitement and richness of vocabulary into modern speech. Although Bunting cuts short his translation of "this drivel" in disgust, the portion he has translated holds its own among more recent attempts. For example, he has compressed twenty-eight lines of the original into only twenty lines. Some of the more recent translations are even more compressed. Phrases such as "bearded the surge" or "in a nimble ship," and "deal sweeps swirling" waste no words. Besides compression, in his favor are the directness and sweeping rhythms of such lines as "The Lady of Citadels shaped them a light hull for darting to windward / and laid the

---

17. *Horace and His Lyric Poetry* (Cambridge, 1951), p. 116.
18. Robinson Ellis, *A Commentary on Catullus* (Oxford, 1876), p. 227.
19. Ezra Pound to T.S. Eliot, Rapallo, March 28, 1935. D.D. Paige, ed. *The Letters of Ezra Pound, op. cit.*, p. 272.
20. Celia and Louis Zukofsky, *Catullus (Gai Valeri Catulli Veronensis Liber*, "Carmen LXIV," [no pagination].

cutaway keel with her own hands and wedded the timbers." However, in spite of successful attempts at compression and simplicity, Bunting's overdraft in general is as overloaded with epithets as the original: "you, heroes, brood of the gods, born in the prime season, / thoroughbreds sprung of thoroughbred dams" and "you, bridegroom / acclaimed with many pinebrands, pillar of Thessaly, fool for luck, Peleus." Repetition of a proper name in the second last line is effective for dramatic emphasis: "to whom Jove the godbegetter, Jove himself yielded his mistress"; however, repetition of two names, Thetis and Peleus, in each line of a three-line sentence adds neither to the rhythm or the overall sound, and little to the sense:

> Forthwith, thus the tale runs, love of Thetis flamed up in Peleus
> And Thetis took Peleus spite of the briefness of man's lifetime;
> even her father himself deemed Peleus worthy of Thetis.

Bunting's greater tribute to Catullus is Ode 7 in his "Second Book of Odes," "*Ille mi par esse deo videtur*" (*C.P.*, 131). The Latin lyric LI itself is partially a translation of Sappho's poem, so that Bunting's suggestion of the Sapphic stanza is singularly appropriate:

> O, it is godlike to sit selfpossessed
> when her chin rises and she turns to smile;
> but my tongue thickens, my ears ring,
> what I see is hazy.
>
> I tremble. Walls sink in night, voices
> unmeaning as wind. She only
> a clear note, dazzle of light, fills
> furlongs and hours
>
> so that my limbs stir without will, lame,
> I a ghost, powerless,
> treading air, drowning, sucked
> back into dark
>
> unless, rafted on light or music,
> drawn into her radiance, I dissolve
> when her chin rises and she turns to smile.
> O, it is godlike!

His version of the Sapphic stanza employs generally exact hendecasyllabic lines in which quantity makes up the eleven beats in some instances. The first two lines, for example, are exactly Sapphic hendecasyllabic; however, in the first line of the second stanza, as in many other lines, pauses or words pronounced slowly by necessity must supplement the actual number of syllables:

<pre>
1 2 3 4 5   6   7 8 9 10 11
</pre>
I tremble. Walls sink in night, voices

Although, as Bunting rightly insists, the sapphic stanza is "a very elaborate affair," he admits his lines are "meant to suggest a distant kinship." The kinship seems more than distant.

In *The Catullan Revolution*, Kenneth Quinn asserts that the polymetric poems of Catullus prepared the way for the Odes and Epodes of Horace. According to Quinn, it is fashionable to disparage both poets for their preoccupation with meter. Besides meter, "structural tightness" and language[21] occupied the attention of both poets. Bunting's interest in the work of these men parallels his concern with technique. The influence of Horace, the third Latin poet represented in the "Overdrafts," is the only one Bunting acknowledges in his "Preface." Even without a discussion of the particular pattern of long and short syllables that gives classic poetry its special characteristic, Bunting's experimentation is evident.

Two translated Odes, 13 in Book III and 12 in Book I, bear the stamp of Bunting's own craftsmanship. The first one, III-13, was for Horace a metrical experiment on a theme from Sappho in the pure Ionic meter.[22] Bunting has experimented in his translation also (*C.P.*, 136). For the long seventeen-syllable first line of each stanza, he has substituted a first line of seven syllables followed by a caesura-like pause which introduces the indented second line. Together this approximates the seventeen syllables of the original. In each stanza the second line sweeps into the third which is invariably twelve syllables. Instead of three-line stanzas, Bunting ends his stanzas with a fourth line of 12-14 syllables.

> Yes, it's slow, docked of amours,
>   docked of the doubtless efficacious
> bottled makeshift, gin; but who'd risk being bored stiff
> every night listening to father's silly sarcasms?
>
> If your workbox is mislaid
>   blame Cythereas's lad . . . Minerva
> 's not at all pleased that your seam's dropped for a fair sight
> of that goodlooking athlete's glistening wet shoulders
>
> when he's been swimming and stands
>   towelling himself in full view
> of the house. Ah! but you should see him on horseback!
> or in track-shorts! He's a first-class middleweight pug.
>
> He can shoot straight from the butts,
>   straight from precarious cover, waistdeep

21. Kenneth Quinn, *The Catullan Revolution* (Melbourne, 1959), p. 57.
22. Paul Shorey and Gordon Laing, eds., *Horace: Odes and Epodes* (New York, 1919), p. 361.

in the damp sedge, having stayed motionless daylong
when the driven tiger appears suddenly at arms'-length.

For this experiment Bunting has no less an authority than Wilkinson who claims that in "rendering the Horatian stanza-poems we must choose or invent some stanza that recalls the movement of the original. Horatian stanzas progress; they cannot be represented by a pair of couplets." He concludes that "there is no easy way of reproducing that effect."[23]

It does not seem that Bunting was working to reproduce the Ionic meter of this Ode, although the feel of it does come through in much of the poem:

> x   x - -   / x   x   -   - / x   x -   -
> 's not at all pleased that your seam's dropped for a fair sight

If the license of using a pause for a beat, as is usual in music, is granted, then this next phrase becomes Ionic:

> x   x   -   -   x x   -   -
> ; but who'd risk being bored stiff

just as it is heard in

> x   x   -   -   x   x   -   -
> He can shoot straight from the butts,

> x   x   -   -
and more briefly in "of the house. Ah!" Since the "Ah!" is added to the original text, it may well be to strengthen the echo of the

> x x   -   -   x   x
Ionic meter just as neatly as the line "in the damp sedge, having

> -   - x   x   -   -
stayed motionless daylong" does.

By compressing the original twenty lines of the second translated Ode, I-13 (*C.P.*, 137), Bunting is experimenting with another style of translation which communicates the contrasting emotions quickly and forcefully. For a more literal and linear version, a reader could go to Joseph P. Clancy's translation,[24] but for a vivid sense of the "sick/badtempered, silly" speaker who "on tenterhooks" begs "Dulcie" to "please stop gushing" about her new lover, he can turn to Bunting's compressed lines:

Please stop gushing about his pink
neck smooth arms and so forth, Dulcie; it makes me sick,
badtempered, silly: makes me blush.
Dribbling sweat on my chops proves I'm on tenterhooks.
- - White skin bruised in a boozing bout,
ungovernable cub certain to bite out a

---

23. Wilkinson, *op. cit.*, p. 152.
24. *The Odes and Epodes of Horace: A Modern Verse Translation* (Chicago, 1960), p. 41.

permanent memorandum on
those lips. Take my advice, better not count on your
tough guy's mumbling your pretty mouth
always. Only the thrice blest are in love for life,
we others are divorced at heart
soon, soon torn apart by wretched bickerings.

The surprising seriousness of the ending of this ode shows where in practice Bunting's open admiration of Horace's "trick" of association and contrast was leading. Wilkinson comments that the "element of surprise plays a large part in some of the odes of Horace which lull a reader into security" in one mood only to awaken him suddenly by an unexpected introduction of another. He believes that Horace was among those who exploited contrasts, and that "indeed he loved contrasts for their own sake."[25] Besides affecting his choice of odes to translate, Bunting's own love of contrasts, influenced by Horace, is most evident in his sonatas.

Not published in the *Collected Poems* but in *Agenda Magazine*, [26] "*Eheu Fugaces, Postume, Postume*," Ode II-14 "from Horace," differs from the other Horatian odes in tone. It is not the voice of an amused or jealous and sarcastic observer, but the reflective tone of a mature and thoughtful persona who speaks with urbane acceptance of the inevitability of death which strips one of everything. The rhythms reflect a far steadier and wiser outlook than that of the younger mercurial persona "on tenterhooks" in Ode XIII for example. This persona can face the inevitable prospect of death with an equanimity reflected in one sentence which goes on steadily for twelve lines through three strophes, and then in a second sentence which carries the reader smoothly through two more sections:

You cant grip years, Postume,
that ripple away nor hold back
wrinkles and, soon now, age,
nor can you tame death,

not if you paid three hundred
bulls every day that goes by
to Pluto, who has no tears,
who has dyked up

giants where we'll go aboard,
we who feed on the soil,
to cross, kings, some, some
penniless plowmen.

25. Wilkinson, *op. cit.*, pp. 133-134.
26. *Agenda*, VIII (Autumn/Winter, 1970), 61.

For nothing we keep out of war
or from screaming spindrift
or wrap ourselves against autumn,
for nothing, seeing

we must stare at that dark, slow
drift and watch the damned
toil while all they build
tumbles back on them.

The finality of the situation is underlined in the direct one-strophe sentences which conclude the ode:

We must let earth go and home,
wives too, and your trim trees,
yours for a moment, save one
sprig of black cypress.

Better men will empty
bottles we locked away,
wine puddle our table,
fit wine for a pope.

The theme of death and the unflinching tone of acceptance has varied expression in Bunting's longer poems.

In 1948 Bunting chided Zukofsky for forgetting the "more permanent values" Horace represented, and suggested that

Horace works wonders with a word order which was crabbed even to his contemporaries, as one may see by reading Lucretius and Ovid on either side of him in time. It is not right to banish such effects, which have their place, one I think too much neglected now, even though we and especially I follow Yeats's example of plain diction and plain syntax. (November 3, 1948)

Included in what Bunting considers "permanent values" is certainly the economy and restraint which is characteristic of the writing of Horace, the use of relatively simple vocabulary, and abrupt transitions, and intentional paradox.[27] All of these values which add to the musical quality of the poetry are also true of Bunting's work. Further, both possess the ability to express the everyday, the commonplace, "so as to make it [his] own"[28] through a metrical art which can be appreciated only by "those who read him aloud."[29] Although these last comments were written about Horace's poetry, they are as easily applicable to Bunting's as this longer quotation is:

---

27. Paul Shorey and Gordon Laing, eds., *Horace: Odes and Epodes*, 2nd ed. (Chicago, 1960), pp. xviii-xxix.
28. *Ibid.*, p. xviii.
29. *Ibid.*, p. xxxvii.

[Those who read him aloud] will observe for themselves in their
favorite passages the reinforcement of the leading thought by the
emphasis of the rhythm, the symmetrical responsions and nice
interlockings of words and phrases, the . . . not obtrusive alliera-
tion, the real or fancied adaptation of sound to sense in softly
musical, splendidly sonorous, or picturesquely descriptive lines.
This kind of criticism may easily pass into the fantastic. It is better suited to the living voice than to cold print.[30]

Italian Adaptation

Besides working with Latin in his efforts to refine his style,
Bunting experimented with translating the Italian of Machiavelli.
However unintentionally, Bunting has added to the statesman's
reputation as a "poet and literary stylist"[31] by translating his
prose report of "A Description of the Method Used by Duke Valentine Contrived" (*C.P.*, 146-152).[32] Ezra Pound admired it
enough to include it in his *Active Anthology*[33] and Bunting collected it as the final poem in the "Overdrafts" section.

As a translation of Bunting's, it is unique—a colloquial but
almost literal version of the prose. By this colloquialism and by
typography, he emphasizes the poetic qualities of the work. According to Gilbert, a modern critic and translator of the Italian
statesman, "Machiavelli subtly exploited the possibilities, including the colloquial qualities, of Florentine speech; such is his
command of word order that through inversion he can get emphasis without appearing to use resources not at the command of
any normal speaker."[34] These are exactly the qualities that Bunting has translated into his twentieth-century poetic version.

If this poem, completed in 1933, was a technical exercise at
all, it must have convinced Pound that Bunting had created the
"new thing" that the older craftsman demanded in a translation.
Goodwin, who is not always complimentary to Bunting, admits
that rather than the more superficial tricks of style that "quite
unintelligent and minor poets" could learn from Pound, "the
less superficial aspects of style, such as the handling of colloquial
rhythms which are less teachable," were learned by only a few
poets willing to devote "intense study" to Pound's work; "one

30. *Ibid.*, p. xxvii.
31. Allan Gilbert, trans., *Machiavelli: The Chief Works and Others*, 3 vols. (Durham,
North Carolina, 1965), I, xi.
32. The title including the subtitle is "How Duke Valentine Contrived *(the murder of
Vitellozzo Vitelli, Oliverotto da Fermo, Mr. Pagolo and the Duke of Gravina Orsini)
according to Machiavelli*
33. Ezra Pound, ed., *Active Anthology* (London, 1933), p. 73.
34. Gilbert, *op. cit.*, p. x.

who did, with limited success, was Basil Bunting."[35] Through colloquial rhythms and diction, Bunting presents insights and nuances which he forces the reader to consider by writing Machiavelli's prose as poetry.

A selection of Gilbert's prose translation, curiously close to Bunting's poetic one, gives a norm for comparison:

> And though Vitellozzo was very reluctant, and the death of his brother had taught him that one ought not to injure a prince and then trust him, nonetheless persuaded by Paulo Orsini, whom the Duke had bribed with gifts and promises, he agreed to wait for him.[36]

Vitellozzo

> was uneasy, he had learned from his brother's death
> not to trust a prince he had once offended,
>> but Orsini argued
>> and the Duke sent presents
>> and rotten promises
>> till he consented. (*C.P.*, 149)

A prose paragraph of description becomes free verse in Bunting's translation. The prose version begins with this sentence:

> Fano and Sinigaglia are two cities of the Marches situated on the shore of the Adriatic Sea, fifteen miles apart, so that he who goes toward Sinigaglia has on his right hand the mountains, the bases of which sometimes are so close to the sea that between them and the water there is very little space, and where they give most room, the distance does not reach two miles.[37]

Bunting's poem economically presents each detail in relief:

> Fano and Sinigaglia are towns of the Marches
> fifteen miles apart on the Adriatic.
> Going to Sinigaglia you have the mountains on your right,
> very close to the sea in some places,
> nowhere two miles away. (*C.P.*, 150)

Details such as the color of a man's clothing or the slight wink of conspirator which only an eyewitness could report with authority are accentuated in the poetic version:

and Vitellozzo

> unarmed, in a tunic with green facings,
> as glum as though he knew what was going to happen
> was
> (considering his courage and the luck he had had in the past)
>> rather admirable. (*C.P.*, 151)

---

35. K.L. Goodwin, *The Influence of Ezra Pound* (London, 1966), pp. 218-219.
36. Gilbert, *op. cit.*, p. 166.
37. *Ibid.*, p. 167.

> The Duke noticed, and tipped a wink to the Reverend Michael
> who was responsible for Liverotto. (*C.P.*, 151)

The quality of Machiavelli's writing that Bunting captures best, the imperturbable, matter-of-fact tone recounting bribery, treachery, and murder by strangulation, creates an understatement laced with sardonic humor:

> Night fell, the rioting abated,
> and the Duke thought it opportune
> to put an end to Vitellozzo and Liverotto,
> and had them led out to a suitable place and strangled.
> Neither of them said anything worthy of the occasion, ...
>   (*C.P.*, 152)

Bunting puts aside the temptation to end the piece dramatically in order to finish appropriately on a very low key:

> Pagolo and the Duke of Gravina Orsini
> were left alive until the Pope sent word
> he had taken Cardinal Orsino, Archbishop of Florence,
> together with Mr. James da Santa Croce:
> upon which, on the eighteenth of January, at Castel della Pieve,
> they were strangled in the same manner. (*C.P.*, 152)

Gilbert comments on the only possibility of an excellent translation in his introduction to his own work:

> The hope to naturalize in his own idiom the stylistic qualities
> and the spirit of a great work is the translator's will-o'-the-wisp.
> So seldom does it happen, that the man who believes he has ac-
> complished it is likely to be a victim of self-delusion. . . . But we
> can suppose translations equivalent to their prototypes only when
> we imagine that translators are stylists with the power of the
> geniuses they interpret, ...[38]

In his version of Machiavelli's report, Bunting is working to present a contemporary view of a shrewd statesman's personality and an episode that seems almost immediate, but he himself downplays the overdraft as an "adaptation" and "a pretty raw one."[39] For all its narrative interest and understated humor, one cannot help being grateful he did not continue in this "prose-poem" mode. Its linear progression with its dramatic necessity of straightforward narration does not allow for Bunting's stronger poetic gift of building more leisurely through a process of incrementation, through repetition and contrast of sounds, rhythms, themes, and visual and aural motifs. This is the kind of poetry for which translations of Persian poetry prepared him further.

---

38. *Ibid.*, p. ix.
39. Basil Bunting to John Matthias, March 23, 1970.

Persian Translations

The sampling in the *Collected Poems*, the few translations published in such periodicals as *Nine*, and those sent to Zukofsky indicate the variety of Persian poetry that Bunting translated: *qasidas*, *ghazals*, a *qit'a*, *rubai*, and large parts of Firdosi's epic, the *Shahnamah*, *The Epic of Kings*. The poets whose works he chose to translate were among the best: Manuchehri, Unsuri, Rudaki, Sa'di, Hafez, and Firdosi. Bunting's familiarity with the Persian language, literary and colloquial, as his household language, as that spoken as a member of the Intelligence dealing with tribesmen, as a diplomat and consul, as a journalist for the *London Times* and Persian newspapers—all this gives his translations an authority and rich immediacy which translations by purely literary scholars generally lack. His knowledge of Persian literature was not merely classical, as may be mistakenly surmised from this list; in a letter to Zukofsky he explains:

> It is no boast to say that I am more widely read in Persian than most of the Orientalists in British and European universities, especially in early poets—Ferdosi, Rudaki, Manuchehri, Farrukhi, etc. whose work is fundamental to a real understanding of Persian literature in the same way that the work of Homer and Aeschylus is fundamental to an understanding of Greek. Lacking it, many Orientalists have lacked proportion in their enthusiasm and run after secondary poets. Hafez, for example, interpreted exclusively in the light of Naser-e Khosro of Khaqani, is less interesting and far less compelling than the real Hafez who never, I think, ceased to listen to the echo of Manuchehri and Onsori. (October 29, 1953)[40]

It is difficult to appreciate Bunting's work in this area without some slight background in Persian literature. Bunting takes for granted that his reader understands that because the themes and various structures of Persian poetry were so fixed by tradition, the outlet for the poet's ingenuity was in perfecting the meaning and rhythm within the framework and themes he chose. For example, in the *qasida*,[41] a lyric of at least twelve lines generally, each unit (*bayt* or distich) is composed of two balanced halves (*misra*)

---

40. This is a copy of a letter Bunting was sending in order to find a job during a time when his family had barely enough to keep alive. William Carlos Williams was in possession of this letter also to try to locate a position for him.

41. Background information about the *qasìda* is compiled from Reuben Levy, *An Introduction to Persian Literature* (New York and London, 1969), pp. 27-30; Jan Rypka, *A History of Iranian Literature* (Dordecht, 1968), pp. 91-94; Omar Pound, *Arabic and Persian Poems* (New York, 1970), pp. 14-16; James Kritzeck, ed. *Anthology of Islamic Literature from the Rise of Islam to Modern Times* (New York, 1964), pp. 52-53; A.J. Arberry, *Classical Persian Literature* (New York, 1958), pp. 8-9, 16; E.G. Browne, *A Literary History of Persia*, 4 vols. (Cambridge, 1902-1924), II, pp. 22-25, 28-33.

corresponding to each other in meter and parallel in theme. The *qasida* is in monorhyme introduced in the opening *bayt*, the only unit in which both halves are rhymed. All the remaining *bayts* repeat this rhyme, but only at the end of the unit. Since the poetry was originally to be sung or recited, the monorhyme could be made acceptable to the ear, although it seems wearisome to the eye. To compose a *qasida* tests the poet's skill in adapting the meter to the theme and rhyming ingeniously.

The half-lines are connected by one thought, or in certain cases by one thought and its underlying argument. Connections can also be the result of merely formal measures, such as parallelisms, the harmony of common images, etc. Rarely are thoughts grouped together grammatically over two or more *bayts*. Since each *bayt* is to some extent independent, the logical connections of the poem are not so clear and obvious as in Western poetry. In Bunting's translation of seven *bayts* from a *qasida* of Manuchehri's (*C.P.*, 143) many of these characteristics are retained:

> Shall I sulk because my love has a double heart?
> Happy is he whose she is singlehearted!
> She has found me a new torment for every instant
> and I am, whatever she does, content, content.
> If she has bleached my cheek with her love, say: Bleach!
> Is not pale saffron prized above poppy red?
> If she has stooped my shoulders, say to them: Stoop!
> Must not a harp be bent when they string it to sing?
> If she has kindled fire in my heart, say: Kindle!
> Only a kindled candle sends forth light.
> If tears rain from my eyes, say: Let them rain!
> Spring rains make fair gardens. And if then
> she has cast me into the shadow of exile, say:
> Those who seek fortune afar find it the first.[42]

In his first *bayt* the question and comment are sides of one thought; here even the monorhyme introduced in each half of the first *bayt* is echoed. The introductory general thought of the stanza supported by the cluster of parallel clauses which are themselves filled with parallelisms illustrate the explanation of Jan

---

42. Also in *Nine*, IV (April, 1956), 10, with this introductory stanza:

> The thundercloud fills the meadows with heavenly beauty,
> gardens with plants embroiders plants with petals,
> distils from its own white pearls brilliant dyes,
> makes a Tibet of hills where its shadow falls,
> San'a of our fields when it passes on to the desert.
> Wail of the morning nightingale, scent of the breeze,
> frenzy a man's bewildered, drunken heart.
> Now is the season lovers shall pant awhile,
> now is the day sets hermits athirst for wine.

This seems a wise omission in the *Collected Poems.*

Rypka, a renowned critic of Persian poetry:

> Persian poetry is seen more as filigree work, full of finely-wrought details, with no strictly logical sequence of verses. . . . The Persian is led far more by imagination than by logic, both regarding description and abstract speculation. Instead of developing one idea from another, he strews them about in apparently haphazard fashion, yet always with the remainder in mind. [However, the verse] is inferior if there is no progress.[43]

Bunting's advice to Zukofsky (April 21, 1945) to examine Upham Pope's beautifully illustrated book of Persian art, especially the pictures of the miniatures and the tile ceilings of domed mosques, is good advice to anyone who would like to see a graphic design of a Persian poem.[44]

Bunting's translation accentuates the contrast between the long-suffering lover and the tormenting beloved, the basic framework of the *qasida*, through internal rhyme in both halves of the introductory *bayt*, "I"–"my love" and "Happy"–"he"–"she." Within this *bayt* he found English equivalents, "a double heart"– "singlehearted," which not only echo the monorhyme of the original through two syllables, "-le heart," but which punctuate the emotional contrast between the shunned possibility of "sulking" in the first line and the impossibility of being "happy" in the second.

He begins a series of *bayts* with the initial word "If," interlocking them further by beginning the second part of each second half-*bayt* with "say." The parts of these half-*bayts* are connected to one another by the repetition of the key word of the first part, in the second part: for example,

> If she has kindled fire in my heart, say Kindle!

And more than once this key word is repeated in the next half-*bayt* with a twist of meaning:

> Only a kindled candle sends forth light.

In this instance Bunting has heightened the key word further through alliteration and imperfect internal rhyme.

As interesting as the technical accomplishments are in this *qasida*, it is difficult to forget the poem is a translation. It never completely fulfills Bunting's own criteria: "a translation in English

---

43. Rypka, *op. cit.*, p. 102. See also his description of a Persian verse as "a completely worked out and independent miniature," p. 101.
44. Arthur Upham Pope, *An Introduction to Persian Art Since the Seventh Century, A.D.* (London, 1930). See also David Talbot Rice, *Islamic Art* (New York, 1965); in A.L. Korn, "Puttenham and the Oriental Pattern-Poem," *Comparative Literature*, VI (Fall, 1954), 289-303, a circular *ghazal* is described and illustrated.

equivalent to [its] original but not compelled to lean on its authority,...."[45] Some of this is traceable to lines dependent on unfamiliar ideas and customs, acceptable in another time and culture, but
difficult for us to respond to; for example, a man exclaiming that
his beloved "bleached my cheek with her love," or "tears rain
from my eyes." However, in most translations Bunting is able to
make us accept naturally, almost without noticing, unfamiliar
ideas or figures of speech:

> The singer is weary of his broken voice,
> One drone for the bulbul alike and the lion's grousing.

or

> Alas for flowery, musky, sappy thirty
> and the sharp Persian sword!
> The pheasant strutting about the briar,
> pomegranate-blossom and cypress sprig! (Firdosi) (C.P., 140)

In Manuchehri's *qasida* Bunting does not quite transform the
combination of unfamiliar ideas and modes of speech and images
into a poem "claiming independence and accepting the responsibility inseparable from a life of its own."[46]

Another *qasida* that reinforces the idea of the "filigree" connections of Persian poetry is Rudaki's famous "Lament in Old
Age" which Bunting translated in 1948 as "A Qasida by Abu'-
abdulla Ja'far bin Mahmud Rudaki of Samarkand" (December 2,
1948). He first wrote to Zukofsky in praise of this poet in August
that year, connecting his poetry with music in his train of thought:

> Rudaki's qasidas have given me great delight, especially the won-
> derful one about all his teeth falling out. One must certainly add
> his name to the list of the world's very great poets, even though
> the remains are so few and fragmentary. I will perhaps send you a
> prose translation if I ever finish it. I have taken a great liking also
> to Persian classical music and wish I could get some records of it.
> (August 2, 1948)[47]

A few months later he added that his translation was of interest "in so far as it gives some idea of the way a Khorassani mind
worked in 950 a.d., I mean in my English. Rudaki's Persian is
delightful" (December 2, 1948). In the same letter he included a
copy of the *qasida* with these brief but enlightening notes inserted
after the title:

> (Monorhyme—every second line—with a good deal of internal

---

45. Basil Bunting, "Modern Translation," *Criterion*, XV (July, 1936), 714.
46. *Ibid.*
47. Kritzeck supports this idea by speaking of Rudaki's "musical poems," *op. cit.*,
p. 105.

rhyming and alliteration. The vocabulary exceedingly simple, the main effects being got by the cross-beat of ictus and stress in an elaborate quantitative measure.)

To the western mind the connections from line to line and within lines in this *qasida* are less obvious than in the preceding one by Manuchehri, but more delightful in their variety. Bunting's translation of the first part of the sixty-four line poem (*C.P.*, 141-142) illustrates this:

> All the teeth ever I had are worn down and fallen out.
> They were not rotten teeth, they shone like a lamp,
> a row of silvery-white pearls set in coral;
> they were as the morning star and as drops of rain.
> There are none left now, all of them wore out and fell out.
> Was it ill-luck, ill-luck, a malign conjunction?
> It was no fault of stars, nor yet length of years.
> I will tell you what it was: it was God's decree.

It would be unusual for a modern western poet to compare his teeth to shining lamps, silvery-white pearls set in coral, the morning star, and drops of rain, yet by piling up these images in extremely simple and forceful statements, Bunting convinces us in the opening lines that this lament for teeth "worn down and fallen out," is a universal and deeply felt one. He reinforces the lamenting quality through a skillful use of incrementation and parallelism by echoing six times throughout the poem the unornamented half-line: "The days are past when. . .", for example:

> The days are past when his face was good to look on,
> . . . .
> The days are past when she was glad and gay
> . . . .
> The days are past when he managed the affairs of princes,
> the days are past when all wrote down his verses,
> the days are past when he was the Poet of Khorassan.

In a section such as:

> . . . . a cure for pain
> and then again a pain that supplants the cure.
> In a certain time it makes new things old,
> in a certain time makes new what was worn threadbare.
> Many a broken desert has been a gay garden,
> many gay gardens grow where there used to be desert.

Bunting proves his adeptness at handling the intricate interlockings in *bayts* which continuously add to the theme, but the passage itself is too general to provide him with the raw material he needs to build vivid, concrete images.

The most general explanation of the *ghazal*,[48] another lyric form, which has something of the character of the European sonnet, is that although it follows the *qasida* in structure and rhythms, it seems more a Persian outgrowth of the fixed Arabic erotic prelude of the *qasida*. The *qasida* begins with the interest-arousing lament that at the place of the poet's desert rendezvous he found only a cold fire; from there on he speaks of the real purpose (*qasida*) of the poem—eulogy, paean, description, etc. In distinction to this Arabic court poetry form, the *ghazal* ("whisperings," "a lovers' exchange"), more radically Persian, from the cultural life of the town, speaks chiefly of love, human or mystical, although anything might be added to the subject matter that stirred the emotions.

Of all the types of Persian poetry Bunting translated, the most numerous are the *ghazal*; and these are works of the greatest writers of the form, Manuchehri, Sa'di, and Hafez. Bunting's translation of "A Ghazal of Sa'di's" (*C.P.*, 145)[49] reveals its more personal nature, as well as the less important tradition of including the name of the poet in the last few lines so that even if a *ravi*, a professional singer, presented the poem, the poet himself would receive his just recognition.

Writing to Zukofsky, Bunting commented:

> I'll type out my last translation, one of the most famous poems in the language in mediaeval times, imitated by Hafez, but now less heard of, one of the finest of Sa'di's long lines in Persian. This prevents the translation being line for line, but doesn't prevent it being almost literal. (July 28, 1949)

> Last night without sight of you my brain was ablaze.
> My tears trickled and fell plip on the ground. That I with
> sighing might bring my life to a close they would name
> you and again and again speak your name till
> with night's coming all eyes closed save mine whose every
> hair pierced my scalp like a lancet. That was
> not wine I drank far from your sight but my heart's
> blood gushing into the cup. Wall and door wherever
> I turned my eyes scored and decorated with shapes
> of you. To dream of Laila Majnun prayed for
> sleep. My senses came and went but neither your
> face saw I nor would your fantom go from me.
> Now like aloes my heart burned, now smoked as a censer.

---

48. Background information for *ghazal* compiled from Rypka, *op. cit.*, pp. 95-106; Levy, *op. cit.*, pp. 33-35; Omar Pound, *op. eit.*, p. 26; Browne, *op. cit.*, II, pp. 22, 25, 27-28; Arberry, *op. cit.*, pp. 8, 13, 276, 298; Najib Ullah, *Islamic Literature: An Introductory History with Selections* (New York, 1963), pp. xiii-xiv.
49. Titled only in *Nine*, II (August, 1950), 219.

> Where was the morning gone that used on other nights
> to breathe till the horizon paled? Sa'di!
> Has then the chain of the Pleiades broken
> tonight that every night is hung on the sky's neck? (Sa'di)

With only a little effort westerners should be able to appreciate that it is "by art concealed behind apparent simplicity that Sa'di demonstrates calculated deliberation,"[50] an art Bunting would be strongly attracted to.

By not using the end-stopped lines of the Persian form, Bunting adds to the emotional effect of uncontrollable lovesickness. Onomatopoetically, "plip" is unsuccessful, adding nothing to an otherwise good line, and the image in "all eyes closed save mine whose every / hair pierced my scalp like a lancet" is not clear. Neither belongs in a poem with lines translated as vividly as

>   wall and door wherever
> I turned my eyes scored and decorated with shapes
> of you. To dream of Laila Majnun prayed for
> sleep. My senses came and went but neither your
> face saw I nor would your fantom go from me.

By not translating the images into more familiar, western terms, Bunting preserves the richness of Sa'di's at the same time that he broadens his reader's enjoyment in such eastern contrasts as "Now like aloes my heart burned, now smoked as a censer" and in the oriental ending:

> Has then the chain of the Pleiades broken
> tonight that every night is hung on the sky's neck?

Even though Bunting includes only one *qasida* of Manuchehri's in his *Collected Poems*, he has translated several of his *ghazals*, two of which are published in *Nine* (1956).[51] Bunting praises no other Persian poet as he does Manuchehri:

> Manuchehri? Haven't I ever pestered you with him? If one puts Homer and Firdosi carefully in one place and then looks for the three or four greatest poets remaining I dont see how anyone who has the luck to read him can omit Manuchehri. His variety is enormous and everything he did he did better than anyone else. You want the directness of some Catullus? Go to Manuchehri. You want the swiftness of Anacreon? Manuchehri. The elaborate music of Spenser? Go to Manuchehri. The formal, full dress ode with every circumstance of solemnity and splendor? Not Pindar, Manuchehri. Satire direct and overwhelming, Manuchehri all

---

50. Rypka, *op. cit.*, p. 101.
51. "A Ghazal of Manuchehri" ("You there, with my enemy, strolling down my street"), *Nine*, IV (April, 1956), 9; "A Ghazal of Manuchehri's" ("Night is hard by. I am vexed and bothered by sleep"), *Nine*, II (August, 1950), 218-219.

alone—no competitor. He was a younger contemporary of Firdosi, and like him went to the Ghaznavi Court—I think probably after Firdosi had left it, for most of Manuchehri is addressed not to Mahmud but his successor. But at that time one man might well have heard both of them, to say nothing of Unsuri and Farrukhi, both also very great poets. I do not know where else at any time a man could have had such an experience. I think Manuchehri began by imitating the great Arabic poet then still recent, Al-Motanabbi, and found he could do it standing on his head. So first he set himself difficult technical problems and solved them, then he began inventing new forms, finally he found he could say what was in him without any elaboration at all and have a great poem. (July 28, 1949)

It could well be his great admiration for the poet that kept Bunting from collecting poems he felt were inadequate translations. A hint of that occurs in a letter which included a translation of Manuchehri's *ghazal*, "Night is hard by. I am vexed and bothered by sleep."

I am going to enclose . . . a literal version of one of Manuchehri's ghazals. The last couplet is very famous and has been quoted or imitated by nearly every notable ghazal writer in Persian history.

We, men of wine are we, meat are we, music . . .
Well, then! wine have we, meat have we, music . . .

But the characteristic of the original is vigour, which has evaporated in the translation and I dont know how to get it back.
(May 28, 1949)

After this letter though, Bunting made only the slightest changes in punctuation, capitalization, and in the omission of words, and clarified the meaning of only one line before the *ghazal* was published in *Nine* (August, 1950). The changes, too slight to vitalize the poem as Bunting wished to do, left the overall effect the same, a translation which only hints strongly at the vigor of the original.

Another poem of Manuchehri's appears only in his private correspondence:

So! I have been reading Manuchehri: bloody fine poet too. The bird that preens its feathers many times a day, going over and over them "like a petty clerk who has made a mistake in his accounts." And the sonority of his musammats. And the wonderful transitions. And his observation of deer and flowers and camel drivers and girls. The tulips that "are a row of parrots asleep with their head under their wings." The names of ancient Arab poets, in a satire—

Amru'l Qais and Labid and Akhtal and blind A'sha and Qais
who keened over the bones of dead encampments and fallen tents,
as we mourn for the ruins of poetry and broken rhymes—
Bu Nuvas and Bu Haddad and Bu Malik bin al Bashar,

> Bu Duvaid and Bu Duraid and Ibn Ahmad. Do you hear
> him who sang "She has warned us," who sang "The honest sword,"
> who sang "Love has exhausted"——?
> Bu'l Ata and Bu'l Abbas and Bu Sulaik and Bu'l Mathil,
> and the bard of Lavaih and the Harper of Herat.
> Where are the wise Afghans, Shuhaid and Rudaki,
> and Bu Shakur of Balkh and Bu'l Fath of Bust likewise.
> Bid them come and see our noble century
> and read our poetry and despair. . . . (May Day, 1939)

Here, in my opinion, is one of Bunting's best Persian-based poems. Only one rough note, "likewise," detracts from the otherwise continuously fluid rhythm of the long lines—

> who keened over the bones of dead encampments and fallen tents,
> as we mourn for the ruins of poetry and broken rhymes—

The series of names which at first seem impossible to incorporate into a mellifluous line, actually enhance the poem through their incantatory effect, if the reader is careful to keep each vowel distinct. With attention to the sound of each "a" pronounced as a long Italian "a" and each "i" as long "e," the reader can appreciate the music of such a line as "Bu Duvaid and Bu Duraid and Ibn Ahmad. Do you hear." The ending, reminiscent of Shelley's "Ozymandias," capitalizes on the accumulation of verb phrases, "Bid them come and see our noble century / and read our poetry," in order to build to the final single word, "despair," an effective satirical anticlimax.

Another poet whose translated *ghazals* Bunting did not publish in his *Collected Poems* is Hafez, the one who after Sa'di brought the form and its musical language to its perfection.[52] Bunting's translation of one famous *ghazal*, "If that Shirazian beauty would lay hands on my heart," bears comparison with all those which both Kritzeck and Arberry present for comparative study in their books. Since Bunting wrote the Persian phonetically for this one along with another *ghazal*, "She said: 'You have been out to see the spectacle of the new moon,'"[53] it was possible for Iranians who compared Bunting's translation with the others mentioned above to evaluate his as one which to them at least presents most aptly to readers in the twentieth century the tone,

---

52. Background information about Sa'di compiled from Kritzeck, *op. cit.*, p. 267; Levy, *op. cit.*, p. 34; Browne, *op. cit.*, III, 271.
53. A sample of this phonetic writing follows:

> Agar an turk i shirazi ba dast arad dil i ma-ra
> ba khal i hinduvush baksham Samarkand u Bukhara-ra.

With these phonetic transcriptions, Bunting sent notes about pronunciation and allusions.

mood, and vocabulary of the originals.[54] With these phonetic versions and the English translations Bunting sent valuable notes on content and form.

Something further will be said about the *ghazal* insofar as it includes music, singing, and dancing interludes when *Briggflatts* is discussed.

The one poem of Hafez's which Bunting did publish in his *Collected Poems* as Ode 28 (*C.P.*, 113), he first wrote to Zukofsky in four continuous lines with the heading, "(Hafez, a rubay)," and the ending note, "(which is nearly a blues)" (September 29,1935). "Epigrammatic in character, severe and Gregorian in effect,"[55] the *rubai* is emphatically Persian, probably originating in Rudaki's poetry. Its form which Bunting purposefully modifies is four half-lines of which line 1, 2, and 4 are in monorhyme; line 3 usually outside the rhyme pattern marks an anticipatory pause before the climactic last line. Two or three long syllables invariably introduce the *rubai*, a fine detail which Bunting retains in his translation. Bunting's poem gains its powerful effect by giving the impression of being "unstudied and spontaneous," yet terse in its revelation of the poet's true feelings:

> You leave
> nobody else
> without a bed
>
> you make
> everybody else
> thoroughly at home
>
> I'm
> the only one
> hanged
> in your
> halter

---

54. Jaafar Moghadam and Khosrow Moshtarikhah, Iranian Midshipmen studying at the University of Notre Dame, spent many hours with me sharing their knowledge of Persian literature, 1971-1972. Khosrow located both poems which Bunting spelled out phonetically in Persian books of literature: اگر آن ترک شیوازی بدست آرد دل مارا ("Agar an turk i" etc.) in لسان الغیب [*The Inspired Tongue*] (Khajehe Sham-saddin Mohammed Hafez Shirazi), Pezhman Bakhtiari, ed., 5th ed. (Teheran, 1345 [1966]), p. 4; and گفتا برون شدی به تماشای ماه نو ("Gufta: Birun shdi ba tamashay i mah i no") in کلیات دیوان حافظ شیرازی حسین بخیاری *The Complete Works of Hafez,* (Housian Bakhtiari, ed.) (Teheran, 1318 [1945]), p. 189. Three published editions served as a double check on Bunting's translation.

55. E. Denison Ross, ed., *A Persian Anthology*. Edward Granville-Browne, trans. (London, 1927), p. 60. Further background information about *rubai* compiled from Rypka, *op. cit.*, p. 96; Levy, *op. cit.*, pp. 35-36; Omar Pound, *op. cit.*, pp. 24, 27; Kritzeck, *op. cit.*, pp. 167-168; Browne, *op. cit.*, II, 22, 25, 34-35.

you've driven
nobody else mad
but me.

By dividing the four lines of the *rubai* into fourteen, Bunting has carefully arranged them for rhetorical and rhythmical emphasis. Although he has translated all three invariably long, introductory beats of the *rubai*, through the typography he has emphasized the first two to gain the keening effect of the Persian *ghazal* singer and to set the modern blues atmosphere. By beginning each section with an echo of the first line, he strengthens the first suggestion of the blues at the same time he underlines the tension between the antagonists ("You leave," "you make," "I'm," "you've driven").

The contrast of the syncopation of the second line in each section, interesting in itself rhythmically, becomes a kind of bridge to the last line, especially in the first, second and fourth sections. In each case he varies the rhythm of the concluding line ("without a bed," "thoroughly at home," "halter," "but me"). Further, he prepares for this by the slight variation in each of the second lines in order to build to the climax of the final line of the poem ("nobody else," "everybody else," "the only one," "nobody else"). By dividing the original lines, Bunting has played the similarities of each fragment against its variations. The following schema shows this more clearly:

You leave	you make	I'm	you've driven
nobody else	everybody else	the only one	nobody else mad
without a bed	thoroughly at home	hanged	but me.
		in your	
		halter	

After reading only two sections, one is aware of the variety of parallelisms; the third section, varied enough to break any suggestion of monotony, prepares by its alliteration and emphatic single-word lines for the climax. This depends on single words alliterated (mad/me) to complete this "blues."

A justification for Bunting's not attributing this poem to Hafez is that his version has such different visual and aural effects it becomes a new poem. The fragmentation of lines emphasizing in an original way content, rhythm and sound creates a poem Hafez would be hard put to recognize. Besides, the new form expresses a universal sentiment found in too many poems and blues lyrics to be attributed solely to Hafez. Bunting's reply to my question about his having created in effect a new poem was "if I'd thought there was very much of Hafez left in the product,

I'd have put it with the other translations."[56]

The *rubai* was, of course, the form used by Omar Khayyam in his great *Rubaiat*, a copy of which Bunting carried with him, along with a pocket edition of Dante, during his war years in the East. Long before that time (August 30, 1933), Bunting had sent a copy of a *rubai* of Omar's to Zukofsky, but only the phonetic Persian and no translation is included:

asrar-i-jihan chunanki dar daftur-i-mast

guftan natavan, ki an vabal sar-i-mast.

chun nist darin mardum [mast]-i dana ahle[57]

natavan guftan haranchi dar khatir-i-mast.

umr-i-khayyam

Written in Persian, the rhyme scheme becomes apparent if the lines are examined from right to left:

ر اضطراری جهان چنانکه دار دفتری مست
لتا نتوان که آن وبا ل سرمست
چونست در این مردم مست دانا اهل
تران کفتن هرآ نچه دار خاطری مست

Bunting has a great deal to say in his letters by way of introduction to the *qit'a*, the "fragment," "attributed, perhaps wrongly, to Sa'di," which he publishes among his "Overdrafts" (*C.P.*, 145). A poem is a *qit'a*[58] if the opening verse, the *bayt* which introduces the monorhyme in both halves of the first unit, is absent. Its theme is arbitrary—philosophical, ethical, meditative— and often based on personal experiences. Bunting introduces his *qit'a* to Zukofsky by filling in the background of the poet who he believes is its true author, Unsuri:

> The most important of Unsuri's poems are lost—they were romances, the first to exist in any language unless we count the Greek novels—but there are a good many qasidas left, and, I think, a powerful short poem which is printed amongst the poems "attributed" to Sa'di. I will try to translate it for you.
>
> (July 28, 1949)

---

56. Bunting to S.V.M. Forde, May 23, 1972.
57. Jaafar Moghadam has supplied a crossed-out word as *"mast."* He also suggests that "daftur-i-mast" in the first line should be "doktur-i-mast." However, according to Bunting, "the word 'mast' would make nonsense of Khayyam's verse and spoils the run of the line too. It means 'drunk,' which is a term of praise with Khayyam and would never be applied to 'mardum-e dana,' learned men, a term of abuse. The sense of the lines is: 'Since amongst these learned men there's not one real person.'" Bunting to S.V.M. Forde, July 4, 1975.
58. Background information about *qit'a* compiled from Rypka, *op. cit.*, p. 95; Browne, *op. cit.*, II, 22-23, 25, 34.

When he sent it to his friend, he added the note: "Attributed to Sa'di: But, I think, possibly by the much earlier and greater poet Unsuri. Unsuri wrote 'Vamiq and Azra' (or translated it from Pahlevi) and may have been the first to write a 'Laila and Majnun.' Sa'di wrote neither" (August 6, 1949).

> This I write, mix ink with tears,
> and have written of grief before, but never so grievously,
> to tell Azra Vamiq's pain,
> to tell Laila Majnun's plight,
> to tell you my own
> unfinished story.
> Take it. Seek no excuse.
> How sweetly you will sing what I so sadly write.

In pencil at the end of the poem, he wrote enthusiastically: "This last poem is song in fullest sense: hope my rendering would be singable. Last line a bit Jacobean, lute cadences all ready for it."

Zukofsky's suggesting a punctuation mark for clarity primed Bunting to reveal his knowledge of Persian poetry and his ideas about its origin:

> You're right, no doubt, about the comma after Azra and Laila in the little Unsuri piece. Too familiar myself, I thought that 'everybody' was familiar with the names and the outline of the story of Laila and Majnun, and that that would explain the preceding verse about Vamiq and Azra. I even thought you had referred to it in your first long work. . . . Laila's parents refused to let her marry him and he went mad, the stereotype of the lovers who go mad all through romantic poetry in Europe as well as the East. Nearly all the main romantic themes seem to come from a group of now lost Pahlevi poems of the fifth and sixth century, of which Vamiq and Azra is one, Xosro and Shirin another, Vis and Ramin the most closely preserved in its Persian version: and Laila and Majnun may or may not have been another: as a source of the romantic subjects it should, by analogy, be one, but it is barely possible that Nezami of Ganjeh invented it in the twelfth century. (September 5, 1949)

Although Bunting translated long sections of Firdosi's epic, the *Shahnamah*, and dreamed of the leisure necessary to complete the long poem, it is only through his correspondence that this work is discovered.[59] Even though Pound sent some of the epic to Eliot to try to publish, in a letter to Otto Bird he commented: "Bunt'n gone off on Persian, but don't seem to do anything but Firdusi, whom he can't put into English that is of any *interest*. More the fault of subject matter than of anything else in

---

59. Some are dated by Zukofsky as "Recvd '35"; other sections not dated.

isolation."[60] The only poetry of Firdosi's that Bunting includes in his collection is the lyrical ode, "When the sword of sixty comes nigh his head" (*C.P.*, 140).

In 1951 Bunting explained to Pound one of his purposes, during that lean time at least, in translating Persian poetry:

> But I'm not hoping for honor and glory, nor expecting to make a living, nor even hoping for translation good enough to approve of: just texts and cribs so that a chap who wants to get at the stuff can. So that another generation may not have quite as many cursed vexations as ours when it sets out to acquire knowledge.[61]

For another generation, in the "Foreword" to Omar Pound's *Arabic and Persian Poetry*, Bunting expressed his matured thoughts more fully:

> Persian poetry has suffered badly, Arabic poetry rather less, from neoplatonic dons determined to find an arbitrary mysticism in everything. . . .
> There are difficulties in the way of a more satisfactory account of Persian poetry. Hafez, for instance, depends almost entirely on his mastery of sound and literary allusion, neither translatable. Manuchehri's enormous vigor and variety expresses itself often in patterns as intricate as those of a Persian carpet. Even dons are put off by the vast size of Sa'di's *Divan*, and fail to find the key poems. . . .
> There is at least as much variety in either of these literatures as in any European tongue. . . .
> Sooner or later we must absorb Islam if our own culture is not to die of anemia. It will not be done by futile attempts to trace Maulavi symbols back to Plotinus or by reproducing in bad English verse the platitudes common to poetry everywhere. Omar Pound has detected something that Moslem poetry has in common with some of ours. He makes it credible. He makes it a pleasure. By such steps, though they may be short and few, we can at least begin our Hajj.[62]

Omar Pound who advises his readers that "Basil Bunting's translations of Rudaki's lament in his old age . . . and one of his quatrains 'Came to me . . . Who? . . .' are superb,"[63] would be one of the first to admit that Bunting's earlier attempts paved the way for his later, smoothly modern translations.

---

60. January 9, 1938. D.D. Paige, ed. *The Letters of Ezra Pound* (New York, 1950), p. 305.
61. Basil Bunting to Ezra Pound, February 26, 1951. Carlton Lake Collection. Humanities Research Library, University of Texas at Austin.
62. Basil Bunting, "Foreword," in Omar Pound, *Arabic and Persian Poems* (New York, 1970), p. 11.
63. *Ibid.*, p. 76.

Japanese Adaptation

Bunting rightly believed that "Chomei at Toyama" (*C.P.*, 75-84) was "a poem which whatever its worth or worthlessness in itself, might have a useful influence: showing, for instance, that poetry can be intelligible and still be poetry, a fact that came to be doubted," he believed, "by the generation that took most of its ideas indirectly from Eliot."[64]

The poem has its basis in a prose work of Kamono Chomei, *Hojoki*, "Life in a dwelling one *jo* (ten feet) square," "the most delicate contribution to the prose of the times."[65] "The times," (1153-1216) so nearly parallel to the times in which Bunting was living, were the late Heian and early Kamakura Periods when the military caste held power and the science of war was taking preference over intellectual matters. However, in his work Chomei describes a series of natural calamities rather than the fighting that also ravaged the country.[66]

Bunting introduced his readers to Chomei in a brief biography written for *Poetry* (August, 1933), the issue in which extracts of the poem were published:

> Kamo-no-Chomei, i.e., Chomei of Kamo, flourished somewhat over a hundred years before Dante. He belonged to the minor Japanese nobility, and held various offices in the civil service. He applied for a fat job in a Shinto temple, was turned down, and the next day announced his conversion to Buddhism.
>
> He got sick of public life and retired to a kind of mixture of hermitage and country cottage at Toyama on Mount Hino, and there, when he was getting old, he wrote his celebrated *Ho-Jo-Ki*, of which my poem is, in the main, a condensation.[67]

Both works, the prose[68] and the poetry, open with the author's view of the mutability of life which underlies all that seems permanent—cities and populations. As illustrations of the changes that men must endure, both works give vivid descriptions of the Great Fire that ravaged the capital of Japan, Kyoto, in 1177, the great whirlwind of 1180, the transfer of the capital that same year and then its relocation to its original site in 1180, the famine of 1181-82, and the earthquake of 1185. Besides these specific

---

64. Basil Bunting to Leippert, September 26, 1932. Ronald Latimer Papers, University of Chicago Library.
65. Roger Bersihand, *Japanese Literature*, trans. Unity Evans (New York, 1965), p. 25.
66. Donald Keene, ed. *Anthology of Japanese Literature from the Earliest Era to the Mid-Nineteenth Century*, UNESCO Collection of Representative Works: Japanese Series (New York, 1955), p. 197.
67. *Poetry*, XLII (August, 1933), 356-357.
68. Keene, *op. cit.*, pp. 197-212.

hardships, both describe the general precarious circumstances of everyday life for the majority of men. All this instability and unrest motivates Chomei, as he leads his reader to believe, to retire from the world as a hermit. Step by step, the lines trace his progress from the ancestral home he inherited before he was thirty, to a small cottage which he left before he was fifty for a ten foot square hut on Mount Hino. The rest is a description of the simple pleasures of the hermitage informed by philosophical attitudes towards the impermanence of all things.[69]

Preserving the design of the whole was something Bunting had to fight for with his editors. Just as critics of Chomei have recognized that it is the systematic design which elevates *Hojoki* above others in the genre *zuihitsu* (fugitive essay),[70] Bunting appreciated the balance which he transferred to his poetic version. In January, 1933, he tried hard to convince Morton Dauwen Zabel, associate editor of *Poetry*, that printing extracts only would ruin the design of the whole:

> First: re Chomei, I'll wait and see the extracts you suggest before making a definite answer. . . . of course I'd best like it to be printed whole, since to me it seems to depend in a high degree on the general design: the balance of the calamities and consolations pivoted on the little central satire, the transmogrification of the house throughout, the earth, air, fire and water, pieces, first physical then spiritual make up an elaborate design, which I've tried not to underline so that it might be felt rather than pedantically counted up. Also the old boy's superficial religion breaking down to anchor it in its proper place.[71]

A few months later Bunting reluctantly acquiesced to its fragmentation, a wise move perhaps in the light of the Honorable Mention the poet received in *Poetry*'s annual awards:[72]

> Alright, you must do as you think best in all the circumstances. I hate to see Chomei cut up, because I think it depends mainly on the balance of parts throughout and the picking out of four somewhat 'poetical' bits rather misrepresents the very simpatico ole Jap.[73]

The *Poetry* notes that Bunting included in this letter explains further his idea of the overall design:

---

69. Keene, *op. cit.*, pp. 129-130.
70. The Kokusai Bunka Shinkokai, ed. *Introduction to Classic Japanese Literature* (Tokyo, 1948), p. 129.
71. Basil Bunting to Morton Dauwen Zabel, January 4, 1933. Morton Dauwen Zabel Papers, University of Chicago Library.
72. *Poetry*, XLIII (November, 1933), 108.
73. Bunting to Zabel, March 24, 1933. Morton Dauwen Zabel Papers, University of Chicago Library.

The *Ho-Jo-Ki* is in prose, but the careful proportion and balance
of the parts, the leit-motif of the House running through it, and
some other indications, suggest that he intended a poem, more or
less elegiac; but had not time, nor possibly energy, at his then
age, to work out what would have been for Japan an entirely new
form, nor to condense his material sufficiently. This I have attempted to do for him.[74]

By teaching that Chomei followed the *yugen*, the "lonesome"
school of poetry, scholars in Japan give some support to Bunting's
judgment.[75]

The design Bunting was trying to save is essential to the
balanced form of the whole. In general, the first part of the poem,
the series of calamities, balances the last part, the consolations of
Chomei's simple life as a hermit. Between these parts, the central
description of Chomei's progressive moves from the Kyoto home
to the hut serves both as a fulcrum and a transition. *Poetry*'s omission of the entire central section about the dwellings of Chomei
disconnects the two large divisions of calamities and consolations,
disrupting the unity of the whole.*

But before this the editors had fragmented the careful design
by omitting the whirlwind and removing the capital sections. The
design includes two natural catastrophes before and two after the
moving of the capital. Thus, the four calamities caused by an element in nature—fire, air, water, or earth—are balanced on either
side of one caused by human whim: "Nothing compelled the
change nor was it an easy matter" (*C.P.*, 76). The three locations
of the capital are also carefully balanced: from Kyoto to the new
site, then back to Kyoto. Though each calamity depends on one
element in particular, Bunting like Chomei is careful to bring in
echoes of the other three; e.g.:

As the wind veered
flames spread out in the shape of an open fan. (*C.P.*, 76)

The design of the first part also includes a transition between
large populations and groupings of houses in the city and Chomei
and his series of individual dwellings by describing the unstable
everyday circumstances surrounding the ordinary man and his
home. By omitting this section also, *Poetry* further disrupted the
balance of the whole. In addition, through their omission, they

74. *Poetry*, XLII (August, 1933), 357.
75. *Introduction to Classic Japanese Literature, op. cit.*, p. 132.

*"The real balancing point of the Hojoki is the bit that begins 'A poor man living
amongst the rich' to 'If he doesnt he passes for mad.'" Bunting to S.V.M. Forde, July 4,
1975.

transformed into a final comment a passage of two lines which is
in fact the connecting link between the large calamities and the
next transitional section, the passage about the precarious existence
of a poor man's life and dwelling:

> This is the unstable world, and
> we in it unstable and our houses. (*C.P.*, 78)

Since the transitional section following these lines leads smoothly
to the central section of the poem (Chomei's progressive moves),
what seems a slight transformation really interrupts the continuity
of the entire design.

After the central description of Chomei's dwellings, the design in the last part continues in the description of Chomei's life
as a hermit. Divesting himself of most unsettling concerns of men
illustrated in the first part, the hermit draws consolations from the
very natural elements which earlier in the poem caused suffering
and death—earth, air, fire, and water. These examples are outstanding in their simple beauty:

> A shower at dawn
> sings
> like the hillbreeze in the leaves. (*C.P.*, 81)

> I rake my ashes.
> > *Chattering fire,*
> *soon kindled, soon burned out,*
> *fit wife for an old man!* (*C.P.*, 82)

Men with their disturbing concerns are kept at a distance. To
highlight this distance, Bunting mentions no particular names of
men; all is vague and unspecific:

> And I hear Soanso's dead
> back in Kyoto (*C.P.*, 82)

> I know myself and mankind.
> . . . .
> I don't want to be bothered.

> (You will make me editor
> of the Imperial Anthology?
> I don't want to be bothered.) (*C.P.*, 82)

In contrast to this, Bunting designates specifically each thing
that contributes to his pleasure; for example,

> The view from the summit: sky bent over Kyoto,
> picnic villages, Fushimi and Toba:
> a very economical way of enjoying yourself.
> Thought runs along the crest, climbs Sumiyama;

beyond Kasatori it visits the great church,
goes on pilgrimage to Ishiyama (no need to foot it!)

one zest and equal, chewing tsubana buds,
one zest and equal, persimmon, pricklypear,
ears of sweetcorn pilfered from Valley Farm. (*C.P.*, 81)

Physical consolations are elevated by being combined with the consolations Chomei receives from poetry and music, from his "books above the window, / lute and mandolin near at hand" (*C.P.*, 80):

Be limber, my fingers, I am going to play *Autumn Wind*
to the pines, I am going to play *Hastening Brook*
to the water. I am no player
but there's nobody listening,
I do it for my own amusement. (*C.P.*, 81)

Chomei's lately adopted religion is more a veneer over the whole picture of an egocentric life rather than something deeply permeating it. Bunting makes this as unmistakable in his poetry as in his note to the poem:

I cannot take his Buddhism seriously, considering the manner of his conversion, the highly suspect nature of his anthology [poems composed at the moment of conversion by Buddhist proselytes], and his whole urbane, skeptical and ironic temperament. If this annoys anybody I cannot help it. (*C.P.*, 158)

By his image Bunting broadens Chomei's attitude to one easily recognizable by men of the East or West:

no one will be shocked if I neglect the rite.
There's a Lent of commandments kept
when there's no way to break them. (*C.P.*, 80)

By typography alone Bunting is able to accentuate Chomei's ironic stance:

I have renounced the world;
have a saintly
appearance. (*C.P.*, 84)

Underlying this balance of calamities and consolations, physical and spiritual, is the deeper irony that Bunting emphasizes to enrich the design of the whole. According to Bunting, this balance "is pivoted on a little central satire."[76] The little central satire he speaks of is rooted in the central section of the poem, Chomei's unsatisfying moves to smaller and smaller dwellings, apparently towards a greater degree of the detachment counseled by Buddha,

---

76. Bunting to Zabel, January 4, 1933. Morton Dauwen Zabel Papers, University of Chicago Library.

but in reality towards a greater, unhampered enjoyment of simple pleasures.

Bunting capitalizes though on the old man's honesty with himself and others to keep his persona throughout the poem a "very simpatico old Jap."[77] In fact, a distinctly original aspect of Bunting's version is his creation of a unique persona, basically the historical writer of the prose work, but one with a much less placid temperament who speaks in a wide range of tones. Appropriately, the elegiac tone pervades the poem, but through his courteous but more colloquial diction, and by means of short, more direct lines which state opinion baldly without apologies or explanations, Bunting creates a persona who expresses himself with a much greater range of feelings: humor, belligerency, haughtiness, melancholy, compassion, condescension, and resignation:

> My hands and feet will not loiter
> when I am not looking.
> I will not overwork them.
> Besides, it's good for my health. (*C.P.*, 83)

> I am out of place in the capital,
> people take me for a beggar,
> as you would be out of place in this sort of life,
> you are so—I regret it—so welded to your vulgarity. (*C.P.*, 83)

> [after a description of a child's death]

> His father howled shamelessly—an officer.
> I was not abashed at his crying. (*C.P.*, 78)

> Oh! There's nothing to complain about. (*C.P.*, 84)

One level of satire is based on the honest old man's admission of a goal in life not quite in line with the highest ascetic practices of his new religion. But beneath this is yet another, deeper irony which Bunting allows his reader to discover with only unobtrusive hints from him. The greatest irony which underlies the situation of the whole poem is that neither an absence of great sufferings nor a wealth of simple consolations gives Chomei the complete happiness he seeks. The same note of sadness and dissatisfaction runs beneath the descriptions of the consolations:

> easy to take it down and carry it away
> when I get bored with this place. (*C.P.*, 79-80)

---

77. *Ibid.*, March 24, 1933.

I do not enjoy being poor,
I've a passionate nature.
My tongue
clacked a few prayers. (*C.P.*, 84)

Bunting deepens the final irony of these last lines of the
poem through the "leitmotif of the House" which includes "the
transmogrification of the house" he mentions. Within the first few
lines he introduces this leitmotif:

Eaves formal on the zenith,
lofty city, Kyoto, (*C.P.*, 75)

and continues repeating it to the end:

Buddha says: 'None of the world is good.'
I am fond of my hut. . . . (*C.P.*, 84)

By means of this recurrent motif which he sees as an indication of
an intended elegy, he tightens the structural design of the whole.
Furthermore, he is able to use it as a basis for the symbolism on
which depends the expression of his ideas about transitoriness and
permanence, sufferings and happiness, life and death. Immediately
after the lines about the eaves of Kyoto, Bunting adds the description of "house-breakers" who in this case are building bungalows.
From this first suggestion of the transitoriness of man's dwellings
on earth until the last lines written from a hut which in many
ways foreshadows the grave, Chomei's final "dwelling," Bunting
continuously combines the mention of houses with the description or suggestion of death. This basic theme of the transitoriness
of all things converts even the innocent-looking epigraph of the
poem to a subtly artistic summary of his thought: "(Kamo-no-
Chomei, born at Kamo 1154, died at Toyama on Mount Hino,
24th June 1216)" (*C.P.*, 75).

In the first part of the poem a catalog of deaths is always
combined in some way with a description of the destruction of
buildings:

Some choked, some burned, some barely escaped.
Sixteen great officials lost houses and
very many poor. (*C.P.*, 76)

Not a house stood. Some were felled whole,
some in splinters; some had left
great beams upright in the ground
and round about
lay rooves scattered where the wind flung them.
. . . .
Lamed some, wounded some.
This cyclone turned southwest.

Massacre without cause. (*C.P.*, 76)

. . . . Dead stank
on the curb, lay so thick . . .
. . . .
That winter my fuel was the walls of my own house. (*C.P.*, 77)

In the rest of the poem Bunting connects the leitmotif of the
House with the transitoriness of life much more delicately. In the
central section of the poem the death of the grandmother begins
the chain of Chomei's moves which ends when he reaches his
smallest dwelling. This one foreshadows the grave with its suggestions of clay and "barrow":

I have filled the frames with clay,
set hinges at the corners;
easy to take it down and carry it away
when I get bored with this place.
Two barrowloads of junk
and the cost of a man to shove the barrow,
no trouble at all. (*C.P.*, 80)

In the final section, whose setting is this ten-foot hut, Bunting
skillfully rounds out our conception of his persona at the same
time that he less directly and vividly speaks of death. It is almost
as if Chomei is unable to speak directly of his own mortality and
death, though he is reminded of it by everything in his past experiences and present surroundings:

Toyama snug in the creepers!
Toyama, deep in the dense gully, open
westward whence the dead ride out of Eden
squatting on blue clouds of wistaria.
(Its scent drifts west to Amida.) (*C.P.*, 80)

Even though the connection of Chomei's thoughts with death here
is explicit, Bunting's notes at the end of his poem in *Poetry* give
further support to my idea:

Amida: in the more or less polytheistic Buddhism of mediaeval
Japan, Amida presides over the earthly paradise, where the souls
of decent dead men repose for awhile. He was reverenced about
as widely as Mary is by Catholics, and Chomei, probably attracted
by the poetic qualities of the Amida myth, professed a special
devotion for him.[78]

Nature, poetry, and music never cease recalling to Chomei the
evanescence of all and the end, death.

---

78. *Poetry*, XLII (August, 1933), 357.

> Summer? Cuckoo's *Follow, follow*—to
> harvest Purgatory hill!
> Fall? The nightgrasshopper will
> shrill *Fickle life!* (*C.P.*, 80)

Bunting enlarges the Japanese image of the cuckoo's promise to guide man on the road of death by combining it with the Dantean image which suggest Chomei's reluctance to follow. Besides the sounds of the insects which seem to him to sing of the transitoriness of life, even the songs hc plays for his "own amusement" underline his constant recollection of the temporality of all things: "*Autumn Wind*" and "*Hastening Brook.*" The single line, "A ripple of white water after a boat," epitomizes the complete thought of Mansei's poem which Bunting merely hints at:

> To what shall I compare
> This world?
> To the white wake behind
> A ship that has rowed away
> at dawn![79]

Bunting deliberately underscores the central satire by adding lines of a poet Chomei only mentions but does not quote:

> Somehow or other
> We scuttle through a lifetime.
> Somehow or other
> neither palace nor straw-hut
> is quite satisfactory. (*C.P.*, 81)

Bunting's note for *Poetry* shows better than those condensed for his *Collected Poems* that he was aware of other specific works of Chomei:

> He wrote: *Tales of the Four Seasons*; *Notes with No Title* (critical essays); and a quantity of poems; edited an anthology of poems composed at the moment of conversion by Buddhist proselytes (one suspects irony); and was for a while secretary to the editors of the imperial anthology.[80]

In one of these works, *Mumyosho*, a section headed "The Modern Style" ("Kindai Katei"), Chomei, "himself one of the most original poets among [his] contemporaries," reports the views of his Master, Shun'e, in the form of answers to questions.[81] In one reply which points to Bunting's own writing, Chomei's Master explains that "the qualities deemed essential to the style are the overtones that do not appear in the words alone and an atmosphere that is not visible in the configuration of the poem."

79. Keene, *Anthology, op. cit.*, p. 93.
80. *Poetry*, XLII (August, 1933), 356-357.
81. Robert H. Brower and Earl Miner, *Japanese Court Poetry* (Stanford, 1961), p. 268.

After illustrating his belief that "these virtues will be present of themselves" in every simple, exact description, he concludes:

> It is only when many meanings are compressed into a single word, when the depths of feeling are exhausted yet not expressed, when an unseen world hovers in the atmosphere of the poem, when the mean and common words are used to express the elegant, when a poetic conception of rare beauty is developed to the fullest extent in a style of surface simplicity—only then, when the conception is exalted to the highest, and 'the words are too few,' will the poem, by expressing one's feelings in this way, have the power of moving Heaven and Earth. . . .[82]

Insofar as it is appropriate to the style and subject matter, Bunting's persona, "Chomei at Toyama," reaches towards a high degree of this compression and simplicity which Chomei also strove for in his writing. Although almost every passage is an example, the following is especially noteworthy:

> My jacket's wistaria flax,
> my blanket's hemp,
> berries and young greens
> my food.
>
> (Let it be quite understood
> all this is merely personal.
> I am not preaching the simple life
> to those who enjoy being rich.)
>
> I am shifting rivermist, not to be trusted. (*C.P.*, 83)

Bunting wrote in *Poetry* (1933) that Chomei "was as modern as, say, Cummings," and in his "redaction and interpretation"[83] he succeeded in writing an adaptation[84] that speaks to us in the twentieth century as simply and easily as Chomei's did to those in the thirteenth. A prose translation of the *Hojoki* begins:

> The flow of the river is ceaseless, and its water is never the same. The bubbles that float in the pools, now vanishing, now forming, are not of long duration: so in the world are man and his dwellings.
>
> . . . of those I used to know, a bare one or two in twenty remain. They die in the morning, they are born in the evening, like foam on the water.
> Whence does he come, where does he go, man that is born and dies? . . . Which will be the first to go, the master or his dwelling? One might just as well ask this of the dew on the morning-glory.

---

82. *Ibid.*, p. 269. "I congratulate you on finding this magnificent passage of Shun-e." Bunting to S.V.M. Forde, July 4, 1975.
83. *Poetry*, XLII (August, 1933), 356-357.
84. Basil Bunting to John Matthias, March 23, 1970. This is the word Bunting used to describe "Chomei" in this letter.

The dew may fall and the flower remain—remain, only to be withered by the morning sun. The flower may fade before the dew evaporates, but though it does not evaporate, it waits not the evening.[85]

Bunting condenses this simply:

> Swirl sleeping in the waterfall!
> On motionless pools scum appearing
>   disappearing!
> . . . .
>
> In the town where I was known
> the young men stare at me.
> A few faces I know remain.
>
> Whence comes man at his birth? or where
> does death lead him? Whom do you mourn?
> Whose steps wake your delight?
> Dewy hibiscus dries: though dew
> outlast the petals. (*C.P.*, 75)

Hugh Kenner admires this "writing that confines itself to discovering what are the essentials of the job in hand and setting them down." He sees that

> Lofty city Kyoto
> wealthy, without antiquities

precisely defines a quality: but six words are apt to be overlooked if one assumes a point to be unimportant unless dilated into witty rhetoric. Mr. Auden would have fashioned this distich into a whole chorus.[86]

It is this kind of writing that enables Bunting through his redaction to condense the material of the original so that the design of the work could be brought out in relief.

As a slight concession to his readers, Bunting comments that Chomei's "Kyoto had a number of curiously detailed parallels with New York and Chicago,"[87] which, he had previously explained to Harriet Monroe, were not his invention and which he did not feel called upon to disguise.[88] Bunting's version emphasizes these parallels by translating "Sixth Ward"[89] as "Sixth Avenue," or sentences such as "Along the banks of the Kamo River there was not even room for horses and cattle to pass"[90] as

---

85. Keene, *op. cit.*, pp. 197-198.
86. Hugh Kenner, "A Resurrected Poet," *Poetry*, LXXVIII (September, 1951), 363.
87. *Poetry*, XLII (August, 1933), 357.
88. Basil Bunting to Harriet Monroe, November 20, 1932. *Poetry Magazine* Papers, University of Chicago Library.
89. Keene, *op. cit.*, p. 199.
90. *Ibid.*, p. 202.

```
. . . . . . . . . . . . . . . . . . . . Dead stank
on the curb, lay so thick on
Riverside Drive a car couldn't pass. (C.P., 77)
```

Bunting modernizes sentences so that a city-dweller anywhere in the world today can empathize with the speaker:

> If a man's house stands in a crowded place and a fire
> breaks out in the neighborhood, he cannot escape danger.
> If it stands in a remote situation, he must put up with
> the nuisance of going back and forth to the city, and there
> is always a danger of robbers.[91]
>
> If he lives in an alley of rotting frame houses
> he dreads a fire.
> If he commutes he loses time
> and leaves his house daily to be plundered by gunmen. (C.P., 78)

Thomas Cole, editor of *Imagi*, admires Bunting's use of the "double image" with which he "ironically parallels . . . the decay and destruction of the ancient Japanese capital Kyoto with, prophetically, present-day New York City." However, he sees this quite narrowly as a technique which allows Bunting to rail "against the ultimate decadence which follows bad government and the overcrowded conditions in great capitals."[92]

A more recent critic, Anthony Suter, offers a more transcendent view:

> . . . Bunting takes an ancient subject—the reflections of Chomei, a twelfth-century Japanese poet, on the disasters that occur during his lifetime—to emphasize the eternal nature of the sufferings of man and the intimate relation of his fate to the cosmic cycle of events.[93]

To my mind, Suter's idea must be combined with Cole's to correctly describe another of Bunting's contributions to Chomei's thought. Besides making the formal intention of the work clearer by bringing out in relief the underlying design, Bunting makes the universality that is only implied in the prose vividly realized in the poetry. Through the "double image," Bunting associates many more eras and cultures than those he or an individual reader may think of. Though he wrote this before World War II and the wars in Korea and Vietnam, by bringing us up shortly to modern times through names and images or by including a metaphor which associates the Renaissance with the subject matter, he forces us to enlarge the scope of the poem to include all eras and cultures.

---

91. *Ibid.*, p. 205.
92. "Bunting: Formal Aspects," *Poetry*, LXXVIII (September, 1951), 367.
93. "Time and the Literary Past in the Poetry of Basil Bunting," *Contemporary Literature*, XII (Autumn, 1971), 522.

Suter goes a step further than the others in judging that Chomei represents a turning point in Bunting's work. He sees it as the first poem chronologically that stands entirely on its own: ". . . from there on, with the exception of 'The Well of Lycopolis' (1935), literature or other source material is no longer required for understanding. . . ."[94] It is certainly true that the enjoyment Bunting's poem, "Chomei at Toyama," provides on one level does not depend on its prose source; however, some knowledge of the original would prevent a critic from such an inept evaluation as this:

> In long poems such as 'Chomei at Toyama,' Bunting sets down data from various sources, without comment and without transition passages, in the hope that an 'ideogram' will result.[95]

Bunting had known stronger criticism long before Goodwin's, however. In a letter to Harriet Monroe, he wrote candidly:

> Re Chomei: Ezra likes it and so does Yeats, but Eliot speaks ill of it because I haven't been in Japan, which seems irrelevant, and because he says it echoes Pound, which, if true, would be a count against it. But Pound supposes it to contain echoes of Eliot. I'm not aware of echoing anybody. Except Chomei: his book was in prose and four to five times as long as my poem. But I think everything relevant in Chomei has been got into the poem.[96]

Pound, nevertheless, besides urging the editors of *Poetry* to print the poem,[97] gave his wholehearted approval through the agency of Eliot at Faber & Faber when he included it without abbreviation in his *Active Anthology* (1933).[98] In my opinion, at least, it is one of Bunting's best long poems after *Briggflatts*.

In most of the translations and adaptations Bunting is experimenting with technique, trying to learn "the trick of it" from Latin and Persian master poets—Lucretius, Catullus, Horace, Hafez, Sa'di, and Manuchehri. In his adaptation of Machiavelli's work, reminiscent of Pound's Canto IX, he successfully transforms a diplomatic report into a poem, but neither its unvaried technique nor its borrowed material allow it to be compared favorably with any sonata, even the shortest. The work that Bunting transforms into the most successful adaptation is Chomei's *Hojoki*. Besides

---

94. *Ibid.*
95. K.L. Goodwin, *The Influence of Ezra Pound* (London and New York, 1966), p. 201.
96. November 20, 1933. Besides Pound, Eliot, and Yeats, Louis Zukofsky and William Carlos Williams were early critics of the poem. See also Bunting to Leippert, October 30, 1932.
97. Ezra Pound to Morton Dauwen Zabel, February 21, 1933. Morton Dauwen Zabel Papers, University of Chicago Library.
98. (London, 1933), pp. 92-105.

passages that look forward to *Briggflatts*, the tone and themes of "Chomei at Toyama" fit in with those in Bunting's own collected works. Awareness of the brevity of life, the beauty of nature and art, the vagaries of fortune, the instability of men—man's acceptance of all of this in view of the inevitability of death are themes that Bunting will develop most fully in his sonatas.

PARVIN LOLOI & GLYN PURSGLOVE

BASIL BUNTING'S PERSIAN OVERDRAFTS:
A COMMENTARY*

For a variety of reasons it has seemed worthwhile to offer here a
relatively detailed commentary on those translations from Persian
which are included in Basil Bunting's *Collected Poems*. (We have
chosen not to discuss other translations which have appeared in
periodicals.) These translations are work of high quality, and appreciation of them can only be enhanced by detailed knowledge
of their relation to the originals. There is an inevitable risk of
pedantry in such exercises as this, and we have probably not escaped it; but the risk has seemed worth taking.

One technical term is perhaps best explained at this point.
The basic formal unit in Persian poetry is the *bait*. This term is
often translated as "couplet," but the correspondence is not exact.
The *bait* is really a single unit of a fixed number of feet, made up
of two symmetrical halves. The *bait* is normally printed or written
in one line across the page. In a number of Persian forms the
initial *bait* contains an internal rhyme, i.e., the two symmetrical
halves (or hemistichs) rhyme. The succeeding *baits* then contain
an end rhyme continuing this same rhyme, but the internal rhyme
vanishes after the opening *bait*.

In translating Persian poetry into English it has been traditional to attempt some sort of rhymed structure—though only a
few hardy souls have attempted to imitate the monorhyming of
the original forms. In the introduction to the Everyman's Library
volume *The Rubaiyat of Omar Khayyam and Other Persian Poems*
(1954) A.J. Arberry writes: "For nearly two centuries now metre,
and usually rhyme, have been thought indispensable to any respectable version of Persian poetry.... So far no successful translation into the modern unrhymed and rhythmic cadences has been
published, therefore none is quoted, though this does not mean
that the editor is convinced that no such renderings will ever succeed." Evidently Professor Arberry had not read Bunting's *Poems*

*Reprinted from *Poetry Information* (No. 19, Autumn 1978).

1950. Sadly, the fact does not surprise. Had he done ~o he would have found there translations enormously superior to the work of the scholar-translators on whom the English reader must normally rely. Compare, for example, the opening lines of Bunting's poem from Rudaki:

> All the teeth ever I had are worn down and fallen out.
> They were not rotten teeth, they shone like a lamp,
> a row of silvery-white pearls set in coral;
> they were as the morning star and as drops of rain.
> There are none left now, all of them wore out and fell out.
> Was it ill-luck, ill-luck, a malign conjunction?
> It was no fault of stars, nor yet length of years.
> I will tell you what it was: it was God's decree.

with the same lines in the frequently anthologised (it appears in the Everyman volume, for example) version from A.V.W. Jackson's *Early Persian Poetry* (1920):

> Every tooth, ah me! has crumbled, dropped and fallen in
>   decay!
> Tooth it was not, nay say rather, 'twas a brilliant lamp's
>   bright ray;
> Each was white and silvery-flashing, pearl and
>   coral in the light,
> Glistening like the stars of morning or the raindrop
>   sparkling bright;
> Not a one remaineth to me, lost through weakness
>   and decay.
> Whose the fault? "Twas surely Saturn's planetary
>   rule,' you say.
> No, the fault of Saturn 'twas not, nor the long, long
>   lapse of days;
> 'What then?' I will answer truly: 'Providence
>   which God displays.'

The first version is self-evidently the work of a poet; the second is that of a well-meaning Orientalist and teeters on the brink of that Wardour Street English that ruins so much translation from Persian.

Demonstration of the quality of Bunting's work is, we hope, implicit in the brief commentaries. In many instances we have provided relevant information and left the reader to form his own conclusions. Since Bunting nowhere specifies the precise location of his originals, and since the works of the Persian poets are often voluminous we have in each case provided the first line of the original so as to make it easier to trace it.

† † † † †

1. *When the sword of sixty comes nigh his head* (Firdosi)

کسی را ک سالئی بدو سی رسید   امید ازجهانش بباید برید

The poem Bunting translates here is a short autobiographical meditation from Firdosi's *Shāhnāma,* the great Persian epic of over 50,000 *baits.* The passage Bunting translates functions in something like the manner of, say, the autobiographical passage which opens Book III of *Paradise Lost.*

The original consists of 20 *baits,* not all of which are translated by Bunting. Diagrammatically the relationship between original and overdraft may be represented thus, where the left hand column refers to the *baits* of the original, the right hand to Bunting:

A:	Omitted
B:	Lines 1-2
C:	Lines 3-4
D:	Lines 7-8
E:	Lines 5-6
F:	Lines 9-10
G:	Lines 11-12
H:	Lines 13-14
I:	Lines 19-20
J:	Lines 15-16
K:	Lines 17-18
L:	Lines 21-22
M:	Lines 23-24
N:	Lines 25-26
O-S:	Omitted

Bunting has thus translated 13 out of 20 *baits* in the original. Of the 7 *baits* omitted 5 contain allusions either to characters and episodes narrated in the *Shāhnāma* or to Islamic theology. The wealth of allusion in Persian poetry is one of the recurrent difficulties for the translator, since the Islamic poet and the western reader have little common property of literary, religious or mythological knowledge. Bunting here adopts the course of omission, and while there is inevitably some loss, the damage to Firdosi's poem is not severe, since the poetic core remains intact. When Bunting uses the same method elsewhere, as in the first translation from Sa'di (entry no. 5 in this commentary) the damage is greater.

All the best of Bunting's Persian overdrafts (of which this is surely one) are marked by the effectiveness with which they demonstrate the poet's belief in the primacy of sound in poetry. Time and again the desire "to trace in the air a pattern of sound that may sometimes . . . be pleasing" (Preface to *Collected Poems*) governs the detail of his translation and his precise choice of word. In line 4 the word *"mal"* meaning "wealth" is well translated "substance" to produce the alliterative half-line "substance spent." In line 20 the phrase *"tābūt-ū-dasht"* which might literally be translated "the coffin and the earth" becomes in Bunting "the bier and the burial ground." Elsewhere Bunting's diction is brilliantly chosen. In line 15 the word *"khosh-āb,"* which the dictionaries lamely gloss as "fresh, full of water" is tellingly translated as "sappy."

One or two quibbles might be registered. In line 5 the word "joust" seems to carry some irrelevant associations. The Persian original talks simply of "the skill to swerve away from the enemy" and the word "joust" seems to be inappropriately concrete. In line 8 the phrase "he used to see there" corresponds to nothing in the original—the contrast between present blindness and former percipience is left implicit in the Persian, where Bunting makes it explicit—perhaps at the cost of a certain diffusion of effect. Bunting's lines 11 and 12 offer a slight puzzle. The original is difficult but would appear to say "if a fast-running horse is eager to run with the speed of an arrow, it finds that the wicked age of sixty will bind it." Bunting's version is certainly a great deal more vivid, but its imagery is not, strictly, that of the original. Some of the very best lines in Bunting are, though, perfectly accurate—such as his splendid lines 16 and 17:

> The pheasant strutting about the briar
> pomegranate-blossom and cypress sprig!

which keep all the sensuous simplicity of the original and provide English verse as beautifully, if very differently, cadenced as the original.

2. *All the teeth ever I had are worn down and fallen out* (Rudaki)

مرا بسود و فرو ریخـت هرچـه دندان بود   نمود دندان لاں جراغ تابان بود

Bunting's overdraft is, on the whole, a faithful and lucid version of an attractive original. Commentary here seems best to take the form of a few observations on details. (The title line in italics is Bunting's own addition.)

Line 2: "rotten" corresponds to no particular adjective in the original, but obviously continues and intensifies the sense of his first line (i.e. of the first half of the opening *bait* in the original).

Line 6: "ill-luck" is repeated more for reasons of rhythm and rhetoric than for reasons of accuracy, though there is a certain, slightly different, element of repetition in the original.

Line 16: Bunting's methods here are interesting. The phrase "*mushkīn mūy*" which he translates as "blackhaired" is literally "musky-haired." The word he translates "beauty" literally means "moon-faced." In each case Bunting has taken one of the conventional conceits of Persian love-poetry and translated the tenor rather than the vehicle.

Line 20: Bunting generalises (with some loss?) an attractively sensuous simile in the original which might literally be translated "The days are past when his face was like silk."

Line 27: The original is difficult here and we would translate "The days are gone when he (i.e. the poet) was happy and glad, enjoying abundant mirth, with his fears diminished."

Line 28: "your lover" is provided by Bunting, the text says simply "he."

Line 29: The figurative writing of the original has again been reduced to literal statement. The original says "a Turki with round swelling breast like a pomegranate." In Persian poetry "Turki" is often used to mean a beloved and beautiful boy or girl.

Lines 30-32: Bunting here rather scales-down the tone of the original which is markedly traditional and rhetorical at this point. By an admixture of Propertian-Poundian irony the original's "many beauteous mistresses" becomes "plenty of good girls" and the original's "lord, powerful man" becomes "husband."

Line 38: Bunting again simplifies the rhetoric of the original which might be translated "my heart was full of pleasure; it was a large meadow of happiness."

Line 45: Again the original's conventional phrases are treated semi-ironically—"moon-faced one" in the Persian becomes "my dear" in Bunting.

Lines 55-58: Once more the rhetorical patterning of the original is simplified. The phrase which Bunting translates as "greatness and gifts" is used twice in the original.

3. *Shall I sulk because my love has a double heart?* (Manuchehri)

ابر آرای چنہا را بر از مرا کند   باغ بو کلبن کند، کلبن پر از دیبا کند

As Bunting's note tells us this overdraft is taken from a *qasīda* by Manuchehri.

The *qasīda* was, in origin, an Arabic form. It's name means "purpose-poem" or "ode." It is a form which uses but a single rhyme through its often considerable length (sometimes over a hundred *baits*) and which therefore calls for considerable virtuosity in its practitioner. In origin the form was used primarily for the public statements of the official poet—panegyric and abuse, congratulation and consolation, etc. Poets using the form largely adhered to a conventional structural sequence, and a conventional order of themes and ideas within the poem. A useful summary of such conventions can be found, for example, in A.J. Arberry's *The Mystical Poems of Ibn Al-Farid* (Dublin, 1956). When poets began to adopt the form to a greater variety of subjects many of these conventions were continued. The poem by Manuchehri, on which Bunting has here turned his attention, consists of 36 *baits*. Of these Bunting translates only the sixth to the twelfth *baits*. Because of its conventional structure sections of a *qasida* can often be readily separated from the whole poem of which they are part and can stand as more or less self-contained poems on their own. Again some few detailed observations are offered:

Line 4: Bunting omits the epithet *"lāla-rukh"*—"tulip cheeked" as he so often omits some of the most conventional features of his originals.

Lines 7-8: In the original *bait* to which these lines correspond the word *"chafta"* is used in each half-line. It is translated literally in Bunting's line 8 in "a harp be *bent*," and it is interesting (and instructive) that in his line 7 Bunting resists the obvious, but trite, phrase "bent my back," which would have enabled him to imitate the repetition of the original, so as to produce the more attractively alliterative "stooped my shoulders."

Lines 9-10: Bunting chooses the verb "kindle" for the original's plainer "light," a choice justified dramatically in terms of the sound pattern produced; on this occasion (as contrasted with lines 7-8) Bunting is also able to reproduce the original's repetition of the verb.

Line 13: The original reads "cast me into the baseness of exile," whereas Bunting has chosen to pick up and continue the image of the candle and the shadow thrown by it.

Line 14: This does not appear to correspond with anything in the original—at least in the text that we have seen. The original poem is a panegyric of the Vizier Hājī. At this point in the original is a line of direct compliment to the Vizier. It might be translated thus: "Although I may be in a far land, still I shall be in the service of my Master Hājī, who exalts me." The line functions as a transition from one section of the *qasida* to the next. Since he does not propose to translate the succeeding *baits* Bunting naturally omits the transition, or *gurīz-gāh*, but substitutes an adaptation of his own to retain the poem's balance of form.

4. *Came to me–* (Rudaki)

آمد برمن که ؟ یا رکی ؟ دقت کجر   تُرسنده زِ که ؟ زغم ،خفتش که ؟ بدر

The original here is a *rubā'ī*. The word means quadripartite and describes a verse form of 2 *baits*, i.e. 4 hemistichs. There are two variations. In one, the first, second and 4th hemistich are rhymed together, thus:

> a ⟵ a ⟵ (first *bait*)
> a ⟵ b ⟵ (second *bait*)

In the second, less frequent, form of the *rubā'ī* all four hemistichs are rhymed together, and it is to this variation that this *rubā'ī* by Rudaki belongs.

Bunting's translation needs little comment in detail. Lines 1-9 of Bunting's version correspond to the first *bait* of Rudaki; lines 11-19 to the second *bait* of the original. "Confide" in Bunting's line 10 is Bunting's addition and corresponds to nothing in the original, but serves, of course, to complete the half-rhyme with "afraid." The addition, with its forceful exclamation mark, perhaps makes the questioner a little more aggressive than he is in the original.

Insofar as the *rubā'ī* is an epigrammatic form, Bunting's brevity and clipped syntax are perfectly apt, and it is perhaps no accident that the aaba rhyme scheme of one kind of *rubā'ī* is approximated in Bunting's version—with the plosives of afrai*d*, confi*de* and swee*t* contrasting with the fricative of mou*th*.

5. *This I write, mix ink with tears* (Sa'di, attrib.)

آب چشم برخون می نویسم   من این نامه که الکرن می نویسم

Line 1: Corresponds to the 1st *bait* of the original. This might literally be translated "Now I am writing this and as I write my eyes are full of bloody tears." Bunting has modified the conceit slightly and has avoided the traditional motif of tears of blood so common in Islamic love poetry and its Sufic analogues. (E.G. Browne in his *Literary History of Persia* comments with a pathologist's dryness: "The Muslim poets suppose that when one weeps long and bitterly all the supply of tears is exhausted, and blood comes in their place, whence the red and bloodshot appearance of the eyes of him who has wept much.") In this particular overdraft Bunting is especially ruthless in stripping away the rhetoric of the original.

Line 2: Corresponds to the 2nd *bait* of the original.

Lines 3-4: Correspond to the 3rd *bait*; in both lines Bunting's economy of words makes the meaning potentially unclear. Azra and Vamiq, Laila and Majnun are two famous and legendary pairs of lovers—the first name being the woman in each case. The sense of line 3 might thus be expanded "to tell Azra (about) Vamiq's pain," and similarly in line 4.

Lines 5-6: The original *bait* begins with a rhetorical address which Bunting omits: "To the beautiful lady / idol, I present my story, though I know not how I write." The poet compares his own "story" with the stories of Vamiq and Majnun. The technique resembles that of Sonnet 45 in Sidney's *Astrophil and Stella* with its concluding line "I am not I, pity the tale of me."

The original of this poem is a very conventional and conceitful piece of work. The conventions, indeed, *are* the poem, and the poem has only slight substance apart from these conventions. In stripping the poem of its conventions Bunting has produced perhaps the least successful of this group of overdrafts.

6. *Last night without sight of you my brain was ablaze* (Sa'di)

دوش بیروی تو آتش بسرم بریست   وآبی از دیده میامد که زمین تربیت

The original is a *ghazal*. This is one of the oldest and most popular lyric forms in Persian poetry (and, indeed, in Arabic, Urdu and a number of other poetries). The *ghazal* consists of a number of monorhymed *baits*, most often between 4 and 20 *baits*. Often the *baits* of a *ghazal* have no obvious connection one with another, and each is complete in itself. It is traditional for the last *bait* to contain the poet's name—this device being known as the *takhallus*.

Of these formal features Bunting reproduces only the *takhallus*. In his earliest published Persian overdraft (no. 1 in this commentary) Bunting largely transfers each *bait* of the original into two full lines in English. In this later version from Sa'di there is no such correspondence between the metrical units of the original and the English version. Here each *sentence* of the English represents a *bait* in the Persian original, with the exception that the second and third *baits* of the Persian are one sentence in Bunting (with the break in the original corresponding, roughly, to the end of line 4 in Bunting).

Not surprisingly, Bunting makes no attempt to reproduce the rhyme scheme of the original. He does, however, produce a pattern of internal rhyme and half-rhyme, of assonance and alliteration which, while it does not have the strictness of the original, has a related, but distinctive, quality of its own; e.g., "Last *night* without *sight* of you my *brain* was *ablaze*." The pattern of internal assonance is very marked in almost every line (trickled . . . plip . . . with; sighing . . . might . . . life; again. . . again . . . name; night . . . eyes . . . mine; etc.); any risk of the metronomic or obtrusive is avoided by ensuring that this tonic pattern does not coincide with the pattern of rhythmical accent; rather the two patterns interlock. At times, as elsewhere in these overdrafts, requirements of sound are reflected in the strategy of translation adopted. In line 9, for example, the phrase "scored and decorated" translates only a single word in the original *"musauwar"* meaning "formed, painted or sculptured." Bunting's expansion produces the intricate pattern of *o*, *c* and *r*.

Bunting's characteristic simplification of the original's texture of allusion here produces occasional difficulties. The sixth *bait* of the original Bunting translates "To dream of Laila Majnun prayed for sleep." A literal version of the *bait* might run: "Whenever Majnun's eyes were shut he saw Laila; even if he wanted to sleep deeply her image claimed his sleep." Bunting has paraphrased and in doing so he robs the following *bait* of a good deal of its point. A related instance is provided by Bunting's final line. Sa'di's magnificent image tells us, in the original, that the chain of the Pleiade hangs "on the neck of the horizon" and the sky is not mentioned explicitly; the periphrasis in Sa'di becomes a slightly more direct statement in Bunting.

Examination of Bunting's Persian overdrafts demonstrates, among other things, how remarkably faithful they are to the "content" of their originals. That is not of course, in itself, an especial virtue. It is something that can be achieved by anyone competent in the language (at whatever poetic cost). It is not, however, something that one might expect of a supposed follower of Pound, and it is not something which Bunting chooses to offer in his translations from Latin, for example. The two overdrafts from Horace which are included in the *Collected Poems* are very much in the tradition of Pound's "Homage to Sextus Propertius" or his "Women of Trachis." In discussing the "Homage . . ." J.P. Sullivan finds it necessary to use such terms as "creative translation" and "imitation":

This consists in a radical rethinking of the theme of the original.

> The original poet's world can never recur, and cannot therefore
> be fully alive for us; the translator proceeds by analogy, sub-
> stituting for remote situations and sentiments some contem-
> porary equivalents to make the whole alive. Attitude and tone are
> contemporary as well as the choice of example and situation: . . .
> Propertius *required* Pound's reinterpretation (and even distortion)
> to bring him within our own frame of reference as a poet. (J.P.
> Sullivan, *Ezra Pound and Sextus Propertius*, 1965)

Pound's translations, as has often been said, constitute a critical
commentary on their originals, by omission and addition, by manipulation of tone, by "playing up a certain aspect of Propertius—
the latent humour and irony—and playing down another, the conventional rhetoric which is to be found in all Latin elegiac poetry"
(A.E. Watts, *The Poems of Propertius*, 1961); something of the
same might be claimed, on their smaller scale, for Bunting's Horatian overdrafts.

Translation, especially of poetry, is necessarily and desirably
a pluralistic activity. No poet can be translated once and for all,
any more than a landscape can be viewed in its entirety from a
single viewpoint. A multiplicity of translations may even constitute something *like* a whole view, and each translator thus contributes to a continuing discussion about the original. Viewed as a
part in such a debate Bunting's Horace:

> If your workbox is mislaid
>   blame Cytherea's lad . . . Minerva
> 's not at all pleased that your seam's dropped for a fair sight
> of that goodlooking athlete's glistening wet shoulders
>
> when he's been swimming and stands
>   towelling himself in full view
> of the house. Ah! but you should see him on horseback!
> or in track-shorts! He's a first-class middleweight pug.

can be seen as a necessary conversational *riposte* to Victorian
understandings of the lines which "distort" Horace in a comple-
mentary (because opposite) direction. Bulwer-Lytton's, for example:

> Neobule, wing'd Love has flown off with thy spindles
>   and basket of wools!
> And thy studious delight in the toils of Minerva is
>   chased from thy heart
> By young Hebrus, the bright Liparaean.
>
> Hardy swimmer in Tiber to plunge gleaming shoulders
>   annointed with oil!
> Sure, Bellerophon rode not so well; as a boxer no
>   arm is so strong;
> And no foot is so fleet as a runner.

Where the translation of Persian poetry is concerned, the terms of the conversation are somewhat different. The relationship between the Latin and English languages and between the two literary traditions is, of course, a long and intimate one. That between the English and Persian traditions is a much briefer and more eccentric one. Classical poetry has had any number of distinguished—even great—translators: Chapman, Jonson, Dryden, Johnson, Pope, etc. Persian poetry has had but one great translator—Fitzgerald— and a few distinguished ones—William Jones, Gertrude Bell, for example. The quality and quantity of preceding conversation which confronts the new translator is therefore very different in the two cases. So are the expectations and foreknowledge of most prospective readers in the two cases. Latin may be a dead language for most of us in the West, but Persian is simply an unknown one. It is perhaps for these and other reasons that Bunting's Persian overdrafts are so different from his Latin ones. In the Latin versions the strategy is to give a particular twist or emphasis so as to bring out these elements in (or potentially in) the original which most interest him, (or in the case of Catullus, which don't!). In the Persian overdrafts he proceeds by a more straightforward, less oblique, path. Rather than recreation by conscious "distortion" these versions present a very direct contact with, and transmission of, many of the most obvious and important features of the originals, and a remarkable fidelity to the content of those originals. Naturally alterations in phrasing, tone, and so on, are made—but these, generally speaking, amount to no more than is inherent in the very act of translation. Some of the rhetoric of the originals is jettisoned—but Bunting does not wholly disguise the poetry's rhetorical bases. The formal qualities of the originals are naturally lost—but Bunting offers us in their place English poetry of a high order. These translations are both an important area of Bunting's achievement and a major, but neglected, contribution to the scanty tradition of distinguished English translations of Persian poetry.

THE TESTAMENT

DANA WILDE

YEAR BY YEAR BIBLIOGRAPHY OF BASIL BUNTING

1924
(prose)

Review of *The Rover* by Joseph Conrad. *The Transatlantic Review* 2, No. 1 (July 1924), 132-134.

1927
(prose)

Throb: An Inquiry. *The Outlook* 59, No. 1516 (February 19, 1927), 188-189.

Alas! The Coster's End. *The Outlook* 59, No. 1521 (March 26, 1927), 328-329.

Review of *London's Squares and How to Save them* (The London Society). *The Outlook* 59, No. 1527 (May 7, 1927), 542.

Review of *The Economics of Small Holdings* by Edgar Thomas. *The Outlook* 59, No. 1530 (May 28, 1927), 674.

Reviews of *The Psychology of Murder* by Andreas Bejerre; *Capital Punishment in the Twentieth Century* by E. Ray Culvert; and *The Convict of Today* by Sidney Moseley. *The Outlook* 59, No. 1531 (June 4, 1927), 717-718.

Readers and Librarians. *The Outlook* 60, No. 1537 (July 16, 1927), 87-88.

Some of our Conquerors, VIII: Lydia Sokolova. *The Outlook* 60, No. 1538 (July 23, 1927), 126-127.

Review of *The Story of the World's Literature* by John Macy. *The Outlook* 60, No. 1538 (July 23, 1927), 132-133.

Review of *Messages* by Ramon Fernandez, trans. by Montgomery Belgion. *The Outlook* 60, No. 1540 (August 6, 1927), 188.

Review of *The Mind and Face of Bolshevism* by Rene Fulop-Miller. *The Outlook* 60, No. 1543 (August 27, 1927), 283-284.

Some of our Conquerors, XI: Nina Hamnett. *The Outlook* 60, No. 1547 (Sept. 24, 1927), 407.

Review of *William Blake, Creative Will and the Poetic Image* by Jack Lindsay. *The Outlook* 60, No. 1548 (Oct. 1, 1927), 453-454.

Review of *Hymen, or The Future of Marriage* by Norman Haire. *The Outlook* 60, No. 1550 (Oct. 15, 1927), 520.

Pianists. *The Outlook* 60, No. 1552 (Oct. 29, 1927), 578-579.

Medium Calibre. *The Outlook* 60, No. 1553 (Nov. 5, 1927), 620.

String Players. *The Outlook* 60, No. 1554 (Nov. 12, 1927), 647-648.

Chamber Orchestras. *The Outlook* 60, No. 1555 (Nov. 19, 1927), 676.

Liszt. *The Outlook* 60, No. 1557 (Dec. 3, 1927), 735.

Beethoven's Quartets. *The Outlook* 60, No. 1558 (Dec. 10, 1927), 815.

The Third Philharmonic Concert. *The Outlook* 60, No. 1559 (Dec. 17, 1927), 815.

Too Many Concerts. *The Outlook* 60, No. 1560 (Dec. 24, 1927), 845.

In the Interval. *The Outlook* 60, No. 1561 (Dec. 31, 1927), 873.

1928
(prose)

The London Programme. *The Outlook* 61, No. 1562 (Jan. 7, 1928), 17.

The Influence of the Ballet. *The Outlook* 61, No. 1563 (Jan. 14, 1928), 56.

Two Wagner Concerts. *The Outlook* 61, No. 1564 (Jan. 21, 1928), 83.

John Gross and John Coates. *The Outlook* 61, No. 1565 (Jan. 28, 1928), 110.

The Graceless Ghost. *The Outlook* 61, No. 1565 (Jan. 28, 1928), 106.

Gurreleider. *The Outlook* 61, No. 1566 (Feb. 4, 1928), 140.

Recent Pianists. *The Outlook* 61, No. 1567 (Feb. 11, 1928), 127.

Recent Fiddlers. *The Outlook* 61, No. 1568 (Feb. 18, 1928), 209.

César Franck. *The Outlook* 61, No. 1569 (Feb. 25, 1928), 236.

Threes and Fours. *The Outlook* 61, No. 1570 (March 3, 1928), 265.

Sackbuts and Harpsichords. *The Outlook* 61, No. 1571 (March 10, 1928), 307.

Song and Folk-song. *The Outlook* 61, No. 1572 (March 17, 1928), 344.

Handel Mishandled. *The Outlook* 61, No. 1574 (March 31, 1928), 404.

Symphonies for Children. *The Outlook* 61, No. 1576 (April 14, 1928), 472.

Review of *Musical Meanderings* by W.J. Turner. *The Outlook* 61, No. 1577 (April 21, 1928), 508-509.

Criticism and Music. *The Outlook* 61, No. 1578 (April 28, 1928), 526-527.

Committing Musical Archaeology. *The Outlook* 61, No. 1580 (May 12, 1928), 594-595.

Review of *Human Values and Verities* by Henry Osborn Taylor. *The Outlook* 61, No. 1581 (May 19, 1928), 635-636.

1930
(poetry)

Redimiculum Matellarum, Milan 1930. *Contents*: Villon-CAR—MINA: I. Sad Spring (Weeping Oaks grieve, chestnuts raise) - II. Foam (I am agog for foam) - III. Against the Tricks of Time (Why should I discipline myself to verse) - IV. Aubade (After the grimaces of capitulation) - V. To Narciss (Narciss, my numerous cancellations prefer) - VI. Against Memory (Empty vast days built in the waste memory) - ETCETERA: Sonnet (An arles, an arles for my hiring) - While Shepherds Watched (Loud intolerant bells the shrinking night flower closes) - Advice to a Lady (Dear be still! Time's start of us lengthens slowly) - Chorus of Furies (Let us come upon him first) - To Venus (Darling of Gods and Men) - Personal Column (. . . As to my heart, that may as well be forgotten).

Villon. *Poetry* 27, No. 1 (Oct. 1930), 27-33.

1931
(poetry)

Nothing. *Poetry* 27, No. 5 (Feb. 1931), 260-261.

Please stop gushing about his pink. *Pagany* 2, No. 3 (July-September 1931), 125.

Please stop gushing about his pink. *The New Review* 1, No. 4 (Winter 1931/32), 385.

Villon (last nine stanzas of first section). *Poetry* 39, No. 2 (Nov. 1931), 110.

(prose)

Scrittori Inglesi Contemporanei. *L'Indice* 1, No. 9 (May 20, 1930), 5-6; trans. into Italian, Francesco Monotti. Reprinted in the original English as "Directory of Current English Authors." *Front* No. 3 (April 1931), 217-224.

1932
(poetry)

Villon (first two sections). *Profile*. Ezra Pound, ed. Milan, Italy: 1932, 13-16.

To a POET who advised me to PRESERVE my Fragments and False Starts—Crackt Records: Number one (Please stop gushing about his pink)—Number Two (Yes, it's slow dockt of amours) - Reading X's Collected Works (I . . .). *Whips & Scorpions: Specimens of Modern Satiric Verse*. Collected by Sherard Vines. Wishart: University Press, Glasgow, 1932, pp. 40-43.

Attis: Or, Something Missing. *An "Objectivists" Anthology*. Louis Zukofsky, ed. France: Maurice Darantiere, 1932, pp. 19-27.

Muzzle and jowl and beastly brow. *Poetry* 32, No. 5 (Feb. 1932), 251.

Verse and Version. *Il Mare* No. 1229 (Rapallo, Oct. 1, 1932), 3.

(prose)

English Poetry Today. *Poetry* 32, No. 5 (Feb. 1932), 264-271.

Mr. Ezra Pound. *The New English Weekly* 1, No. 6 (May 26, 1932), 137-138.

Review of *Gemini* by John Collier. *Poetry* 40, No. 5 (August 1932), 293-295.

Lettera Aperta a Sherry Mangan, Esquire. *Il Mare* No. 1223 (Aug. 20, 1932), 3; trans. into Italian, Fr. Monotti.

Lit. Sup. *Il Mare* No. 1225 (Sept. 3, 1932), 4; trans. into Italian, Fr. Monotti.

Mr. T.S. Eliot. *The New English Weekly* 1, No. 21 (Sept. 8, 1932), 499-500.

Diagnosi. *Il Mare* No. 1227 (Sept. 17, 1932), 4.

Some Limitations of English. *The Lion and the Crown* 1, No. 1 (Oct. 1932), 26-33.

L'Accademia Irlandese. *Il Mare* No. 1321 (Oct. 15, 1932), 3; trans. into Italian, Maria Agosti.

Come Acquistare uno Stile. *Il Mare* No. 1239 (Dec. 10, 1932), 3.

Periodici. *Il Mare* No. 1241 (Dec. 24, 1932), 4; trans. E.D.

1933
(poetry)

Villon — Attis: Or, Something Missing — How Duke Valentine Contrived — They Say Etna — Yes, it's slow, docked of amours — Weeping oaks grieve, chestnuts raise — Molten pool, incandescent spilth of — The Passport Officer — Fruits breaking the branches — Chomei at Toyama — The Complaint of the Morpethshire Farmer — Gin the Goodwife Stint. *Active Anthology*. Ezra Pound, ed. London: Faber and Faber Ltd., 1933.

Chomei at Toyama. *Poetry* 42, No. 6 (Sept. 1933), 300-307.

Selections from Chomei at Toyama (I-V) — Fruits breaking the branches. *The Observer II*, No. 1 (Oct.-Nov. 1933).

(prose)

"Testimonial" article on Ezra Pound. *The Cantos of Ezra Pound: Some Testimonies by Ernest Hemingway, Ford Madox Ford, T.S. Eliot, Hugh Walpole, Archibald MacLeish, James Joyce and Others*. New York: Farrar & Rinehart, 1933.

(prose)

Definiri i nostri Termini. *Il Mare* No. 1243 (Jan. 7, 1933), 4; trans. E.D.

Borgesimi. *Il Mare* No. 1243 (Jan. 7, 1933), 4.

Uno dei Mali dell' Inghilterra. *Il Mare* No. 1253 (Mar. 18, 1933), 3.

Settimana Mozartiana. *Il Mare* No. 1268 (July 1, 1933).

1934
(poetry)

Mesh cast for mackerel. *Poetry* 45, No. 1 (Oct. 1934), 13.

(prose)

Carlos Williams's Recent Poetry. *The Westminster Magazine* 23, No. 2 (Summer 1934), 149-154.

1935
(poetry)

Aus dem Zweiten Reich (Section III) — Light of my eyes, there *is* something to be said — Southwind, tell her what-You leave. *Bozart — Westminster* 1, No. 1 (Oglethorpe University, Georgia, Spring/Summer 1935), 10-11.

1936
(poetry)

From 'Faridun's Sons' by Firdusi. *The Criterion* 15, No. 40 (April 1936), 421-423.

(prose)

The Roots of the Spanish Civil War. *The Spectator* No. 5639 (July 24, 1936), 138.

Review of *Modern Translation* by E. Stuart Bates. *The Criterion* 15, No. 41 (July 1936), 714-716.

Review of *Aspects of Modernism* by Janko Lavrin. *The Criterion* 15, No. 41 (July 1936), 762-763.

Reviews of *The Paradise of Fools* by Michael Mason; *Adventures in Algeria* by Brian Stuart; and *The Scourge of the Desert* by Operator 1384. *The Spectator* No. 5648 (Sept. 25, 1936), 510-512.

Review of *The Earnest Atheist: A Study of Samuel Butler* by Malcolm Muggeridge. *The New English Weekly* 9, No. 25 (Oct. 1, 1936), 411-412.

1938
(prose)

Reviews of *Chinese Lyrics*, trans. Ch'u Ta-Kao; and *Some Greek Poems of Love and Beauty*, trans. J.M. Edmonds. *The Criterion* 17, No. 68 (April 1938), 557-559.

1939
(prose)

Review of *Allied Propaganda and the Collapse of the German Empire* by George C. Bruntz. *The Nation* 149, No. 2 (July 8, 1939), 51-52.

1941
(poetry)

You leave. Appears in *The Journal of Albion Moonlight* by Kenneth Patchen, with no indication of the poem's authorship, p. 26.

These tracings from a world that's dead. *Poetry* 58, No. 6 (Sept. 1941), 304.

1948
(poetry)

Night swallowed the sun — Darling of Gods and Men, beneath the gliding stars. *A Test of Poetry* by Louis Zukofsky. New York: The Profile Press, 1948.

The Complaint of the Morpethshire Farmer. *Four Pages* No. 5 (May 1948), 3.

1950
(poetry)

Poems: 1950. Galveston, Texas: The Cleaner's Press, 1950. *Contents*: SONATAS: Villon — Attis: Or, Something Missing — Aus dem Zweiten Reich — The Well of Lycopolis — CHOMEI AT TOYAMA: Chomei at Toyama — ODES: 1. Weeping oaks grieve, chestnuts raise — 2. Farewell ye sequent graces — 3. After the grimaces of capitulation — 4. I am agog for foam — 5. Empty vast days built in the waste memory — 6. . . . As to my heart, that may as well be forgotten — 7. The day being Whitsun we had pigeon for dinner — 8. Loud intolerant bells (the shrinking nightflower closes — 9. Dear be still! Time's start of us lengthens slowly — 10. Narciss, my numerous cancellations prefer — 11. Chorus of Furies — 12. An arles, an arles for my hiring — 13. Muzzle and jowl and beastly brow — 14. Gin the Goodwife Stint — 15. Nothing — 16. Molten pool, incandescent spilth of —17. Now that sea's over that island — 18. The Complaint of the Morpethshire Farmer — 19. Fruits breaking the branches — 20. Vestiges — 21. Two Photographs — 22. Mesh cast for mackerel — 23. The Passport Officer — 24. Vessels thrown awry by strong gusts — 25. As apple-blossom to crocus — 26. Two hundred and seven paces — 27. You leave — 28. Southwind tell her — 29. The soil sandy and the plow light, neither — 30. Let them remember Samangan, the bridge and tower — 31. Not to thank dogwood nor — 32. These tracings from a world that's dead — 33. Search under every veil — 34. See! Their verses are laid — OVERDRAFTS: Darling of Gods and Men, beneath the gliding stars — Yes, it's slow, docked of amours — Please stop gushing about his pink — All the teeth ever I had are worn down and fallen out — When the sword of sixty comes nigh his head — HOW DUKE VALENTINE CONTRIVED: How Duke Valentine Contrived — THE OROTAVA ROAD: The Orotava Road — THEY SAY ETNA: They Say Etna.

All the teeth ever I had are worn down and fallen out — Night is hard by, I am vexed and bothered by sleep — Last night without sight of you my brain was ablaze. *Nine* No. 4 (vol. 2 no. 3) (August 1950), 217-219.

1951
(poetry)

Empty vast days built in the waste memory. *Fragmente* 1, No. 1 (Freiberg im Breisgau, Germany, 1951), 7; trans. Rainer M. Gerhardt.

The Spoils. *Poetry* 79, No. 2 (Nov. 1951), 84-97.

Now that sea's over that island — The soil sandy and the plow light, neither. *Imagi* No. 14 (vol. 5 no. 3, 1951).

1956
(poetry)

You there, with my enemy, strolling down my street — This I write, mix ink with tears — The thundercloud fills meadows with heavenly beauty. *Nine* No. 11 (vol. 4 no. 2, April 1956), 9-10.

1959
(poetry)

Let them remember Samangan, the bridge and tower — Vestiges. *The Art of Poetry* by Hugh Kenner. Holt, Rinehart & Winston, 1959.

1960
(poetry)

Darling of Gods and Men, beneath the gliding stars. *Poetry for Pleasure: The Hallmark Book of Poetry* by the Editors of Hallmark Cards, Inc. Garden City, New York: Doubleday and Company, Inc., 1960.

1963
(poetry)

All the teeth ever I had are worn down and fallen out (excerpts from stanzas one, two, and five) — When the sword of sixty comes nigh his head (first stanza). *Bottom: On Shakespeare* by Louis Zukofsky. Out of the Ark Press, 1963.

1964
(poetry)

Gin the Goodwife Stint — The Complaint of the Morpethshire
Farmer — (five lines quoted from "They Say Etna," beginning
"the sea is his and he"). *Confucius to Cummings: An Anthology
of Poetry*, Ezra Pound and Marcella Spann, eds. New York:
New Directions Books, 1964.

1965
(poetry)

The Spoils. Newcastle upon Tyne: The Morden Tower Book
Room, 1965. *Contents*: The Spoils.

First Book of Odes. London: Fulcrum Press, 1965. *Contents*:
same as ODES in *Poems: 1950*, with the following additions:
On highest summit dawn comes soonest — The Orotava Road
— On the Fly-leaf of Pound's Cantos.

Loquitur. London: Fulcrum Press, 1965. *Contents*: same as *First
Book of Odes*, with SONATAS and CHOMEI AT TOYAMA
from *Poems: 1950*, and with the following additions: Verse
and Version — Shall I sulk because my love has a double heart
— Came to me — This I write, mix ink with tears — How Duke
Valentine Contrived.

Gin the Goodwife Stint — Fruits breaking the branches — Mesh
cast for mackerel — Not to thank dogwood nor. *Sum* 5 (April
1965).

A thrush in the syringa sings — Came to me. *Paris Review* No.
34 (Summer 1965), 92-93.

Now that sea's over that island. *The Newcastle Journal* (July
17, 1965), 7.

Villon — Dear be still! Time's start of us lengthens slowly — The
Passport Officer — Not to thank dogwood nor — Search under
every veil — See! their verses are laid — Mesh cast for mackerel
—Southwind tell her what — You leave — The Orotava Road
—Two Photographs — The soil sand and the plow light, neither.
King Ida's Watch Chain: Link One.

On the Fly-Leaf of Pound's Cantos. *Agenda* 4, No. 2 (Oct.-Nov. 1965), 28.

Nothing — Molten pool, incandescent spilth of — Now that sea's over that island — Two hundred and seven paces — The soil sandy the plow light. *Granta* 71, No. 12457 (Nov. 6, 1965), 13-14.

1966
(poetry)

Briggflatts. London: Fulcrum Press, 1966. *Contents*: Briggflatts.

Villon (The last nine stanzas of the first section, beginning "Remember, imbecile and wits," and all but the last six lines of section two). *The Penguin Book of Modern Verse Translation*, George Steiner, ed. Penguin Books, 1966.

Briggflatts. *Poetry* 107, No. 4 (Jan. 1966), 213-237.

Birthday Greeting — Carmencita's tawny paps. *Agenda* 4, Nos. 5 & 6 (Autumn 1966), 3.

(prose)

The Poet's Point of View. *Diary* of Northeastern Association for the Arts (April-Summer 1966), 2.

1967
(poetry)

Two Poems. Unicorn Press, 1967. *Contents*: Birthday Greeting — All you Spanish Ladies (Carmencita's tawny paps).

What the Chairman Told Tom. Cambridge, Mass.: The Pym-Randall Press, 1967. *Contents*: What the Chairman Told Tom.

Darling of Gods and Men, beneath the gliding stars. *Grok* No. 2 (Isla Vista, Cal., May 19, 1967), 5.

(prose)

Preface to *High on the Walls* by Tom Pickard. London: Villiers

Publications, 1967.

<h2 align="center">1968
(poetry)</h2>

Collected Poems. Fulcrum Press, 1968. *Contents*: Version of Horace—Stones trip Coquet burn—and all previously published poems except the following: Against the Tricks of Time (*Redimiculum Matellarum*, 1930), Reading X's Collected Works (*Whips and Scorpions*, 1932), They Say Etna (*Active Anthology*, 1933, and *Poems 1950*), Light of my eyes, there *is* something to be said (*Bozart-Westminster* I, No. 1, 1935), from 'Faridun's Sons' by Firdusi (*The Criterion*, April 1936), Night swallowed the sun as (*A Test of Poetry*, 1948), A Ghazel of Manuchehri's (*Nine*, Summer 1950), and A Ghazel of Manuchehri and From a Qasida of Manuchehri (first stanza) (*Nine*, April 1956).

<h3 align="center">(prose)</h3>

Descant on Rawthey's Madrigal: Conversations with Basil Bunting, by Jonathan Williams. Lexington, Kentucky: Gnomon Press, 1968.

<h2 align="center">1969
(poetry)</h2>

You can't grip years, Postume. *Make* No. 9.

You can't grip years, Postume. *Sunday Times* No. 7646 (London, Dec. 14, 1969), 51.

<h3 align="center">(prose)</h3>

What about Herbert Read? *Agenda* 7, No. 2 (Spring 1969), 41-45.

<h2 align="center">1970
(poetry)</h2>

Yes, it's slow, docked of amours. *Erotic Lyrics* selected by Anthony Howell. London: Studio Vista, 1970.

Briggflatts (stanzas 2, 3, 4, & 5 of section III, beginning: "I am neither snake nor lizard"). *Junior Voices: An Anthology of Poetry and Pictures*, Geoffrey Summerfield, ed. Butter Market, Ipswich: W.S. Colwell Ltd., 1970.

The Spoils. *British Poetry Since 1945*, Edward Lucie-Smith, ed. Great Britain: Cox & Wyman, 1970.

You can't grip years, Postume — Stones trip Coquet burn. *Agenda* 8, Nos. 3 & 4 (Autumn-Winter 1970), 61-62.

Southwind, tell her what — These tracings from a world that's dead — See! Their verses are laid — A thrush in the syringa sings — O, it is godlike to sit selfpossessed. *Anglia* No. 36 (No. 4-Oct. 1970), 54-55.

Mesh cast for mackerel. *The Ubyssey* 52, No. 19 (Nov. 20, 1970), 13.

Weeping oaks grieve, chestnuts raise — Fruits breaking the branches — Mesh cast for mackerel — Empty vast days built in the waste memory — Two Photographs — Dear be still! Time's start of us lengthens slowly — Darling of Gods and Men, beneath the gliding stars — Last night without sight of you my brain was ablaze — Came to me — See! Their verses are laid — Villon (last eight stanzas of Section I) — I am agog for foam — The day being Whitsun we had pigeon for dinner — Attis: Or, Something Missing (the last two stanzas of section 1) — The Spoils (last twelve lines of section 2) — Briggflatts (stanzas 13-16, section 2, and coda) — Southwind tell her what — Birthday Greeting — The Orotava Road — What the Chairman Told Tom — The Well of Lycopolis — Stones trip Coquet burn. *Writing (Georgia Straight, Writing Supplement)*, No. 6 (Nov. 18-25, 1970) (whole issue).

(prose)

Foreword to *Arabic and Persian Poems in English* by Omar S. Pound. New Directions Books, 1970.

Introductory remarks to reading of Wordsworth's "The Brothers." *The Listener* 84 No. 2176 (Oct. 8, 1970), 484.

Reviews of *More Collected Poems* and *A Clyack-Sheaf* by Hugh

MacDiarmid. *Agenda* 8, Nos. 3 & 4 (Autumn-Winter 1970), 117-121.

1971
(poetry)

Vestiges – What the Chairman Told Tom – Briggflatts (section I and coda) – Chomei at Toyama. *23 Modern British Poets*, John Mathias, ed. The Swallow Press, Inc., 1971.

A thrush in the syringa sings. *Poetry Brief: An Anthology of Short Poems*, William Cole, ed. New York: The MacMillan Company, 1971.

Vestiges – What the Chairman Told Tom – Briggflatts (section I and coda) – Chomei at Toyama. *Tri-Quarterly* 21, (Spring 1971), 34-51. (Reissued in book form as *23 Modern British Poets*.)

(prose)

Preface to *Selected Poems: Ford Madox Ford*, Basil Bunting, ed. Cambridge, Massachusetts: Pym-Randall Press, 1971.

1972
(poetry)

What the Chairman Told Tom. *Say It Aloud*, Norman Hidder, ed. London: Hutchinson, 1972.

(prose)

Response to editor's questionnaire on rhythm. *Agenda*, Autumn-Winter 1972.

A tribute to Ezra Pound. *The Sunday Times*, Nov. 12, 1972.

1973
(poetry)

On the Fly-leaf of Pound's Cantos – Chomei at Toyama – What the Chairman Told Tom. *Oxford Book of Twentieth Century Verse*, Philip Larkin, ed. Oxford University Press, 1973.

Came to me. *A Book of Love Poetry*, Jon Stallworthy, ed. New York: Oxford University Press, 1973.

To abate what swells. *Epitaphs for Lorine*, Jonathan Williams, ed. Champaign, Illinois: The Monkeytree Press, 1973.

A thrush in the syringa sings — The Well of Lycopolis (section I) — Villon (last nine stanzas of section I) — The Orotava Road — Briggflatts (last stanza of section II, and last 26 lines of section I). *The Best of Modern Poetry*, Milton Klonsky, ed. New York: Pocket Books, 1973. (Second printing, 1975. Originally published under the title *Shake the Kaleidoscope*.)

(prose)

Review of a book on Persia. *The Sunday Times*, Oct. 7, 1973.

1974
(poetry)

You can't grip the years, Postume — Stones trip Coquet burn — Two Photographs — Carmencita's tawny paps. Modern British Poetry Conference Booklet, Oct. 18-20, 1974.

Briggflatts (first 10 stanzas of section I, first stanza of section II, and stanzas 2-5 of section IV). *100 British Poets*, Selden Rodman, ed. New York: The New American Library, Inc., 1974.

All the carts they peddle. *Agenda*, Summer 1974.

(prose)

Yeats Recollected. *Agenda*, Summer 1974.

1975
(poetry)

On the Fly-Leaf of Pound's Cantos. *Faber Book of 20th Century Verse*, J. Heath-Stubbs and D. Wright, eds. Faber & Faber, 1975.

At Briggflatts Meeting House. *Poetry Review*, Vol. 65, No. 4, 1975.

1976
(poetry)

At Briggflatts Meeting House. *Montemora*, no. 2 , 1976.

The Spoils (last 12 lines of section II) — Briggflatts (stanzas 14-17 of section II, and Coda) — Birthday Greeting —What the Chairman Told Tom. Pamphlet of St. Andrews College reading, Laurinburg, N.C., April 15-19, 1976.

(prose)

Introduction to *Joseph Skipsey: Selected Poems*, Basil Bunting, ed. Sunderland: Ceolfrith Press, 1976.

Presidential Addresses: An Artist's view on Regional Arts Patronage (Bunting's speeches to Annual Meetings of Northern Arts; 2 pamphlets, the first with 3 speeches dated Nov. 1974, Nov. 1975, & July 1976, the second with 2 speeches dated 1976 and 1977).

1978
(poetry)

Now we've no hope of going back — Snow's on the fellside, look! —You, with my enemy strolling down the street. *Agenda*, Spring 1978.

Collected Poems. Oxford University Press, 1978.

ROLAND NORD

A BIBLIOGRAPHY OF WORKS ABOUT
BASIL BUNTING WITH EXTENDED COMMENTARY

"There is no excuse for literary criticism"—Basil Bunting.
If so, bibliographers must be doubly cursed!
For locating the majority of the works on Bunting, I am deeply indebted to Roger Guedalla whose "Articles on Basil Bunting" appeared in *Poetry Information* 19, Summer 1978, pp. 81-82. I also wish to thank Carroll F. Terrell [C.F.T.] for some critiques, as well as Burton Hatlen [B.H.] and Winifred Hayek [W.H.] for annotating those articles which were written in French, and William Milne [W.M.] for annotating a number of articles which were difficult, if not impossible, for me to obtain.

Following the format established in *Louis Zukofsky: Man and Poet*, the bibliography has been organized and numbered, *seriatim*, according to the date that the critical pieces appeared. If a date is ambiguous, the order has been alphabetical. Each of the items treated has been numbered for easier reference. The work has been preceded by an index alphabetized by author and followed by the number of the item.

‡‡‡‡‡‡

‡‡‡‡‡‡

1. Swabey, Henry. "Basil Bunting." *Four Pages*, 3, March 1948 (Galveston, Texas), pp. 2-3.

> In this short two-page review, Swabey laments the unavailability of Bunting's poetry. Furthermore he suggests a parallel between Britain's neglect of its farmers, as reflected in Bunting's poems "Gin the Goodwife Stint" and "The Complaint of the Morpethshire Farmer," and Britain's neglect of its poets, in this case specifically Bunting.

2. Williams, William Carlos. "On Basil Bunting's Poem in *Four Pages.*" *Four Pages*, 8, August 1948 (Galveston, Texas), p. 3.

> This one paragraph response concerns Bunting's poem in *Four Pages* [Cf. 1 above]. Williams' response is a short anecdote about a case of income tax abuse (involving real estate) in Vermont.

3. Hall, Anthea. "Basil Bunting Explains How a Poet Works." *The Journal* (Newcastle), 17 July 1965, p. 7.

> There is the usual account of Bunting's travels and sojourns here. He tells a story about sitting in a café with Tristan Tzara, writing poems all afternoon without words. He says they were "Just any damn sounds like Brrrrrr! Grrrrrr! Arrrrrr!" They managed to palm them off on

highbrow papers as serious efforts. "Its all been done before and, no doubt, since." He talks about meeting Isadora Duncan. He says that he wanted to lead a life like that of Sir Walter Raleigh; he wanted to do every damn thing. He says that "You can't write about anything unless you've experienced it: you're either confused in your subject matter or else you get it wrong. . . . You dont set out to make a poem of your experience. You set out to make a shape, a shape of sounds. . . . Poetry is a craft which you learn by trying. . . . Unless you work very hard at it you won't get anywhere." He talks extensively about *Briggflatts*. He says that he must have originally written 10,000 to 20,000 lines and cut them down eventually to 700. He invariably writes in the early morning, starting about 5:45. He states that he had a plan for the composition of *Briggflatts* (this is outlined in great detail in the opening essay in the Basil Bunting Special Issue of *Agenda*, Spring 1978). He says that "In one part I knew the effect I wanted but I had no idea of the words. Then I read the Song of Songs. . . . and after a week I got it. And sometimes you get bits of luck. One day I was filing away the gas bills and receipts and I came across a poem on the back of a bill that I had written three years earlier and quite forgotten about. It was obviously the epilogue to the whole thing, and after one day's alterations it was all right." He thinks *Briggflatts* is the best thing he's done. [W.M.]

4.   Lucie-Smith, Edward. "A Man for the Music of Words." *The Sunday Times*, 25 July 1965.

> Lucie-Smith recounts the salient facts of Bunting's life. Like most of the journalistic accounts of Bunting's life and work it adds little to our sum of knowledge outside of that comprehensive account given by Jonathan Williams in *Descant On Rawthey's Madrigal*. Bunting tells Lucie-Smith that "It takes the experience and reading of a number of years to provide material for a serious poem. . . . After a while I became confident that my poems wouldn't be allowed to perish. Someone would collect them sooner or later." Lucie-Smith says that Bunting seems a little astonished that recognition has arrived so soon. [W.M.]

5.   Clare, John. "A Critical Look at Bunting's Poems." *The Journal* (Newcastle), 1 September, 1965, p. 6.

> This article opens with a review of *King Ida's Watch Chain*, a miscellaneous collection of Buntinginia. Clare complains that Bunting's poems have been inaccessible in England for too long. He states that Bunting is not a prolific poet but is certainly a painstaking one. His verse is more remarkable for its craftsmanship than its inspiration he says; and that the influence of Pound is too marked. It is precisely with Eliot and Pound that Bunting must be compared. He goes on to argue that Bunting is not a provincial poet. He compares his lyrical poems with those of Hopkins. He says that Bunting speaks with passion in his voice. He concludes: "If Mr Bunting achieves a permanent resurrection. . . . it will be because poets at least will always remember a man who has done a few things exceedingly well." [W.M.]

6. Creeley, Robert. "Basil Bunting: An Appreciation." *Granta* (Cambridge), 6 November 1965, p. 12.

> Creeley says that he has never been able to understand why a man of Bunting's accomplishment should have so little use in his own country. He argues that Bunting made a useful distinction between organizations of sound as one meets them in a lyric where the briefness of the poem's length gives them a necessarily emphatic situation and in a long poem, where their texture may accumulate relationships without the reader being fully aware of their singular conditions. He feels, in addition, that Bunting's work offers the most significant occasion for the work of younger poets now writing. He concludes that the possibilities of poetry for himself had become most evident when he first realized that the modulation of sounds in a poem might be the agent of emotions as actually as any other. [W.M.]

7. Ginsberg, Allen. "Studying the Signs: An Exercise in Composition, Basil Bunting's *Briggflatts* in Mind." *Isis* (Oxford), 26 November 1965, pp. 12-13.

> A forty-four line poem concerning Bunting's poem. The relationship between Ginsberg's poem and Bunting's is remote in the least. [W.M.]

8. *A Moving Anthology*; Link One: Basil Bunting Issue, *King Ida's Watch Chain*. Ed. Tom Pickard (Newcastle), Autumn 1965.

> The following description of this work was given in the Select Bibliography found in *Descant on Rawthey's Madrigal*:
>
> > A magazine of loose sheets placed in an envelope, edited by Tom Pickard and published by The Morden Tower Book Room in Newcastle-upon-Tyne. This issue reprinted poems by Bunting and published essays on his work by Zukofsky, Gael Turnbull and Hugh Kenner.

9. Ure, Peter. "The Sound of Poetry: A Rejoinder to Basil Bunting." *Diary* of Northeastern Association for the Arts, May-Aug. 1966, p. 368.

> This is a reply to Bunting's essay "The Poet's Point of View." Ure says that Bunting's position is a bad parody of that adopted by some poets earlier this century. He says Bunting is turning against the discursive intellect in poetry. He argues that words cannot be like notes: they have necessary connotations. He says that a poem should not be viewed as an artifact: a poem should be seen as a structure of meanings. Ure continues this line of argument by stating that sound is only one of the vital constituents of poetry: poetry is speech and also a branch of rhetoric. He concludes that Bunting has restricted the possibilities for poetry by stressing its musicality alone. This remains the most comprehensive criticism of Bunting's aesthetic, but one must say that Ure's tone is as entrenched in its

scholarly prejudices as Bunting's tone is in its own way in "The
Poet's Point of View." [W.M.]

10. Woof, R.S. "Basil Bunting's Poetry." *Stand 8*, no. 2 (Newcastle), 1966, pp. 28-34.

Woof begins his fairly short article on Bunting's poetry by referring
to Bunting's statement that "poetry is seeking to make not meaning,
but beauty; or if you insist on misusing words, its 'meaning' is of
another kind, and lies in the relation to one another of lines and
patterns of sound, perhaps harmonious, perhaps contrasting and
clashing, which the hearer feels rather than understands. . . ." In
response to Bunting's statement Woof says of *Briggflatts*:

> It is a poem carefully musical in the variety of its verbal effects;
> it draws upon diverse styles of poetry, is persistently allusive
> and doubly compels our making reference to music by having
> music as a continuous image. There is something of an old no-
> tion at work: stars and men, beasts and things, flowers, all make
> singing and music, so that these arts seem not just decorative,
> but the art, the one measure of truth, the poet knows. He is
> not making beautiful sounds merely, but seeking with an obses-
> sional intensity what harmonies he can discover in all the con-
> flicting elements he is conscious of.

However, the majority of Woof's article does not deal with "the
music" of *Briggflatts* but rather deals with an explication of the
narrative line of the poem. Although Woof deals with the themes of
death and the rural versus the marketplace in *Briggflatts*, it is only
when speaking of Bunting's treatment of art that Woof returns to
his original concern as stated above:

> He finds greatness in art, and there follows, with an exciting lift
> in the mood, a stanza on Scarlatti which demonstrates that, in
> the context of music (as always Bunting's catalyst for vision),
> reality can be seen for what it is, and that is a total harmony:
>
> > As the player's breath warms the fipple the tone clears.
> > It is time to consider how Domenico Scarlatti
> > condensed so much music into so few bars
> > with never a crabbed turn or congested cadence,
> > never a boast or a see-here; and stars and lakes
> > echo him and the copse drums out his measure,
> > snow peaks are lifted up in moonlight and twilight
> > and the sun rises on an acknowledged land.

11. Cox, Kenneth. "The Aesthetic of Basil Bunting." *Agenda*,
Autumn 1966, pp. 20-28.

Cox begins his discussion of Bunting's poetry by noting its most
salient characteristic: its compression of language. Cox, however, is
quick to point out that,

> the method which gives his style its individual mark is not at all
> scrimping or casual. His aesthetic, his sense of the beautiful, does
> not depend on mechanical measurement, although the criterion
> of brevity may be used as others might use metre or consonance,
> to prompt revision and suggest improvements.

Cox suggests that Bunting's compression of language is intimately
connected with a compression of meaning: "The meaning is given in

full and at one go, in a quick and as far as possible inclusive shot."
To illustrate his point, Cox discusses Bunting's poetry by referring to
Bunting's use of the concept of the turn (tropos, trope) and by arguing that Bunting's poetry in its narrative or dramatic method is
more akin in its origins to Norse verse than to Old English verse, and
by pointing out similarities between Bunting and Wordsworth insofar as the "compression of language can be regarded as a compression of emotion."

With his usual discrimination, Cox places Bunting firmly in an
old tradition. But,

> For all its artistry the poetry of Mr Bunting stays . . . close to
> the state of inarticulateness. Such a state may arise from concen-
> tration, passion, madness, sleep or even stupidity: any of these
> can turn into a matrix of poetry, because free of sophistry. The
> resulting speech utters what has only just escaped being un-
> spoken, almost as if speech were painful or inappropriate to the
> circumstances, and it bursts under strong pressure but strict
> control into the nearest expression capable of speedy termina-
> tion.

The work of such a devotee of the tradition may raise questions in
the minds of those critics who stress "Bunting's acknowledged obli-
gations to Ezra Pound and who ask to what extent and in what manner the example of the American master can be assimilated to a
native heritage." The question is legitimate. But,

> One of the paradoxes of the situation is that a direct transcrip-
> tion of the vernacular easily looks false. Mr Bunting's Cockney
> imitation of Villon rings untrue. It is hard to say why: it seems
> that the feel of living speech comes through only when some of
> the subtlest elements of movement and intonation join in a
> meeting governed by rare and unpredictable conditions, similar
> to those which govern the evanescent existence of the elemen-
> tary particles, and that these conditions commonly escape the
> meshes of the grammarian's net, fine as these are now. The pres-
> tige of Wordsworth's theory, the political movement of which it
> is part and our modern interest in radio and the tape-recorder
> may temporarily have obscured the truth that even the collo-
> quial style is acquired by sedentary toil oblique stroke and by
> the imitation of great masters. The real, it seems, is not to be
> won by direct assault but is to be wooed with humility and dis-
> play. It is demonstrable that the most authentic achievements of
> colloquial utterance usually crown a lifelong exercise in revision,
> imitation and translation.

Cox is one of the few critics who can engage the concepts of
natural rhythm such as Pound developed in Great Bass and his
Treatise on Harmony. Thus, he is able to be graphic about similar
ideas at work in Bunting.

> Few of Mr Bunting's rhythms depart from the limits ordinarily
> set by the internal movements of the human body—systole and
> diastole of the heart, expansion and contraction of the lungs—
> which set the norms for expression of the emotions. But there
> is also to be found in his verse a slower movement keeping time
> not with the movements or gait of the body but with the longer
> stronger motion of the sea. When drained of feeling or evoking
> a reality outside human life it is to this movement, as to a pre-
> natal source, that his verse returns, for example in the coda to
> *Briggflatts*.
> It may be doubted whether anyone can really (without losing

his personality) step outside his own personal rhythms, whatever the nationality of the vocabulary he may temporarily employ. Mr Bunting's rhythms offer great variety within a small compass: the delights of perfect freedom of movement are difficult to combine with the satisfactions of remaining close to earth. His verbal concentration also precludes certain auditory effects. Although it may be lightened by playfulness, his verse is occasionally also clogged by the ornament the Arabs call *jinas*, correspondence of consonants without correspondence of meaning. (It differs from the *cynghanedd* of Welsh poetry in that it does not constitute an organic part of the structure of the verse but only knits it closer together.)

Cox points out that, "After economy the next most notable characteristic of Mr Bunting's verse is risk." This risk is manifested by the omission of intervening or supporting structures and by a word choice which tends towards the slightly unexpected. According to Cox:

The constant undercutting of his expectations may excite in the reader a pleasure continually reactivated and mingled with a suppressed apprehension. When he sees that an exercise of skill and daring has been successfully performed his pleasure is complicated by relief that the danger has been avoided and by amusement that it could ever have been overestimated.

Slight deviations from the expected can achieve a new coherence:

When the ewes go out
along the towpath striped with palm-trunk shadows
a herdsman pipes, a girl shrills
under her load of greens.

Flute,
shade dimples under chenars,
breath of Naystani chases and traces
as a pair of gods might dodge and tag between stars.

Shepherds follow the links,
sweet turf studded with thrift;
fell-born men of precise instep
leading demure dogs.

Cox comments with the nicest discrimination on these few lines:

The phrases succeed one another easily, without hurry or slip, with *never a boast or a see-here*, but with extraordinary marksmanship. Though bare of ornament the diction is rich by virtue of economy and enterprise; what may be called its specific gravity must be one of the highest in English. This is the accomplishment of *Mauberley*, poetry of the second order but the finest quality.

The felicity of the descriptions shows that the focus of interest is an observation half created, half acutely perceived and exactly recorded. The fascination exercised by some incidental aspect of the physical world constitutes the tenuous but unexpectedly solid foundation of the art. We know how such perceptions obsess the attention and govern the appetites, without understanding how they operate. Those of *The Spoils* are principally visual, those of *Briggflatts* aural, but both convey a perception of total grace not easily communicable by means other than verbal, unless the essential force of these percepts may be reduced to the equation of a curve.

Cox goes on to explore other concerns of Bunting's poetry as illustrated by his perceptions, both sensual and as a close observer:

Mr Bunting's verse is not only concerned with *the angle a slut's blouse / draws on her chest*. As in the example given above, it also honours those who themselves acknowledge and manage these perceptions. From the girl with *delicate ignorant face (preoccupied rather / by the set of her stockings)* it goes on to celebrate a Persian miniature painter, Italian fiddler, Cumbrian dogtrainer. This cultivation of the senses has two extraneous consequences of some importance. First, by progressively increasing the definition of the verbal record, the expression of observation drives the language to its primal resources, till it draws upon the qualities which bind words to things. Secondly, by monopolising the mind these observations act as a preservative against propaganda of all persuasions and so make possible the commemoration of innocence achieved in the first section of *Briggflatts*.

To live in a flood of images, feelings and observation, all discrete, poses a problem to the poet:

The problem is to fit the bits together. Some of Mr Bunting's longer poems look like tesserae or catenae of particulars. *Briggflatts* arranges them in patterns copying musical forms. To both matter and pattern the world, both animate and inanimate, created and manufactured, is made to contribute. From its opening line (*Brag, sweet tenor bull*) the poem plays on the whole realm of sound, inarticulate but not inexpressive, and on the gesture related to it by rhythm, harmonising the units into a chorus of selfpraise:

Under sacks on the stone
two children lie,
hear the horse stale,
the mason whistle,
harness mutter to shaft,
felloe to axle squeak,
rut thud the rim,
crushed grit.

But the work poses problems not unrelated to unity and design. Mr. Bunting's designs require a unifying vision, but can the reader say, "Splendid! It all coheres!" As Cox says:

The underlying themes of Mr Bunting's poetry are not easily brought to the surface because the volume of his preserved work is small and sudden perfections discourage thematic analysis. Certain deductions may be permitted. In its description of the external world much of his writing is concerned with appearances of desolation: the deserts of the Middle East, the borderlands of northern England, the Paris of Villon, the thirties, the sea. In these settings man comes close to facing the conditions beyond which life is not possible:

Bound to beasts' udders, rags no dishonour,
not by much intercourse ennobled,
multitude of books, bought deference:
meagre flesh tingling to a mouthful of water,
apt to no servitude, commerce, or special dexterity.

If he survives he can say with the quiet arrogance of the bedouin: *What's to dismay us?* The impoverishment of the actual world stems the flow of the verses, reducing them to a pure trickle of which every drop is to be valued. Economy, the free use of few resources, is seen to be another aspect of the same concern, thematic as well as technical.

Such risks also appear thematically in *The Spoils:*

The dominant theme of this poem is that of opposition between the calculating and the reckless. The calculator (moneylender, administrator, policeman) imposes arbitrary rule and measure; the reckless (singer, soldier, seaman) gives without counting. The difference between them is determined by the presence of death. The calculator works to an end beyond the scope of an individual lifespan, but it is the risk of death that gives zest to life: without death life is not worth living. This bourgeois-romantic dichotomy is counterpointed by a secondary opposition running in the contrary direction. In spite of the care and precision of their operations the art of the calculating is rhetorical and false: *Roman exaggeration and the leaden mind of Egypt*. But the art of the gay in the shadow of death is cool and fine: it is by taking risks that we preserve proportion. The thesis is illustrated by reference to Persia and the second world war.

These speculations among others bring Mr. Cox to some astute observations.

> *Briggflatts*, somewhat unfairly, makes Mr Bunting's earlier poetry look like preparatory work. Its subject is repossession after long absence: *Heureux qui comme Ulysse*. . . . It returns to the north country with English both purified and enriched, the past and its studies absorbed. Here and there is a southern warmth, an eastern courtesy, the skill of a Latin poet in placing a long word, the audacious finality of Dante:

> > *One*
> > *plucked, fruit warm from the arse*
> > *of his companion, who*
> > *seeking to beat him, he screamed*

> But in general the debts are present only as harmonics. Yet it is the long practice of the translator, the persistent testing of every word, which has probably made possible the unfailing discretion with which the life and appearance of the country is represented without trace of provincialism or lapse into the banal. In addition to romantic theory and symbolist technique it infuses into the native tradition the sensuality of oriental poetry and attains, not by imitation but by a revival of its primitive elements, the standard of the King James version of the Old Testament:

> > *My love is young but wise. Oak, applewood,*
> > *her fire is banked with ashes till day.*
> > *The fells reek   of her hearth's scent,*
> > *her girdle is greased with lard:*
> > *hunger is stayed on her settle, lust in her bed.*

Cox concludes his observations by demonstrating that whatever changes Bunting may have experienced as an artist living, looking, and thinking in the world, human or non-human, the same poet early and late is always there:

> Skills and accidents by which we make contact with poets distant and past, or by which we seem to establish a relation with the non-human world, convince us that in cultivating the art we are not just playing with words, toys of our own invention, but that we do indeed perform, in ways we cannot understand but know for sure, parts in a rite able to dignify and perpetuate our common life. It may also be allowed that in obeying its laws we do a little to appease the dead. The achievement of Mr Bunting is to have demonstrated yet again and by concrete example the classic conclusion of his early poem:

> > *The Emperor with the Golden Hands*

> > *is still a word, a tint, a tone,*
> > *insubstantial-glorious,*
> > *when we ourselves are dead and gone*
> > *and the green grass growing over us.*

We must conclude that a critic so astute as Kenneth Cox makes us look again at Bunting's statement, "There is no excuse for literary criticism," and enter this caveat: A critic such as Mr. Cox who throws light upon and brings the reader closer to the work of art deserves the thanks of an inquiring reader whose own living, looking, and thinking in the world is as stimulated by a criticism which is itself the nicest of art. [C.F.T.]

12. Creeley, Robert. "A Note on Basil Bunting." *Agenda*, Autumn 1966, pp. 18-19. Reprinted in *A Quick Graph: Collected Notes and Essays*, Four Seasons Foundation, San Francisco, 1970.

Robert Creeley observes certain qualities and insistences in Bunting's work: its firm entrenchment in local English roots, its "almost flat pessimism," its "insistence on death." He then asks some interesting questions:

> In short, I am curious to know if an implicit quality of language occurs when words are used in a situation peculiar to their own history. *History*, however, may be an awkward term, since it might well imply only a respectful attention on the part of the writer rather than the implicit rapport between words and man when both are equivalent effects of time and place. In this sense there is a lovely dense sensuousness to Bunting's poetry and it is as much the nature of the words as the nature of the man who makes use of them. Again it is a circumstance shared.
> I am caught by the sense of himself Bunting defines:

> > . . . I hear Aneurin number the dead and rejoice,
> > being adult male of a merciless species.
> > Today's posts are piles to drive into the quaggy past
> > on which impermanent palaces balance.
> > (*Briggflatts*)

Only a discriminating poet with Creeley's ear could follow those observations with these remarks:

> It is the heirarchal situation of poet going deeper in time than one could borrow or assume, and hence the issue of some privileged kinship with the nature of poetry itself in one's own language. Pound's 'heave', with the trochee, proved him sensitive to it and makes clear one aspect of the relation between Bunting and himself. Bunting, from the earliest poems in *Loquitur* to the greatness of *Briggflatts* itself, is closely within the peculiar nature of his given language, an *English* such as one rarely now hears. In the earlier poems he makes use of a Latin, call it, appropriately enough:

> > Narciss, my numerous cancellations prefer
> > slow limpness in the damp dustbins amongst the peel
> > tobacco-ash and ends spittoon lickings litter
> > of labels dry corks breakages and a great deal

> > of miscellaneous garbage picked over by
> > covetous dustmen and Salvation Army sneaks
> > to one review-rid month's printed ignominy,
> > the public detection of your decay, that reeks.

> > ("To a Poet who advised me to preserve my fragments and false starts")

But the insistent intimate nature of his work moves in the closeness of monosyllables, with a music made of their singleness:

Mist sets lace of frost
on rock for the tide to mangle.
Day is wreathed in what summer lost.
(*Briggflatts*)

Having traced these sounds of Bunting in the air, Creeley safely concludes: "Presumptuously or not, it seems to me a long time since English verse had such an English ear—as sturdy as its words, and from the same occasion." Creeley believes it is precisely Bunting's kinship with the nature of poetry itself—the words—within the English language in which his greatness lies. [C.F.T.]

13. Read, Herbert. "Basil Bunting: Music or Meaning?" *Agenda*, Autumn 1966, pp. 4-10.

Herbert Read cites some of the key statements Bunting has made insisting that the music of poetry is the one thing poetry cannot do without. Poetry may have a meaning ranging from the high-serious to the trivial which could be expressed in prose, but the one thing it must have in addition, to be poetry at all, is music and such qualities of music as rhythm, cadence, tone, timbre, harmony etc. He concludes his quotes from Bunting with one of the most controversial: "Poetry is seeking to make not meaning, but beauty; or if you insist on misusing words, its 'meaning' is of another kind, and lies in the relation to one another of lines and patterns of sound, perhaps harmonious, perhaps contrasting and clashing, which the hearer feels rather than understands; lines of sound drawn in the air which stir deep emotions which have not even a name in prose."

Read then cites the rejoinder of Professor Peter Ure as an expert who holds an opposing point of view by giving us key sentences: "A poem is a structure of meanings . . . poetry a branch of the art of rhetoric; . . . words are extremely ineffectual instruments for providing . . . the pleasure of sounds—which is an enormously subtle and moving one when it is provided by the right means, such as fiddles, drums, trumpets, or bassoons." Read suggests that Ure has a point but that he has in effect changed the subject. But in making the musical analogy Bunting entered upon dangerous ground because "verbal music is quite distinct in tonality and every other characteristic from instrumental music—even the familiar comparison of architexture to 'frozen music' is not so misleading." Here no confusion between different kinds of sound is likely. Read points out that Heidegger was correct to insist that since words come into existence to establish being, "the sounds of words have ontological significance." "So," says Read, "do the tones of music." Thus Professor Ure makes the mistake of using the word "moving" as if the intent of art is to *move* us, an old confusion of art and rhetoric which even Longinus in his day dealt with and Stravinsky in our day (*The Poetics of Music*) tried to settle for all time.

Since these considerations strike at the heart of the music-meaning controversy, Read gives an extended quotation from "one of the greatest of modern musicologists, Victor Zuckerkandl":

Music has often before been interpreted as a language. Since it is of the essence of a language to say something, the question arose: What does music say? The usual answer was: As the words of language have factual meaning, the tones of music have emotional meaning; music is the language of feeling. According to this conception, the musical meaning of our Beethoven melody would lie in its expressing the feeling of joy, with a power far exceeding that of Schiller's poems and of all words. This interpretation cannot be ours. The key to understanding the processes that make the tones of this melody a melody at all, a piece of music, we found not in the relation of the tones to any particular feeling but in the relation of the tone e to the tone d. That the dynamic qualities of tone, in which we recognized the genuine musical element, have nothing to do with the expression of feeling, or with the expression of anything whatsoever, follows from the mere fact that they clearly appear even where absolutely nothing is meant to be expressed or stated, namely, when a scale is played.

Music and language, then, have one thing in common—that tones, like words, have meaning and that the "being in" of the meaning in the word, like that of the musical significance in the tone, is of a nonmaterial nature. But beyond that, the relations that connect the word with its meaning, the tone with its musical significance, are quite different. The word and its meaning are independent things. *Here* is the word—a complex of sounds or signs; *there* is what it means. The two are separable; each exists by itself, the word without the thing, the thing without the word. The same thing is designated in different languages by different words. We can refer to a thing otherwise than through a word—through a symbol, for example, or a sketch. The tone and its meaning, on the other hand, are connected in a far more intimate way. The accoustical event and its musical meaning are in no sense two independent phenomena, existing by themselves. They cannot be imagined separate. To be sure, it is possible to imagine a tone that means nothing, that is a simple acoustical phenomenon; but it is impossible to imagine the musical meaning of a tone, its dynamic quality, without the tone. . . . What tones mean musically is completely one with them, can only be represented through them, exists only in them. Except in the case of creative language (in the biblical sense of Adam's "naming" things) and of poetic language, where other, more "musical" relations come into play, language always has a finished world of things before it, to which it assigns words; whereas tones must themselves create what they mean. Hence it is possible to translate from one language into another, but not from one music into another—for example, from Western into Chinese music. Hence too the number of words, of the smallest meaning units of language, corresponds roughly to the number of things: languages are rich in words; whereas twelve tones suffice to say everything that has ever been said in our music.

(*Sound and Symbol: Music and the External World.*
New York (Bollingen Series), 1956, pp. 66-8)

Read believes that with these words Zuckerkandl "powerfully supports Basil Bunting's contention." Poetry is indeed creative language in the biblical sense of Adam's "naming of things" but with other more musical relations coming into play. If so, then poetry may be said to "*create* what it means." Read caps this climatic statement with an italicized conclusion: "*this is proved by the impossibility of translating poetry from one language to another.*" He offers us supporting arguments:

A minor indication of the same truth is found in the

dependence, for its full musical effect, of poetry on regional
speech or traditional accent, upon which Bunting insists in one
of the notes at the end of *Briggflatts*. He himself speaks the
Northumbrian tongue, "which sometimes sounds strange to the
koinè or to Americans who may not know how much Northumberland differs from the Saxon south of England. Southrons
would maul the music of many lines in *Briggflatts*." Luckily the
present reviewer was born north of the Humber, enured in childhood to the accents in which this poem must be spoken and
heard. (The accents, incidentally, in which Wordsworth's verses
must be spoken and heard, or forever remain an unknown poetry.) But he despairs, except in speech, to render the particular
quality of the diction of this poem, which partly depends on a
select vocabulary. Saxon in its roots, partly on a traditional
pronunciation (broad, soft vowel sounds), partly on a crisp
enunciation that seems to carve the syllables out of crystal
rock, writhing lips and tongue with a gusto unfamiliar to slurred
Southern speech.

Read concludes his piece with a number of quotations from
Bunting's poetry to illustrate and develop the points he has made.
Since he is a native of the land north of the Umber, he speaks with
a knowledge, experience, and authority most of us "southrons"
or aliens from other continents cannot have.

14. Tomlinson, Charles. "Experience into Music." *Agenda*,
Autumn 1966, pp. 11-17.

Tomlinson deplores the long lack of availability of Bunting's work,
gives a brief chronology and then quotes Hugh Kenner's claim that
from Pound and Williams "he [Bunting] has learned techniques
where others have borrowed voices." After dealing with Bunting's
use of these techniques in the Odes, Tomlinson transfers his attention to similarities between Bunting's and Zukofsky's work. Tomlinson says:

Bunting's art, like Zukofsky's, 'aspires to a condition of music'—
'accompanying tones of the words' that 'are their own experience'—and in coming to *The Spoils* (1951) one sees time and
again how the music achieved there was of the greatest possible
transitional importance for the all-over musical structure of
Briggflatts, published fourteen years later.

In the second half of his paper Tomlinson analyzes Bunting's
use of motifs to support the musical structure of *Briggflatts*. He
says:

The music of *Briggflatts* lies not only in tones, rhyme, the articulations of syntax, but in the use throughout of recurrent motifs.
A number of these—spring, bull, slowworm, a mason chiselling
letters on a gravestone—are introduced at the opening in a landscape of space and time, and analogous with the entry of the
various voices in a madrigal:

But for Tomlinson the central incident of the poem, the love scene
between two adolescents as remembered by the poet fifty years
later, supplies the main motif—the conflict between Then and Now.
On Tomlinson's account:

The music Bunting refers to for his imagery (Byrd, Monteverdi, 'Schoenberg's maze') suggests voice against voice, line against line—madrigal and canon, not impressionistic sound-painting. The achievement of the poem—and here one is reducing to abstraction all that is art and art's particulars—derives from the attempt to bring Then into as close a relation with Now as possible. The aligning of the two comes about by the central device of imitating 'the condition of music'. Then and Now are brought to bear upon each other as are the different voices in a madrigal. In the poem this cannot be done simultaneously; but, by juxtaposition, Now can be played over against Then as Then—summoned up by motif and left echoing in the mind— stands forth, counterpoised rather than counterpointed, against the ensuing motif of Now. And yet, in the beautiful image of the slowworm, simultaneity can be and is achieved, by a radical innocence that has persisted as a possibility in the poet's own mind:

> light from the zenith
> spun where the slowworm lay in her lap
> fifty years ago

Tomlinson ends an astute critique with an astute overall view:

From the measured quantities of *Loquitur* through the more intricate rhyme and line of *The Spoils,* Bunting has come, in his late poetry, to a music that combines strength and delicacy in patternings that to the reader are a constant delight and that to the young poet should prove of intense and liberating technical interest. Not least among the poem's achievements is the way an erotic incident that could have been sentimental or, in the manner of some of the *Loquitur* poems, trivial, has been made as real for the reader as for the poet, realised, as it is, with a novelistic specificness. We can completely accept, for the purpose of the poem, his valuation of it, which is a measure of how far Bunting has come since "the teashop girls" of his earlier verses.

It takes a poet of Tomlinson's own stature to cut through so neatly to the heart of the matter. [C.F.T.] .

15. Ginsberg, Allen. "On Basil Bunting." *International Times,* 16-19 January 1967, p. 14. [Reprinted, *Some of it,* Knullar Publishing Ltd., 1969]

Ginsberg says that from reading the small collection of Bunting's early work he got the impression he was one of the masters of the age of poetic invention that starred Pound and Williams. Ginsberg says that Bunting is the most alert prosodist in England and that poetry has been a ghost there because Bunting's poetry has been ignored. [W.M.]

16. "Grok." "Basil Bunting: An Interview." *Grok,* no. 2, 19 May 1967, pp. 4, 5, and 7.

[Unavailable for comment.]

17. "Pooter." "At the Tower in Newcastle," *The Times,* 3 August 1968, p. 19.

The tower referred to in the title of the article is Morden Tower in Newcastle. The article, for the most part, deals with Tom Pickard;

however, four paragraphs deal with Basil Bunting's relationship to Tom Pickard and other young 'northern poets' who have been connected with or read at the Tower.

18. Unsigned. *Palatinate: Durham University Newspaper*, 24 October 1968, p. 14.

> A very short interview with Bunting. The poet says here that his first excitement was Wordsworth and that "there is a lot of work in poetry." He says that he is often thinking of the architecture of poems and that once he has "the shape" of a poem he fills it out with material. [W.M.]

19. Hall, Anthea. "The Irony of Bunting's Climb to Fame." *The Journal* (Newcastle), 6 December 1968, p. 8.

> Anthea Hall writes that with the Literary Fellowships awarded Bunting in the mid-sixties the poet could give up his job sub-editing the financial page of the *Newcastle Evening Chronicle*. Bunting says of his early poems that they are not as skillful as they might have been. Bunting says that "I regret to say there is no way of teaching people how to write poetry; you can just point out the obvious faults of composition and suggest reading." He says that poetry is part of every male's nature, that it is the brag of the bull (and this obviously links up with the opening section of *Briggflatts*), a delightful thing to see, showing off in the pleasantest sense of the word. [W.M.]

20. Williams, Jonathan. "Notes: One and Two," *Descant on Rawthey's Madrigal: Conversations with Basil Bunting*. (Lexington, Kentucky), 1968.

> The opening epigram to this short book runs as follows:
>
> > Jonathan, I am surprised at you. What the hell has any of this to do with the public? My autobiography is *Briggflatts*—there's nothing else worth speaking aloud.
>
> Nevertheless, Williams is able to coax about 30 pages of information, mostly biographical, out of Bunting. The plan of the interview was to begin with Bunting's birth in 1900 and to proceed to the present (1968). The interview, for the most part, does simply that. The book also includes "A Statement" on poetry by Bunting, the now famous (or infamous) statement that "Poetry, like music, is to be heard...," as well as a select bibliography of works by and about Bunting.

21. Norman, Philip. "A Necklace of Chamber Pots." *The Sunday Times*, 19 January 1969, Supplement pp. 34 and 38.

> This article again recounts the standard biographical accounts of Bunting's life. Interviewing Bunting, Norman discovers that Bunting's father gave him an early interest in the Bible and Wordsworth; in Bach, Scarlatti and Dante. Norman argues that the slimness of Bunting's output is due partly to indolence and partly to the exquisite editing that was one of the great lessons taught by Pound.

Norman says that *Briggflatts* is "a sonata poem with a mystic introduction like Debussy, and full of hard landscapes, bloody myth and
cold-breath lovemaking". The title of this article is a translation of
the title of Bunting's first book, published in Milan in 1930, *Redimiculum Metallarum*. Bunting concludes the interview in his usual
mischievous manner, by saying "I'm a great swallower of tea when
there is any." [W.M.]

22. Webster, T. B. "Basil Bunting—A Poet in Our Time." *Courier*
4, 5 February 1969, (Newcastle University), p. 6.

This piece was written by a student at Newcastle Upon Tyne University when Bunting was the Literary Fellow there. It is concerned
with all the standard biographical details of Bunting's life. Webster
writes that "Obscurity seems to have given him a freedom that few
major poets have had and a means for personal expression without
the inhibitions of public taste and morality. Bunting has never sought
publicity or recognition, nor has he tried to impress us with a flood
of work." There are verbatim reports included in the article concerning Bunting's views on poetry. Bunting says that the poet or poetry
serve no specific purpose to society and that "Meaning consists in
sounds and the emotions sounds rouse." Bunting also talks to Webster about the standard influences on his work: Pound, Eliot, Yeats,
Malherbe and Dante. He says that he admires Malherbe and Dante
for their precision of language. He also talks of the necessity for
compression in poetry. He talks at some length on the Northumbrian
dialect and its effect on his poetry. Of *Briggflatts* he says "The bull
that begins *Briggflatts*, I noticed some fifteen years ago, strolling
around a field. It struck me that no-one had ever publicly noted that
the bull's voice is a tenor one, unlike the contralto of the cow, and
that when he is with the cows, showing off, he does in fact dance."
In conclusion he says "I've been a poet all my life, I've never really
thought of being anything else." [W.M.]

23. Cox, Kenneth. "A Commentary on Basil Bunting's 'Villon.'"
Stony Brook (New York), Fall 1969, pp. 59-69. [reprinted:
Agenda, Spring 1978, pp. 20-36]

Although Bunting wrote "Villon" in 1925, at the age of 25, Cox suggests that many of the permanent qualities of Bunting's poetry are
already in evidence. Cox concludes his article with the statement:

> Backward in his ideas, in technique Bunting was at twenty-five
> among the most accomplished poets of his time: *Hugh Selwyn
> Mauberley* and *The Waste Land* had been published only a few
> years before. *Villon* is a masterpiece not in the conventional but
> in the original sense of the word: work done by an apprentice to
> demonstrate his mastery of the craft, though a man yet unformed.
> It is the proof-piece of a stubborn antinomian with an acute ear,
> brought up a Quaker in the north of England in the first quarter
> of the twentieth century, who finds intolerable contradictions
> between the actual and the imaginary, between what the body
> suffers and what the mind holds, neither of which he will deny.

Following a brief description of the lives of Bunting and Fran-
çois Villon, a fifteenth-century Parisian poet, and of each man's imprisonment, Cox begins a section by section, and at times a line by
line, analysis of "Villon." On Cox's account, the relation between the
actual and the imaginary forms the basic subject matter of the poem.
Part I of *Villon* immediately poses two themes:

> The two opening themes are structurally related: living speech
> as against dead literature, inward experience as against outward
> semblance, the immediate as against the remote, the bare as
> against the ornamental, listening as against looking. The opposi-
> tions can be grouped:
>
> | | | | |
> |---|---|---|---|
> | VILLON | LIFE | MAROT | DEATH |
> | SOUND | TRUE | IMAGE | FALSE |
>
> The rest of the poem will develop these themes. It will not only
> vary the words used to state them and apply the oppositions
> established to elements as yet unmentioned. The poem also re-
> groups the themes, inverts them, revalues and resolves them. The
> development is effected by way of renewed attacks on the raw
> stuff in which the poem originated. What turns, recurs and
> changes as the poem proceeds is not so much the words them-
> selves, their rhythms or syllables, as the poet's grasp of his sub-
> ject.

Part I then closes with a restatement of the opening themes but with
a reversal of their values: "The living die and the dead are only a
faint memory. Absent from the actual, the image of the lost ideal
remains present in art outlasting mortal life." Parts II and III then re-
work the oppositions and contradictions of Part I by evolving further complications and by attempting finer definitions.

Cox, however, does more than simply trace themes throughout
"Villon." He is also concerned with Bunting's technique and Bunting's imitation of Villon's poetry, specifically Bunting's free rendering of lines from the *Grand Testament*. But most importantly, his
primary task is to show that,

> Many of the permanent qualities of Bunting's writing can already
> be observed in *Villon*. It is remarkable for its freedom, in the
> sense one says a drawing is free, for the variety of its rhythms
> and the width of its reference, above all the quality Marot prized
> in Villon: *sa veine*, something between wit and daring, partaking
> of the nature of cheek. Apart from an occasionally juvenile ac-
> cent the language is assured, nimble, new.

24. Suter, Anthony. "Un «Raleigh» moderne: Introduction à la
     vie et l'oeuvre poétique de Basil Bunting." *Annales* 6, No.
     1, (University of Toulouse), 1970, pp. 121-132.

This article offers a useful summary of the principal events in Bunting's life and a brief synopsis of Bunting's major poems, from "Villon" to *Briggflatts*. [B.H.]

25. Johnson, Carol. "The Poetics of Disregard: Homage to Basil
     Bunting." *Art International*, October 1970, pp. 21-22.

> As the title should suggest, Johnson spends a considerable portion
> of her article talking about England's neglect of Basil Bunting. Her
> conclusion, after having read *Collected Poems*, is that, "Forty years
> of going his own way have not diminished this poet's receptiveness
> to life, vitiated his sense of humor or precipitated a sterile retreat in-
> to sensibility at the expense of intelligence." For the most part, the
> remainder of the article serves as evidence for the preceding assertion
> and as an opportunity for the author simply to quote portions of her
> favorite poems. But why not? The article is also a "Homage to Basil
> Bunting." In Johnson's opinion, "England does not deserve him,
> whether she likes it or not: the only worthy successor to Hopkins—
> who also had to wait."

26. Lucie-Smith, Edward. "Basil Bunting." *Contemporary Poets
     of the English Language*, ed. Rosalia Murray, London & Chi-
     cago, St. James Press, 1970, pp. 161-62.

> This article contains a brief biography of Bunting and a few general
> remarks about the dominant themes in his poetry. It also contains
> a bibliography of Bunting's verse publications.

27. Suter, Anthony. "*Chomei at Toyama*: Commentaire Critique
     du poème de Basil Bunting." *Annales 7*, No. 1, 1971, pp. 77-
     87.

> Suter here compares Bunting's poem to its principal source: to Muc-
> cioli's version of Chomei's *Ho-Jo-Ki*. Suter argues that Bunting puts
> to effective use certain principles of narration that he learned from
> Pound, and that the poem exemplifies the ideogrammic method at
> work. In the process of developing this argument, Suter spars briefly
> with K.L. Goodwin's judgment that Bunting's attempts to employ an
> ideogrammic method are unsuccessful. "*Chomei at Toyama* offers a
> mixture of ideogrammic techniques and narration.... The union of
> those two modes represents an important step on the way toward
> the symphonic structure (which incorporates, furthermore, narrative
> fragments) of his last long poem, *Briggflatts*." [B.H.]

28. Cawley, Tom. "...And Suddenly, He's Prominent." *The Sun-
     day Press* (Binghamton), 7 March 1971, p. 5.

> This short but amusing article contains Bunting's views on a number
> of issues as diversified as his sudden prominence, his views on Viet-
> nam and student protests and his grandchildren. The interview was
> conducted during Bunting's brief (one semester) stay at the State
> University at Binghamton, and while Bunting's responses do point
> out interesting aspects of his personality, there is little in the arti-
> cle for the serious student of Bunting's poetry.

29.   Suter, Anthony. "Time and the Literary Past in the Poems of
Basil Bunting." *Contemporary Literature*, Autumn 1971 (University of Wisconsin), pp. 510-25.

Suter sets up the problem his article is to deal with in the following
way:

> Bunting has only very rarely expressed himself in writing on the
> subject of poetry and has never gone so far as to theorize about
> literature in general. Why he uses material from other literature
> in his work has to be studied from the poetry itself. However, it
> can at least be said that Bunting conceives of literary material as
> subject matter to "fill" the structures or shapes that he
> has in mind for his poems.

Suter places Bunting in a Pound-Eliot tradition and claims that the
most obvious characteristic the three share in common is that in their
use of the literature of the past they are almost always respectful.
Suter immediately adds that this respectful use of the literary past
does not rule out parody (and here he quotes Bunting's note to "Attis: Or, Something Missing") because "an author rarely parodies
another writer within the framework of a serious piece of literature
if he does not think that the other is worth parodying." Parody then
may be respectful, or it may be done tongue in cheek as a literary
joke. According to Suter, Bunting's parodies of Villon in "Villon"
and "The Well of Lycopolis" and of Anglo-Saxon verse in *Briggflatts* fall into the first category, parodies of Milton in "Attis: Or,
Something Missing" and of Eliot in "Aus dem Zweiten Reich" fall
into the second category.

Although many more examples are given, the important
point to note, in Suter's view, is that,

> Bunting himself admitted in conversation that the public for po-
> etry has changed since he began writing. What one could expect
> in terms of erudition from one's audience, he claims, was far
> greater a generation ago than now. His present poetry, thus, has
> changed with the times in minimizing erudite reference.

Thus Suter sees a shift occurring in Bunting's use of the literary past
beginning with "Chomei at Toyama" and "Odes" and culminating in
Briggflatts. "What distinguishes 'Chomei at Toyama' from all of
Bunting's other long poems prior to its composition, apart from 'Aus
dem Zweiten Reich,' is that it stands entirely on its own. The reader
need have no acquaintance with its source, the *Hōjōki*, which is
entirely assimilated into both the design and subject matter." What
distinguishes the "Odes" is their almost total lack of literary reference. What Bunting is evolving toward, according to Suter, is not a
denial of the past that is behind him but rather an attempt "...to
give an extra dimension to both past and present by juxtaposing
them like interreflecting mirrors." *Briggflatts* then is the culmination
of Bunting's efforts insofar as the theme involves a juxtaposition of
past and present. In this way the use of the literary past does not become sterile or merely a technique but rather it aims at the renewal
of the past for the present. "Art that draws on literary sources of
the past shows at least a faith in, if not the accomplishment of, a
power to overcome time."

30. Butters, Brian. "Don't keep Poetry to Yourself–Read it Aloud." *Victoria Daily Times*, 13 October 1971, p. 3.

> [Unavailable for comment.]

31. Thomas, Bill. "If You Want Riches, Poetry Isn't Your Bag." *Daily Colonist*, 17 October 1971, p. 48.

> This short newspaper article laments the inability of poets in general, and Basil Bunting in particular, to make a decent living:

>> It could be that the very character of the poet predicates his own economic status. Bunting says the poet who is good "is always a shock and a surprise to his contemporaries."
>> There is little doubt that the shock waves the poet sets up also sets society against him.
>> The life-style of the poet, as seen by Bunting, doesn't fit the regular cast.
>> He insists the poet should be as lazy as possible and that there is no merit in sitting down to a daily routine of writing. The best work comes when the poet feels there is no peace to be found until what he has inside forces itself out.
>> The eight-hour society can't reconcile itself with this attitude where productivity is programmed to the clock. The world of the structured day has no place for the poet.

> Besides all this, Thomas avers:

>> Academics make a better living writing criticism of the works of men like Bunting than the original creators of the works ever made.

32. Jones, Douglas. "Basil Bunting: The Line of Succession." *Odysseus* (Portland, Oregon), Oct.-Nov. 1971, pp. 1-2.

> This article is a very brief and general introduction to Bunting's *Collected Poems*. Jones stresses Bunting's early associations with Pound and Zukofsky and his adoption of the sonata form for his longer poems. To the article is added a note from Denis Goacher, another poet who knew Pound and Eliot as well as Zukofsky and Bunting. He says:

>> Stress *thoroughness*: that is Ezra Pound's real lesson, even though he was not always able to live up to his ideals. Most followers of Pound in verse deploy only a few superficial technical tricks. By thoroughness I obviously don't just mean painstaking acquisition of knowledge. Anyone can do that. A poet's business is to discover the area for which he is fitted, then plough, sow, pluck, watch the skies, be flexible to change but only in his area. Grubbing and guzzling every or any foreign body available through what journalists call "mass media" will only be shot out as journalism or fashion, dated as soon as stated.
>> So far Basil Bunting is the only one of Pound's close associates to have managed a long poem (*Briggflatts*) which will hold a permanent place in our literature. Note well that Bunting was 65 when he achieved this. If we take talent as given (wishful thinking?), *stamina* and *thoroughness* are the only body guards which can hope to stem the erosion of western civilization.

33. Durand, Regis. "Quelques aspects de la poésie de Basil Bunting." *Études Anglaises*, XXIV (Oct.-Dec., 1971), pp. 405-15.

Durand touches on several of Bunting's poems in order to show the importance of seemingly conflicting images within the poems. The images which Durand finds are closely linked and help to explain the chief tension on which Bunting's poetry centers, the tension between a need for change and a desire for unity and order. A stone mason, for example, is a creator, an artisan, but he is also associated with death, with cold stone, with sterility. The sea, an even more important symbol, is a mason which carves the land. The sea is on one hand a symbol of change, fertility, and excitement but is also linked with empty, barren expanses. Bunting, according to Durand, is searching for an equilibrium among contrary impulses. Therefore, "brackish" becomes a central word: salt water and sea water incompletely mixed. The salmon which moves from salt water to fresh water is one related image. Contrasting with the sea, the land in Bunting's poems is often a desert. The gods are dead or dying. Durand finds that in working to resolve the conflicts he expresses, Bunting uses approaches similar to those of Pound (the use of masks) and Eliot (the need to go through a period of dryness or death before regeneration can take place). [W.H.]

34. Brooker, P. J. M.A. thesis, University of Birmingham, 1971.

This is decidedly not a run-of-the-mill thesis. Rather it is, both as a piece of literary theory and as a contribution to Bunting criticism, an original and important piece of work. Brooker's thesis develops "a theoretical and operational model for the study of style, particularly style in poetry." Brooker argues that "a division has been too often wrongly drawn between literary stylistics and linguistic stylistics. Stylistics . . . is rather the area in which the evaluative and interpretative approach of literary criticism can be expected to combine with the system and the descriptive authority of linguistics." From linguistics, Brooker borrows two methods of analyzing syntax: category/scale grammar and transformational grammar. But in developing this "model" Brooker also seeks to move beyond "the purely textual approach to a poem." "It has," he says,

> long been a tenet of especially British linguists that the levels of language be studied in terms both of the internal relations of a text and relations in its "context of situation". It is commonly held in linguistics, moreover, that the status of meanings which occur at this outer level of contextualisation be recognised as "cultural". Literary criticism also, has long been interested in the social, historical and ideological background to literature, and more recently in the ideas and assumptions about society and culture that are implicit in a literary text. The relations between a level of cultural meaning, and the levels of "formal" and "expressive" meaning, for example, that might be identified "below" the cultural, are extremely problematic and as yet barely systematised by linguistics or literary studies. One can assume, however, that these levels are fluid and interdependent. I hope to suggest that a stylistics which combines the virtues of descriptive rigour with an interpretative approach to poetic structures, will be better fitted than either a linguistic or literary stylistics alone to direct analysis towards meanings in the context of situation.

In the last half of his thesis Brooker applies his new "syntactic/

contextual" method of analysis to a specific poem: the coda to *Briggflatts*. This exhaustive (75-page) analysis demonstrates the value of Brooker's powerful critical model and offers valuable insights into Bunting's work. Brooker offers an indispensible starting point for the study of how Bunting's poetry works, *as language*. Any serious student of Bunting's work should take the trouble necessary to secure a copy of this thesis. [B.H.]

35. Cox, Kenneth. "An Introduction to *Briggflatts*." *Tuatara* (Vancouver), Spring 1972.

> This is a short, page-and-a-half, poetic introduction to *Briggflatts*.

36. Suter, Anthony. "Basil Bunting, Poet of Modern Times." *Ariel*, October 1972, pp. 24-32.

> Suter argues that insofar as Bunting has never been associated by his few critics with "thirties" poetry, it may seem surprising to some to label him as a "poet of modern times." Bunting's own tendency to state that thematic preoccupations are of secondary importance and only necessary to "fill" the structures of his poems, Suter takes for *prima facie* evidence for this view. Yet after citing passages from *The Well of Lycopolis* in which Bunting attacks both the "committed" poets of the thirties and the members of the Bloomsbury Group, Suter goes on to argue that both Bunting's prose and poetry show him to be a man of many social concerns: economic, scientific, political, and military.
>
> "The neglect of the social aspect of the poet's work perhaps comes from the negative form that it takes. Bunting has never espoused the cause of any particular group or proclaimed any political doctrine." Failure to espouse a particular doctrine, however, does not rule out social concern; rather, Suter argues that Bunting's social concern "is more often than not accompanied by profound pessimism." Suter cites as evidence Bunting's anti-scientific bias and hatred of bureaucracy both as evidenced in "Villon"; his distaste for the dictates of economics is exemplified in "Gin the Goodwife Stint" and "The Complaint of the Morpethshire Farmer"; his distaste and yet indifference to war is evidenced in his report on the Spanish situation in 1936 which was published in *The Spectator*. Yet as Suter is quick to point out, "One surprise of the political aspect of Bunting's poetry is that it does not condemn warfare." Instead, as in *The Spoils*, war is often a means of regeneration, even if only temporary.
>
> Finally, Suter argues that even though Bunting fails to put forward a political program, he does have a poetic ideal of a better world. He cites *Odes I*, 32:
>
> > Let them remember Samangan, the bridge and tower
> > and rutted cobbles and the coppersmith's hammer,
> > where we looked out from the walls to the marble mountains,
> > ate and lay and were happy an hour and a night;
> >
> > so that the heart never rests from love of the city
> > without lies or riches, whose old women

> straight as girls at the well are beautiful,
> its old men and its wineshops gay.
>
> Let them remember Samangan against userers,
> cheats and cheapjacks, amongst boasters,
> hideous children of cautious marriages,
> those who drink in contempt of joy.
>
> Let them remember Samangan, remember
> they wept to remember the hour and go.

Thus Suter concludes that for Bunting, "The poet returns to his art as the only force for good in a corrupt world."

37. Forde, Sister Victoria Marie. "Music and Meaning in the Poetry of Basil Bunting." Ph.D. thesis, University of Notre Dame, 1972. [Available from University Microfilms.]

Sister Forde's thesis is divided into five chapters: (1) Biography, Poetics, and Major Influences; (2) The Odes; (3) Translations and Adaptations; (4) Sonatas; and (5) Conclusion. Chapters two and three may be found elsewhere in this book [pp. 125-144 and 301-342]. The "Abstract" of the complete thesis is given here:

> For Basil Bunting poetry is inseparable from music. When he acknowledges poets who have influenced him, he is referring to those whose techniques help him realize in his own work qualities he finds in such composers as J.C. Bach, Scarlatti, and Corelli—informally balanced structure, clear outlines, a variety of contrasts and associations. For example, from Horace, Dante, Wordsworth, Villon, Whitman, Zukofsky, and Pound, he learned ways of creating economical poetry, using ordinary diction and speech patterns. Dante taught him to say a thing once, sharply and precisely; Spenser, to use music suited to his theme. From Wyatt and Malherbe, who both used a lute to create poetry, he learned metrical inventiveness. With Zukofsky Bunting believed in Pound's pronouncement that poetry fails when it gets too far from music and that the best poetry is composed in the sequence of the musical phrase.
>
> Although Pound's place in Bunting's technical development is assuredly an important one, in his own evaluations Bunting himself seems never to place him far above such poets as Malherbe and Manuchehri. Besides insisting on direct treatment of the thing, it was Pound who encouraged Bunting to translate and adapt poems in order to learn techniques from great writers of other languages—Latin, Italian, French, Persian, and Japanese —a means of technical refinement he used only for a time.
>
> Even though Bunting has continued to write odes for fifty years, the highest points of his development are the sonatas. The early sonatas depend to some extent on the material of other, older poets, but their expression is modern and the themes are personal concerns. By 1951 both the material and the musical techniques are uniquely his own and used with originality to develop themes which are personal but more broadly universal.
>
> For Bunting to share experiences in a fully human way—sensually, emotionally, and intellectually—requires poetry as close to music as possible for its fullest expression. His insistence that his poetry be read aloud is underpinned by Pound's theory of melopoeia. To achieve the melopoetic quality, Bunting creates a basic surface simplicity by means of ordinary but exactly precise diction and economically compressed syntax. His concentration on these qualities to stress what is immediate, particular,

and concrete is a source of strength but also at times the basis for just charges of obscurity. This surface simplicity combines with complexities of rhythms, varied stanzaic patterns, subtle vowel modulations and alliterations to create poetry that helps the audience share more than the connotative meanings of the words, but rather emotions which are, in Bunting's words, "too deep to name."

In the sonatas, above all, and in *Briggflatts* especially, the balanced architecture of the whole provides the necessary framework for the full development of Bunting's art. The form through which he has gained the freedom and spirit of Scarlatti's sonatas allows scope for the overall development of themes throughout several large movements. The means are best described in musical terms, i.e., incremental repetition of themes and recurrent motifs, contrasting rhythms, tempos, and texture of sounds, and tone color. Within each movement subordinate thematic and technical developments through contrasts and associations parallel the larger ones. For Bunting all this is necessary for the fullest expression of the human experience he is communicating.

The thematic and technical relationships among all his sonatas, in fact among all his collected poems, create a unity in his work that comes near to his dream of finally creating something in poetry like the *Art of the Fugue*. The musical development has obviously an essential unity and the predominant themes can be grouped around the tensions of life and death, art and experience, permanence and impermanence, with the individual's responses to these as the unchanging focal points.

38. Suter, Anthony. "Basil Bunting et deux poètes américains: Louis Zukofsky et William Carlos Williams." *Caliban IX*, Tome VIII (Toulouse), 1972, pp. 151-57.

This article attempts to show that Zukofsky and Williams provided models for at least some of Bunting's poems. Suter sees "The Orotava Road" as a direct "imitation" of Williams' work, in its verse form and in its attempt to achieve a "direct presentation of the thing." And Suter finds an equally strong Zukofskian influence in Ode 33 of the *First Book of Odes*. [B.H.]

39. Suter, Anthony. " 'Attis: Or, Something Missing,' a commentary on the poem by Basil Bunting." *Durham University Journal*, March 1973, pp. 189-200.

Suter suggests that *Attis: Or, Something Missing* is interesting for its presentation of literary sources, its connections with Eliot, and its beautiful imagery. Suter has previously discussed Bunting's use of the literary past in his article "Time and the Literary Past in the Poems of Basil Bunting" [reviewed above], but in this article, as the title suggests, he confines his discussion of Bunting's use of the literary past to a discussion of *Attis: Or, Something Missing*. Much of what he has to say, however, about both the use of the literary past and of Bunting's connections with Eliot follows from the earlier article.

Suter's method is to go through the poem section by section, part by part, pointing out Bunting's use of themes and techniques as he goes. From Bunting's note in *Collected Poems* ("Parodies of Lucretius and Cino da Pistoia can do no damage and intend no disrespect"), the reader immediately recognizes the importance of Lucretius and Cino da Pistoia to the poem. Part II is followed by the parenthetical remark "Variations on a theme by Milton." But in addition to these three poets, Suter also finds Bunting borrowing themes or techniques from Catullus, Dante, Mallarmé, Pound, and Eliot.

It is with Eliot though that Suter thinks Bunting is particularly concerned, and on this topic Suter is especially outspoken as the following two paragraphs should show:

> The third part of *Attis*, and particularly its conclusion, indicate what should be our general interpretation of the whole poem. At first we are somewhat doubtful as to the meaning of this elaborate treatment of the Attis myth. However, it is obvious by the end that the story of Attis is symbolic here of poetic sterility and failure. If we want to be more precise, the target of Bunting's satire is probably T.S. Eliot. All the similarities between the work of Eliot and Bunting in the first two parts of the poem are not just imitations of technique if we see them in the context of the satire, although—unfortunately for Bunting's purpose—this is not always immediately obvious to the reader; also, the serious element represented by the Lucretius counterpoint prevents us from seeing everything in a light-hearted way. Certain parts of the poem, other than the parodies already mentioned, can be seen as references to Eliot. The decay/renewal imagery near the beginning of Part I shows thematic preoccupations similar to those of Eliot. More mocking are the references in Part III, where the prizes Attis receives at the "sports and flower show" are Eliot's rewards in the literary field, and where the religiosity of the castrated priests is a parallel for Eliot's conversion to the Church of England coinciding with what Bunting considers to be a diminishing of his poetic powers.
>
> This view of Eliot is not one shared by the present writer, but one can perhaps understand the feelings of a struggling, unrecognized writer concerning a successful poet being expressed in this way. However, the criticism is unfair when one considers how much Bunting really owes to Eliot and the partly parallel development of their two careers towards summits of musical form in poetry, *Four Quartets* and *Briggflatts*. It is not entirely paradoxical, but rather ironic therefore, that Bunting should attack a poet with whom he has so much in common.

40. Gardner, Raymond. "Secret, solitary, a spy. . . ." *Arts Guardian*, 27 June 1973, p. 10.

This short article was the outgrowth of an interview with Bunting previous to his speaking (a tribute to Ezra Pound) at the Poetry International. The article touches on Bunting's acquaintance with Pound and Zukofsky and gives a short synopsis of Bunting's views on a number of twentieth-century poets including Zukofsky, MacDiarmid, and Pickard. As is usual with such articles, it also gives a brief biographical description of Bunting. The title comes from *Briggflatts:*

> Poet appointed dare not decline
> to walk among the bogus, nothing to authenticate
> the mission imposed, despised
> by toadies, confidence men, kept boys,
> shopped and jailed, cleaned out by whores,
> touching acquaintance for food and tobacco.
> Secret, solitary, a spy . . . .

41. Suter, Anthony. "The Sea in the Poetry of Basil Bunting." *Forum for Modern Language Studies*, July 1973, pp. 293-97.

[Unavailable for comment.]

42. Suter, Anthony. "With Basil Bunting in Berlin: A Study of 'Aus dem Zweiten Reich.'" *Proof*, Spring 1975, pp. 5-10.

[Unavailable for comment.]

43. Woolford, John. "*Briggflatts*: A Poem shaped like a Tombstone." *Mews*, No. 1, April 1975 (Cambridge), pp. 41-45.

The author writes of *Briggflatts* that it is Wordsworth's artistic dilemma of the interaction of memory with the threatened substance of life renovated. He compares Bunting's laconic style with that of Wordsworth's "Essay on Epitaphs" arguing that both poets are concerned with the grand expression of immortality. Writing of Bunting and his long poem, Woolford concludes that "his life, being complete, takes on that outer coherence and inner harmony that only complete structures attain." [W.M.]

44. Mottram, Eric. "Out Loud." *Listener*, 28 August 1975. An abridgement of Eric Mottram's radio interview with Bunting of 7 March 1975. The interview is reprinted in full in *Poetry Information*, 19, Summer 1978.

Mottram and Bunting begin the interview by talking about what it means for Bunting to be a Northumbrian poet. From this topic they progress to Bunting's views on the sound of poetry—the necessity to read poetry aloud—and on the poet as a singer. Other topics discussed include music and poetry (from the perspective of Bunting the music critic), the structure of long poems, and as seems to be inevitable in these interviews, the effect other poets and musicians had on Bunting's poetry:

M: With Pound, for instance, it must have been very strong—it's a highly individual voice and set of structures, isn't it?

B: I don't think that that is what had the effect. What has the effect is that one sees the processes a man uses, whether he's a living man or a dead one, and one then attempts to make use of them oneself. They are useful tools. Now Pound has provided a box of tools, as abundant for this generation as those that Spenser provided for the Elizabethans, and a man who is not influenced by Pound, in the sense of trying to use at least some of those tools, is simply not living in his own century.

M: Would you feel the same way about Zukofsky?

B: Zukofsky has some things he does with *extreme* skill. Others are experiments which are justified in that an experiment is as well worth making if it doesn't come off as if it does. It shows you at least that in that direction there is no progress to be made. But the thing which to me seems most important about Zukofsky, and the thing which delights me all the time, is the extreme economy of his lyric poems. That is something

> that he was able to show to Carlos Williams—greatly improved
> Carlos Williams' poetry—and it is something which I have, oc-
> casionally, tried to rival. I haven't, I think, succeeded but at
> any rate it helps one to shape something.

Other poets who are discussed include Lucretius, Ferdosi, Manuchehri, Joseph Skipsey, Swinburne, Whitman, and MacDiarmid; discussion of musicians centered around Byrd, Scarlatti, and Corelli.
One final series of exchanges begs quotation here:

> M: . . . Well, let's move to something else—something I know you
> are fiery about—and I'm going to quote a phrase, to provoke
> you, out of your little book with Jonathan Williams: "There
> is no excuse for literary criticism." Now why not?

> B: It distracts attention from the work almost always. There are,
> of course, exceptions. One overstates things as a rule. But
> there are not very many exceptions. I think that a man who
> will read DE VULGARI ELOQUENTIA will have got most of
> the literary criticism he's ever going to require.

> M: Nothing since Dante.

> B: Well, bits and pieces, but not much.

> M: Yes. As you know, it's an enormously big trade. . . . Are
> there any articles that have appeared on your work that
> you've approved of at all?

> B: I think that Kenneth Cox generally shows considerable in-
> sight into anything he writes about, and he has written about
> me. That's all I can really say. Others—well, if they're polite,
> one is grateful; if they're not polite, one takes no notice.
> Mainly if anything is printed about me I don't ever even see
> it, so that it doesn't matter.

Luckily, Mottram did not ask any questions about bibliographers.

45. Suter, Anthony. "Basil Bunting et Mallarmé." *Annales/Uni-
versité de Toulouse-Le Mirail*, 1976, pp. 137-40.

Suter here traces to the influence of Mallarmé certain recurrent poetic devices in Bunting's verse: the cultivation of a deliberate syntactic ambiguity, the use of punctuation to define rhythmic rather
than syntactic units, and the use of the "white spaces" on the page
to indicate "silences," thereby "regulating the tempo and the tonality of the verse." In general, Suter sees both Mallarmé and Bunting
as exponents of a "musical" approach to poetry. [B.H.]

46. Reagan, Dale. "An Interview with Basil Bunting." *Montemora*, Spring 1977, pp. 67-80.

The Dale Reagan interview [1975], different from most others, con-
centrated on intellectual and ontological questions. Reagan begins
by asking Bunting about a number of writers seldom mentioned in
earlier interviews: Swift, Wittgenstein, and Niedecker. Bunting ap-
proves of Swift because, of all men, he is "easily the chief master
of English prose and particularly English syntax." He thinks that
anybody who wants to write good English, prose or poetry, should

"turn to Swift's prose and see what the language is capable of."
Reagan asked him also about his affinity with Swift's "view of life"
or "the kind of pessimism that is found in *Gulliver's Travels*."
Bunting replied:

> Yes, I was addicted to Swift and his look of things, an outlook
> which is grimmer than is often realized. Swift didn't admire the
> species man and neither do I. It's true that by considering one-
> self as just a product of the various chemicals that one is made
> up of, it is easy not to bother. So long as you stay clear of hu-
> manism there is nothing to complain of. But if one is obliged to
> judge things from a humanistic point of view, there is no escape
> from pessimism. The Middle Ages distorted God, making a God
> who cared only for humans. Then the Renaissance came along
> and substituted man for God at the centre of things. If you do
> that, Swift's pessimism is inevitable. The universe is very large
> and in it man is no more important than animals or trees.

Upon this startling response, Reagan asked, "Is there any place in
your world for God or religion?" And he received an answer of
equally telling force:

> I have no use for religion conceived as church forms or as be-
> lieving as historical fact what are ancient parables, but I do be-
> lieve that there is a possibility of a kind of reverence for the
> whole creation which I feel we all ought to have in our bones
> if we don't, a kind of pantheism, I suppose. If the word "God"
> is to have any use it must include everything. The only way to
> know anything is to consider yourself a student of histology,
> finding out as much as carefully controlled commonsense can
> find out about the world. In so doing, you will be contributing
> to the histology of God.

This response led to a question about Wittgenstein.

> I can't say that I know much of his writing, but when I was a
> student *Tractatus Logico-Philosophicus* appeared and although
> parts of it were, and still are, beyond my comprehension, the
> thing as a whole has always pleased me, and the final conclusion,
> "Wovon man nicht sprechen kann darüber muss man schweigen"
> is so amusing a piece of irony after that long book that, well, I
> felt a fondness for Wittgenstein.

From here the dialog went on to remarks about Lucretius ["able
to make poetry out of scientific lingo"] Catullus ["nearer in time to
the old Roman stuff . . . than the other lyrical writers"] and other
writers such as Hugh MacDiarmid and Joseph Skipsey, until it came
to Lorine Niedecker. Reagan observed that she has very few readers
and asked, "Do you see any hope of that changing?"

> I think that is bound to change. People do get completely for-
> gotten sometimes, but on the whole people get resurrected with-
> in a short while. It's very rarely that they have to wait as long as
> Father Hopkins or Emily Dickinson, and in Lorine's case, since
> she was known to, and praised by, a number of good poets, a
> number of people who have a say in what is regarded, I think
> it won't be too long before it is recognized that America had
> there a very fine poetess. Zukofsky was her friend most of her
> life. She had correspondence with a number of other people, I
> can't tell you exactly which, but I think Dr. Williams was one.
> She was known to me and Cid Corman and others. Jonathan
> Williams was taking an interest in her before she died.

The conversation then went to Zukofsky and the "Objectivists" and the fact that Zukofsky always said no such thing as an objectivist movement ever existed. Since *An "Objectivists" Anthology* had a lot of Bunting in it, Reagan asked if he thought his poetry "had much in common with that of the other poets in the collection." Said Bunting:

> Precious little. That was also Zukofsky's view. I think that he would probably have omitted me altogether but submitted me to pressure from Pound, possibly also from Reznikoff. I wasn't anxious to be with them because I didn't like the manifesto he had decided on. And this in spite of the fact that so far as there is any having things in common, some general principles which were very much akin to the same general principles Ezra had laid down long before, and Wordsworth a hundred years before that again, apart from a few general principles, there wasn't much to have in common; but those I did have with Zukofsky. Some of the others, though, seemed to me at that date not to have made terms with the elementary demands of straight vocabulary and straight syntax, and so forth. I still have much the same feeling. I have a very great admiration for Zukofsky and find a great deal to admire in Reznikoff, but the others, well, they're just poets.

Reagan then asked about the editing Pound did on "Villon" which led to an interesting dialog:

> R: I would like to pick up on your reference to Pound and ask you about the kind of influence he had on your writing. It's well known that he had something to do with the final shape of your first long poem, "Villon", inasmuch as he edited it for you. Do you remember what was involved in his editing?

> B: Well, he must have chopped out at least one fifth, perhaps one quarter of the first two parts, maybe more than that. He didn't touch the third part because he said, "I don't know what you young fellows are up to nowadays!"

> R: Did he suggest changes in any of your other poems?

> B: Except that he rescued one or two of them from the wastepaper basket which they were destined for, no, I don't think so.

> R: In these early years did Pound encourage you to work on translation as a means of learning your craft?

> B: Yes he did, but it was the obvious thing to do in any case. When you are young and haven't anything to say except perhaps, "I feel so bad but I don't know why," it's as well to apply yourself to the job of learning what has been done in poetry. It gives you standards to measure your own work against.

> R: How do you approach the task of making a poem written in another language available in English?

> B: It isn't in fact possible. The business of translation seems to me a very good exercise but one which I now feel it's perhaps a pity to carry further than the wastepaper basket. I think, of course, if I started over again about half my book wouldn't be there, including most of the things which figure as translations. What you might do with a great deal of luck is to pick up the accent of somebody and reproduce that more or less. I tried to do it with a translation of Horace recently and I don't know that it was really any good; but it's a slight

change from the usual things, which would give you the meaning of what Horace *said*, which wasn't what Horace meant, of course.

R: One poem of Pound's that seems to have been particularly important to you as an example of what might be done in poetry was "Homage to Sextus Propertius". In a review of Pound's poetry in 1932 you remarked that it was "the most important poem of our time, surpassing alike 'Mauberley' and *The Waste Land.*" What qualities made this poem special for you?

B: I think "Homage to Sextus Propertius" was the first poem which is consciously using the rhythmic material of music in the manner in which it was used, in a small number of his best poems, by Walt Whitman, but possibly with greater skill, and shows a rhythmic variety which is very pleasing and very important to my mind. People have spent their time thinking instead about irony and so forth. That's there, but the thing that is important is a change in the view of rhythm and in the use of rhythm. "Propertius" is the first poem he wrote in that way.

These remarks led to questions about music as a formal model for poetry, in particular Pound's use of the fugue and his own use of the sonata. Since Bunting's response was the most detailed we have, I give it in full:

I don't think Pound was interested in the fugue more than other things. Zukofsky took great pains over the fugue. Pound did indeed think of the possibilities of the fugue as the only kind of polyphonic music he was really familiar with for wedding lots and lots of different themes together. I thought that it was foolish, for me at any rate, to think in terms of polyphonic stuff when I have in fact only one voice and can't sing a duet with myself; and what I hoped to get from music was a form which, however indescribable, is recognizable, and which allows a great variety and a great deal of contrast. At first, when I was very young, I tried to write something that would give the same kind of impression as Beethoven sonatas, but in fact Beethoven, as perhaps I should have known, at the height of the Romantic period, goes in for contrasts which are far too violent for poetry and depends a great deal on things that you can't easily reproduce such as changes in dynamics, and so on. The early eighteenth century composers, particularly the Italians, treated the sonata much more simply. Not only did they not elaborate the actual form itself in the way it was elaborated later on, but you could play through the works of Scarlatti, let's say, in a fairly even way, without exaggeration, and still get an enormous variety of movement, of life in it. I thought that to be able to marry themes, perhaps a little in between what Scarlatti did and what was being done sixty or seventy years later, but to keep more easily within hailing distance of Scarlatti than of Mozart and Beethoven, might give a chance to make shapes; and though of course poetry has different problems than notes, and having once started the thing one moves in a way which is not exactly the same way that music moves, I think that right from the start I did have things which had some of the simplicity of the Italian stuff without having its skill; and at the end I probably got something which has got the skill of the early Italian stuff, but perhaps not the simplicity.

The dialog then went on to observations about other poets and groups. Bunting liked the earlier Auden better than the later

after he had gone in for a "terrific gush of words." Earlier he thought
Auden showed promise:

> When Auden sent his first book to Rapallo I thought there was
> something there that ought to be encouraged. Pound didn't.
> Pound thought there was nothing there and there'd never come
> out of it anything but bunk. I tried to write and suggest to
> Auden the way I thought things should go. He wrote back, quite
> pleasantly, but stating that what he really wanted to do was go
> on teaching rugby football at a prep school.

As for the group as the whole [Auden, Spender, MacNeice *et al*]:
"When you begin to take three pages to say what someone who
writes like Zukofsky would say in four lines, well . . .":

> The didn't even, I think, understand the kind of thing they were
> attempting to do. During the years in which they were wishing
> to stir up the multitudes, or professing to wish to stir up the
> multitudes, they might surely have taken a lesson or two from
> Rudyard Kipling who understood how to do it and who didn't
> waste words at all.

As for Bloomsbury? Well, again . . .:

> What I resented about the Bloomsbury group in particular might
> be said to be two things: one, a certain cocksureness which in
> particular made me distrust Maynard Keynes. The other was that
> they were all of that well-to-do middle class, bordering on county
> gentry who felt that if you couldn't afford to live in Blooms-
> bury or Regent's Park or some similar, desirable, but very ex-
> pensive part of the world, well, poor devil, there wasn't much to
> be expected from you. Then also, their patronage was something
> I didn't like the smell of. They took up a fellow like Lawrence,
> for instance, and Lawrence was, unfortunately, very willing to be
> taken up by the rich. I think they spoilt what chances he had of
> being a good writer. They were quite considerable at the time.

And what about poetry becoming "too arcane":

> Yes, things go wrong from time to time, fashions are carried too
> far, habits are pushed to a limit, and so forth. You could say if
> you like that Dante encourages, he doesn't actually require but
> he certainly encourages, the commentator standing beside you
> all the time to tell you just who everybody is, what everything is,
> how the shape goes, and so forth, and you would say that that is
> carrying things to an absurd point. The same would be true with
> Ezra Pound's *Cantos*. So far of course we haven't had six cen-
> turies, which have gone by since Dante's poem, of continual
> commentary to reduce Ezra Pound to a series of footnotes. But
> there's something both to be said for writing so that footnotes
> are not going to be required and something for writing in a way
> which does, I'm afraid, appeal to footnote writers but which
> doesn't make them absolutely necessary. Pound is dependent
> really and truly most of the time upon the noise that his poem
> makes and every time you interrupt the noise to go and look up
> a commentator, or even simply to recollect in your mind what
> the commentator might have said, you get in the way of the flow
> of noise, the flow of sound.

The dialog then went on about stanzaic forms of poetry and
returned to the extraordinary importance of Dante for any serious
poet:

> When I became acquainted first with the work and then with
> the persons of Pound and Eliot what astonished me and made
> me so enthusiastic was that here were men who were doing and

who had been doing all the time, though I had been unaware of it, the things which I had painfully worked out for myself were the things necessary to do with poetry, but we'd arrived by quite different roads at this conclusion. Only a very small part of my road to these ideas coincides with Pound's road or Eliot's road. The chief part of that would be that we were all three very enthusiastic readers of Dante. I think that for anybody who has enough Italian to read Dante, Dante is always going to be one of the chief influences on them, whoever they are, whenever they are.

Reagan noted that in the early Odes Bunting over and over draws on Cantos 7 and 8 of the *Inferno* and asked why?:

The whole of the *Divina Commedia*, not only the *Inferno*, is something which no man can forget, no man can be uninfluenced by, and different people possibly get more attracted to different parts of it and for different reasons. My reasons for having a special affection for certain parts are simply the enormous power of the words in Dante which is most manifest of all, I suppose, in the final Cantos of the *Paradiso*, which everybody knows, where he is dealing with the light of the final godhead and so forth, but which has many other places where the sheer enormous skill of the choice of words and the choice of the sound the words make carries you along, gives you a feel of the thing. One of those spots happens to be the one at which Dante and Virgil were held up outside the city of Dis by the devils who brought Medusa to turn them into stone and who are quelled by the arrival of an angel floating over the Styx. Quite marvellous. They are amongst the very greatest moments of poetry and one remembers them in the same way that one remembers some passages from other poets. The one in Firdosi which I made use of in *Briggflatts* of Alexander climbing the mountain and seeing on the top the Angel of the Resurrection ready to blow the trumpet and put an end to the world. And it's not merely because the incident itself is striking but because the words make it so much more striking.

The interview closed with a fascinating interchange which might seem to reinforce Bunting's dogged pessimism. But if one listens to him long enough, one is led to think that he is pessimistic about particular moments in history rather than history teleologically: A million years in the future? Man, as presently designed, may well be a momentary aberration among the species and destroy himself. But the earth and the universe will continue to unfold in all its mystery and splendor. Reagan noted Bunting's remarks that "God is the dividing sword" and that "order is no more than an unfortunate accident that sometimes hampers civilization," and asked could he explain. He certainly could:

B: "God is the dividing sword" is a quotation from my poem "The Spoils." It means what it says, that all this sweet peace and brotherhood and so on is not the way things work, not by any wickedness of human kind, but by the way the world is organized. What progress is made is always made as the result of violent disturbances of one sort or another, whether you begin by talking about an amoeba or by talking about men. Once you settle down into the kind of thing that the Chinese had for centuries and that the Russians are trying to inaugurate, progress will be near nil in the end; nothing new will happen in such a society. So far as that particular aspect of things go, you might say that I prefer even the horrors of capitalism, but there are better things than either. That order is an unfortunate accident you can verify at once by seeing what happened when the Roman Empire succeeded in establishing itself a "pax Romana" on Mediterranean lands. Everything went flat. Things had been going fine up till then.

R: A final question: You have been accused by some critics of lacking a concern for social man, for the problems and realities of the twentieth century man in society. In the first place, do you think this is true, and if it is true, do you think it's a shortcoming?

B: I don't think it matters in the least one way or the other, but I think that what the critics mean is that I am not naive enough to pick up the party battle cries of current students and other superficial people. I don't think that what is wrong with the world is that there is a war in Vietnam. There isn't any longer and things are just as bad with the world; or I don't feel that I am called upon to join the Communist Party or any of these sort of bloody things. Why the hell should I? I am allowed to feel that history is a very complicated thing indeed and that all these easy ways of putting things right are a lot of bloody nonsense.

And that, we may say, takes care of that—at least from one fascinating poet's point of view. [C.F.T.]

47. Johnstone, Paul. "Basil Bunting: Taken from two interviews, recorded by Paul Johnstone in April 1974 and April 1975." *meantime*, April 1977, pp. 67-80.

Broadly speaking, these two interviews deal with Bunting's reaction to various modern poets and the course that poetry has taken in the twentieth-century. Bunting responds to the work of such poets as Dorn, Snyder, Duncan, Creeley, J. Williams, S. Smith, and Herrick. Pound, Eliot, W.C. Williams, and Zukofsky are dealt with at great length, but here Bunting is not reacting so much to their poetry as to their poetic techniques. Johnstone's interests, as reflected in his questions, lie not so much in discussing particular poems or themes of Bunting's as in discovering the sources of his methods or those persons who were important in influencing his use or adoption of certain methods.

48. Metz, Roberta. "Touched By The Poet." *St. Andrews Review*, Spring/Summer 1977, p. 43.

This is a very short (3 paragraph) article containing a couple of anecdotes expressing Roberta Metz's fond memories of time spent with Bunting.

49, Swann, Brian. "Basil Bunting of Northumberland." *St. Andrews Review*, Spring/Summer 1977, pp. 33-41.

Swann begins his article which records his meeting with Basil Bunting in 1974 with a quote from a previous interview with the Regional Arts Director of the Northern Arts Council. The Director is speaking of Bunting:

"I think his efforts in that direction are a bit fatuous. He's got no followers and has had no effect. He is rather an eccentric. And I think it's nonsense when he says poetry is just sound and that meaning is hardly ever important. As for dialectic, I myself have none and I cannot read anything in dialect. I'm thrown off by dialect words. I think it's affected. . . . Northumberland is dead, and it's so-called folk-culture. . . ."

"No poets?" I said.

"Poets. Well, there's Fred Reed. I think he's quite good. There's Sid Chapin, but he's a novelist. There's, let's see, Tom Pickard, whom Bunting regards as his successor, but he's played out before thirty. There isn't much local talent. . . ."

The Director then handed Swann a brochure put out by the Northern Arts Council:

It was full of imported arts, mostly music and dance. Northumberland was still a kind of outpost of the empire. What Basil Bunting had written in his introduction to Tom Pickard's *High on the Walls* began to take on meaning: "He has to endure the hatred of art which persists in the North of England, the insolence of officials and of those who pirate the money suscribed 'for the arts'." When I went home I re-read "What the Chairman told Tom."

These comments serve as a background for Swann's meeting with Bunting at his home in Wylam and for Swann's discussion of Bunting as a Northumberland poet. He says:

In some ways, Bunting is an American poet, since his closest modern ties are to Pound, Williams, Oppen, Zukofsky. But to me he was something particularly Northumbrian, even in his internationalism.

Swann concentrates neither on Bunting's biography nor on his poetry, but rather he tries to give the reader some insight into "Basil Bunting *of Northumberland*" (italics mine). Part of Swann's attempt is simply to show Basil Bunting at home in Northumberland. But in addition to merely describing Bunting's home life, Swann also goes on to relate portions of his conversation with Bunting which deal with Joseph Skipsey, the use of dialect in poetry, the Lindisfarne Gospels and art-history to name but a few of the topics dealt with. But no matter what the topic, Swann's focus is consistent and might best be summed up by the quote of Bunting at the beginning of the article: "I belong to Northumberland, I want to finish in Northumberland, if the bloody Northumbrians will let me."

50. Williams, Jonathan and Tom Meyer. "A Conversation with Basil Bunting." *St. Andrews Review*, Spring/Summer 1977, pp. 21-32. [Reprinted in *Poetry Information 19*, Summer 1978.]

This interview took place following a reading by Bunting at St. Andrews Presbyterian College on April 16, 1976. Due to the public nature of the conversation, the questions and answers are fairly general and often center on topics discussed at greater length in previously published interviews. The sound of poetry, the (im)possibility of writing long poems, and the use of literary allusions are just a few of the topics covered.

Two questions and answers deserve mention here. Jonathan

Williams questioned Bunting about the anthology of poetry he had brewing:

> The plan was not to put in the best poets necessarily, or the best poems, but to try and demonstrate, from the English everybody knows—without going to Old English, and even excluding Middle English—to try and show the principles on which poetry works.
>   . . . Right up to 1640 you can say that a poet wasn't a poet unless he was capable of playing a musical instrument and composing his poems to that. . . .
>   If you will read Wyatt and Sidney and Campion you'll get a good idea of poetry as song. But Sidney's slightly older contemporary, Spenser, invented a new thing which has given a complexion to English verse ever since, so one must have Spenser there also. Spenser made the words produce their own music, instead of depending on the musician to do it.

Skipping to the twentieth-century, Bunting says of his contemporaries:

> I should say Yeats and Pound and Eliot with David Jones, the Welshman, Hugh MacDiarmid, the Scotsman, and Louis Zukofsky, the son of an immigrant Jew in New York, provide a galaxy of poets as splendid as any century can show, and I hope that when things get filtered down by time they will all be clearly visible still.

In answer to a question from the audience, Bunting states that he would include the following female poets: Lorine Niedecker, Marianne Moore, and Christina Rosetti.

Finally a member of the audience asked: "Do you think that Pound was crazy at all?" Said Bunting:

> How many of us are not crazy? I don't know. I know very few people who are not crazy, and I think that unless my friends are a bit daft and I can laugh at them, they're not likely to be friends. Pound always had in him some things which were awkward, hard to explain and so forth, and a very great deal which was sheer generosity and kindness to everything around him. Ah well, Jonathan—Jonathan is obviously mad—what on earth! But Jonathan is one of the kindest men I'm sure you'll find in North America, I'm quite sure, so we've got to put up with his occasional madness.

And Basil Bunting???

51. Davie, Donald. "English and American in *Briggflatts*." *PN Review*, No. 5, 1977, pp. 17-20. [Reprinted in *The Poet in the Imaginary Museum*, Garcarnet Press, 1977.]

Davie begins his article by questioning how the critic should classify Bunting; he seems to be a unique poet in that, "His sensibility is profoundly English—not British but *English*, and Northumbrian English at that; and yet his techniques, his acknowledged masters and peers in the present century, are all of them American."

Davie builds his argument by first tying Bunting's use of techniques into the Objectivist school of thought and then secondly showing what is uniquely English in Bunting's use of those techniques. Much of Bunting's allegiance to the Objectivist doctrine—the necessity of form, the objectification of the poem—is obvious from what he has said about his poems in various published interviews (for example, the discussion of the form of *Briggflatts* is treated at length in Bunting's interview with Warren Tallman and Peter Quartermain, reviewed below).

But the interesting twist in Davie's article concerns the way in which Bunting differs from his American friends and peers:

> When Basil Bunting says, "Pound has had a great influence on me, of course, but Wordsworth has had a steady, solid one all my life on everything," he declares an allegiance that none of his American associates, not excluding Pound, would subscribe to. And it is somewhere here that one starts differentiating this English "objectivist' from the Americans, and envisaging the possibility of a distinctively English version of this otherwise all-American movement.

Davie ends by suggesting "that for the English poet the writing of poems is a public and social activity, as for his American peers it isn't." What Davie finds so amazing in Bunting's poetry is the degree to which these two aims are combined:

> I will show my hand without more equivocation, and assert that it is writing of this quality—so compact, having no syllables to spare for nudges or tipping the wink—that English poetry needs to assimulate and build on. Only when we have done that shall we be able to deny Oppen's and Kenner's contention that the whole Objectivist endeavour is "an American movement". Why should we want to do that? For our own good, I think. And, heaven knows, the matter that Bunting packs into *Briggflatts*, the content of it, the experience that it re-creates and celebrates, is indelibly and specifically English enough to satisfy anybody. He has shown us that the achievement is abundantly possible, if only we choose to emulate it.

52. Williams, Jonathan, ed. *Madeira & Toasts for Basil Bunting's 75th Birthday.* Jargon Book no. 66, The Jargon Society, North Carolina, 1977.

Just as the title suggests, this book is a collection of toasts, both prose and poetic, to Basil Bunting on his 75th birthday. The book is amusing and delightful as many short anecdotes about Bunting slip out in the course of the toasts. Close to 90 people contributed, including Cid Corman, Kenneth Cox, Robert Creeley, Guy Davenport, Allen Ginsberg, Hugh Kenner, Hugh MacDiarmid, Thomas Meyer, Eric Mottram, Tom Pickard, Charles Reznikoff, Jonathan Williams, and Celia and Louis Zukofsky. The problem with such a book as this is aptly set out by Russell Banks in the very first toast:

> How do you chat with the author of poems that have made it impossible for you to use the language the same way ever again? You can't really *thank* him for it.

And his solution:

> And then it occurred to me that the best reason for a young writer to meet an older writer is the possibility that he might learn a few manners. *Practically everything of consequence is in the work.* [Italics mine.]

That sounds a lot like . . . Cheers!

53. Dale, Peter. "Basil Bunting and the Quonk and Groggle

School of Poetry." *Agenda*, Spring 1978, pp. 55-65.

Dale begins with two quotes from Bunting concerning *Briggflatts*:
"The attempt to find any meaning in it would be manifestly ab-
surd." And, "Southrons would maul the music of many lines in
Briggflatts." Dale responds:

> . . . since it is Bunting's purpose as a poet to move us by sound,
> arguing that this is what all poetry does, pure and simple, one
> should so be moved in order to speak fairly of the work. Unfor-
> tunately, I am not moved consistently by the work, finding a
> touch of obscurantism and what music it has of a rather primi-
> tive and contrived kind. The remarks and reflections which fol-
> low may thus be discounted as those of a hostile witness. . . .

Dale first tries to show that "Bunting massively contradicts himself
in that meaning is easy enough to detect in *Briggflatts*." In support
of this assertion, he merely sums up some of the main themes of the
poem. Unfortunately, this short paragraph gives the reader no more
information as to the poem's meaning than Bunting has been willing
to supply to the reader in his various interviews.

What Dale does set out to attack, in some force, is Bunting's
analogy of poetry with music. Dale states:

> The analogy of poetry with music is a dangerous one for two
> basic reasons: first, poetry has severe limits in pitch, key, tone,
> and range; nor can it orchestrate; second, it does not have notes
> devoid of referrents as music largely does. Words mean—if the
> poet discards their meaning the hearing mind puts them back,
> just as it picks up echoes of its own tongue in an unknown
> foreign speech. It is interesting that the sound-merchants never
> go as far as creating neologisms in English phonetics nor aban-
> don entirely the syntactical structures of their native tongue.
> Another thing that makes it a dangerous analogy is that users
> slip between two aspects of music: one as a set of scale-systems
> of sounds, the other as a set of structural principles like sonata-
> form. This use of musical form is ultimately a mere metaphori-
> cal usage. There's a touch of both aspects in *Briggflatts*. In
> general, the musical approach is nearly always a form of anti-
> rationalism.

What Dale goes on to try to show is that "The purely musical or
sonic effects of poetry are a much more limited lingo than that of
music itself." To do so, he quotes from Johnson's *Life of Pope*,
often changing Johnson's examples as he goes.

Finally, Dale suggests that *Briggflatts'* claims to musicality
prompt a comparison to works by Chaucer, Shakespeare, Milton,
Tennyson, Pound and Eliot, "the closest comparison actually being
Four Quartets which clearly by contrast illustrates a coarsening in
Briggflatts of the musical tradition."

> The most obvious way in which *Briggflatts* is not a step for-
> ward in the tradition is the poverty of its use of syntax. The
> poem is tediously dominated by the simple sentence, extended
> by appositional developments to subject and object. In addition
> to this the custom of English in excising a repeated subject pro-
> noun makes this appositional effect sound worse. Along with
> these appositions goes a considerable reliance upon present par-
> ticiples.

As further examples Dale cites Bunting's use of trite rhyming bobs

(In the grave's slot/he lies. We rot.) and mid-line rhymes.
Dale concludes:

> In Davie's book of essays, *The Poet in the Imaginary Museum*,
> he suggests that the musical and sculptural analogies for poetry
> were conveniences of thought he personally had found useful
> though they should be discarded by anyone who found them less
> than useful. This is clearly the way in which Bunting has used
> them. His peak diagram, his Scarlatti, and his insistence upon
> music have been ways to enable him to extrude the matter of
> *Briggflatts*, some of which he suggests in interview, lies too deep
> in the subconscious for his rational explication. Such crutches
> have their uses. Bunting's error is his persistence in trying to give
> poetry the same crutches. . . . The way forward, for some, may
> not be the obligatory *Briggflatts* but the way back into the full
> articulations of metric and syntax or the grand old English com-
> promise of strong meaning and haunting music that Geoffrey
> Hill masters.

54. Hamburger, Michael. "A Note." *Agenda*, Spring 1978, pp.
    99-100.

   This short note is reprinted from *Medeira & Toasts for Basil Bunting's 75th Birthday* and is entitled "Gratulatory Variation for Basil
   Bunting with an Inaudible Ground-Bass, Growled." The note—or
   toast—is an elaboration on the phrase, "Minor poet, not conspicu-
   ously dishonest."

55. John, Roland. "Basil Bunting: A Note." *Agenda*, Spring 1978,
    pp. 101-105.

   This short article explores some of the possible reasons for the critical neglect of Bunting's work. One paragraph deserves quotation
   here:

> We have then an expert, a master craftsman, a witty transla-
> tor and explainer, a poet whose rhythms move towards music
> and with all these talents it is hard to see why Bunting is not a
> major poet. Admittedly the output is small; but there are splen-
> did long poems like *The Spoils* and *Briggflatts*, so often the mark
> of a major poet. I believe that he fails due to his lack of didacti-
> cism, he does not preach nor demand disciples, he has founded
> no school. In the preface to the *Collected Poems* he says, "With
> sleights learned from others and an ear open to melodic analogies
> I have set down words as a musician pricks his score, not to be
> read in silence, *but to trace in the air* a pattern of sound that
> may sometimes, *I hope be pleasing. Unabashed boys and girls
> may enjoy them.* This book is theirs." (My italics.) The phrases
> I have noted show the debt to Pound; but also the lack of a
> distinct base, there is almost a take it or leave it attitude; but
> more important it shows that Bunting has never crawled after
> success. It calls to mind the lines from his famous poem "on The
> Fly-Leaf of Pound's Cantos."
>
>> There they are, you will have to go a long way round
>> if you want to avoid them.

56. Makin, Peter. "Bunting and Sound." *Agenda*, Spring 1978,
    pp. 66-81.

   Makin begins his article with a general question about poetry: given
   that emotion is of interest, to what degree can the sound of the

poem communicate emotion? Speaking of Bunting, he says:

> His line, for example, only exists as an aural event. He insists that the way his words are cut up the page has no significance except as a minor aid, for the reader, to grasping how the words should be read. Were the age less ignorant in reading, he would prefer to write his verse out like prose (as, for example, the scribes who wrote Provençal verse did), so that patterning of sound might come through of itself, if it were strong enough to do so, and might sink if it were not.
>
> With a traditional regular English metric, layout of words on the page very clearly reflects sound: a graspable number of stresses is made to coincide more often than not with a syntactical event, and so one notes very clearly the moment when the line has ended. But Bunting's verse is "freer"; perhaps his talk of sound inhering in his line should be treated with gentle scepticism, as interviewers have tended to treat his talk of sound in general.

By citing examples of sound patterning in Bunting's own works and by comparing Bunting's techniques to other writers (Dante, Creeley, Reznikoff), Makin tries to show that Bunting does not betray his own claim that what matters in poetry is sound. Makin suggests that for Bunting,

> There is no sound-element that is not necessitated by the overall development of the meaning; nor is there any sound-element that is left out of the patterning; the patterning cannot be resolved except into a scheme that is essentially cruder than it. [Here he considers a passage from *The Spoils*.] . . . The demands are two: that there should be constant surprise, or invention; and that emphases, tensions, etc., produced by the whole patterning should add to, not hinder, the development of the thought. If ever, in the immediate area, any one of these types of sound-repeat is done again, it is never in the same "location" of other structural elements. The trick is to set up an expectation and then defeat or twist its fulfilment. . . . The art of this interweave is like the cunning surprises of the Lindisfarne manuscripts, which take their barbarous sinuosities from the animal motifs that are found across the Asian landmass from Sinkiang to Scandinavia; but also like those of the interweave of sounds in Old English verse. Like all rules of patterning, the rule "never repeat identically" is only an expectation itself, which can be defeated with even greater effect. . . . [Here he quotes from *Briggflatts*.]

In addition to Bunting's use of techniques found in the Lindisfarne manuscripts and Old English verse, Makin also argues that, like Pound, Bunting made use of the patterning of long and short syllables as used in classical Greek and Latin poetry. The range and sophistication of Bunting's techniques are summed up by Makin in these words:

> A principle of Bunting's verse, then, is vowel and consonant sound producing tendencies of inherent speed, in tension with speed produced by stressing, in tension with speed suggested by syntax; and all the aural elements—pitch and colouring of individual syllables— are brought out and flexed and given their due weighting by the attention drawn to them by these patternings. The human voice once more is an instrument whose modulation will carry complexities of emotion equivalent to those implicit in any orchestral work.

Voila!

57. Quartermain, Peter and Warren Tallman. "Basil Bunting Talks about *Briggflatts*." *Agenda*, Spring 1978, pp. 3-19. [This is a slightly amended version of the interview which first appeared in *Writing (Georgia Straight, Writing Supplement)*, No. 6 (Vancouver, B.C.), November 18-25, 1970.]

> According to Bunting, before he so much as wrote a line of *Briggflatts*, he had a notion of its structure in his mind. In this interview, Bunting draws out his peak diagram for *Briggflatts*:
>
>> You're going to have five parts because it's got to be an uneven number. So that the central one should be the one apex, there. But what is new, the only new thing that I knew of in, in doing it, was that instead of having one climax in the other parts you have two. In the first two the first climax is the less and another immediately comes out of it when you're not expecting it. So you have it for those two. In the others the first climax is the greater and it trails off. . . .
>
> Each of the five peaks also had a Latin motto (of the five mottoes, Bunting recalls only one), and with the exception of the middle peak, the other four correspond to spring, summer, autumn, and winter. This diagram of the climaxes provides the emotional and chronological structure of the poem. But according to Bunting, there was a second shaping influence: "The other thing is that the *B minor fugato* sonata of Scarlatti is in my mind from the same time as the diagram."
>
> This interview provides an interesting look into the creative process; but Bunting allows the interviewer and reader only a quick glance, for when quizzed as to the poem's meaning or definitive interpretation, he replies: ". . . oh what the hell, I don't know. You're asking for things which are too far down, hid in the subconscious, to be brought out without falsifying it in a way."

58. Suter, Anthony. "Musical Structure." *Agenda*, Spring 1978, pp. 46-54.

> Suter begins his article with a reference to the dispute between Basil Bunting and Peter Ure over the nature of poetry, the latter having claimed that by reducing poetry to sound alone, Bunting has overlooked the importance of the structure of meaning. The point of Suter's article is to show that, ". . . the paradox of the whole situation is that inevitably Bunting's poetry does deal in the structure of meanings and, moreover, the meanings are organised according to a musical architecture—that of sonata form."
>
> Suter begins his analysis with "Villon" and "Aus dem zweiten Reich," trying to show in each case how the main themes of each part of the poems fall into the sonata form ABA. He then tries to show how "Attis" and "The Well of Lycopolis" "represent a testing ground" or transitional stage between the early sonatas which have a relatively simple form and *The Spoils* and *Briggflatts* which have more complex forms. Suter states:
>
>> As the sonata becomes more complex, it does so from the inside, from Bunting's own development of sonata form. He took a

fixed model to begin with, but when he found that model too limiting he did not seek a more complicated one that was ready-made for him (such as a Beethoven sonata); he sought to expand and experiment the basic form he had chosen in the beginning.

Thus, the reader can still find the basic sonata elements—statement, recapitulation and development—found in the early poems, but he will not find them in such strict parallels. For example, *Briggflatts* ". . . treats its thematic material in reverse. Whereas *The Spoils* states its theme at the beginning like a classical symphony, *Briggflatts* hides the real nature of its central thematic ideas until the end." Suter ends his paper with a discussion of "symbolism of a musical nature" as found in *Briggflatts*.

59. Suter, Anthony. "Imagery & Symbolism." *Agenda*, Spring 1978, pp. 82-98.

In this fairly straightforward article on images and symbols in Bunting's poetry, Suter draws examples from all of the major poems and many of the *Odes*; special emphasis, however, is given to examples drawn from *Briggflatts*. Suter begins with a discussion of Bunting's fairly conventional use of images in his early works. He then quickly moves to a discussion of music imagery in *Briggflatts*, "where he [Bunting] frequently sees a musical pattern in nature."

Suter soon moves on to a discussion of Bunting's symbolism, for he says:

The sea in Bunting's poetry shows how the boundary between image and symbol is sometimes ill-defined. Also, it indicates that his symbolism is not referential in a facile way: it is definitely post-"Symboliste". It avoids, however, obscurity, because the context of the long poem informs symbol (and vice versa). Sometimes the whole of a poem becomes a symbol.

Odes I, 13 (1929) Suter suggests is symbolic of the dangers of Fascism, and "Even the long poem, *Briggflatts*, could be considered in its totality as a pure symbol in that it is the autobiography of *any* artist, just as the whole of a Shakespeare play, such as *King Lear* or *A Winter's Tale*, can be seen as a symbol of the total human condition." Specific symbols drawn from *Briggflatts* which Suter discusses include the rat (used as a "shock" image), the mason, and the slowworm.

60. Wainwright, Jeffrey. "William Wordsworth at *Briggflatts*." *Agenda*, Spring 1978, pp. 37-45.

Basil Bunting has mentioned on numerous occasions the influence William Wordsworth's poetry has had on his life, and as Wainwright says, "Basil Bunting holds the matter of northern England so much in common with his predecessor." In light of these facts, it seems odd that no one chose to write on the Wordsworth-Bunting connection until Wainwright did which makes Wainwright's article significant.

He focuses mainly on technique and structure in "Tintern Abbey" and *Briggflatts*. Wainwright argues that Bunting has "the same feel for the simple word and the solid power of the

monosyllable" that Wordsworth had and, furthermore, that Bunting's use of an Old and Middle English vocabulary is an attempt to
recover, at least partially, the language of northern England.

In terms of structure, both poems open with the sound of
water, in one case the Wye, in the other the Rawthey. And while
Wainwright is quick to point out differences in the two poems'
structures:

> The fundamental and indeed traditional elements of *Briggflatts*,
> some of which I have stressed so far, would not appear to in-
> clude the poem's structure. Its sequential structure, the juxta-
> position of different times and scenes and statements without
> an overt narrative or discursive procedure is notably modern.

He is also intent on pointing out similarities:

> "Tintern Abbey" itself is, like *Briggflatts*, a poem of recall and
> recovery, following the movements and shifts of the poet's con-
> sciousness in response to the physical world and the world of
> memory. To the extent that this movement is characterised by
> "transitions, and the impassioned music of the versification,"
> then we might see, besides other resemblances, some structural
> similarity between the two poems.

61. Gardner, Raymond. "Put out more Bunting." *Arts Guardian*,
March 10, 1978 [p. 10, c. 1,2].

This short, 10-paragraph newspaper article announces a party for
Bunting to celebrate the republishing of *Collected Poems* by Oxford
University Press. For the most part, the article deals with the English
public's neglect of Bunting and his work.

62. Loloi, Parvin and Glyn Pursglove. "Basil Bunting's Persian
Overdrafts: A Commentary." *Poetry Information* 19, Summer 1978, pp. 51-58. [Reprinted elsewhere in this book,
pp. 343-353.]

63. Meyer, Thomas. "*Collected Poems* (1968): A Few Observations, Some Remarks." *Poetry Information* 19, Summer
1978, pp. 30-36.

Meyer begins his article with a thorough analysis of vowel and consonant patterns in the third part of "Villon." But he goes on to
make the following disclaimer about his analysis:

> Understand though, all my talk remains semaphore, and when I
> make so bold as to pick out consonants, vowel schemes, images
> or tones of voice I am doing no more than waving a green, red
> checkered or yellow kerchief hoping the flurry of color may
> result in a closely read stanza and the poem (not my message
> about it) begins to click. With that we must also bear in mind,
> no poet, no honest poet ever intends his verse to be scrutinized
> in so awkward and exasperating a manner. When it is, the self-
> appointed critic, at best innocent only of career grubbing and
> name puffing (if he is) is a man who can't contain himself but
> must tell someone, tell the world what delights him.

Meyer certainly comes across in this article as a man possessed by the delights of Bunting's poetry. His purpose in writing on Bunting he says is as follows: "'Sleights learned from others with an ear open to melodic analogies,' if I've been able to point to the simplest, I'll be pleased, but don't count on that pleasure." In attempting this task, Meyer looks at the influences of Pound's poetry, Eliot's poetry, and Latin poetry on Bunting's work. But most importantly, Meyer looks at Bunting's poetry and quotes from the Persian overdrafts, *Briggflatts*, *The Spoils*, and *The Odes*; it is precisely this enthusiasm to look at, to read (aloud), to hear Bunting's poetry that assures the reader that he will profit by having read Meyer's analysis.

64. Mottram, Eric. "'An Acknowledged Land': Love and Poetry in Bunting's Sonatas." *Poetry Information* 19, Summer 1978, pp. 11-19. [Reprinted elsewhere in this book, pp. 77-105.]

65. "Mr. Bunting and the Critics." Ed. Eric Mottram and Peter Hodgkiss, *Poetry Information* 19, Summer 1978, pp. 65-69.

This "selection of criticism" contains excerpts from articles or reviews on Bunting's work by Zukofsky, Kenner, Read, Creeley, Connolly, Brownjohn, Holmes, Dale, Toynbee, Fraser, and Booth (as well as two anonymous authors). The earliest review is dated 1931 and the latest 1978. The majority of the excerpts run two to three paragraphs in length.

66. Quartermain, Peter. "Basil Bunting: The Poet as 'Magnanimous Man.'" *Poetry Information* 19, Summer 1978, pp. 48-50.

The main focus of Quartermain's article is the music/meaning debate which has evolved, at least in part, from Bunting's statements about the purpose of poetry: "poetry is seeking to make not meaning, but beauty; . . . prose exists to convey meaning, and no meaning such as prose conveys can be expressed as well in poetry. This is not poetry's business." From the preceding thought, Quartermain unpacks the following:

> Thought, ideas, passions, meaning, are *not* dismissed from the poem: the poem simply does not *seek* to "make" them; the poem does not serve *them* so much as they serve *it*—much to the chagrin, no doubt, of the interpreters and symbol-hunters. If you read a poem by Basil Bunting, it is indeed identifiably *about* something (there is *matter*—though it is worth noting Bunting's phrasing: "the matter comes after," and is thus, I presume, secondary. And anything at all, it would follow, can be fit matter for poetry), and it arouses *feelings*. It takes some time, a number of readings often, for the poem to work, for the matter to be clear, for the feelings to emerge; the sound, however—if we can voice poems properly—is there from the start.

At this point, Quartermain cites Ode 5, "To Helen Egli," and analyzes the poem's diction—patterns of sound. As Quartermain takes great pains to show, the idea of the poem is really quite simple, *but* "If, reading or talking about the poem, you explicate that idea, you have a great deal less than you started with, and in the process you have quite possibly given yourself the impression that the poem exists for the sake of what it says, for the sake of what the poet wanted to say." Hence, rather than becoming a tool for the advertisement of the poet's thought, the poem achieves a certain sense of independence from the poet. Here Quartermain's quote of Zukofsky is particularly apt: " 'Magnanimity,' Louis Zukofsky says in *Bottom: On Shakespeare*, is 'by nature difficult' when the artist 'loves his own handiwork more than it would love him if it visibly came to life.' "

67. Anderson, Alexandra. "Basil Bunting." *The Poetry Project Newsletter* (New York), No. 31, n.d. pp. 4-7.

> Anderson laments that "only a handful of graduate students know much about Bunting. Combine them with a few poets, poetry addicts and literary archeologists and you have 'a poets' poet'—a figure whose name is familiar to few and whose work is almost totally unexposed." Anderson goes on to give a brief biography of Bunting and a brief analysis of Bunting's use of poetic techniques in hopes of spurring interest in Bunting's work.

68. Slade, V. "*Briggflatts.*" *Tarasque*, No. 3 (Nottingham), n.d., n.p.

> Slade argues that while the inability of the experience of the past, the poet's memory, to comprehend what may be forged out of the newness of living may form "the logical deliberation of the poem," the true achievement of the poem lies elsewhere. For Slade, the achievement of the poem "lies in the way Bunting exploits the strength and penetration of the English language, its syllabic, alliterative qualities, its intonations and gestures controlled in speech, song and metre; his awareness of the accomplishments of other verse as a medium for his own consciousness." Slade compares *Briggflatts* to Old English poetry and Bunting to Chapman, but his final conclusion is that,
>
> > The predominant voice in this poem is that of the skald, the song of the early poet, "before the rules made poetry a pedant's game", the skelping nature of our inherited speech modified by an awareness of the dances and songs of the Renaissance. It is one of the tensions of the poem that, for some experiences, no song, no dance can be found; a galliard by Byrd, a madrigal by Monteverdi appropriate certain vivid occasions,
> >
> > "But who will entune a bogged orchard,
> > its blossom gone."

69. Banks, Russell. "Going to the Source: A Lesson in Good Manners." *Paideuma*, Vol. 9, No. 1 (Spring, 1980), pp. 17-18. [Reprinted from *Madeira & Toasts for Basil Bunting's 75th Birthday*. Ed. Jonathan Williams. Reviewed above.]

> This short anecdote concerns Banks' first encounter with Bunting.

70. Bayes, Ronald. "Balancing Act." *Paideuma*, Vol. 9, No. 1

(Spring, 1980), p. 19. [Reprinted from *Madeira & Toasts for Basil Bunting's 75th Birthday*. Ed. Jonathan Williams. Reviewed above.]

> This is a short, 13-line poem subtitled, "On the Occasion of Basil Bunting's Birthday."

71. Creeley, Robert. "Basil Bunting." *Paideuma*, Vol. 9, No. 1 (Spring, 1980), pp. 13-14.

> Creeley concludes his short tribute to Basil Bunting by quoting "At Briggflatts meetinghouse" to which he replies:
>
>> And for the *art*—such particular sounds of human voice so tuned, to the weaving rhythm, the *dance*-ing *transcience*. . . . What to say *not* said by it? And what else is there ever to say.

72. Dale, Peter. "Bunting and Villon." *Paideuma*, Vol. 9, No. 1 (Spring, 1980), pp. 101-107.

> In "Bunting and Villon," Dale picks up on an argument he made in the previously published "Bunting and the Quonk and Groggle School of Poetry" [reviewed above], namely,
>
>> . . . that in verse the "use of musical form is ultimately a mere metaphorical usage," and that the musical approach is nearly always a form of antirationalism. It is these two points which I hope to amplify in the discussion of Bunting's adoption of "sonata" form for his "Villon."
>
> Dale begins by considering three ways of using musical form in words: 1) by establishing a series of sounds and varying them by inversion or retrogression, 2) by balancing rhythm against metre, and 3) by devising a sort of semantic use of musical form. Dale suggests that Bunting has rejected the second alternative "by largely eschewing metric, English, Greek or otherwise, in favour of a free verse whose music is at worst most subjective—a point illustrated by the eccentricity of the poet's own readings." Furthermore,
>
>> In all these "musical" methods, the literary difficulty is that these things would have to be immediately and sensuously apprehended from the text. In the last method, the problem would also be to confine the perceivers' minds to the aspects of the words, which need to be foregrounded for the musical structure to be apparent.
>
> With the preceding serving as a brief background, Dale goes on to part-by-part analysis of the poem. He argues that "The opening section has no obvious theme-line memorable enough to ring in the mind through the rest of the reading in order to catch the variations as it resonates in the ear." Here he cites a remark made by Kenneth Cox in "A Commentary on Bunting's 'Villon'" [reviewed above]:
>
>> What turns, recurs and changes as the poem proceeds is not so much the words themselves, their rhythms or syllables, as the poet's grasp of his subject.
>
> Thus musical form becomes a set of variations on ideas, and, as Dale says, "It is here that one's bafflement returns for one must deal with

ideas by logic, reason, and some sort of syntax.

Movements II and III are dealt with very briefly: II is often marked by bad poetry, "which one can only assume to be deliberately bad—but why?" Here Dale is referring to Bunting's imprisonment written in octosyllabic couplets. Part III, insofar as it ends with an invocation to precision, stands self-condemned.

> Wherever Villon's lines are cogent and concrete, the results in Bunting are inchoate and vague. Bunting's own lines with their *hardness* and *darkness*, their suppression of sources, their nondescript seas and mountains are not a little vague. This is not to mention the vagaries of the free verse passages. In addition, the poem as a whole lacks conciseness; it is far longer than it should be to imply that the present is better than any abstraction of history and that imagination, particularly musical, has mighty powers. . . .

73. Davenport, Guy. "For Basil Bunting." *Paideuma*, Vol. 9, No. 1 (Spring, 1980), p. 21. [Reprinted from *Madeira & Toasts for Basil Bunting's 75th Birthday*. Ed. Jonathan Williams. Reviewed above.]

Davenport ends his poem with the following stanza:

> Great men have been among us
> a few are with us still.

No doubt the last line refers back to his opening lines:

> Northumbrian master
> of number and pitch

74. Davie, Donald. "But to Remember." *Paideuma*, Vol. 9, No. 1 (Spring, 1980), p. 20. [Reprinted from *Madeira & Toasts for Basil Bunting's 75th Birthday*. Ed. Jonathan Williams. Reviewed above.]

"But to Remember" is a five line poem written to Bunting.

75. Gordon, David. "Bunting *Obiter*." *Paideuma*, Vol. 9, No. 1 (Spring, 1980), pp. 149-53.

This article is an account of Gordon's first meeting with Bunting which took place at the University of Maine in 1976. As one would expect from Gordon's close association with Pound, much of the conversation of this piece centers around Bunting's association with Pound. But overall, it is simply a recollection of Gordon's first impressions of Bunting and a recollection of a congenial conversation held over a lobster lunch.

76. Gordon, David. "A Northumbrian Sabine." *Paideuma*, Vol. 9, No. 1 (Spring, 1980), pp. 77-87.

Gordon argues that many of the techniques of Bunting's later poetry, for example his use of rhythm and idiom, were already apparent as early as the 1931 Overdrafts of "Yes, it's slow, docked of amours" and "Please stop gushing about his pink." Gordon points out that both in the case of the first poem whose Latin metre is the *ionic a minore* and in the case of the second poem whose metre is the Second Asklepiadean, Bunting convincingly develops an English cadence that adapts Horace's metre to the stresses of Bunting's line. Furthermore, Horace's tone in these poems is reinforced by Bunting's replication of assonantal patterns found in the poems and by Bunting's carefully selected idiom.

Gordon's task in the second part of this article is to show how "Bunting's word-carving of the episode of the murder of Bloodaxe at Stainmore (pp. 46-47 [of *Collected Poems*]) exhibits many qualities that make up the whole of *Briggflatts*, and reveals something of the early influences that have shaped his poetry." Gordon's analysis here is threefold: an analysis of the rhythms of this section, an analysis of the unusual degree of assonance present in this section (maintenance of the assonanting long *i* sound throughout all 24 lines of this section), and an analysis of Bunting's moral message in this section. Hence Gordon concludes: "In shaping the history of a little known king's mysterious death, Bunting's many years work in developing a Northumbrian Horace has been predominant in universalizing this episode into a significant comment on the way modern man meets his fate."

77. Gustafson, Ralph. "Music Thinks Sensuously, Words Can't." *Paideuma*, Vol. 9, No. 1 (Spring, 1980), p. 15.

> This short poem, dedicated to Bunting, makes frequent reference to *Briggflatts* and Bunting's poetics.

78. Jones, F. Whitney. "Basil Bunting in America, 1976." *Paideuma*, Vol. 9, No. 1 (Spring, 1980), pp. 142-48.

> Jones, here, recalls Bunting's visit to St. Andrews for a reading in 1976. Although much of the article is anecdotal, Jones draws a specific conclusion from his meeting with Bunting:
>
>> Hearing Basil read *Briggflatts*, I take him seriously. I believe the poem began as a sound, then developed into a series of sounds. . . . Sound is as primary to the poem as it is to a song. . . . The primary experience afforded by *Briggflatts*, however, is in *hearing* it.
>> I have heard many poets read from their work, and in each case the reading has enriched my response to the text. The text, however, has always been my primary interest. In the case of Basil's work, the text serves to enrich my original response to hearing his work, and hearing him read the work is my primary interest.
>> . . . He is more the last great poet of the spoken word.

79. Kenner, Hugh. "The Sound of Sense." *Paideuma*, Vol. 9, No. 1 (Spring, 1980), pp. 9-12.

> This short article, which easily might be subtitled "A Distinct Voice," concerns, not so much the sound of Bunting's poetry, as the sound of Bunting himself—his voice. Bunting is a man who

sounds like a poet. As Kenner points out,

> Frost . . . said, "A sentence is a sound in itself on which other sounds called words may be strung." Those are Bunting's priorities too: the tune, then the words.

Thus, those who have not *heard* Bunting read are the losers, even though his words are preserved, for "The voice of Basil Bunting was not shaped by all those decades of craft to the end that its simulacrum might lie pressed flat on a page."

80. Kleinzahler, August. "Throw it Out and Try Again." *Paideuma*, Vol. 9, No. 1 (Spring, 1980), pp. 27-29.

> Kleinzahler's article is an attempt to provide the reader with some idea of both the joys and problems of being a student in a class taught by Bunting. Given this much of a hint, the reader might very well guess what the title refers to.

81. Lewis, Peter. "*CUNTO CLI.* . . . from *SARTORIS.*" *Paideuma*, Vol. 9, No. 1 (Spring, 1980), pp. 23-25. [Reprinted from *Madeira & Toasts for Basil Bunting's 75th Birthday*. Ed. Jonathan Williams. Reviewed above.]

> On the whole, a bawdy poem—made by parodying some of the most familiar cadences of Pound, mostly taken from the Libretto section of Canto LXXXVI or from the Usura Canto [XLV].

82. Pickard, Tom. "Serving My Time to a Trade." *Paideuma*, Vol. 9, No. 1 (Spring, 1980), pp. 155-63.

> Although Bunting claims not to have any disciples or apprentices, Tom Pickard could claim the right to that mantle if anyone could. "Serving My Time to a Trade" is an account of Pickard's introduction to poetry and Basil Bunting and presents a brief view of how difficult a task-master the two are.

83. Suter, Anthony. "The Writer in the Mirror." *Paideuma*, Vol. 9, No. 1 (Spring, 1980), pp. 89-99.

> The subtitle of this article, "Basil Bunting and T.S. Eliot: Parody and Parallel," more adequately reflects the content of the article than its main title. Bunting's parodies of Eliot and his parallels with Eliot are topics that Suter has dealt with previously in such articles as "Time and the Literary Past in the Poems of Basil Bunting" and "'Attis: Or, Something Missing,' a reading of the poem by Basil Bunting" [both reviewed above].
> Suter claims that,
>
> > By constant parody, Bunting makes it probable that Eliot in particular is the target for his attack on the inadequacy of much of modern art. The choice of the Attis story is in itself a reference to the background material of *The Waste Land*. Various incidents in the poem can be interpreted as specific references to the progress of Eliot's life and career.

Bunting's next poem, "Aus dem zweiten Reich," according to Suter, is an Eliot influenced poem. "It has Eliot-like, sudden 'cinematographic' changes of scene . . . and the same sort of tone as the early, pre-*Waste Land*, Eliot poems." Suter later describes the poem as "a sort of minor, flippant and more lighthearted *Waste Land*."

Progressing from parody to parallel, Suter discusses three possible parallels in the two poets' works. First, Suter suggests that there is considerable exploration of the theme of literary creation within the works of both poets. Second, he briefly discusses both poets' use of personae (whether historical or fictional). Third, and most developed of the three points, Suter argues that the

> . . . final parallel between Bunting and Eliot again comes to its climax in *Briggflatts* and *Four Quartets*, but has its roots in the early works. These lie in the extensive use of literary material by Bunting in much the same manner as Eliot in *The Waste Land*. I have already remarked upon the fact that the use of literary sources has the effect of opening the poetry onto the past. More than this, it shows in Bunting's poetry the same acceptance of the culture of the past as exists in Eliot. Even more important, the literary references, creating inter-reflecting mirrors of past and present, show a preoccupation with the theme of time, and the part of time that survives in the present.

84. Terrell, Carroll. "Basil Bunting in Action." *Paideuma*, Vol. 9, No. 1 (Spring, 1980), pp. 33-76.

This article is, without doubt, the most enjoyable piece written on Bunting to date. But the major problem with the article is one of classification. Is it criticism, biography or Romance? Professor Terrell, with tape recorder in hand, sets off for England to do a series of interviews with Bunting, but at some point the tape recorder is retired from the action (largely due to Bunting's disdain of such machines). Thus, rather than a transcription of a series of interviews, the reader is presented with Terrell's recollections (from his notes) of his talks and adventures with Bunting.

The article is divided roughly into five sections. In Part I Terrell recalls snatches of the conversation held between himself and Bunting at Bunting's home in Washington. The main subjects of this conversation were Douglas' *Economic Democracy*, Pound's manner of reading poetry, and Alfred Richard Orage. This section also contains the account of the ill-fated attempt to record the conversations.

Part II aptly might have been called "On the Road with Bunting and Terrell" as the pair set out to visit Jonathan Williams and Briggflatts Meeting House. Here Terrell plays Sal Paradise to Bunting's Dean Moriarty (or Sancho Panza to Don Quixote—I'm not sure which); note here the following description:

> Basil settled himself behind the wheel and we were off. He was a picture sitting there upright, far enough back so that his arms were straight, one hand on each side of the wheel. He seemed quite comfortable as he picked up speed and darted in and out of traffic like a maniac. . . . I asked, "Do they have any speed limits in England?" It seems that they have them, but nobody, especially lorry-drivers, or ageing poets, pays any attention to them. Basil said that up till the last few years, he used to drive

> those roads at eighty miles an hour, but recently he'd slowed
> down quite a lot. "Age," he said. "With age you slow down in a
> lot of ways." I thought to myself, "It's probably lucky for me
> we aren't taking this trip when he was a youthful seventy-five."

Part II also contains the story of Bunting sending Terrell out on an adventure with perhaps a distant relative of that sweet tenor bull made famous in the opening lines of *Briggflatts*, but no more can be said of that here without ruining the reader's pleasure in reading that anecdote himself.

Parts III and IV relate Bunting's and Terrell's meeting with Jonathan Williams and Tom Meyer and the resulting trip to Briggflatts Meeting House. Part V concerns the return trip to Bunting's home.

The article, however, is more than simply the retelling of the escapades of this dangerous duo, for the emphasis is always, as the title suggests, on *Basil Bunting* in action. Furthermore, Terrell is always careful to preserve portions of conversations illustrating Bunting's views on a number of persons and topics which only a small list may be made here: Margaret de Silver, Dickens, Chaucer, Spenser, Shakespeare, Wordsworth, modern writers and modern verse. No doubt many of these subjects have been dealt with in more detail in other articles, but none have been dealt with in such an enjoyable context as the reader will find in this article.

85. Williams, Jonathan. "Eighty of the Best. . . ." *Paideuma*, Vol. 9, No. 1 (Spring, 1980), pp. 121-39.

Here, Williams asks Bunting 80 questions, presumably one for each of Bunting's 80 years. The questions range from the whimsical, such as the first question, "What do you dislike most?" and the last question, "Isn't it time for a Dog's-Nose?", to the serious, such as questions dealing with literature, music, and politics. All in all the questions and answers are great fun; one question and answer might bear quoting here:

> Q. A research fellowship at Queen Mary College, University of
> London, is advertised in *The Guardian* this morning. The
> subject is "Laser Measurement of Bovine Spermatozoa
> Motility." What should be done with old poets who are un-
> employed?
>
> A. They might become subjects for research. Or, perhaps turned
> into cat's meat.

INDEX OF PEOPLE, BOOKS AND THINGS

The Index includes mainly the names of people and the titles of books or musical compositions. It also lists most other capitalized words or concepts, except for the names of cities and publishing companies or other routine names used in bibliographical notes. Bunting's works are indexed alphabetically under his name: the titles of books are given first followed by the titles of individual poems and other works in quotation marks except for the odes which are listed numerically. The "Year by Year Bibliography" of Bunting's works has not been indexed.

The spelling of most names has been standardized, except for transliterations from the Persian such as Firdausi which Bunting writes as Firdosi because in Northumberland speech that comes closer to the correct sound than other variants found in the literature do. For similar reasons we allow Bunting to spell Wyatt as Wyat [one of its old forms] and authorities from Iran to spell *The Rubaiyat* in their own special way: a few other eccentricities for similar reasons have been allowed in the text and cross-referenced in the Index.

‡ ‡ ‡ ‡ ‡ ‡

A